Charles N. Bamforth, 1921

# Iron Jaw:

## A Skipper Tells His Story

Captain Charles N. Bamforth (1895-1975)

compiled and edited by

Charles A. Bamforth and Richard A. Bamforth

*R A Bamforth*

DORRANCE PUBLISHING CO., INC.
PITTSBURGH, PENNSYLVANIA 15222

Cover photo courtesy of the Board of Directors of the Alumni Association of the Massachusetts Maritime Academy. Used with permission.

ISBN # 0-8059-5417-1
Printed in the United States of America

*First Printing*
For information or to order additional books, please write:

Richard A. Bamforth
P. O. Box 5068
Augusta, ME 04332  USA
(207) 626-0073          pbamforth@aol.com
Or                                                        om

# Dedication

To those
who go down to the sea in ships
and ply their trade in deep waters

*Psalm 107*

# Contents

# Editor's Acknowledgments

In addition to thanking Pat and Dick Bamforth for their substantial contributions, I thank my tireless editor, Kitsey Canaan, who spent a year making sense out of my narrative and reduced it to readable proportions. My wife, Jan, put up with my preoccupation, ten years of it. As for finances, she was a full partner. There are others whose constant and enthusiastic support kept me going. Jack Greenley tried to make me computer literate and has never given up trying. Dad's sisters, Grace Corrao and Beatrice Snelling, have answered my questions and clarified the family tree. Uncle Chester, who suffered under the captain's command that he "Stand by to open the Golden Gate" as the S. S. *Pennsylvanian* approached San Francisco Harbor, has enthusiastically endorsed the project. Margaret Bamforth Adam and Anna Lee Bamforth have typed and encouraged me. Andrew Adam has offered invaluable computer assistance. Jeanne Bamforth has helped with layout and graphics. Don Russell, Carol Andlauer, Freeman Condon, and Terry and Maren Ryan have kept me enthused. My daughter Judy Jervis and daughter-in-law Debbie Bamforth head the list of many who have criticized and made helpful suggestions. I thank them all.

April 1998
Charles Allan Bamforth

# Editor's Prologue

My father, Captain Charles Nathaniel Bamforth, fascinated his family and friends with stories of his life at sea. Two notable members of his audience encouraged him to write a book about his experiences. One was Lieutenant Albert Seechts, a Navy man who had taken part in Dad's training. Another was Dad's friend David Ryder, a writer. In the late 1920s, Mr. Ryder suggested that Dad use his diary entries to trigger his memory and then write down every detail he could remember. Dad began the process in 1930, working from the first of his diaries, a small, leather-bound volume with "Daily Reminder 1915" in gold lettering on the cover. On the back of the flyleaf, in the captain's hand, is written, "Charles N. Bamforth from Aunt Grace, Xmas 1914." On January 1 it begins,

> All of us cadets went to the annual banquet at the Sailor's Haven.
> We all had a fine time. We returned to the ship at 9:30, bringing
> with us 104 pairs of warm gloves, presents from the Haven. I had to
> stand watch until 12 o'clock when I saw the old year out and the
> new one in. We made all the noise we could.

Among his papers (he was a saver) are typewritten sections titled, "My First Fifteen Years at Sea," and "My first Twenty-five Years at Sea." Some of his stories were typed during free time aboard ship, using the hunt-and-peck system. Other parts were handwritten and filed in his scrapbook. He began writing his memoirs in earnest in the late 1960s, transcribing his diaries onto yellow legal pads and expanding the entries with remembered details. As with his diaries, each entry began with the weather and location. He included every haircut, stomachache, and visit to the dentist. Somewhat later he set down the facts of his beginnings.

In 1975, the year Dad retired from the sea for good, I spent much time at home recuperating from surgeries. During this period, Dad offered me access to his writings. I'd take ten of his yellow pads home with me to read. I'd write comments and questions in the margins to discuss later in the privacy of his basement den. He began many stories that went nowhere, leaving the reader at a loss, because he was forever protecting the guilty. I worked hard to draw him out so that these stories and anecdotes could be concluded. I got no response to certain sensitive issues and, respecting his reticence, I did not press him. There was a new closeness between us. He treated me as an equal for the first time. We enjoyed a wonderful camaraderie.

When Dad died suddenly on November 19, 1975, I was devastated. My new friend had left me. I knew, however, that it was up to me to tell his life story. In the back of my mind were the words my Aunt Jean had written to me and my brother Dick in 1943, as she was dying of cancer: "Someday perhaps you'll write a book about your father. Think of what an unassuming man he is."

In 1989 I began editing the manuscript my father left behind. Dick and his wife, Pat, have helped me enormously in this, the story of my father's life.

Charles Allan Bamforth

# List of Photographs

# List of Maps

SEATTLE
PORTLAND
SAN
FRANCISCO
LOS ANGELES
PORT of WILMINGTON

QUEBEC
BOSTON
NEW YORK

FALMOUTH
BREST

GIBRALTAR
CAPE BON

PEARL
HARBOR

~Panama Canal

PORT
OF SPAIN

FREETOWN

*
TORPEDOED
HERE 1942

CAPE
SAN ROQUE

SALVADOR
(BAHIA)

RIO DE
JANEIRO

MONTEVIDEO
BUENOS AIRES

CAPE TOWN

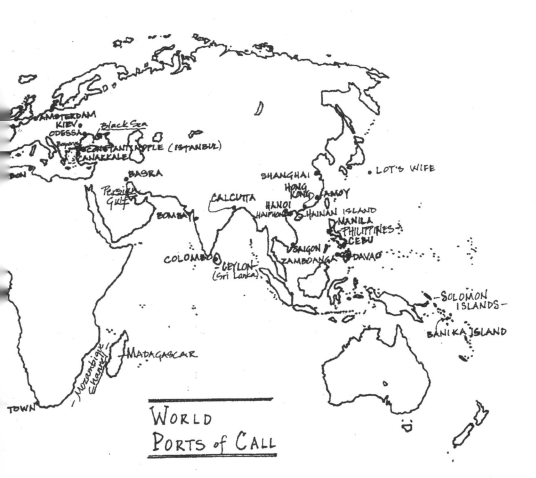

AMSTERDAM
KIEV
ODESSA
Black Sea
CONSTANTINOPLE (ISTANBUL)
CANAKKALE
BASRA
Persian Gulf
BOMBAY
CALCUTTA
COLOMBO
CEYLON
(Sri Lanka)
SHANGHAI
HONG KONG
HANOI
HAIPHONG
HAINAN ISLAND
AMOY
MANILA
PHILIPPINES
CEBU
SAIGON
ZAMBOANGA
DAVAO
LOT'S WIFE
SOLOMON ISLANDS
BANIKA ISLAND
MADAGASCAR
Mozambique Channel
TOWN

# WORLD
# PORTS of CALL

3

# CHAPTER 1

# BOYHOOD AMBITIONS

When I was about a year old, Mother, Father, and I lived in a one-room flat in Lawrence, a textile town twenty miles north of Boston. It was 1896 and my father, Charles Henry Bamforth, then eighteen years old, had a job working as a cobbler at $5 a week. The shop owner had to close his business, and Father lost his job. He walked twenty-five miles over dirt roads to his parents' home in South Lincoln. His shoes were poor and he developed bad blisters on his feet. He left my mother and me alone in Lawrence. We had only meager possessions and no money. Father planned to send money as soon as he could. In desperation, my mother wrote to her father and mother in Upper Lincoln for help, and we went to live with them. Thus my grandparents, all four, became prominent in my life.

My mother, Alice Maria, was the tenth of eleven children and was married at eighteen. She was lame, having had spinal meningitis when she was very young. Her folks, the Cousins family, were farmers of old New England stock. Grandma and Grandfather Cousins always had plenty of everything. Barrels of potatoes and apples were stored in the cellar and in the pantry off the kitchen, where there were three more wooden barrels under the counter. One was a flour barrel, one a sugar barrel, and the third a cookie barrel. Grandma used to give us remnants of woolen cloth for Mother to make a dress for my sister Grace, or a pair of pants for me. After we moved to our own house, sometimes I stayed at Grandma's for a few days. On arrival she would say to me, first thing, "Do you have a jackknife?" Often I did not, having lost the last one. Each time she found another to give me. She never scolded me. I was spoiled from the beginning.

My father's parents lived in South Lincoln. They came from England. My grandfather was a highly skilled welder who worked at the Boston Navy Yard, which made all the anchor chain for the Navy. Each link was forged and welded by hand. Grandma Bamforth was a dress designer with a shop in Boston. Grandfather and Grandma Bamforth lived just a little over a mile from the railroad station at South Lincoln and went to town six days a week. They walked to and from the station, as there was no other means of transportation.

My father's parents gave him a half-acre of land five hundred feet beyond their place to build a house. Father worked at odd jobs and in his spare time dug the cellar for our new house, which became a wooden structure with two rooms downstairs and two rooms above. He borrowed $1,000 at 6 percent interest to build it.

As the family grew, the house expanded. First came a new back shed. Later a third room was added on the first floor and a third room on the second. I gained a small bedroom to myself over the front stairs. Later we added a henhouse out back, and planted a few apple and cherry trees. Under one apple tree we had an air-conditioned "reading room." In each gable, high up, was a quarter moon cut out for daylight and essential air. In this structure there were always newspapers and the Sears Roebuck catalogue. Every year this "room" was moved a few feet.

Like most houses in this end of town, there was a black iron sink in the kitchen with a single cold-water faucet. Hot water had to be secured from the big kettle on the kitchen stove. Grace and I had the job of doing the dishes. I stood on one chair and washed the dishes in a pan while Grace, a year and a half younger, stood on another chair and dried.

Light was provided by kerosene lamps, and heat came from the black iron kitchen stove in which we burned either wood or coal. On the coldest nights, the water pipe to the kitchen sink often froze where it passed through the cellar. To thaw it in the morning, my father wrapped a rag around an iron poker, poured kerosene on the rag, lighted it, and went to the cellar to warm the pipe with his torch. It was a messy, smoky job. Later on we avoided this by insulating the cellar with piles of pine boughs and banks of leaves a foot thick outside the stone foundation and as high as the sill of the house. This was one of my fall chores.

Each summer, when fruits and vegetables were plentiful, my mother preserved as much as possible for winter use. Our cellar had a sand floor, so Father fashioned two old wooden doors as shelves which hung about a foot from the ceiling. By fall these doors were full of preserves put up in Mason jars. Toward spring all that would be left were two or three jars of sour picalilli made from green tomatoes, so that by early spring the sandwiches we took to school or to work consisted of that unappetizing filling between two slices of bread.

The mail was delivered by a horse-drawn carriage. Everyone was required to have a roadside mailbox. When things got better, we had the *Boston Herald* delivered with the mail. Things improved when Father got a steady job as a coalfireman on the Boston and Maine Railroad. The Fitchburg division ran through South Lincoln. Lincoln was the highest point in elevation between Boston and Fitchburg. All freight trains pulled uphill to Lincoln, stopped for water, and then rode down grade in either direction. Father was studying to become a railroad engineer. I was about four years old at the time.

My mother knew about what time my father's train regularly stopped at Lincoln, and we would be at the station to see him. When Father greeted us, he reached down, grabbed me from my mother's arms, and showed me things like the fire end of the boiler on the locomotive. He would open the door to the firebox and show how he could place a shovel of soft coal on the exact part of the fire he chose. He demonstrated how he could bank the fire or slice it and make it give its maximum heat.

Fire tube boilers were in use in those days. I remember him telling me how he coped with leaks. Sometimes during a run they got so bad that they had to stop the train, go into the woods, and cut a green sapling of the right size to match the inside diameter of the leaking tube. Then he would bank the fire, crawl over it through the heat and suffocating coal gas, and drive the sapling into the leaking fire tube on the firebox end. The repair was essential but temporary at best.

Railroading was hazardous. All passenger cars at the turn of the century were built of wood, and the overhead lights were fired with kerosene. There were no block signals to control traffic. Whenever there was a collision, great fires took place and many people were burned to death. I remember several such accidents near home. There were very few specified or enforced safety practices. After a few hours' sleep in a room at the round-house at the end of a run, the crews were often ordered out on another run without having had sufficient rest. Many times my father arrived at the roundhouse after a long, tiring run only to be ordered to make another trip, and then another. This was before labor unions and laws made it compulsory for a man to have a specified minimum rest each day. Many accidents on the railroad were caused by men whose judgment was impaired due to fatigue.

About 1901 there was a big coal strike. Hard coal, desirable for use at home, was impossible to buy. The railroads burned soft coal, and Father carried a burlap bag with him to work. During the trip he filled the bag with lumps of soft coal. Passing through Lincoln, he tossed the bag off into the bushes at a predetermined place. Later, instead of walking home from the station, he used Matthew Doherty's carriage service. That way he recovered his bag of coal and got it home for twenty-five cents.

Many residents of Lincoln commuted to Boston for work. The engines burned soft coal and used a steam jet for forced draft. With doors and windows open in warm weather, the coal gas and soot in the air was thick. Long passenger trains of coaches went into Boston around seven each morning. About half of the coaches were designated "smokers," and in these cars smoke from pipes and cigars was thick. A few men smoked cigarettes of the roll-your-own variety. Big brass spittoons were everywhere on these trains. Spitting was not prohibited and was a common habit. In each railroad station and at the end of every car was a water tank with a metal dipper fastened on a chain for all to use as a common drinking cup. The tit-ta-tit sound of the telegraph could always be heard in the station office.

Lincoln was a dry town. In fact, liquor could not be bought any closer than the city of Boston. The last train out of Boston on any weeknight was at ten, but every Saturday there were several trains that left Boston about midnight, and another brought the theatergoers home at one in the morning. On these last trains, many men brought home a bottle on the hip. On a sunny summer Sunday morning, it was common to find a man lying under a tree asleep somewhere between the railroad station and his home, his empty bottle beside him. I learned early in life that drinking liquor was about as low in life as one could get.

In the spring of 1901, when I was six, Father quit the railroad and went to work for Thomas Giles, a carpenter and builder who lived nearby. Mr. Giles was also a whistler. As he and Father walked to work, their progress could be monitored for miles, Mr. Giles whistling all the way. Father learned the carpenter trade from him and eventually took contracts for jobs on his own. Often he took me along to help. His jobs included shingling barns and the roofs of houses. He usually had another man with him who carried the bundles of wooden shingles up the long ladders to the roof. I worked on the staging ahead of my father, laying the shingles against a straight edge. Father followed along, nailing like a machine. We would lay tier after tier, beginning at the eaves, at last reaching the ridge. After shingling was completed, we had to clean up the grounds around the building. I did my share of this work too.

Sometimes we walked as many as three and a half miles to work. Going home, those walks were painfully long, but I felt like a man. I was my father's partner. There was no money involved for me. Gradually, my father took on more skilled carpenter work, even becoming a contractor for whole dwellings.

As a small boy, I was often asked to help in the neighborhood. When strawberries were ripe, lots of laborers were in demand. Oftentimes I picked strawberries and earned nearly a dollar a day. I helped Grandmother Cousins with the garden in the summertime and also worked for Sam Farrar, who had a cornfield near our house. When he cultivated with a

Young Charlie in his Sunday best

horse-drawn affair, he used to get me to ride the horse and guide it down the rows of plants. At the end of each row, we'd turn around and come back up the next row. I rode the big horse bareback. It was not easy because the horse was so wide that my legs had to be spread unnaturally, and the horse's spine was very hard. It was disheartening to make only thirty-five or fifty cents for a whole day of this activity and to have aches and pains afterwards.

When strawberries were in season in June, Sam Farrar got me to help him market them. I arrived at his house early. He had a small market wagon loaded with quart baskets of berries to sell retail. We drove six miles to Waltham and arrived in the residential district around ten o'clock. He took one side of the street and I took the other, and we peddled berries door to door. The price was fifteen cents a quart or two quarts for a quarter, cash only. We usually sold out by four o'clock and drove the six miles back to Farrar's place, arriving at about six. In June, on a fair day, it was a pleasant occasion. I received seventy-five cents for my efforts.

Late in the season I picked wild cherries, and when apples came in, I got jobs picking those. Some Saturdays in the fall, after the fields had been harvested and frost was in the air, I went to Waltham again with Sam Farrar. The one-horse wagon was loaded with all sorts of homegrown fruits and vegetables. We walked the horse most of the way because the gravel road was rough, and if we went too fast the produce would be damaged. At that slow pace it took us two hours to make the six-mile trip. Again, we peddled door to door. There was little traffic on these streets so the horse was given its head, and it moved the wagon slowly forward, stopping and starting as ordered by Mr. Farrar. Farrar and that horse had worked this route many times together, and the horse recognized his voice.

By the middle of the afternoon, we sold out and began our cold ride back to Lincoln. Although Mother had seen that I was dressed in long underwear, I suffered terribly on those return trips. Mr. Sam was a big fat man and seemed to be able to ride and keep warm enough. I, on the other hand, had to walk or run alongside to keep warm. I did not have gloves or mittens and my hands nearly froze. On one of these trips I stopped several times by the country roadside to urinate, but I couldn't. When we reached Farrar's, I was given my wages and set out for home in the dark by way of the shortcut over a stone wall and through the woods. I was in utter distress. My hands were so cold that I couldn't unbutton my pants. I just couldn't move another step and at last wet my pants. Such relief! Then I ran home, crying, to my mother's arms. She understood.

In the fall, the farmers cut their feed corn and popcorn. They bundled the stalks in stacks at regularly spaced intervals in the fields to dry. Later, labor was secured to shuck the corn into bushel baskets. I had my turn at this job. It was very hard on the hands and darned cold work, especially on cloudy days with a wind blowing.

9

I usually had my Saturday jobs lined up in advance. I remember once my assignment was to drive a neighbor's wagon to his relatives in Waltham. These relatives kept a horse, and my job was to fill the wagon with the horse's discarded bedding of hay mixed with manure. I had to fork this mixture out of the stable cellar, fill the wagon, and drive it home to my employer. This was a full day's work, for which I earned $3.

Another time I worked for this same farmer on a Saturday in the fall. My job was to pick up the horse and wagon, load it with wind-fallen apples, and drive to a cider mill in the town of Stow, eight miles west. I unloaded the apples at the mill and loaded barrels of cider back on the wagon. The exchange was so much cider for so many hundred weight of apples. It was interesting to see how the cider was made. The apples were layered in burlap, then squeezed in a wooden press. The cider ran out of spigots at the bottom of the press.

In driving to Stow I had to pass through the center of the shopping district of Concord. My family had arranged for me to stop at the shoe store on one of these return trips to buy a new pair of shoes, but this was not a successful venture. In cool weather we boys wore pants that ended below the knee, and long stockings. In summer we went barefoot most of the time, but as cold weather approached we wore our shoes and the stockings. When the foot of the stocking got so worn that it wasn't worth mending, the foot was cut off. Since everyone wore high shoes, no one could tell that our stockings had no feet unless, of course, the shoe was removed. On this trip to buy shoes I forgot to wear a good pair of stockings. I went into the shoe store and sat down among other customers on the long row of seats and unlaced my old shoe. As I pulled it off, I was shocked to find I had on footless stockings. Embarrassed, I quickly slipped my foot back into my shoe and ran out of the store to the surprise of the customers and clerk. I got my new shoes on a subsequent trip, remembering to wear good stockings. I was about seven years old at the time.

Uncle Harry Cousins had a grocery store near the railroad station. He kept several nice driving horses and some good-looking express wagons. Each day of the week the two Watson brothers made deliveries for the store, taking a different route each day. They took orders in the morning and delivered the merchandise the same afternoon. I was given this job for two weeks at a time to fill in for their vacations. It was a pleasure to drive such nice horses. Mornings we took orders in an order book, and back at the store the groceries were put up in baskets with a copy of the written order. Then we were given a white cloth bag with a drawstring and money to make change for those who paid cash. A day did not end until we had balanced the money against the orders delivered, to the penny. This was my first lesson in bookkeeping. If I was short, I had to make up the difference out of my own pocket.

One day when I was driving back to the store with one of those fine horses, a gig, a two-wheeled vehicle used for driving race horses, tried to overtake me. I could not resist. I had my horse open up to meet the challenge. Of course, the driver of the racehorse succeeded in passing me. During this short race my horse stumbled a bit, but I never dreamed that her knee ever touched the ground. As the racehorse and driver pulled ahead, I slowed my horse so it could cool off because I was sure that Uncle Harry would not approve of behavior such as mine, and he would know if I brought the horse back in a sweat.

Back at the store I put my horse up for the night in the stable, balanced my books, and went home. On arrival at the store the following morning, Uncle Harry asked me if the horse had fallen down when I had driven her the day before. I answered, "No." He told me that before he had gone home, he checked the horses, and in running his hand down the front leg of the horse I had driven, he found some sand and pebbles buried in one knee. I don't remember volunteering any further information at that point. I do remember clearly, however, that I was darned careful to drive the horse with the utmost care from then on.

The Bamforth side of my family spent all they made, so when hard times came and there was no work, we were in trouble. Some years when my father had plenty of work, he had my mother buy nothing but the best. Then in winter when work was scarce, with little or no money coming in, the grocery bill often ran up, and we got in debt to Uncle Harry to the tune of several hundred dollars. I also remember that in such hard times we couldn't buy regular milk, instead we bought large cans of skimmed milk. Potatoes were bought cheaply, too, from a nearby farmer for fifty or sixty cents a bushel. There were times when we had little else to eat but skimmed milk and potatoes.

Every few years another relative of my mother died, and Mother received a small portion of the inheritance. It all went to pay back grocery bills.

One day when Father was working in Concord as a carpenter, he asked me to do an errand for him. He didn't tell me that he was in debt to the local butcher, but he gave me a dollar with instructions to give it to the butcher on my way to school the next day. Apparently he had agreed to pay the butcher a dollar a week on his back bills. I forgot to give the butcher the dollar.

Father got paid every Saturday night. The next Saturday night he came to collect his pay but couldn't get a cent. His pay had been attached for failing to pay the dollar to the butcher as had been agreed. When he came home that night, much distressed, he asked me, "Charlie, did you pay the dollar I gave you for the butcher?"

I said, "No, I still have it in my pocket." I had never seen him so depressed as he was that night. He said hardly a word, but his condition was obvious.

Some winters Father had no work at all and spent most of his time reading. Such were the things that shaped my future life. I saw what a hard time my mother had. She could never make plans for the days ahead.

With me, my sister Grace, and my brother Ralph, Mother had more children than she could handle. Then she had a fourth child, Beatrice. After that, Mother swore to me that she would never have another. I seemed to be her confidant in these matters. I kidded her and reminded her that she had told me that one before. Then she had her fifth child, Albert. She repeated her promise to me again. This time, to emphasize her determination, she bet me a hundred dollars. I laughed it off. I doubted that Father would have approved of her being so open with me about such things. Then Mother gave birth to twins, Clara and Chester. It was then that I made up my mind not to get married until I could have a home and give my wife a regular allotment. That is what I did. I cannot say, even today, that it was the perfect solution, but I have always stuck with it.

The Cousins side of the family were always able to take care of themselves. My cousin Ashley's father was Uncle Fred Cousins. He handled coal and stored great warehouses with burlap bags of grain. In the early 1900s, most people used coal for heat and grain to feed their horses, cattle, and poultry, so this was big business for Uncle Fred. When I became old enough, I was hired as extra help during school vacations. Several cars of grain would come in on the railroad siding or spur track at the station. The cars had to be unloaded in three days or demurrage was charged and added to the freight charges. With practice I was able to lift and sling a hundred-pound bag of grain neatly up on top of a six-foot pile in the warehouse. I also became expert at driving a wagon up to the platform and shoveling in a ton of coal so accurately that when I drove the wagon onto the scales, I had to place only one or two shovelfuls on or off to make the exact weight.

About one mile from home there was a red schoolhouse where I attended the first six grades. The boys' entrance was on one side and the girls' on the other. During recess we played baseball behind the school. I was the catcher. During one of these games, I squatted and outgrew my trousers all at the same time. The seam gave way from crotch to belt. Without a word I jumped over the red fence, streaked through the apple orchard toward home, changed my pants, and ran back to school. I was in my seat, breathing heavily, just as the bell rang.

Miss Farnsworth taught the first three grades. One afternoon when I must have been eight or nine years old, she had parked a nice driving horse outside. We had been told not to touch it, but, in admiring the horse, my chum Arthur Rice and I lifted and examined the horse's anchor. Miss Farnsworth saw us and called us into the schoolroom. She scolded us and gave me the only licking I ever got in school. She used a leather strap. It tapered to a point at the free end. She held my fingers at the tips and laced me across the knuckles about three times so that it stung. She gave Arthur the same treatment.

I did not tell my parents because it was well understood at home that if I was naughty enough to be punished by the teacher, worse was waiting for me at home. My father always backed up the teacher. For every strike the teacher gave us, he promised two strikes with his razor strop across the bare bottom.

We children toed the mark. We were taught to say "Yes, Mother" and "No, Father." We always had to sit up straight at table. If we ate too fast, we were required to take thirty chews to the mouthful. We were taught to behave at home, so we behaved away from home also. Mother often complained to Father of our misdeeds and expected him to back her up. Father ruled with an iron hand. If we deserved punishment, he went for his wide razor strop, folded it, laid us over his left knee with our bottoms up, and slapped us with the folded strop. It made a horrible sound. He never did hurt us physically, just our egos, but he got his point across. If we were about to be spanked, we would yell blue murder before he ever struck us. That brought Mother to our aid, and she would warn him, "Don't hurt him, that is enough, that is enough!" We children took full advantage of the situation, yelling as loudly as we possibly could.

It was customary in our home for all to be seated together for meals. No one started to eat until grace had been said by my father or, more often, by us in unison: "For what we are about to receive, may the Lord make us truly thankful, for Christ's sake. Amen." Then no one started to eat until all were served. After the meat and vegetables were eaten there was often some simple dessert. No one, however, was served dessert unless he or she had a clean plate. Nothing went to waste.

I often came home from school in the afternoons feeling very hungry and would search the pantry for something to eat. It was usually raisins from a cardboard box. I had been warned not to touch them, but I just couldn't leave them alone. One evening, to my surprise and distress, on my plate at dinner was a half-empty box of raisins. No explanation was necessary. Others were served dinner. I had raisins, period. My tears flowed in humiliation and embarrassment until at last I was excused from the table and sent to my room. Never again did I touch anything I was not supposed to touch.

By 1909 the elder Bamforths had passed on, and we moved into their house. We rented our smaller house to a family named Coffee. I got a job working with Mr. Coffee. In the New England states, people were much concerned about the gypsy moths that were stripping the leaves from trees. After a few annual strippings, great old and beautiful trees would die. The town of Lincoln prized its beautiful trees, so public money was allocated for containing the pests. Mr. Coffee was employed to kill the moths at a good standard pay of twenty-eight cents an hour and was allowed a boy to assist.

I got the biggest pay that I'd ever had until then, twenty cents an hour. I had the job all through my summer vacation.

I contributed my share toward the cost of running the home. My mother planned the rest of my take: so much for Sunday School, so much into the savings bank, and the balance for clothing or the materials to make them. I felt very proud to be doing my part. Although many boys of today think that all they earn is their own, I think my parents' system was better. Even after I left home, it was not a hardship to help out my family. I sent money home in the same manner until I married at age twenty-seven.

When Father worked as a carpenter, he and I got up at five in the morning. I made the fire, his breakfast, and put up his lunch. I cut his plug tobacco, "Master Workman" brand, and then I filled his pipe and saw him off at six. This early departure gave him time to walk to the station, ride the train to Concord, and then walk to the job site, ready to go to work at eight. When Father took on building and repair contracts, several times he had me fill in on such jobs as a regular helper. I did nailing of subfloors, lathe work, and roof shingling. From an early age I became accustomed to heights.

Before going to work each morning, Father cut what he thought was enough wood for a day. Frequently, however, this failed to suffice. Mother and I had to cut more to keep the stove going through the evening meal preparation and clean-up. Secretly, during the days when Father was away on the job, Mother had me saw up great quantities of stove-length wood from the cord piles and stow it away in the cellar. One Sunday Father discovered what I had done. From then on he cut no more wood himself. I had demonstrated my ability and that became my job for as long as I lived at home.

When I was in the eighth grade, I attended a new school in the center of Lincoln. We took the barge, a type of horse-drawn wagon, which stopped a quarter mile away at John Farrar's place. We were always there ahead of time to be sure not to miss the ride to school. My teacher was Miss Chapin. She had taught my mother. When I was in high school in 1909, I had so many chores to do and so much outside work that I barely had time for homework. All during summer vacation I had a job as a laborer driving work horses.

In the spring of 1910, I was obliged to leave high school and go to work full time to support the family. I might have gotten in some more schooling, but one after the other of us came down with the mumps, and the Board of Health quarantined us at home. To continue school in the fall, I would have had to repeat the ninth grade.

I began to look to the future. Since my father's business was either a feast or a famine, he could not give my mother a regular stipend to run the house. I remained determined to secure a regular job and not marry until I could give my wife a steady sum so that she could plan ahead.

I worked at various jobs, earning a man's wages. I was big for my age, appearing much older than my fifteen years. As always, half of what I made went into the much-needed funds used to run the household. I built a back porch and steps for Bert Farrar. Later I worked for my uncle, Rodman Snelling, who was in the coal and ice business. There I received $10.50 a week. It was supposed to be a twelve-hour day, but I had farther to walk to work. Many times the day did not end at six but only when the job was done, sometimes as late as eight-thirty. Frequently I did not get home until everybody was in bed. Even my father disapproved and scolded me for coming in late.

One afternoon in early spring, when the gravel roads in town had started to thaw, I was given orders to drive to the railroad station and load three and a half tons of hard coal from a railroad car that had been on demurrage. The scales for weighing the coal at the railroad yard belonged to my mother's brother, Uncle Fred Cousins. The Snellings owed him so much money that he didn't let them use these scales, so I was directed to drive up to the center of town and get the weighing done on the town-owned scales, double back to South Lincoln, and deliver the coal at John Farrar's place, near home. Although I had good heavy horses, a load of two and a half tons, not three and a half as ordered, would have been enough to carry on those gravel roads.

As I was driving toward the center of town to weigh the coal, I got stuck going up a long hill. The horses simply refused to pull the load. It was by then well after six, already dark, and neither I nor the horses had had supper. I got down from the wagon and found that the wheels on the low side had settled in the soft gravel. I dug a trench in front of the right-hand wheels, down two or three inches to hard frozen ground, got back on the load, and the horses were then able to pull. I was in a hurry to get to my destination, so I did not stop to fill in the trench that I had dug in the road. It was only a couple of inches deep, and I didn't think it would be dangerous to others. I figured I had not been seen doing it anyway. Normally, however, it was courteous and good practice to fill in such diggings.

Once started, I continued up the long hill, afraid to stop for fear of getting stuck again. I reached the town scales and weighed my load. It was very close to the specified three and a half tons ordered. It was then nearly eight o'clock. I proceeded over hilly country and gravel roads successfully until I got within about a quarter mile of my destination. There was quite a steep hill to climb, and the surface of the road had thawed. The horses stopped. They would not even try to pull. I left them and walked ahead to Farrar's, hoping to get the loan of a horse or two to help get the load up to their house. When I arrived there, I found my father paying a call. He was embarrassed and angry that I, his boy, was working such ungodly hours. Father insisted that I eat the supper offered to me. Then he and young Bert Farrar took a pair of horses with them and went to the foot of the hill, put the new pair of horses on the lead, drove the load of coal to its destination, and unloaded it. I was disappointed at being unable to complete my mission. My father had taken over my job.

The Farrars had a telephone by then. Father put in a call to the Snellings to tell them the situation and then arranged with the Farrars to feed the horses and put them up for the night. It was agreed that I would pick them up in the morning. I went home tired and much put out with my father. Now I know that he was correct in what he did. I learned also how not to run a business. It was only prudent to take care of both horses and men. A couple of days later the road commissioner took me to task for failing to fill in the trench I had dug in the road.

Some days I delivered ice, even though it was winter time. Nobody had electric refrigerators then. When ice was about a foot thick, we cut it on Beaver Pond using horses and ice plows. After it was cut, large cakes were floated in strings toward a line of icehouses on shore. We pushed the cakes onto chain belts that carried them up the bank, and men stood at different junctions to guide the cakes to a solid pile in the icehouse. When one layer was completed, the guide shoots were lifted up a foot, and the next layer was slid in. The walls of the icehouses were of wood filled with sawdust for insulation. When the icehouse was full, a foot of hay was spread over the top. When the ice was taken out to be delivered, these cakes, stored in great blocks twenty feet high, melted very little, even in hot weather.

When we made a delivery, we first looked in the customer's icebox and removed what was left of the old ice. Then we went to the wagon and cut a piece just the right size to fit the ice chamber completely. We used an ice pick to make stress holes in the big block, and the piece split off easily. It was a wet job. We wore rubber aprons, one in front and a second one over the shoulder. We picked up the cut piece with iron tongs and then, with the ice hanging from the tongs, hung one handle on the hook of the scales. We charged according to weight. Next we washed the new piece with water from a bucket, carried it to the house, and placed it in the icebox using the same tongs. Finally we cut the old piece into small pieces, packed them in around the new piece, and closed the lid.

Many times on the road that winter, driving horses for long days, my lunch consisted of bread with the last of the preserves in our cellar, sour piccalilli. All I had to drink was cold water whenever I could find some. Dismal though those days were, I was learning and formulating what I wanted for the future, consciously or not.

Aunt Grace and Uncle John Danner lived next door. Uncle John was away at sea much of the time, and Aunt Grace, being crippled, needed my help. I stayed many nights at her house to keep her company. Her house was wonderful, with central heating and a nice bathroom with hot and cold running water. Aunt Grace was very interested in my welfare. She did not approve of my driving horses instead of attending school. She told me that

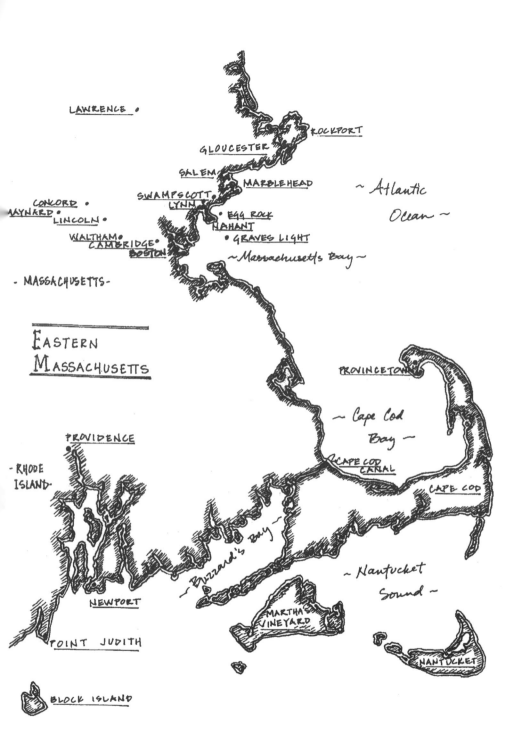

Eastern Massachusetts

if I continued, I would be nothing more than a day laborer for the rest of my life. She expected better things of me. Although I said nothing in reply, her talks made me think.

On September 11, 1911, at age sixteen, I went to work for Mr. Frank Wheeler, a prosperous market gardener in Concord. It took a good deal of explanation before Father grudgingly gave his permission for me to board at Wheeler's rather than at home. The job was a three-mile walk, and Father seemed at last to see the logic of my living away from home.

On a knoll shaded by an immense horse chestnut tree, the main house at Wheeler's had a big porch extending all across the front. From the back door towards the barn stood the traditional carriage shed. Beyond the carriage shed were a big barn, a windmill over a water tank, and a heated garage. To the rear of the house was a small orchard with various fruit trees. Everything was beautifully kept up. The main buildings were all painted yellow with white trim.

To the east was an icehouse, and beyond were long greenhouses painted white. In the middle of these long greenhouses were three boiler rooms. From each of these rose tall red brick chimneys. Adjoining the center boiler room was a packing house. Mr. Wheeler had many greenhouses and grew things scientifically. All the time that I worked for him, he was in close correspondence with the Rhode Island Agricultural College.

The main highway between Boston and the town of Maynard ran in front of Wheeler's. Beyond the gravel road extended forty acres of rich, level, highly cultivated farm land which at some distance sloped gradually to the Concord River. The estate continued on the other side of the river.

At the extreme east end of the property was a two-and-a-half-story house housing nine men who were employed year-round. This boarding house was run by a man who also looked after the main house and stable. He and his wife were Irish and lived in the front part of the house. They had no children. There was one woman employee who lived in another room at the front of the house. On the first floor there was a big dining room with a table long enough to seat ten easily. At mealtime the boarding master sat at the head of this table. The washroom for the hired men was also on the first floor, with living quarters for them above it. On the second floor, eight men lived in four rooms, two to a room. The men were mostly in their thirties and forties. One was a Swede and one a Norwegian. These two roomed together and, for the amusement of us all, played the accordion and other musical instruments. I roomed with a Lithuanian. The others were all from Nova Scotia, fishermen who had had a bad year or two of fishing. Some had lost their boats in storms or had had to give them up to pay debts. They planned to work a few years at Wheeler's and, if they could save enough money, return to Nova Scotia for another go at fishing. These men had lived a hard life and expected to continue to do so. I was taken in as a chore boy to care for the animals, the lawns, keep the iceboxes full of ice, and so on.

The Wheelers had six daughters and no sons. One of the daughters was already married, the other five were in high school or college. Mrs. Wheeler was very kind to me and invited me to social affairs. I usually declined, thinking it better to keep my place as a hired hand.

As chore boy, I had eight work horses and one riding horse to look after. There were also eight pigs that I tended to, and one milk cow. I kept the main house and boarding house supplied with ice and the carriages clean and greased.

After three months as chore boy, the boarding master took over my chores, and I was assigned work like the men were doing. At that point I realized that Mr. Wheeler intended me to learn the business and become his partner. He saw to it that I got to study all the scientific literature from the Agricultural College.

We worked from 5:00 A.M. to 6:00 P.M., six days a week. We took turns on Sundays tending the greenhouse boiler rooms. The greenhouses had to be kept between seventy and eighty degrees at all times. On a sunny day, the fires would be banked with soft coal and the ventilators in the green-houses placed in the open position. On dull, overcast days, the fires were kept burning all day. I felt pretty smart, as young fellows do, and didn't think that I had to be shown how to do anything.

One Sunday when I was responsible for controlling the temperature in the greenhouses, I closed the vents as the sun set and tried to start the fires but had absolutely no success. I did everything I knew to get them started, to no avail. I stirred the coals, added kindling, even tried newspaper. Not a flicker. There was just no draft. Nothing would burn. The temperature in the greenhouses was beginning to drop below seventy degrees and, in desperation, I ran to the mansion to explain my problem to Mr. Wheeler. I think he knew the cause and remedy from the start. He accompanied me to the boiler room where he proceeded calmly to rumple up a newspaper. He walked to the foot of the chimney, opened the iron door at the base, lit the newspaper, and held it in the opening. Very quickly, the air started to rise in the chimney, and with little attention the fires started to burn. How easy it was to get a draft when one knew how. Mr. Wheeler said to me, "Now I think you will have no more trouble." He smiled and left. He was quite a gentleman.

After I had been at Wheeler's a year or more, a young, fresh, strong, talkative Irishman came over from Ireland and, through the boarding house master, got a job at Wheeler's. He was about twenty-seven years old, ten years my senior. To get along with the men, I had learned to say little. This Irishman, to make himself feel important, I suppose, had to pick on someone, and he chose me as his target.

19

We were in the back of the boarding house washing up, combing our hair, waiting for the landlady to call, "Dinner is ready." I was sitting on the long wooden bench with the other men, waiting to wash at the black soapstone sink which only accommodated two men at a time. Mike, the noisy Irishman, had been making sarcastic remarks about me all morning as the two of us were helping the carpenters shingle the boiler room roof. He continued to needle me in the washroom. I made no reply, but when he began to dry himself on the roller towel and I stepped to the sink to take my turn, I must have had enough. I had not yet taken off my eyeglasses but was filling my basin with water full to the rim. Without saying a word, and to the surprise of everyone present, myself included, I picked up my basin with both hands and swung the contents in an upward motion so that Mike got the water full in the face. He swore at me and came at me with both fists flying. My glasses flew off. I was still clutching the basin overhead at the top of my swing, and I came down hard with it on top of Mike's head. I didn't realize how hard I had hit him until later when I saw the misshapen basin. We were both at each other with fists until the boarding master appeared, stopped the fight, and chased me out of the house, yelling, "Troublemaker!"

I was standing a few yards from the back door, amazed that I had escaped unhurt, when Mr. Wheeler appeared. He settled things, told me to go in and eat my dinner, and said that there was to be no more fighting. I retrieved my glasses unharmed. One of the men had rescued them from the floor.

All went well at dinner. At one o'clock, all nine of us met Mr. Wheeler at the boiler room door for our afternoon work assignments. Mike and I were again assigned to assist the carpenters on the roof. Mike wore a cap with a peak pulled over his left eye. Oh, what a big black-and-blue shiner he had, and all afternoon those carpenters rubbed it in.

Mike and I got on well after that, but it wasn't long before he began making fun and jokes about the Irish boarding master himself, who at one point came after Mike with an asparagus knife. Mike stayed only a few months after that.

Before cucumbers were planted in the greenhouses, the soil had to be prepared. First, chemical fertilizers, humus, and horse manure were thoroughly mixed with the soil. Then this augmented soil was steamed to kill weeds, seeds, and vermin. This was done by running steam through perforated pipes buried in the soil. The cucumbers grew on vines planted in rows. They reached six feet in height by the time the 'cumbers were ready to pick in May and June. All of us, including Mr. Wheeler, started picking them before breakfast and then carried them to the packing room in half-bushel baskets. We only picked them when they were of a size that when a man grasped them in the middle, his thumb and middle finger couldn't quite touch. If the fingers touched, the cucumber was left to grow another day. If it had the right color and shape, it was a number one grade and was so packed. Oddly shaped cucumbers were packed as number two or number three class. Although the twos and threes were just as good to eat, it was the number ones that brought the best price.

Rhubarb stalks were also sorted. Only the long, full red ones nearly as long as a bushel box were packed as number one quality. We set the rhubarb plants close to one another and tried to keep their temperature near forty-five degrees. When they were ripe, we pulled all the stalks. The stalks were completely pulled three times. At each pulling they got smaller. After the third pulling, the roots were replanted outside, north of the greenhouses, where they remained for two years, renourishing themselves. Rhubarb must be allowed to freeze seasonally or it will not produce.

We cut the asparagus in early spring, using a long knife to cut the sprouts well below the surface of the soil. Each man carried a half-bushel basket. All of us were at it early in the morning, including Mr. Wheeler. When the baskets were full of cut sprouts, we sorted them to send fresh to market every day. They were carried to the packing room where all ten of us sat around a large table at which we selected the nicest shoots and made them into bunches with the aid of wooden forms. I operated the binding machine, which wrapped and tied a piece of raffia around each bunch when a pedal was pressed. Then I trimmed the root end square with my knife and placed each bunch in a tray of water. Then we packed the bound bunches in clean new boxes, ready for shipment to market. Only the nicest sprouts or spears were sent. We threw the crooked spears aside in a box, and I often met my friend Elizabeth Wheeler when she came to the packing house to pick over the culls, taking the best for use at the home. The rest were for us to eat.

When Elizabeth sat on the big porch at the residence, and I was working in the field in front where we could see each other, we always exchanged a secret wave. Years later when I was at sea and she was a teacher and then later a secretary and treasurer for a private girls' school in Concord Junction, we exchanged letters occasionally. I had to be careful what I wrote, as I was already married by then. Finally, in 1953, Elizabeth's sister replied to one of my letters, telling me that Elizabeth had passed away. Elizabeth was the only one of the six girls who never married.

When Frank Wheeler had two new greenhouses built, contractors put in the foundation and did the woodwork, glazing and painting, but we did our own plumbing, which included setting up the boilers and the pipe work. All of this work was under Mr. Wheeler's direct supervision. For nearly three months, I worked as a pipe fitter with the other men except, of course, when we had to pick cucumbers, and every fourth Sunday when it was my turn to tend the greenhouses. Most of the piping was six inches in diameter, which made for rather heavy work. Although I was a farming apprentice, I also learned a lot about pipefitting.

At the end of my first year's work I asked Mr. Wheeler for an increase in pay. He replied, "On the first of the month, I increased your pay to $27 a month."

Nearly every day throughout the year, Wheeler's sent a load of produce—whether cucumbers, asparagus, celery, mint, chives, or squash—to the Boston Market. At eleven o'clock in the morning, the big load, drawn by four horses, started for Boston. A second driver rode for the first five miles, which had the steepest hills. He then unhitched the two lead horses and took them back to Concord. The remaining two horses were driven at a fast walk all the rest of the way, but never trotted. This was better for the horses and the load. They actually covered more ground per hour than if trotted. They had been trained to walk. If a new horse could not be so trained, it was sold.

While most drivers refrained from letting their horses drink cold water, too much of which could make them sick, Mr. Wheeler gave specific instructions that we were to stop at every watering trough. His theory was that if the horses drank often, they would not overdrink. He must have been correct because we never had a horse get sick from overdrinking.

Since the big-wheeled trucks could not be turned sharply, as might be necessary in heavy traffic, the driver delayed his arrival until after five o'clock when the traffic lightened up. Our route took us through Waltham, Watertown, Harvard Square, over Craigie Bridge, and through the North End and Dock Square, arriving at last at Faneuil Hall where the produce was unloaded by the driver himself. The boxes of produce were piled on the sidewalk in front of commission merchants.

Unlike regular farmers who sold their produce in the market themselves, Mr. Wheeler had us drivers leave the produce on the sidewalks in front of four different brokers who did the selling. It was a big job to unload the boxes from the high wagon. It required lots of climbing up and down.

After the driver had unloaded his produce, he drove around to Blackstone Street, left the empty wagon in the alley, and then put his horses up in a boarding stable adjacent to the Blackstone Hotel. There he unharnessed the horses, fed them, and then went out to find supper for himself. By then it would be 9:00 P.M. Money for all of this was provided to us in a small, white, cloth drawstring bag. The $10 given us was to pay for supper, breakfast and hotel room for the driver, and board for the horses. We drivers were allowed $1.50 for sleeping in the ten-bed room at the Blackstone, where there was no privacy. We were always provided with nice clean blankets by Wheeler to have with us on the trip. Having parked the wagon in the alley, we had to take these blankets into the stable office for safekeeping.

For the first week or two of my assignment as a market driver, I hired a bed at the Blackstone. I was in bed from 10:00 P.M. to 3:00 A.M., but I couldn't relax because the lights were on all the time, the men kept coming and going. I finally fixed it with the stable manager that I could sleep on the floor of his office wrapped up in my own blankets, and he would call me at three in the morning. For this favor I bought him an occasional beer, and I saved the $1.50 a night, or $9 a week, which was far more than I earned at the job. In this way I slept better and felt more secure, as well as richer.

We market garden drivers got up at 3:00 A.M. but, instead of selling what we had brought to market, we went directly to the stable, fed and brushed down the horses, and went out to get breakfast nearby while the horses ate.

The bar-restaurants in this area were open by four in the morning. After breakfast the driver got his horses hitched to the empty wagon and drove down to Long Wharf to the wooden box factory. He aimed to get his wagon under one of the chutes before five when the factory opened. If he was not there that early, he might be delayed several hours waiting his turn. Although many farmers used secondhand, dark, dirty-looking boxes, Frank Wheeler always bought brand-new boxes, clean and white. Although they cost a few cents more apiece, they made the produce bring a better price. By six the driver had his load of new boxes lashed down and started off to Concord. In cold weather he had to walk fast or run alongside to keep warm.

On the ground floor of the Blackstone Hotel was a barroom facing Dock Square. Although I was barely seventeen years old, I looked older and was seldom challenged. Often on Sunday nights, when most other restaurants nearby were closed, I enjoyed a big oyster stew for my supper. It was cooked individually right there at the bar. It cost fifty cents and came with all the oyster crackers I could eat. I sat up on a high stool at one end of the bar where only food was permitted to be served.

Sometimes I sat at the tables with the men and bought the stable man a drink. If I were challenged by the waiter for being underage, several men would speak up, saying that they knew me and that I was of age.

Once in a while I attended an entertainment. The only theater I remember attending was the Old Howard. I sat in one of the last two rows in the balcony, then known as "Nigger Heaven." Those seats cost only fifty cents. While there, I was always afraid that some drunk might vomit on me. About the most daring sight on the stage was Molly, who wore a low-necked dress and sometimes bared her fat knees. We all hoped that she would show us more. I was disappointed and felt cheated because the advertisements had promised so much.

One Sunday evening, after I had unloaded and put my horses up for the night, I took a walk into the Public Gardens and sat on a settee, watching the swans in the pond nearby. It was a nice moonlit night and I was enjoying relaxing. I had on me what was left of the $10 expense money and some money of my own to buy tobacco. (To make extra money, I bought tobacco wholesale when I was in Boston for resale to the men at Wheeler's.) After a while a middle-aged, well-dressed man sat down beside me and got friendly. I was suspicious of him, fearing that he was a pickpocket. I was on guard. Then he moved closer to me and slapped me gently on the thigh and said,

"That's a good-shaped leg you have, son." I did not reply but got up and walked toward Blackstone Street as quickly as I could.

On our trips back to Concord, we arrived by 10:30 A.M., put up the horses and ate our dinner. The truck was then reloaded with boxes of produce for the next trip. Fresh horses were harnessed, and all was ready to make the next trip to market by 11:30. A load was sent daily, except Saturday. At certain slack times in midsummer there were just three trips a week instead of the usual six.

I had very little spare time after a long day of work and study, but I spent most of what time I had making a little extra money. I never used tobacco myself. Instead, I set up a store to sell it to the other men. In winter I did some trapping. In summer I picked wild cherries and sent them to market by the bushel. In the fall I harvested wild grapes. I also planted tomatoes at home. Those that were in excess of what my family could eat I packed in bushels and carried, a bushel at a time, on the handlebars of my bicycle the three miles to Concord to be sent to market with the Wheeler produce. One night, about ten o'clock, I was riding down the long hill toward Concord with a nicely packed bushel of tomatoes on the handlebars when my front wheel got caught in a rut, and over I went. I had no thought of saving myself, only the tomatoes. I repacked them and carried on, although a bit painfully.

In the fall came my big project. There were great spans of meadow on either side of the Concord River. Here I raked wild cranberries after dark by lantern light. Many of the berries had frozen and were well mixed with hay. However, I raked many burlap bags full of the mixture and stowed them in the boiler room at Wheeler's. Later, when the weather got too cold to work outside at night, I went to the warm boiler room and picked over my berries until I had a bushel box full, which I sent to market along with the rest of the produce. These extra projects produced money that I considered my own. I shared none of it with my father.

During the winter months, Wheeler purchased many freight car loads of soft coal and green manure at the railroad siding at South Lincoln Station. The men worked like machines loading the wagons. A man with a wagon and a pair of horses could make four roundtrips a day, a total distance of fourteen miles, transporting three tons per trip, twelve tons a day. The coal was loaded to the wagons by shovel from the freight cars and then in turn from the wagons to the boiler room.

The manure was full of hay and was more difficult to shovel than the coal. The Wheeler men who did this work had to be young and tough. They all took pride in their work and never had to be prompted. I had my turn at driving and loading coal and manure, and I nearly killed myself in the process. I finally was able to keep up with the others loading coal, but not the manure. I thought that I was a man, but I wasn't able to do as much as the others. I managed to make my four trips each day, but instead of going fishing at six with the others, I kept at it until 8:30 or so before I got my last wagonload emptied. Then I had to grease the wheel bearings, as I was required to have the wagon ready for the next day.

I continued helping out at home with half of my wages from Wheeler's, but since he only paid twice a year, there were seven months in summer and five during the winter when I had no pay. That meant that Father went for long periods without my help.

One day in the early summer while I was cultivating young asparagus seedlings in the field near the road, I noticed a horse-drawn carriage stop in the road opposite. As I reached the end of a row, I looked up and discovered that one of my relatives was in the carriage. My father's sister, Aunt Marian, had come with a message for me from Father. He needed money. It was then the middle of the week. I was to meet him on Saturday night at nine in the evening on Lee's bridge. That afternoon I notified Mr. Wheeler that I needed $75 by Saturday. He advanced the money, and I met Father that night on the bridge as arranged. He was on foot, and with him was Nurse Allan, who had helped my mother when Chester and Clara were born. I didn't ask, of course, but I supposed that he needed the money to pay Miss Allan. I know that he wouldn't have asked for it unless he really needed it.

Massachusetts Schoolship *Ranger* under sail

"Iron Jaw" Bamforth in the foreground with fellow cadets
aboard the Schoolship *Ranger*, 1914

Photo courtesy of the Board of Directors of the Alumni Association of the
Massachusetts Maritime Academy. Used with permission.

## CHAPTER 2

# TO THE TOPMOST BUNT

The longer I worked on Wheeler's farm, studying and reading about the agriculture business, the more I realized that there were very few advancement opportunities for me. Without capital or good land to inherit, I was on the wrong track. I could have married into the Wheeler family, and I was not altogether dissuaded from this possibility. However, I decided that I should get into a field in which I could advance on my ability alone.

A few years previously, my Aunt Grace's husband, John Danner, a Navy officer, had shown me the Massachusetts Nautical Training Ship *Ranger*. When he had been the ship's executive officer, he had taken me on board for the annual governor's inspection. I had a chance to see the drills demonstrating the working of the ship. Becoming a cadet on her seemed my best hope.

In September 1913, at age eighteen, I wrote to the Secretary of State in Boston and got the list of the schoolship entrance requirements. The fall class had just begun. I would have to wait for a vacancy and then be admitted in competition with other applicants. In a few weeks I received a notice of a vacancy. I had to appear for a scholastic and physical examination. I had been out of school for two and a half years, during which time I had had no practice with figures other than tallying my earnings and savings. On the train ride to Boston, I studied a sample examination and came across a problem involving square root. I had forgotten how to do it. In desperation I introduced myself to a woman across the aisle, and fortunately she was able to help me. The examination lasted all day and included writing a letter

28

about why I wanted to join the school. That night I went back to Concord to await the results.

In just a few days, I was notified that I had been accepted. Mr. Wheeler was disappointed but wished me well. I had hoped to say goodbye to Elizabeth, but she was not there.

I reported to the *Ranger*, which was then lying at North End Park, Boston. I found myself one of 104 cadets. My joining late made me ripe for hazing, and I certainly got my share. I sang before the crowd and was doused with a bucket of water from behind. They put boxing gloves on me and matched me with an opponent. Since I did these things good-naturedly, their fun with me soon wore off.

The training was a two-year course. The first year, each cadet took the general course of deck navigation and engineering. The second year, with adequate grades, a cadet could choose either deck or engineering course. If he did not have good enough grades, he was assigned to one or the other. I was used to working for what I got, and I was ready to work here. It was, in fact, hard work. Most of the other cadets had had far better schooling and found the studies little more than a review of what they had already learned in high school. I found the studies very difficult, however, the more so because I had joined the class two months late. There were fifty-four cadets in my class. Most of them, I believe, could have easily surpassed me had they been so motivated. I worked and studied nearly every minute possible. In spite of having started from behind, I was first in my class in engineering and second in my class in the deck course material. I was urged to stick with the engineering course, but I was determined to go on with the deck training in preparation for becoming a ship's officer.

Each year before the ship went on a regular summer cruise, it took a short trip in April, which is cold and rainy in New England, to weed out undesirables or those who had simply joined for a nice summer's boat ride. The short cruise began just after a new class was taken in. We went only as far as Provincetown Harbor, at the end of Cape Cod, where the ship remained at anchor. We took a wagonload of bricks and a load of sand. For most of the two weeks, we were on our hands and knees with half a brick in each hand, sanding the wooden decks to remove the weathered surface which had developed during the winter. This was part of the hardening-up process to make seamen of us. Some of the less determined boys quit right there, forfeiting their down payments.

On the annual three-month cruise, we put our theoretical training into practice. I was on the verge of being seasick many times during my first cruise. I would look at the waves and wonder what was the matter with the earth's gravity. Why didn't it exert more control over this vessel?

My previous jobs ashore had almost always afforded me a regular night's sleep. Now I found that the ship's schedule made no distinction between day and night, at least when we were at sea. We were divided into two watches, half on the port watch and half on the starboard watch, serving four hours on and four off duty. This routine went on continuously at sea. There were always things to do off duty as we followed the orders: Shorten Sail, Make Sail, Trim Sail, Lifeboat Drill, Man Overboard Drill, Fire Drill, Collision Drill, Scrub and Wash Clothes, Wash Down Fore 'n Aft, Inspect Locker Drill, Signal Drill, Captain's Mast (deck court), Navigation Drill, Mend Sails, Shift Sail, and Change to Storm Sail. When not occupied with these drills and operations, those on duty performed the tasks of running of the ship: steering, lookout, firing the boilers, coal passing, oiling the machinery, general cleaning, and orderly (or guard) duty.

Every morning at sea we stripped off our clothing, and the bos'n turned the saltwater fire hose on us. That was our daily bath. Freshwater was reserved for drinking and for cooking. If we struck a rain squall, we were ordered to strip and wash. Rainwater made a better-feeling bath, but it seemed anything but warm, especially with a fresh breeze blowing.

Each cadet had a small steel locker where all personal effects were neatly kept. As was Navy custom, we slept in hammocks fastened to hooks overhead. Each hammock had a thin hair mattress, a mattress cover, and a single blanket. We had no pillows. When not in use, these hammocks were made up with timber hitches and stowed in the netting beneath the ship's rail. (Hammocks with their mattresses were traditionally stowed this way to provide protection from small-arms fire if a ship were engaged in battle.) When we hung our hammocks for sleeping, we lashed the foot ring to the foot hook. It was a form of hazing for senior classmen to let this lashing go free or to cut it with a knife, if they felt mean enough. When a cadet had his foot rope cut, he might be lucky to fasten himself back up to finish his sleep using only pieces of cut line. In any event, he would find it very embarrassing in the morning, not being able to hide the fact that he had been cut down. My rope was never cut, but many times I was let down from my perch, feet first, after I was asleep. The foot of my hammock would fall seven feet to the deck. I was never hurt. I assumed one of the upperclassmen was responsible, but I never caught anyone.

Cadets were punished for minor offenses with a number of demerits. Each demerit meant one half hour of extra duty to be performed during liberty hours. Extra duty work was always unpleasant. I was fortunate because I was put on report only once. The ship was at anchor in Gloucester Harbor. I was the officer on duty on the main deck, amidships. It was night, and I was standing clear of everything (not leaning against anything), with a telescope under my arm. Officer Ware claimed that he walked past the middle of the ship, my area of responsibility. He put me on report, "Asleep on duty."

This was a serious offense, although my first. At Mast, the captain's court held every morning, Captain Atwater read the charge and asked me if it were true. I denied it. Mr. Ware asked me if I had seen him pass from the quarterdeck to the bridge at 2:14 A.M. I replied, "No, sir."

The captain said, "First offense, ten demerits." That hurt, but perhaps it did me good to have been punished at least once. I had a lot of respect for Mr. Ware and thought it was possible he had passed me that night, but to this day I don't believe I was asleep.

While I was a junior cadet, a regular Navy officer joined the staff. Lieutenant Seechts, a man who had been in sail and had worked up through the ranks to warrant officer and then lieutenant, was a friend of my family. He was determined to make a sailor of me. One day when we were having the drill, "Make Sail and Furl All Sail," Lieutenant Seechts spied me from the quarterdeck.

He called, "Bamforth, what are you doing back here?"

"I am in charge of the spanker, sir," I answered.[1]

"Never mind about the spanker. I want to make a sailor out of you. Up in the topsail bunt!" he shouted and swung his foot at my behind as I ran to the mast.

On Navy square-riggers[2] like the *Ranger*, the fore topsail bunt is the position in the middle of the fore topsail yard, where the really hard work takes place. It is the position where the sail, neatly made up, makes a good appearance. I was glad I was used to working at great heights from my experience shingling roofs. From then on Seechts saw to it that Cadet Bamforth was toughened up and made a real sailor, whether it was according to regulations or not.

When the *Ranger* was on a cruise, she anchored a distance from shore. Liberty parties went to and fro in boats either under oars or towed by a motorboat. The motorboat ran on hourly schedules with passengers, usually officers. As a junior cadet, I was often the coxswain[3] of the motorboat. Once, on a run between the *Ranger* and a landing float, I had to make a rather difficult starboard landing. Starboard landings are inherently more difficult than port landings in single-screw boats with the usual right-turning propeller. I was using bell signals to communicate with the cadet operating the engine. When we reached the desired position on approaching the float, I rang three bells, calling for the engine to be operated full speed astern. The cadet operating the engine did just the opposite, full ahead. We crashed square into the side of a moored four-masted wooden sailing vessel. Fortunately, I helped check some of the force of the collision by assisting the bowman with his boathook. There was no damage, but it was mighty embarrassing, I can tell you that. At least one senior officer among the passengers had difficulty keeping a straight face.

During the winter season, the ship tied up at North End Park in Boston Harbor. Classes were held on the ship and in an adjacent building ashore. Doctor Cob, the ship's medical officer, taught English and Hygiene. He was well liked by the cadets. He warned us of the many hazards, especially vene-real disease, to young men visiting foreign ports.

On weekends, boys who wanted to and could afford it went home to visit. Those who stayed had to do a certain amount of ship care but were allowed liberty during much of Saturday afternoon and most of Sunday. About seventy boys went home, which left about thirty-four cadets who either lived too far away or who did not have money to travel. I stayed and studied because I was determined to succeed.

I not only worked hard at my studies, I also took my other assignments very seriously. One evening I was on duty as a junior deck officer, in uni-form and carrying a telescope under my arm as an emblem of my office. I noticed Linnehan, one of my classmates, sitting on the engine room comb-ing.[4] Half a dozen senior classmen started to pester him. Linnehan had lit-tle sense of humor and took their joshing as a personal offense. I came to his defense and ordered the seniors to break it up. To my surprise, they turned on me for not respecting their seniority. They dragged me to the forward deck near the scuttlebutt[5] and laid me on the deck, face up. They opened my belt, pulled my shirt up and my pants down, and then took turns filling their mouths with cold water at the fountain and squirting my bare middle. When I was thoroughly soaked, they left me alone and beat it. Generally I showed little sense of humor myself, but this time I took it all as a joke and carried on as though nothing had happened.

Eventually I acquired the nickname Iron Jaw. I never knew just why they called me that, but I realized that it probably described me to the others: a firm, serious conformist. (Of course, I also had a prominent jaw.) I was like that, I think, because Father taught me that rules were to be obeyed to the letter without question or compromise.

On October 2, 1915, I completed the Massachusetts Nautical Schoolship course, making me eligible to serve as quartermaster or junior officer of the watch on any merchant vessel. I was second in my class, behind Earle Hammond. The management of the schoolship offered me a job as master-at-arms at about the same pay as a ship's officer, but I was not interested. Just making a living was not my goal. I had set my mind to advancement in the Merchant Service. I started my search for a job as quartermaster. I inquired at all the shipping companies whose addresses I had previously gathered. I wrote to all the companies in New York for employment appli-cations, and I visited those with offices in Boston. Some of them sent appli-cation forms, which I filled out and returned. This activity offered me hope of employment.

The graduation exercises were to take place aboard the *Ranger* on October 6, but I was free to go on my own by the second, having com-pleted all academic requirements. That Saturday I called on a past employer to collect money owed me, and in the evening I joined my fam-ily for supper at St. Anne's Church. Sunday, after services, I helped my father with a gasoline engine and later joined the gang for a baseball game in the hollow behind the house. In the evening I studied a correspondence course in English.

Monday morning I went to Boston for the day, job hunting. No luck. I called on Mr. Dimmick, secretary to the schoolship's commissioners, for advice. The next day I went to Concord, withdrew $20 from my savings account, and went to Boston once more. This time I went to the Navy Yard, hoping to get a job on a Navy collier.[6] There were no openings but, back at home, I found a telegram from Mr. Dimmick: "SS GEO HAWLEY ARRIVED STOP SAILING EARLY IN MORNING STOP BE ON BOARD EARLY READY TO SAIL STOP."

The ship was discharging coal at a pier in Fort Point Channel near South Station. I was there with my things promptly at eight. I met the master, Captain Moses, and was hired as quartermaster at $40 a month. We sailed at four o'clock on October 6, 1915. I missed the graduation exercises, but I was very happy to have a job.

## The S.S. *George Hawley*

Captain Moses was an able shipmaster who did most of his own piloting, docking, and undocking. The *George Hawley* was a "laker," built on the Great Lakes, 240 feet long, just short enough to fit in canal locks. She carried 4,200 tons of cargo. With her steam power she made about nine knots average speed and steered like a box when loaded. The charter was to carry a load of coal from Baltimore to Galveston and to return with a load of sulfur for Philadelphia.

I had the wheel on the way out of Boston. Steering was by magnetic compass; there was no gyro or other automatic gear.[7] The captain and officer of the watch could not see directly ahead from their vantage point in the small wheelhouse far aft, so the bow had to be put off course for a "jiffy" so they could see to take bearings. I was hardly a good steersman, but I understood the orders "port" and "starboard helm." Fortunately, my first time at the wheel was when she was loaded and therefore was relatively easy to steer, at least when there was little or no wind. The bow rode high in the air. Since I kept overcorrecting amateurishly, there were frequent enough "jiffies" with the bow off course.

There was one other quartermaster on the ship. My partner was an experienced seaman who had served on this ship for two years. He and I were to divide the days between us, four hours on and four hours off while at sea, twelve on and twelve off in port. At sea, the quartermaster's duties included steering the vessel and maintenance work around the ship's bridge, boat deck, lifeboats and navigational gear, all done under the strict supervision of the senior officers. In port the quartermaster often stood the gangway watch, where he was responsible for safety and security. We ate with the captain and officers. The food was the best I had ever eaten, and there was all the ice water one could drink. We bunked with the crew, who worked days. Since we had to try to get our sleep at odds with the crew's waking hours, it was very difficult to get our needed rest. The forecastle was alive with lights and damned noisy.

In New York we went on dry dock.[8] We quartermasters stood our twelve-hour watches in the wheelhouse, which had windows all around. From this perch, we could observe everyone who came on board or went ashore. We were high enough to see the Statue of Liberty, the waterfront, and all ships leaving or entering the harbor. Many of the ships were under foreign flags. I picked out attractive ships under the American flag and fixed my hopes on the future.

While I was on duty one day, I noticed a young woman on board going from room to room. I asked her what business she had there.

"I'm selling," she said.

"What are you selling?" I asked.

"Thread," she replied. That didn't sound reasonable to me, thread bringing so little profit, but since she was going from one officer's room to another, the officers obviously knew of her presence. She seemed familiar with the surroundings and not likely to get hurt, so I left her alone.

On October 15, the shipyard work was completed, and we sailed for Baltimore, arriving on the seventeenth. After loading 3,800 tons of coal, we set sail on the nineteenth for Galveston.

Because we wanted to make trips in as little time as possible, we gave careful consideration to the currents. On our trip to Texas, we were traveling against the Gulf Stream. The captain carefully avoided the head current by staying in close to the Keys. This was not without hazard, since coral reefs skirt the Gulf Stream. Captain Moses remained on the bridge most of the way down the Florida coast.

We arrived in Galveston following a hurricane. The storm had left the city largely in ruins. Buildings on the high seawall facing the ocean had been destroyed. At the entrance to the harbor, we saw the Southern Pacific liner *El Sud* lying on her side, high up on the beach. The tide had been so high that the vessel had floated there and was left stranded when the tide receded. As we sailed further into the harbor, we saw another merchant ship high and dry on shore, resting across railroad tracks. Our pilot told us two other merchant ships had been driven twenty miles inland by the wind and extra high tides and were now resting on meadowland. A channel was going to be dredged to a nearby river to free them.

We unloaded our cargo of coal at the pier at the foot of Twenty-fourth Street. In port we quartermasters stood the usual twelve hours off and twelve hours on watch by the gangway. As daylight broke, I made out several men asleep on tops of railroad boxcars, perched on the narrow catwalks. They had covered themselves with newspapers against the dampness. It looked dangerous to me. Off duty, I went to mail letters. I was struck by the incredibly high watermark, well above my head, left by the hurricane on the inside walls of the customs house.

In port we were all free to come and go when not on watch, but when we two quartermasters were off duty, we had to use much of our spare time trying to get sleep. The ship stayed in port only twelve hours before we were off on another trip. This left little time for sightseeing. I couldn't rest in the forecastle, which had no natural light, no portholes, and inadequate ventilation. Then there were the noisy crew members. So whenever I could, when the ship was in port discharging, I swung a hammock on the poop deck under the awnings. I found it much easier to sleep, in spite of the ever-present coal dust.

There was a fruit ship nearby taking on a full load of bananas from freight cars. They had to be shipped green. Any that had become bruised or that had started to ripen were removed. I was crazy about bananas. After asking permission, I took a bunch of the rejects from the pile on the dock. I hung them up by my hammock, picked off those nearest to being ripe, and ate them with enthusiasm. I ate too many and suffered considerable distress.

On November 5, we finished discharging, took on three hundred tons of bunker coal,[9] and sailed for Port Arthur. The crew worked day and night cleaning the holds in order to be ready to load sulfur on arrival. The next day we tied up to a Union Sulfur Company pier. On shore was but one low-lying building. This structure housed the machinery that brought the powdered sulfur up from underground. It was delivered by means of a powered endless belt. The sulfur just poured in. The dust burned our eyes, nostrils, and throats. We were fully loaded on November 8 at six in the morning and sailed immediately for Philadelphia. The crew secured ship and tried to wash off the dreadful sulfur dust, but we were bothered by it all the way to Philly.

On November 9, I was so sick to my stomach from eating green bananas that I could hardly stand up to steer. Captain Moses gave me a dose of calomel and followed this with a dose of Epsom salts. I was allowed to sit on a tall stool to steer. Luckily it was nice and smooth in the gulf. Even so, I nearly fell off the stool and out the wheelhouse door. I had to be tied in to steer at all. Part of the time the officer on watch had to steer for me. By the next day I felt better. I was then able to stand my full watch, but, being so weak, I was allowed to sit on the stool. Finally I had to give up the stool as the ship gained motion in the small sea.

We rounded the Keys on the twelfth, only this time the captain kept the ship far enough offshore to give us the benefit of the Gulf Stream currents. This made it dangerously difficult to see landmarks, but the officers knew the course well. (The *George Hawley* had no chart room. The captain kept charts in his office and the officers had them in their rooms. I was disappointed not to be able to study them.) They would navigate close to a light vessel or buoy, then shape a course directly for the next one. If, when the calculated time was up, the aid had not been sighted, they would haul out[10] one half point. Then, when they sighted the buoy or light vessel, they hauled close again so as to make a good departure for the next one. It was not uncommon to pass close enough to a light vessel for a newspaper to be tossed on board.

On the sixteenth we reached Philadelphia. The cargo had to be weighed, and unloading was a very slow process due to rain. The weather was so very different from the warmth of the South, and my face was sore from the northwest wind. I was chilled. I wrote letters while on the long watch in the wheelhouse. I had fully recovered from my bout with bananas and swore never to eat green ones again. However, the sulfur dust seemed even worse than before. On the nineteenth, the captain paid off the whole crew. I received $57.33.

The crew washed the ship as we finished discharging, and on the twenty-second we sailed for Newport News. The crew finished washing down the sulfur residue inside and out. This made it easier, at last, on the nose, eyes, and throat.

On November 23, we anchored off Newport News to wait for a clear berth. We were among many vessels at anchor waiting to get to the coal docks. At about eleven in the morning I was alone on the bridge. Others were busy about the decks. Although we were at anchor, all of a sudden I noticed that the ship was forging ahead through the water. I called the captain, who came up from his room two steps at a time, grabbed the telegraph handle and swung it through STOP to FULL ASTERN.[11] Before we got the headway off, we struck the side of an empty sailing ship anchored ahead, provoking angry protest from its captain. Fortunately the stem[12] of the *George Hawley* was vertical, and we did no damage. Better to be boxy than fine of line in this instance. You can imagine how emphatically Captain Moses instructed the engineers never again to test the engines unless there was an officer on the bridge.

That evening the ship was assisted to the coal berth. This was a great high pier where the coal cars on railroad tracks were high above the ship. The cars dumped the coal through chutes to the ship below. It was a mighty dusty job. All rooms and vents had to be closed tightly. Even then the dust found its way inside.

On the twenty-fourth we sailed for Boston. When we arrived I got leave for the weekend. At home the next day, Sunday, I appreciated the full night's sleep. I had stood four-hour watches for two long months. After church and a family dinner at home, I took a walk through the woods with my brother Ralph. We visited more family and friends, returned home by foot, and I enjoyed another delicious full night's sleep. Monday morning I was up early and returned to Boston on the first train. We finished discharging and sailed in ballast[13] for New York. When we arrived on

December 1, we were received directly onto a floating dry dock for repairs. In the afternoon I visited three American-Hawaiian ships that I had recently admired, the *Virginian*, the *Alaskan*, and the *Mexican.*

We sailed for Newport News in fine cool weather, and there we loaded coal for Providence, Rhode Island. Soon after midnight on the sixth, we started up the Narragansett River. I was at the wheel for the four-to-eight watch. The weather was clear and the tide was strong flood.[14] At 4:20 A.M. the messboy had just brought us all coffee. It was still dark. We were about two miles up Narragansett Bay with the captain piloting. As the messboy handed the captain his cup of coffee, we came upon a sharp bend to the left. There was no light on the buoy at Bull Point, making the turn very difficult to see. Captain Moses ordered, "Port the wheel." I put fifteen degrees on her, but the ship did not respond since she was deep in the water and sluggish. The full tide didn't help either. The red light on Fort Adams indicated we were on a dangerous course. The captain then ordered, "HARD A-PORT!" and set his coffee mug on top of the compass binnacle.[15] I was tense and knew something was wrong. The captain still expected the ship to make the turn, and she did, almost. She slid up onto Pinnacle Reef, south of Rose Island, and there she sat. No blame rested upon me for the grounding–I had done just as the captain had ordered–but was concerned nonetheless. I was proud of this ship and of Captain Moses, who was always a gentleman and kept his head. At the next high tide, the captain directed back-and-fill maneuvers[16] and, with the tide turning to ebb, he was successful in working her off the reef. We proceeded to Providence some eight hours later.

At Hancock (now Melville), halfway between Newport and Providence, the Navy Yard had a coaling station. We heard that the Navy, noting our grounding, had sent a tug to assist us. I arranged for my partner to take my twelve-hour watch, and I went to call on my Uncle John Danner, who was then in command of the coaling station that we had passed. I told him and Aunt Grace how proud I was to be a quartermaster on such a fine ship as the *George Hawley.* I admitted, of course, that she was much smaller than the Navy colliers that came to his station. I was terribly let down, however, when my uncle told me that there had been a coal barge stranded on Rose Island and that he had ordered a Navy tug to assist in floating her. I had to admit that the vessel aground had been my ship and, though not a barge, she was barge-like to look at.

From Providence we sailed empty to dry dock at Erie Basin in New York. The insurance company insisted on examining the bottom. Sure enough, bottom plates and some frames had to be replaced. For having damaged the vessel, Captain Moses lost his license for a few weeks. Luckily he had it back by the time the ship was repaired and ready to sail once more.

The cold northwest wind was severe, but we quartermasters were allowed to stand watch in the warm wheelhouse. While on watch we painted the inside. I could view New York with all the fine ships going to and fro.

Directly across the channel stood the Statue of Liberty welcoming all the immigrants who poured in from Europe every day. I took the time to become familiar with charts and navigation equipment. This was a good opportunity for me, one I would not have had if the ship had been active.

I had put in applications with the many different companies for a quartermaster position before getting my present job. I hoped that I would hear from some of them. I longed to get better jobs on larger ships traveling to far-flung ports of the world. I was particularly interested in the clean, well-painted American-Hawaiian ships I had seen.

## The S.S. *Montanan*

On December 15, when I had the day off, I went to the Customs House to get my seaman's license and lifeboat certificate. As I hadn't been a full three years at sea, I had to go to the Navy Yard and be examined by the chief bos'n. My knowledge was found satisfactory, and I was issued a certificate.

While ashore I met my classmates Hammond and Nichols. They were quartermasters on the American-Hawaiian ship *Montanan,* and I went on board with them for a visit. I was so impressed with the better quarters that, on leaving my friends, I went to see Captain Bennett at the American-Hawaiian marine superintendent's office on the upper level of the dock and applied for a job. I was given an application to fill out and questioned as to my reason for applying. At the time Captain Bennett was looking for officer material but told me that candidates must have served at least a year on American-Hawaiian ships before being allowed to take charge of a watch. He told me that if a quartermaster proved himself reliable, he would have a chance for promotion.

All of this sounded good to me. There was a quartermaster vacancy on the S.S. *Pennsylvanian,* and Captain Bennett gave me a note to take to her chief officer. The mate, a big, blustering fellow, asked me the usual questions. In those days captains favored candidates who had square-rigged sailing ship training, which I had. I thought surely the mate would choose me. Instead he said, "Get out of here. I've got too many schoolship men here already.

I returned to the *George Hawley* and stood my twelve-hour watch. Still determined, I returned to Captain Bennett's office next day and reapplied to his assistant, Mr. Singleton. Captain Bennett overheard me and bellowed, "Young man, come in here." I went into his office.

"Didn't I send you to the *Pennsylvanian* yesterday?"

"Yes, sir, but the mate would not have me."

"Why?" Bennett demanded. I told him exactly what the mate had said to me.

Bennett thought for a moment and then said, "Report to the mate of the S.S. *Montanan*," the very ship on which I had visited my classmates.

The mate of the *Montanan* was a Mainer, truly brought up on sail. He was a man of few words. He simply looked me up and down and hired me to report for duty the following day. I was elated. I returned to the *George Hawley*, stood my twelve-hour watch, then had Captain Moses pay me off. I never forgot my experiences with that gentleman.

The *Montanan* was a package freight carrier fitted out to carry twelve passengers as well as cargo in the intercoastal trade.[17] When I came aboard, she was discharging general goods from the Hawaiian Islands, canned pineapple and sugar; and from the Pacific Coast, dried fruits, lumber, and canned fruits and vegetables. This was surely a nice clean cargo compared to the coal and sulfur I had been dealing with. Her next charter was to carry manufactured goods to South America and bring back rubber, coffee, hardwoods, beef, and linseed. Good charter rates were available, but South American countries had difficulty getting supplies, since the bulk of shipping was carrying war materials to Europe.

The ship was commanded by Captain George Wright, and I became one of his four quartermasters. On December 17, I started work at eight in the morning. I was assigned to a room with four berths and an adjoining bath. The room was not big enough for a chair for each of us, but it did have a wooden bench so those of us assigned to upper bunks had a place to sit other than on one of the lower bunks. Since we owned very little, we had enough room. There were never more than two of us in the room at any one time anyway. It was a pleasant room, comparatively speaking, principally because it was on deck, with portholes on two sides. It was, in fact, very nice compared with most other ships of that era. The only drawback was that the steering room was right next door. In it, a large quadrant on the head of the rudder moved to and fro by means of a pair of compound steam engines, which made considerable noise while we were at sea.

Next day the *Montanan* had completed loading and we sailed. Even though there were four of us instead of two, we quartermasters still stood watches of four hours on and four off. Instead of standing at the wheel for four hours straight, the two of us on duty at the same time stood two hours as lookout and then swapped places for two hours at the wheel. Most quartermasters at the time were young schoolship graduates like me. I was happy to be serving with Hammond and Nichols. Stoltz, a fine fellow, was the fourth.

The *Montanan* was a modern ship for her day. She had a ten thousand ton capacity, 10 percent refrigerated; a reciprocating, quadruple expansion steam engine with twelve knots speed; and a Telefunken radio direction finder.[18] We didn't have powered window wipers in the wheelhouse, just manual ones like on a model-T Ford.

We had a full load of general cargo destined for three ports in Brazil: Bahia (now Salvador), Santos, and Rio de Janeiro. After loading at Philadelphia, Baltimore, and New York, we headed south. We crossed the Gulf Stream in delightful summery weather and sighted flying fish, dolphins, and whales. On December 22 we ran through the center of a twister, at which point the wind calmed, and then an hour later it blew just as strongly in the opposite direction. During the worst of the storm, the captain had the ship hove-to[19] the sea. On the twenty-fourth we passed San Juan Light and changed course to the east for St. Thomas of the Dutch West Indies. At daylight on the twenty-fifth, the pilot boarded and took us in. It would be my first of many Christmases away from home.

St. Thomas was a valuable fueling station situated on a direct approach to the Panama Canal from Europe. The people of St. Thomas were mostly colored and very poor. It was common to see them on the main street sucking on the end of a sugar stalk.

While we were tied up at the dock on the day after Christmas, I went below at midnight and was back on duty at four in the morning. Although the rules forbade unauthorized persons aboard, about an hour into my watch I heard women's voices and giggling coming from the crew's quarters. I looked around and discovered two Negro girls in their late teens. They were dressed in short skirts and wore no shoes or stockings. They seemed to be well pleased with themselves and were carrying several pairs of old shoes and dungarees, evidently gifts from the crew. I was embarrassed. I wasn't supposed to allow them on board, but there they were. Since they had with them nothing of value, no ship's gear, I was relieved and very glad that they were on their way ashore. They got off before any officer discovered them on board on my watch. Their true mission barely entered my mind.

War news: On December 30, we heard by wireless that the British steamship *Persia* had been sunk in the Mediterranean, a war casualty.

As our ship passed through the northeast trade wind belt, we entered the doldrums, a belt extending around the earth from five degrees south to five degrees north latitude, in which the trade winds meet. It is an area of hot, muggy weather, subject to squalls and small tornadoes. Sailing vessels had great difficulty crossing the doldrums due to lack of a steady wind; but steamers welcome the lack of wind, which means smooth seas, and they make good time in these waters.

When we passed the mouth of the great Amazon River, we were too far off to see land, but we could see the black, muddy waters from its outpourings for miles. After leaving the doldrums, we found ourselves in the gentle southeast trade wind belt, and there in the South Atlantic, we saw the graceful great albatross with a wing span of almost seven feet. Porpoise sighted the ship and rushed to play under the bow. They would roll, dive, jump, and squeal as they broke the surface. Occasionally we saw a whale or two blowing in the distance. As we passed down the Brazilian coast, we saw tops of mountains faintly in the distance.

The first port of call was Bahia. We anchored several miles from shore, and the only contact with land was via open boat. The fare going ashore was three pesos, but to get back, the fare was at least ten pesos, or all the money you had. I didn't feel I could afford it so stayed aboard. The general cargo was discharged into barges which were towed alongside by tugs. We loaded raw rubber in balls one to two feet in diameter.

In port we quartermasters worked directly for the second mate, Mr. McGill. He helped us with our studies. The quartermasters lived in the extreme aft end of the ship. Mr. McGill's room was near the bridge some two hundred feet away. He made communication between his quarters and ours easy by rigging a Morse code system between the two. This gave him much needed practice and helped us become ready to pass the examination for our officer's licenses.

Earle Hammond, my partner and schoolmate, was a radio ham who often listened to a radio signal through a crystal set that he carried. The European war was in progress and, in order to maintain neutral status, Brazil required that all radios be sealed in port. Earle's listening device had to be used secretly, making it all the more interesting.

Our second port of call was Rio de Janeiro, a beautiful harbor surrounded by high coastal mountains. It was in Rio that I learned an important lesson in navigation. What I should have done when I first went ashore was to get the name of the quay where the ship was tied up, thus establishing my point of departure. I failed to do this when I decided to explore the city one evening. I wandered about, taking in the sights by myself. I couldn't speak the language, and I couldn't find a soul who was able or was willing, to speak English, but I kept trying. Finally I asked a German salesman for help. He knew the city very well and figured out where I wanted to go. I got into a taxi, and he gave the driver directions in Portuguese.

While in Rio we loaded from lighters[20] tied alongside. One of our deck engineers in charge of loading became very angry with the Brazilians, particularly with a very officious customs officer who strutted about, dressed in his white uniform. At one point the engineer made an insulting gesture to this contemptuous officer on the shore. As a result, the customs officer stopped the loading and demanded that he be compensated. Time is money to a ship, so the captain and the agent agreed to give the customs officer all the dunnage at the completion of the unloading of the ship. The dunnage, wooden boards used to separate and protect cargo in transit, amounted to fifty thousand board feet of lumber. The Brazilian officers worked all angles and took advantage of every opportunity to use their authority for personal gain.

War news: January 20, 1916, William Jennings Bryan, former Secretary of State under President Wilson, argued for American neutrality in the European war.

War news: January 24, a British Naval victory off Doggerbank. On the twenty-eighth, we heard of the first American ship to be sunk by the Germans, the *William P. Frye.*

When the Rio cargo was discharged, we sailed down the coast to Santos, the port of São Paulo. A local pilot took us up the narrow, crooked river, and at last we tied up to a long quay wall. On the left-hand side was a modern long dock that could service many ships at once. A series of corrugated iron-roofed warehouses stretched along the shore in a continuous line from which several endless belts extended to the ships. The coffee was mechanically transferred from warehouses to ships even in 1916. Longshoremen handled the bags of coffee on board, storing them one at a time in the hold.

São Paulo, the new capital of Brazil, was not far from Santos, but I could not take time to see it. After standing my watches and supervising the stowage of cargo, I needed my time off duty in this hot weather for resting, washing clothes, and studying. The study was particularly essential since I intended soon to sit for examination to get an officer's license.

We sailed back to Rio where we loaded the lower holds with manganese ore bound for Baltimore. Manganese was in demand for alloying with iron to make the superior steel needed for armaments in the war effort. The ore was loaded from barges surrounding us. The natives, dressed only in sandals and trousers, shoveled ore by hand into buckets which they hoisted up over the ship's side to the hatches, and the ore was dumped into the holds below. From there it was trimmed to the wings by other laborers using shovels. Loading continued at all six hatches day and night.

The local workmen were a tough lot who seemed to live on nothing but black coffee and plain dark bread.

Once, the ship was so closely surrounded by lighters that Chief Mate Dennis Sullivan was worried they might damage the ship's propeller or rudder. He asked them to move one or two, but they insisted on mooring at the stern. Mr. Sullivan, not always diplomatic, got into a shouting match with the natives on the barges. More than ever they refused to do what he commanded. Sullivan sent me down onto the barges to have me let go their lines. I showed no fear and proceeded down the side over rope ladders where these angry men were gathered. I let the wires go, and the lighters floated clear of our rudder. Two officers stood on the ship's deck above, ready to dump big lumps of ore onto those below if they molested me. I judged it was all a misunderstanding due to the language difference.

On the northbound passage, the *Montanan* stopped at Trinidad for a few hours while we took on oil and fresh water. We were allowed no shore liberty, but Captain Wright arranged with the agent to have the ship supplied with fresh fruit, vegetables, and fish. Then we sailed for New York. The ship tied up at her regular berth at the foot of Forty-second Street, Pier Six, a double-decker. Twelve gangs of longshoremen, twice as many as could be used at a single-decker pier, worked cargo on both levels. The bags of coffee were valuable cargo, and when a bag got torn, the leaked contents had to be swept up and saved. The ship worked cargo all night, and the following day the crew was paid off.

By the second evening, all cargo except the manganese ore had been discharged. We sailed for Baltimore, where the ore was removed, and the *Montanan* was chartered for another voyage to Brazil, my second. The new contract, which we had to fill out and sign, included such specifications and admonitions as "voyage to end within six months at a port north of Hatteras," "no women allowed," "no liquor allowed," and "lime juice to be provided." Lime juice was the standard means for preventing scurvy, which was caused by lack of vitamin C.

This trip to Rio took seventeen days. We sailed the same route as before, stopping at St. Thomas on our way south for fuel and water, and at Trinidad on the way back. On the *Montanan*'s return to the States, I longed to get home and see my mother and small brother and sister, the twins Chester and Clara. The ship was to be in New York overnight. Normally, if the ship worked cargo during the weekend, we had no time off. However, I asked the chief mate if I could get off on Sunday to go home. He agreed, but I had to get the captain's and marine superintendent's permission also. I took a crowded Saturday midnight coach to Boston. I had to sit on my suitcase until there was a vacant seat. From Boston I took the train out to Lincoln, and at nine in the morning surprised Mother and the twins. I loved them all. They were my encouragement on my long trips at sea.

We had a great day together, but it was all too short. In order to be back on board ship at eight on Monday morning, I had to take the 5:20 P.M. train from Lincoln to Boston, then wait six hours for the midnight train to leave for New York. During this wait I tried to see Dorothy Allan, a girl I had met at the Sailors' Haven. She lived in nearby Everett. I had made no appointment, and she and her family were away for the evening. I was back on the *Montanan* by eight on Monday as agreed. It was not until a few years later that I finally caught up with Dorothy, and it changed our lives forever.

On my third trip to South America, we had to run blacked out and keep radios silent because German commerce destroyers were known to be about. This made all ships at sea suspicious of each other. Although the U.S. was still a neutral country, German submarines were attacking merchant vessels they believed might be carrying war supplies to Germany's enemies.

On my fourth trip south, the *Montanan* was chartered to the Barber Line for one round trip to Buenos Aires. Our cargo consisted largely of steel rails and barbed wire. Many other ships were headed to Europe carrying the same things, but as materials of war.

On this run we heard stories of German and British sea battles. It was rumored that the *Minnesotan*, manned by foreign-born officers and men, was on a secret mission with a cargo of coal from Norfolk. She was reported to be carrying big timbers on deck, which could be used between ships as rolling fenders when fueling at sea. She was said to have been at anchor for weeks at the mouth of the La Platta, waiting to perform her mission. We also heard that the German fleet making repairs in the Falkland Islands had been destroyed by the British fleet. Apparently the *Minnesotan* had been waiting to refuel some of these German vessels. After a while the *Minnesotan*'s cargo of coal was sold through a local broker and the ship returned to legitimate trade. We got reports daily of sea battles and the sinking of ships by German U-boats.

In order to get the ship into Buenos Aires, we had to cross the shallow La Platta River. This meant lightening the vessel by discharging cargo first at the deep water port at Montevideo, the largest city in Uruguay on the La Platta. The city was modern and attractive, with broad, tree-lined boulevards and parks. There are many white sandy beaches and fancy hotels.

We discharged two thousand tons at Montevideo on a beautiful sunny day. During my time off, I decided to take a walk straight over the hill. It appeared to be a fine residential section of town extending nearly down to the waterfront. I was alone and had no idea what I might be running into. I walked straight up the hill for about a mile, reached the crest, and, looking ahead, could see the ocean a mile or so beyond. The fine houses were close together and came within a few feet of the tree-lined street on both sides. As I walked down the hill, I thought the elaborate front doors of these houses to be conspicuous, up three or four steps from ground level. As I got halfway down the hill, I began to hear rapping sounds inside these doors as I passed them. The doors never opened and I saw no one. I thought this to be very strange indeed.

At the bottom of the hill the street ended, so I turned to the left on a street that ran parallel to the beach. Carefully I noted the name of the street that I had turned from to be sure I could find my way back to the ship. There were few people and no wheeled traffic on this street, although it was paved and had tree-lined sidewalks. Though there was no motor traffic, there was a policeman in uniform in the middle of the street about half a block behind me.

As I walked along the right side of this street, the rapping became more intense, and sometimes I could hear Spanish voices from behind the closed doors. I was curious but did not stop. As I passed one of these buildings, a young, scantily clothed woman stepped to the small verandah to entice me. Then another and another stepped into the open. Apparently these business ladies were not allowed to expose themselves except behind closed doors, and the policeman was there to enforce this. I gazed and smiled but kept walking. I stopped when a nice-looking lady stepped outside her door and said in English, "Oh, you nasty thing, won't you come in?" I hesitated, but I was challenged, and followed her inside.

We entered a spacious hall and she led me into a large bedroom. She offered me a drink. Teetotaller that I was, I refused. We stood by the bed and she asked me to sit down. I was afraid of being caught in a trap and remained standing. Somehow she maneuvered me so that I stood with my back close to the bed. She got her foot behind mine, gave me a sudden shove, and I fell back on the bed. I sat up immediately, but I was enticed, and we talked some more. She said, "What is the matter with you, are you sick?" Then a little later, "Perhaps you prefer it the French way." After about ten minutes of this talk, she realized that there was no prospect of business. She must have given a signal because I heard another woman's voice coming from the back room, saying excitedly, "Hurry, hurry, here comes your husband!"

The woman with whom I was keeping company said, "Hurry! Give me money!" I had a few dollars in my billfold, but in my pocket I carried a small change purse. I dumped all the change I had into her hands and fled through the open door. I felt lucky that I had not lost the contents of my billfold. I had not forgotten the schoolship lectures concerning the hazards confronting young men in foreign ports. I headed back to the ship, satisfied that I had at last experienced a red-light district.

The ship sailed, with a pilot, across the wide mouth of the Rio de la Platta to Buenos Aires. The fine stone harbor was beautifully kept, with green grass extending right down to dockside. Since we were tied up in the city, it was easy to explore Buenos Aires with just a short walk. Earle Hammond and I went ashore together one evening to see the beautiful city. In many places we saw familiar signs advertising Coca-Cola and Lux soap. Somehow we found ourselves in the red-light district. I don't believe that this was entirely by accident. It was natural to be curious about such places, young men that we were. On the street corners there actually were red lights high up on the fine, three-story masonry buildings We entered what appeared to be a theater, bought tickets, and were interviewed by a madam. We were then escorted to seats in a sparsely filled auditorium. At once girls joined us and became very familiar.

The girls got us to order drinks for them while movies of dancing men and girls played on the screen. What they were doing was obscene. This was, of course, to stir up our animal instincts. Then the girls offered to take us to their rooms. Failing to break us down, the madam ordered other girls to try their luck with us. We were both strict New Englanders and from the same training ship where we had been properly warned of such places (or was it our pocketbooks that held us back?). The madam came and asked us if none of the girls pleased us. We took this as an invitation to be on our way. At last we left, to the madam's disappointment. Our curiosity had been satisfied.

Most of our cargo from the north was discharged, and the *Montanan* loaded a full cargo, 1,500 tons of frozen beef, as well as linseed, pickled and dried hides, horns, and bones.

After four round-trip voyages to South America, all in one year, Earle Hammond and I got paid off. We took officers' rooms at the Seamen's

Institute in New York. After three days of written examinations in the Customs House, on December 10, 1916, we received our second mate licenses.

With my license in my pocket, I searched for an officer's job. Captain Bennett, the marine superintendent of the American-Hawaiian Steamship Company, who had hired us quartermasters, never lost interest in us. He advised me, "Get your license, and ship out on short trips coastwise.[21] When there's a vacancy, I'll call you." There being no immediate openings, I went home for the Christmas holidays. I needed a vacation after having been away for sixteen months. Being with my family was a joy. Grace had graduated from high school and was working. Beatrice was in private school. Ralph was about to enlist in the Navy. We were all there together with young Albert and the twins, Clara and Chester.

Just before the first of the year, I applied in writing to all of the steamship companies in Boston and New York, hoping for a reply by mail. While at home waiting for a berth at sea, I spent my time working at various chores. I cut down trees, hired a horse, and hauled the logs out of the woods. My pay was one half of the wood produced, which I cut into stove lengths, enough to last the family a year. Ralph worked with me, and we had fun. I worked at Beaver Pond for Rodman Snelling, cutting ice and getting it into the icehouses. With fifteen other men, I worked daybreak to dusk for eight days. I earned $19.50. On January 27, 1917, I went with Ralph to the Navy recruiting station in Boston where he signed up to be a sailor.

I spent the rest of my time with my family, going to church on Sunday, and once to Uncle George Cousins' for dinner, where Esther and Evelyn Cousins made fudge. I had also called several times on Miss Martha Weir. On New Year's Day I took her to the Rex Theater in Waltham. After the movie we rode the train as far as Baker's Bridge. I saw her home and walked the rest of the way to Lincoln. A week later I had another date with her. This time I took her to an evening dance at the Armory in Concord. The last train home left about eleven o'clock, and at quarter to eleven I told Martha that we would have to be going.

"Why?" she asked.

"If we don't leave now," I said, "we'll miss the last train."

"Oh, let's stay," she said. "We can go home in a taxi."

Well, we stayed. Halfway home in the taxi, she complained of a draft on her side. I reached over and said, "I don't feel any draft." I started to take my arm away, but she leaned back against it. I failed to respond except to keep my arm out stiff behind her. How dumb I was.

I was anxious for a job at sea. On January 28, I sent a telegram to Captain Bennett. The next day I received a reply that there were no vacancies and that I should try to get something coastwise on a temporary basis. So I drew $60 from the bank (most of my savings) and traveled to New York, where I got a room at the Seamen's Institute.

War News: January 31, 1917, Germany declared it would attack any and all vessels in the war zone, including ships of neutral nations.

I started looking for a job in person, going from pier to pier, working my way down the Hudson River. All of the supers had me fill out applications. I was back at the Institute for the night. On the following day I continued my visits. I finished with the Hudson River offices and went over to the Brooklyn waterfront, where I applied to Captain Munday of the Puerto Rico Line. He gave me encouragement. He had me fill out an application and said he hoped to have something in a few days. I didn't take this very seriously and kept plugging. I spent another night at the Institute and on February 1 went back to the Hudson piers. About noon I called once more on Captain Parks, the operating manager of the Clyde Line, and got the job offered, third mate on their ship *Philadelphia*. She was berthed near the Battery. I went aboard and went right to work at $65 a month.

## The S.S. *Philadelphia*

Captain McKinnon was the master. She was chartered to the Puerto Rico Line for a round trip to the Dominican Republic. I found that I was not only the third mate but also the bos'n, which meant that I had the job of supervising the crew of Curaçaoans. I now had to be a leader.

The ship was being fumigated with cyanide gas to kill vermin. For safety reasons, the crew was sent ashore. I, being the junior officer, was detailed to stay and look after the ship. Although the deck crew had been ordered back on board at three in the afternoon to assist in opening up to ventilate, they didn't show up. By myself, I attempted to get the process of venting the deadly gas underway. In an hour's time I had the doors and cowl vents open. I also had the corners of the hatches uncovered. Then I went to the foot of the gangway on the dock for a much-needed breath of fresh air and to give orders to the crew in case they showed up. At that moment Captain Munday, the marine superintendent, was making his rounds. Coming upon me, he asked if the ship were being ventilated.

I said, "Yes, sir, and she will be ready to load at eight in the morning."
He recognized me and said, "Weren't you in to see me a few days ago?"
I replied, "Yes, sir."
"Didn't I say that I would have something for you in a few days?"
"Yes, sir."
"Well, how come you are here?"
"Captain Munday," I said, "I had to have a job as soon as possible."
"Young man," he answered me, "another time when you need a job, come and see me. I won't make you wait; I'll put you on the payroll immediately. You are the kind of man I want."
I went back on board and began uncovering hatches with new vigor.

We loaded general cargo, then sailed for the West Indies on February 2, 1917. The S.S. *Philadelphia* was up-to-date for her time, with radio and electric lights. Although electricity was used to light the quarters, the running lights were fueled by kerosene because at the time it was more reliable. Being the junior officer, many a rainy, windy night I was called out to climb the mast to relight the lantern. One day out of New York, we found ourselves in a blizzard. For the next forty-eight hours, the captain had the ship hove-to, and she barely made steerageway.[22] She was small, with only 2,500 tons of cargo and the big waves battered her about mercilessly until we were well past Hatteras. Only after passing the Gulf Stream did the sea and temperature moderate, at which point the exhausted officers and crew got to bed and actually rested.

Only a person who has been at sea in a storm understands what a buffeting about a ship can get in a rough sea. The vessel is in constant jerky motion, rolling and tossing violently, pitching and pounding. One minute the stern comes out of the water. The engine races with the propeller and rudder in the air. Next moment the bow is high in the air, then dives, pounding into the sea with such a force that it seems the bottom will surely be driven right up through the main deck. This is followed by a sudden lurching to one side, and with a jolt she stops and a huge wave comes right over the top. To keep the ship from breaking up, the engine must be slowed to provide steerage and the ship quartered to the wind[23] to ride the waves. In such a sea the vessel labors to keep upright and afloat. The people on board cannot walk, stand, sit, or lie down. Meals cannot be served. Every piece of equipment has to be fastened down, tied, chocked, or wedged in place. It is impossible to rest. Only when utterly exhausted might one be able to sleep fitfully, wedged between two fixed objects. When the weather finally moderates, it does so gradually until, at last, it is once more a pleasure to be alive.

War news: February 3, the U.S. severed diplomatic relations with Germany.

During this storm we had been set off course. The skies remained cloudy, the wind picked up some, and the spray it created doused the wheelhouse, making visibility nil. Determining the ship's position with any accuracy was impossible. The deck officers and the master were desperate for an opportunity to get a good glimpse of clear sky and the horizon. Our destination was Turk's Head Island in the British Bahamas. It was surrounded by dangerous low shoals which could not be seen from a distance even under the best of conditions. As we approached the West Indies, we needed to pinpoint our position so that we could set a course between low sandspit islands and sunken shoals. There were hardly any aids to navigation, such as buoys or lighthouses.

We arrived at Turk's Head on February 8. By prearrangement, forty natives arrived in sailboats and boarded. These men were experienced in the discharge and loading of cargo at the Dominican Republic ports. The process would take about three weeks, and these men lived on board the whole time. Two cooks among them used the galley, when it was not being used by our own steward personnel, to cook rice and corned beef. Together with a large can of coffee, this mixture was left in barrels outside the galley door. Each laborer had been supplied with a plate and a tin cup. No other food was provided, but they did have plenty of ice water to drink. Toilet facilities for these men were rudimentary. The mate had a board fastened over the stern for them to sit on as a toilet. They were not allowed to use the crew's facilities. I did not find out what these men were paid, those arrangements having been taken care of by the local agent. Whatever their pay, I'm sure it was better than living on the island. The only jobs there involved making salt for export by evaporating sea water.

From February 9 until March 1, we worked cargo at seven Dominican ports: Monte Cristi, Puerto Plata, Samana, Sanchez, La Romana, San Pedro de Macoris, and Santo Domingo City, the capital. In order to do my work well, I had to be on duty continuously for three weeks, getting rest as I could. Opportunities to go ashore on this voyage were rare. Directing the crew was difficult since the Curaçaoans had no initiative. I had to work with them to get anything done.

There were sixty U.S. Marines on duty at Puerto Plata. They couldn't buy liquor ashore, so they lined up on the *Philadelphia* and bought it from Captain McKinnon. Twenty-five U.S. Marines were stationed at La Romana as a peacekeeping force. This was in accordance with the 1907 agreement between the Dominican Republic and the U.S. whereby we were to collect customs revenue, assist the local government in maintaining peace, and act as an intermediary between the Republic and its foreign creditors. The Marines had been landed in 1916 after a series of revolutionary outbreaks. We saw thousands of guns, rounds of ammunition, revolvers, and pistols that the Marines had seized. They were being packaged for shipment to the capital.

At Santo Domingo City we spent two days discharging, and I had a rare afternoon off. I went ashore and saw the cathedral where Christopher Columbus was buried. I also visited the fort, which was flying the American flag and had a thousand Marines camped inside. They had 152 prisoners in their custody. By way of a plank from shore, I went aboard the old U.S.S. *Memphis*, a stranded wreck on the rocky beach, and was shown around by a U.S. authority from the fort.

For our return trip to the U.S., we loaded cargo (raw sugar, dye wood, tobacco, honey, wax, and hides). At Sanchez we loaded cocoa for three days before proceeding to Turk's Head Island. The sea was rough outside Samana Bay, and we were running short of fresh water for the boilers. At one place we had several open boats loaded with water towed down the river, but the engineers were unable to suck it up over the side. Giving up, the chief engineer agreed to proceed with what little water we had left.

On March 1, we returned to Turk's Head Island, anchored, and sent our forty laborers ashore in their sailboats. We obtained water in six large wooden hogsheads from a wooden sailing barge that tied up alongside. I refused to drink the beer that the captain sold from his slop chest. I drank the water no matter how bad it tasted. The captain and officers made fun of me and tried to break me down. They reminded me that if water rusted iron, there was no telling what it would do to my stomach. From the taste of the water, I doubt that the hogsheads from which it came had been anywhere near clean.

That evening we sailed for New York. For the first few days I made slings for cork life preserver rings. There was no chance for me to practice navigation, which I longed to do.

We reached New York on March 7 and anchored at quarantine. On entering the harbor we had to clear the submarine net.[24] So ended my first voyage to foreign ports as a ship's officer. Off duty, I bought a secondhand sextant, nautical almanac, and officer's whistle at Bliss's.

The *Philadelphia* discharged all cargo and went off hire. The boilers had to be repaired because the fresh water had run out on the voyage, and the engineers had resorted to the use of sea water. We got a new chief engineer for the next voyage. (The original engineer was incompetent on two counts: he miscalculated the remaining water, and he didn't know that he could have placed a pump on the barge and pushed the water up, even though he couldn't suck it from above.)

Next day, with boilers repaired, the ship was ready to go back to work for the Clyde Line, and the articles[25] were signed. We loaded general cargo for Brunswick, Georgia.

War news: Germany declared war on Portugal. By March 12, armed guards were being placed on many American merchant ships as a precaution against enemy activity, even though Germany had sent a memo to all neutral powers: "Any armed merchant ship will be treated as a warship and will be sunk without warning."

Brunswick, Georgia, was a town of unpaved streets, with a post office, a drug store, and a movie theater. Hardly a soul could be seen on the main street. Even the movie house was nearly empty of people, though filled with plenty of gnats. The insects drove us crazy. They were everywhere and came right through the screens. I tried burning rags in my room, but I couldn't sleep for the stink. Finally I got hold of some citronella. We did not like being in Georgia.

On the thirteenth, while we were discharging cargo, a barrel of molasses was dropped in hold number one. In no time the hold was swarming with bees in search of the sweet syrup, making cleanup difficult. After discharging we loaded wooden railroad ties. We sailed for New York on March 15, happy to leave. The whole town must have felt safe again as the Yankees were leaving, because hundreds of girls, women, and whole families lined the hillsides to wave goodbye and to throw us kisses. We young fellows felt good about being noticed. We would have happily stayed another night, in spite of the gnats.

In New York the master paid off the crew. I received $32 for the voyage. On the twentieth, Captain McKinnon recommended that I be promoted to second mate, and I was made such immediately, with my pay boosted to $85 a month. When I had taken the third-mate job, I had made it clear that I wanted it only until there was a vacancy at American-Hawaiian. Therefore I thought it strange that I had been promoted, especially since I had refused to join the company union, the Licensed Officers' Association, to which all officers of this line belonged. I had been told that if I did not join, I would never get promoted, but here I was, promoted already.

There were several other changes aboard. Captain McKinnon was transferred to the S.S. *Comanche*. The first and second mates were also transferred, and the *Philadelphia* was assigned to the New York to Philadelphia run, a distance of less than four hundred miles, and therefore the number of mates required dropped to two (no third mate). Captain Rich and Chief Mate Townsend joined the *Philadelphia*. These two men had sailed together on this run for nineteen years. They did all the piloting and docking. They brought their own taffrail log[26] to measure distance, mounting it on the wing of the bridge where it was easily read. Captain Rich relied on the taffrail log, chronometer,[27] and the magnetic compass to navigate. The captain and officers were required to know the route without reference to charts, so there were none available for me to study.

The chief mate and I were to stand watch, four and four, at sea. I was to have all port time off in New York, and the chief mate had all port time off in Philadelphia, his home town. Arriving in Philadelphia, the chief mate went home, and the cargo went out and in again so fast that I didn't even get a chance to check the bilges. This sort of thing would not be allowed on an offshore vessel.

War news: The British transport *Minneapolis* was sunk by a German submarine. The U.S. recognized the new government of Russia. The French steamer *Sussex* torpedoed with eighty passengers killed or injured, while the American steamer *Petrolite* was sunk by an Austrian sub.

I made several trips on this run. The ship never stopped working cargo while in port. In those days longshoremen were available at any hour of day or night. They made fifty-five cents an hour on coastwise vessels and a nickel more working offshore cargoes.

## Notes on Chapter 2

1. Spanker: the fore-and-aft sail on the aftermast of a square-rigged vessel.
2. Square-rigger: a vessel carrying square sails.
3. Coxswain: the person who steers the ship's boat.
4. Combing: raised portion, or rim, surrounding an opening.
5. Scuttlebutt: a wooden barrel containing drinking water.
6. Collier: a ship carrying coal.
7. Gyro compass: more accurate than a magnetic compass, a gyro compass receives its directive power from an electrically powered gyroscope, the axis of which comes to match the axis of the earth, thereby indicating true north.
8. Dry dock: a dock from which water can be emptied, allowing examination of and work on the bottom of a vessel.
9. Bunker coal: coal to fuel the ship, as opposed to coal transported as cargo.
10. Haul out: change course.
11. Engine room telegraph: a mechanical device with a dial and two indicators, one having a handle attached, on the bridge, and a similar device in the engine room. The dial shows the various speeds, which are sent below according to the setting of the indicator. The engineer, hearing an automatic bell, notes by his indicator the desired speed of the engines.
12. Stem: foremost steel bar or timber of a vessel.
13. In ballast: a ship sails in ballast when she is loaded with a low-value material, such as sand or water, in order to weigh the ship down in the sea so that she will handle safely and efficiently.
14. Flood: the period when the tidal current is flowing toward land. Ebb is the period when the tidal current is flowing away from land. The different phases are referred to as the first of the flood, the strength of the flood, and the last of the flood.
15. Compass binnacle: a box container for the compass with lamps for night work and fitted with gimbals or a gimmal to allow the compass to remain level.
16. Back-and-fill maneuver: a maneuver comparable to parallel-parking a car.
17. Intercoastal trade: plying waters from one coast to another, usually through the Panama Canal.
18. Radio direction finder: pre-radar technology in which a radio operator turns a directional antenna to beam in on the signal sent by an onshore station.
19. Heave to: to head up to the sea, turning the engines just enough to maintain the ship's position; to lay a vessel where it takes the seas most comfortably in order to ride out the gale rather than make progress on the voyage.

20. Lighter: a barge used for discharging or loading vessels when it is not possible to load or unload from a dock.
21. Coastwise: along or following a coast.
22. Steerageway: enough speed through the water so that the rudder can control the ship's direction.
23. Quartered to the wind: positioning the ship so that the wind is on the forward quarter.
24. Submarine net: underwater steel mesh to keep enemy submarines out of the harbor. It was opened only to allow surface craft to enter or leave.
25. Articles: the contract for a specific voyage, signed by officers and crew upon joining a merchant vessel.
26. Taffrail log or patent log: a mechanical device that measures the distance a vessel has sailed.
27. Chronometer: a seagoing clock of superior accuracy.

East Coast and Carribean

## CHAPTER 3

# CROSSING THE LINE

### The S.S. *Californian*

Upon docking in New York on March 28, 1917, I had a telegram from Captain Bennett, and I paid him a visit. He told me to lay off and go to Charleston to meet the American-Hawaiian ship *Californian*. I had to go before Captain Rich to get paid off. He objected, but I reminded him that I had hired on with the understanding that I wanted the job only temporarily. Captain Rich tried to get me to stay, saying, "Stay in this company, and you will be master as soon as you get your license." But I was determined to go, and he finally paid me off. I packed my duds and stopped at the Seamen's Institute for the night.

Next day I telephoned the Wistrands in Irvington-on-the-Hudson, a little north of New York City. The Wistrands had rented our first house in Lincoln after we moved into our grandparents' house. The whole family had become our good friends and remained so after they moved to New York. That night I had a good time dancing with Esther and her sister Ethel. I spent the night with their brother Clifford. On April 1, I took the afternoon train for Charleston.

The *Californian*'s capacity was ten thousand tons, with a steam reciprocating engine and enough power to make about ten knots speed. Her boilers were coal fired. She had been built to carry manufactured goods to California and the Hawaiian Islands and to return with sugar. She had been running with just two deck officers because the injured third mate had been left in the Canal Hospital at Panama. I was to replace him.

War news: April 6, 1917, the U.S. declared war on Germany. Our government seized all German ships in U.S. ports. The American-Hawaiian ship *Missourian* was sunk by a German sub behind Belle Island on the French coast. German raiders were reported just outside the port of Charleston.

My job as third mate began while the ship was discharging nitrate, tin, and copper in Charleston. I stayed on board to help with the annual inspection and also stood the watch of the new second mate, Mr. Harrington, whose wife had arrived in town. I had a room all to myself. I ate with the other deck officers in the saloon, wearing a white collar, tie, and coat. This all was very grand compared with what I had experienced before.

We sailed on April 6 for Newport News. The country was now officially at war. Captain Curtis was very alert to the danger of commerce destroyers and had us run blacked-out at night. We posted extra lookouts, and the whole ship was being painted grey to reduce its visibility to other vessels. The lifeboats were swung out, ready to be lowered promptly.

A few months before I joined the *Californian*, Captain Curtis had been master of the company's ship *Columbian*, which was carrying horses to Bordeaux with pig iron in the bottom for discharge at Genoa. On her passage between Bordeaux and Genoa, the ship had been stopped by a German sub. The sub commander had the *Columbian's* papers examined, and finding no evidence of contraband, had let the ship proceed. (Germany had a policy of sinking even neutral vessels carrying contraband, i.e., supplies which could aid Germany's enemies.) That night the *Columbian's* British-born radio operator radioed a nearby British man-of-war the position of the submarine. A few hours later another German sub surfaced and halted the ship once more. The Germans boarded her and protested to Captain Curtis that he had committed an act of war by having sent the offending message. Captain Curtis denied it, but the Germans got his radio operator to admit the deed. The ship's company was ordered at gunpoint to board the lifeboats, and the Germans blew up the *Columbian*. The submarine towed the lifeboats near the coast and cast them adrift. Captain Curtis was kept aboard the sub, and three days later he was put aboard a fishing vessel off the coast of Spain. After that experience, Captain Curtis was very cautious in his running of the *Californian*.

On the nineteenth we arrived at Newport News, and I sent money home. The *Californian* was chartered to carry coal to Rio de Janeiro. We had to wait our turn to berth and then loaded a full cargo of coal. The coal piers provided the labor to trim the coal in the ship, a certain number of men to each thousand tons of coal. The ship had several decks for carrying general cargo and was not built for bulk cargo, which made for extra work in trimming the coal. The charterer's agent was anxious to get quick dispatch each time, so he speeded up the shoveling, or trimming, of the coal within the decks by rewarding the coal trimmers with liquor (which he had bought in Maryland since Virginia was dry) if they did a good job.

We proceeded down the coast to Bodie Island, then shaped a course for Cape San Roque, on the eastern tip of Brazil. We continued blacked-out and kept double lookouts. When we were free of coastal shipping, we turned the colored side lights on. They were only visible for about two miles. I spent my off-duty time sewing canvas ventilator covers.

We kept our radio silent except for receiving the time from Washington to check our chronometers, the accuracy of which was essential in calculating our position. We also received Navy weather reports and news bulletins. The radio officer placed a printed sheet of news in each mess room once a day while we were at sea.

By April 30, the slow-moving *Californian* seemed to be on an endless voyage. She was one of the slowest vessels that I was ever on. Our twenty-four hour runs averaged only 225 miles. On May 1, while standing watch, I wondered what I would be doing if I were at home. I imagined I would be hanging May baskets on all the girls. I supposed that other fellows would be making them happy in my absence. But in reality, if I'd stayed home, I probably would soon have been drafted into the army and sent to the trenches in France.

War news: American destroyers had begun cooperating with the British Navy.

At last I was doing some navigation. I relieved Mr. Griggs, the chief mate, one afternoon when he went for his supper. He had taken a sighting of the moon and asked me to work it out. He was trying me out to see if I could do it. I succeeded.

Careful checks had to be made each day to be sure that the coal cargo did not heat in the confined spaces in which it was stored. The temperature of each hold was taken and recorded twice a day. This ship was equipped with fire-detecting devices consisting of a tube from each cargo compartment to the bridge. If the officer on duty were alert, he could detect a fire from smoke or fumes coming up the tube.

We sailed down through the northern trade winds, then through the squally doldrums, where we sighted several water spouts. In the northern hemisphere they turn counterclockwise around the low pressure center. In the southern hemisphere they revolve clockwise.

On May 5 there were no stars or sun evident for sights except at noon when the sun peeped out, and we got our latitude fixed. Next day we crossed the Line (the Equator), and the weather cleared as we reached the southeast trade winds.

There was a wonderful friendliness and esprit de corps among the officers on this ship. In the evenings we got together, punched the bag, sang songs, and played shuffleboard, cards, or checkers. Some members of the crew had their own phonographs with records to play, and there were always several among the crew who played musical instruments. Sometimes, in port, there might be a baseball game.

The atmosphere among the men, however, was not always peaceful during these long trips. I remember two confrontations. We carried six firemen and three coal passers. Their work was hard, and the company was careful to feed them plenty of good food. However, one night a fireman came to the galley and hit the cook in the face with his steak because he'd found it tough. The cook in turn knocked him cold with a wooden potato masher. Another time a fireman came to the galley door, holding a steak he didn't like, and tried to get the cook's attention. The cook pretended to pay no notice, but he pulled the big pot of frying fat over the center of the stove to get it good and hot and began stirring it with a big ladle. All the while he kept the corner of his eye on the fireman to be sure he did not step over the threshold into the galley, which was a forbidden place for anyone not officially assigned to the stewards' department. We were in the tropics at the time, and the fireman wore only trousers and a skivvy shirt. The fireman yelled, "Why you feed me this plank-like-a-board meat?" Then, gaining confidence, he placed one foot inside the galley, and the cook threw a full ladle of hot fat splashing over his chest and arms. That fireman screamed blue murder and fled. I don't believe that he or any of his colleagues ever set foot inside the galley again.

Southbound rounding Cape Frio, we struck cooler weather, and mountainous swells made the ship roll, pitch, and labor to keep upright. We could see the mountains in the distance, a relief after nothing but sea and sky for so long. At last, after steaming slowly outside Rio de Janeiro and waiting to pass quarantine, we passed inside the entrance to the harbor and picked up the pilot whose native language, like most in Brazil, was Portuguese. Next came the boarding party. In many other ports, these people went up the pilot ladder and boarded without fanfare, but in Rio the captain went down to meet these government officials on their boat. They were all in white uniforms, very dignified in manner, and were easily hurt if shown the least lack of respect or courtesy. They expected to be given free cigarettes or more. The captain was anxious to get the quickest dispatch possible, so he never hesitated in granting them their wishes. The boarding officers sealed the radio so that there was no chance of it being used for any purpose of war. No agent or businessman was allowed on board until the boarding party cleared the ship.

As soon as the gangway was down, the agent, stevedore, ship chandler,[1] tailors, and laundry men all came aboard to perform their jobs. The customs officers were given a room and served meals. These men had to be handled like prima donnas or they would delay the work.

The chief mate got the hatch opened, the wedges out, and all spare gear locked up securely. The cargo lights had been made ready for night work, and he had made sure that there was steam on the winches. Cargo lighters tied alongside using wire instead of Manila rope, which might be cut and disappear. (Pilfering, as in other foreign ports, was rampant.) One hundred or more native longshoremen boarded to work the cargo. Company checkers reported to the chief mate, and they too were given an office and fed on board.

The crew were allowed to go ashore at any time so long as they were back aboard in time to stand their watches. They received no overtime compensation, so it was the custom to give them at least a day off in port whenever possible.

As soon as the longshoremen trimmed the booms and uncovered the hatches, cargo was discharged to the dock and to the lighters on the offshore side. The docks at Rio were equipped with cranes. These were rarely seen in the States in 1917. Discharging continued around the clock. About two thousand tons were discharged each twenty-four hours. In five days the cargo was all out. This was hard on the old deck winches. They were badly worn in the bearings and had to be shimmed frequently to make them run anywhere near smoothly.

On these trips as third mate, I had the 6:00 P.M. to 6:00 A.M. night watch while in port. It was my duty to look after the ship, see that no one got hurt, provide proper lights, and the like. Usually I had a quartermaster on duty to assist me. (Some of the work I did not delegate but performed myself, a practice which would later be forbidden by the unions.) I had to see that there was no cause for delay, particularly from failure of deck winches. If so, it was up to me to get repairs made and to keep account of the downtime to the minute because the stevedore or charterer would charge the ship for all lost time. It was very important to have our own accurate figures and to know of all legitimate delays in order to get a fair deal with the stevedores. I was also responsible to see that nothing was pilfered, that lighters did not damage the ship's propeller or rudder, and to see that tugs did no damage. The *Californian* depended on cargo for her existence, and careful measurement of the number of tons handled per hour had to be made to be sure that the rate was within established guidelines.

Ordinarily the dunnage[2] would be used in stowing the return cargo, but it wasn't needed for the manganese ore we loaded for the return trip. The chief mate sometimes found a customer for eighty thousand board feet of lumber; otherwise it was dumped overboard at sea.

With the cargo out and the longshoremen gone, the cargo holds were swept, the bilges cleaned, and the rose boxes[3] were inspected and tested. The chief engineer and chief mate together inspected the holds to make sure that they were ready for the next cargo. The carpenter protected the drains so they would not be plugged.

War news: May 18, President Wilson signed the Selective Service Act.

We loaded manganese ore continuously, stopping only for meals and changing of gangs. We loaded until the ship was just about touching the bottom. Then we were towed to deeper water to allow loading the maximum amount that the ship could safely carry. The charterer always wanted to get every ton possible into the ship, but the captain didn't want the ship to be as much as a single inch below her allowed draft.[4] The mates had to check the specific gravity of the water in the harbor and apply this factor to the draft level. It was important also to be sure that the ship was in proper trim.[5] I had to watch the water level at the marks. Invariably the wind kicked up a chop when I was trying to get a reading, requiring judgment on my part as to how near the limit we really were. Not only did we have to be sure that the ship lay parallel in the water with the proper trim, but we also had to be sure that the load was distributed so as not to bend or "hog" the hull fore and aft.

Manganese ore is very heavy and has to be loaded with great care to be sure the ship will be seaworthy. Cargo ships were built to carry material, such as coal, at forty cubic feet to the ton, filling a ship while providing trim both fore and aft, up and down, making for stability and subjecting the hull to the least stress and strain at sea. Manganese ore, being much denser than coal, stows less than ten cubic feet to the ton, requiring that a certain weight had to be put in each compartment to minimize stress on the vessel. The proper amount of ore had to go in the upper decks. If all the weight were in the bottom of the ship, she would right herself from each roll so fast that it would be dangerous.

Once loaded, we lost no time in setting sail. The ship was underway while all hands were still securing gear for sea. We carried the minimum amount of fresh water and bunker coal required to get to the next port in order not to take up profitable tonnage space. Sometimes we had to make a stop after leaving port to pick up the captain from a launch if he had been detained while getting papers cleared at the customs house.

Feeling that the charterers had been well served, their representative handed me a $10 bonus before we left.

War news: On May 30, the American armed steamer *Silvershell* exchanged sixty rounds with a submarine in the Mediterranean.

During the first mate's watch, the island of Barbados came into view. He called me to relieve him so that he could get the gear ready for coaling the ship on arrival. We anchored in Bridgetown Harbor, and coal barges came alongside with bumboats[6] among them. The natives on these boats were anxious to sell their wares. There were many naked Negro boys who wanted us to throw coins into the water. They dove for them and almost always were able to pick them out of the water before they reached the bottom.

War news: On June 9, the steamers *Manchester* and *Southland* were sunk. The American steamer *Morenic* was sunk after a running, two-hour fight. General Pershing was sent to France.

On our return voyage, we anchored several times due to fog near Cape Henry at the mouth of the Chesapeake Bay. The submarine net was open only during daylight hours, and about thirty steamers rushed to get through at the end of the day. We were a few minutes late, but the pilot took a chance, and we made it. We docked at Canton Lower Docks, East Baltimore, after passing quarantine, and started to discharge cargo. I received $301 for the voyage. That was based on $85 a month plus a war bonus. I sent $200 home.

On June 16, although I had been up all night, I went ashore and registered for the draft at the courthouse and sent a card to the Lincoln town clerk. The registration clerk couldn't understand why I hadn't registered before. He took me for a slacker until I finally made him understand that I had been on the high seas. On June 21 we were off on another trip to Rio.

When the *Californian* left port, regular sea activity replaced the hustle and confusion of port routine. When the ship was clean, stores in place, and all was running smoothly, maintenance work was carried on as weather permitted. Each officer had his regular duties to perform. The watch maintained the position of the ship and determined and recorded currents, wind, sea, clouds, speed, fuel, and water consumption. Safety inspections were made twice a day, including sounding to determine if there were any leaks. Ventilation, temperature, and humidity of the cargo holds was determined and recorded at regular intervals. The compass error, if any, was also determined and recorded. Weather reports were sent by radio to the weather bureau.

Much of the maintenance work at sea consisted of chipping of rust and repainting, an ongoing necessity for steel ships in salt water. Cargo handling gear and safety equipment had to be maintained, and there were scores of other chores (inspections, cleaning, logs, and records to be kept). The *Californian* carried the minimum number of personnel, enough to run the ship safely, no more. We all kept busy and the time just flew.

War news: On June 26, the first American troops arrived in Europe. On July 14, 348 wooden ships and 77 steel ships were to be built in America to support the war effort.

We entered Rio on July 18 at sunrise. As a war measure, no ships were allowed to enter during darkness. We took a pilot after passing quarantine, went to anchor, and once again discharged coal to barges.

I had all the night duties in port and slept during the day. I had a very good quartermaster on duty with me so that my work was made easier, and

61

I was more relaxed than would otherwise have been the case. However, I had to be on deck to check on any delays.

We had some delay because of a longshoremen's strike. Otherwise we discharged coal continuously, and our old winches groaned in protest. On July 27, the strike was settled, and we started loading ore.

Back at sea on this trip we found two stowaways, one in the crew's quarters and another in the donkey boiler furnace.[7] They were put to work. During the next few days I painted the walls and ceiling of my room white with straw yellow around the ports. Later, in fine weather, I varnished the woodwork.

War news: Three more American vessels were reported sunk in the Pacific. The German raider *Sea Adler* became stranded and a total loss. An American tanker was reported sunk off the west coast of France. On August 9, the food supply control bill was enacted by Congress.

Arriving in Barbados, we took on forty-five tons of fresh water and two hundred tons of bunker coal, some fresh fruits, and fish. While in port, the mate got rid of the wooden dunnage from the deck. Since wood was in great demand for housing on the island, I judge that the mate made himself a little extra money.

War news: French planes dropped fourteen tons of explosives behind the German lines. Another report told of twenty German airplanes bombing England. Nicholas II was deposed as czar of Russia and exiled to Siberia.

We arrived in Baltimore on August 21, completing my second trip to Rio as third mate aboard the *Californian.*

I sent $50 to my mother for her personal use. She had taken ill in the spring and had been hospitalized for months with a nervous breakdown. Grace had had to leave her teaching job in New Hampshire to take care of the family. By the time Mother was released from the hospital, Father had taken work in Greenwich, Connecticut.

On my third trip to Rio we were cautious about each of the many vessels we sighted and everyday we awaited the radio operator's bulletin.

War news: The American steamer *Headton* was sunk by a sub off the coast of Holland, having been attacked without warning. September 6, a German sub was sunk by an American destroyer using a depth bomb. September 7, the Rainbow Division of 27,000 troops was reviewed at Camp Mills, New York. A German sub off our coast sank the British passenger steamer *Staphano.* New York police arrested three men found placing bombs on American ships bound for Europe. American steamer *Lewis Luckenback* was sunk by a sub, with a loss of nine lives. A sixth merchant ship was sunk by German subs off

Nantucket Island, Massachusetts. A total of 1,253 ships had been sunk by mid-September, 1917. Only two hundred of these were carrying contraband.

Returning northbound, we passed through the submarine net at Cape Henry on October 30. The pilot boarded and we took the *Alaskan*'s berth as she sailed. Three days later I tried to join the Naval Reserve but was referred to New York. On November 1 I was paid off. Mr. Harrington and I went ashore and tried to join the Naval Reserve but couldn't find the right authorities.

On November 4 we went outside the nets to change pilots and anchored off Sewells Point all night, awaiting orders. We were told that the American-Hawaiian ships *Alaskan* and *Pennsylvanian* had been taken over by the Navy.

War news: American patrol boat *Oleida* was torpedoed and sunk, with twenty-one lives lost.

We saw the *Pennsylvanian* and the *Alaskan* nearby, loading men and horses for France. Many airplanes buzzed overhead as we entered New York Harbor and anchored. A Coast Guard boat came alongside and ordered us not to leave the anchorage without specific instructions.

Saturday, November 10, 1917, we docked at the foot of Twenty-ninth Street, Brooklyn, and loaded general cargo under a new charter. Captain Bennett came on board and told me that there was a second mate's opening on the S.S. *Kentuckian* and suggested that I see her master, Captain Blackwell. But when Captain Curtis found this out, he said, "No, Bamforth, you are to be promoted to second mate on this ship." And so I was. I took the train to Boston and went home to see my mother and the twins. At home I bought stores and made repairs for Mother.

Back in New York it took several days to get exemptions from the Draft Board. As second mate and navigator, I secured the tools of my trade: charts, tide tables, current tables, and almanacs. I went for a medical examination and again tried to secure a passport, which was now required. One evening I visited the Wistrands in Irvington. I sent money to my sister Grace.

Confusion reigned as the country geared up for more active participation in the war. I finally got my passport at the customs house. With the rest of the crew, I signed the articles for another voyage to Brazil on the *Californian*. Our cargo included machinery, steel rails, hundreds of tons of barbed wire in rolls, and kerosene. Hazardous cargo, such as paints and chemicals, was stored on deck so that it could be jettisoned easily in an emergency. Any heavy machinery too large to fit through a hatch was also carried on deck. The carpenter and his helpers did the shoring and securing with lumber, strapping wires, and turnbuckles. They built steps and passages over the deck cargo, allowing the crew safe places to walk. On November 23 we sailed down the harbor and through the net in dense fog.

War news: An American destroyer captured the crew of a German submarine and then sank the sub. New York Harbor was placed under military control.

Our trip began in foul weather so there could be no celestial navigation to determine our position, and we had to rely on dead reckoning. We ran blacked-out, with extra lookouts. With good weather we crossed the Gulf Stream and got the extra bunker coal off the deck and washed down. However, we had to stop the engines for an hour and a half to make repairs, making us a sitting duck for an attack.

As we neared the Equator and Thanksgiving Day, awnings were stretched over the bridge and quarters so the men could sleep on deck.

War news: The Rainbow Division reached France. December 6, the American ship *Jacob Jones* was sunk in the North Atlantic, sixty-nine lost. The American steamer *Aztec* sunk without warning. The U.S. declared war on Austria.

As second mate, I made sure the proper charts were on the chart table, corrected and ready for use. I had the canvas dodger, the windbreak to protect the wheelman, taken down, scrubbed, dried, and bent on[8] again.

It was my duty to wind the chronometers at 8:00 A.M. and to report this done to the captain. I did the usual second mate duty of winding and resetting the common clocks throughout the ship. As the daily longitude changed, the local time changed. I had to estimate this change and then set the clocks accordingly. At sea, when making east longitude, we set them ahead each day; and when making west longitude, we set them back. On this run it would be about twenty minutes a day.

December 9, in the tropics again, with temperatures in the low eighties, we wore lightweight clothing. Our shirts had hard, detachable collars, which we wore only at meals and when in port. We arrived at Rio at daybreak on the fourteenth.

From our position at anchor we discharged general cargo to lighters. I had one quartermaster at the gangway duty and another washing paint in the wheelhouse. I overhauled the hand and steam steering gear, took azimuths[9] as the ship swung with the tide twelve points, and I made a new deviation table.[10]

On the eighteenth, I had a starboard lifeboat lowered into the water to be sure that it would float. After it was raised again, I had a quartermaster paint it inside. On the twenty-second, we passed inside São Sebastião Island Lighthouse, picked up the pilot, and entered Santos.

War news: British destroyers were sunk by mines, with 183 lives lost.

We tied up at the quay wall and discharged cargo. It rained so hard that discharging had to be stopped for fear of damaging the cargo, in spite of our using tents at each hatch. I went ashore on the twenty-fourth, got some local money, and visited the barber. I bought some egret feathers as souvenir gifts and returned aboard. There was no cargo worked this Christmas Eve. On Christmas Day cargo was worked as usual until midnight, when it had to be stopped due to more heavy rain. We did get a real turkey dinner that day, with gravy, cranberry sauce, fresh fruit, and nuts. The mess rooms were decorated for the occasion.

War news: On December 31, New York and Massachusetts fuel administrators ordered six lightless nights in order to save available fuel. German submarine crews mutinied and thirty-eight German officers were killed. Seventy-two public schools were closed in New York due to lack of fuel for heat.

After taking on fresh fruits and vegetables, the *Californian* sailed north on January 2, 1918. On January 18, we stopped at Barbados to take on fuel from lighters. We dropped the pilot, and each department head got to work making up repair lists. Repairs that could be handled on the ship were taken care of on the way home, and those that required action in port had to be well defined in writing.

As we proceeded north, the fresh trade winds slopped the clear blue sea water on board. Our men were warned to pass on the lee side. Sometimes a flying fish landed on the lower deck, and a crew member would grab it and take it to the steward to serve at the next meal.

Further north, across the Gulf Stream off Hatteras and the high pressure thirties of latitude, the wind shifted to the northwest and blew a gale of cold air. We took all precautions against enemy attack. The sea got really rough and the ship started to labor. The captain wired ahead his estimated time of arrival, and some of the men sent wireless messages home for their wives or sweethearts to meet them. But the wind and sea slowed us, and the weather got colder. The wind howled and frigid sea water sprayed over everything. It hit the stack and left white salt streaks as it dried. The canvas screen rigged to protect the wheelman from the biting wind offered little comfort.

We broke out our oilskins and put them on over our warmest clothing to help keep out the cold spray. The seaman on lookout forward moved up the mast to the crow's-nest (a barrel-like lookout station) to keep from being washed overboard. It was difficult to move about the deck as the wintry wind blasted us off our feet.

In spite of our effort to push the ship and get into port, on checking our position we found that the speed had dropped to eight knots. We were bound to Baltimore via Cape Henry. As we passed Diamond Shoals Light Vessel and Cape Hatteras, Captain Curtis shaped the course a little closer to the shore to get in smoother water in the lee of the land. He went as close as he dared without risking striking the hull on one of the many outlying shoals. In the smoother water the ship picked up a knot in speed.

As we approached Cape Henry and the mouth of the Chesapeake Bay, we began seeing broken ice. We finally reached Cape Henry. With great difficulty, the pilot boarded from a small boat by a Jacob's ladder.[11] He had the latest newspapers and docking instructions with him.

We passed cautiously through the mine fields and in through the submarine net. Inside the bay the surface was fairly smooth, but the pilot warned the captain that the ice was very thick.

There were two battleships acting as icebreakers, running back and forth to Baltimore. With their immense power, they had no difficulty plowing through the ice. Most of the buoys and other aids to navigation were off station or had been completely carried away by the ice. The wind picked up the tops of the waves and blew them like mist, so it was very difficult to see. We doubled the lookouts. Men stood by the anchor. We relied on soundings to keep in the bay channel. Making these soundings was very difficult and hard on the hands, with the temperature in the teens and wind blowing. Once or twice we managed to get the lead down between ice cakes only to have the ice cut the line, and we lost our lead. When the ice got so thick that we couldn't sound over the side, I stood with a crewman at the stern trying to get soundings in our wake. Eventually we lost all our leads and were reduced to using old iron grate bars from the fire room as sounding weights.

We crept by Wolf Trap and could barely see the lighthouse. At last we came to the mouth of the Rappahannock River. The buoy was carried away, nowhere in sight, and we couldn't see Windmill Point Lighthouse. We just managed to get clear of Tangier Lamp Shoal and up to Smith Point. The light was out. We were off the Potomac River. The ice was so thick we could hardly move. Stopped completely, we backed the engine and then pounded into the ice. With our heavy load, the momentum carried us a short distance. Although there was no danger of damaging the propeller since it was well below the ice, there was danger of damaging the hull and putting a hole in her, so Captain Curtis was cautious. He ordered the anchor down until daylight. We were only halfway up the bay. It was two in the morning of the second night, January 28. Our exact position was in doubt. As many of the crew as could be spared were allowed to rest, but in a short while we discovered that the anchor was dragging. We knew this not because we could see the ship move in relation to some fixed object on shore (we could see none) but because the anchor chain jumped every few minutes. We were in danger of being carried into Gangier Bar. The captain ordered the anchor hoisted, but the chain parted, and the anchor was lost. We still had the port anchor up and ready to let go again.

We got underway, and soon one of the battleships passed within a half-mile of us, indicating the center of the channel. We backed and filled to get the ship into the wake of the battleship. It wasn't long before the ice closed in and nearly stopped us once more. Daylight came and we crept by Point No Point. As the bay got narrower, we saw the land at last. We had trouble passing Cove Point, a narrow part of the bay, but the battleships were passing more often. Off Sharp's Island the engineers had to stop the engines because the condenser was full of ice. We passed Bloody Point Bar and Sandy Point, twenty miles from Baltimore.

It had taken us two and a half days to make 130 miles. Everyone was exhausted. There was still plenty of ice, but the channel ice broken behind the battleships didn't shift as quickly as before, and we were better able to follow in their wake.

After taking three days to make 150 miles, we arrived at last at Canton, East Baltimore, and docked under the big ore cranes in the evening of January 29. We were the first ship to arrive in Baltimore in three days. I wasn't married, but I could imagine that most of the waiting wives were exhausted, too. This year, 1918, was the year of that terrible cold spell that covered the American continent and Europe. It was the only time I ever saw the bay frozen so far down to the capes.

During the icy passage up the Chesapeake, I was too busy to think about what my life might have been like had I stayed in the farming business, perhaps married to Elizabeth, and residing safely in Concord. I knew, however, had I not gone to sea, I would likely have been in the trenches in Europe.

On January 31, I went to town, got a draft questionnaire, filled it out, had it sworn to, and mailed it to the Exemption Board in Lincoln. At the customs house and the ship chandler, I secured weather data, pilot charts, and notices to mariners. I also got a primer on income tax and then bought shoes, underwear, gloves, a diary, valentines, garters, and shirt studs. I sent a check to Mother and valentines to several girls. Back on board, I filled out my income tax return.

We discharged the manganese ore from South America around the clock. The temperature remained below zero. We were empty on the seventh, but the thick ice delayed us from moving. On the ninth the empty ship was finally towed to a berth at a lumber dock, as other loaded ships needed our berth.

The U.S. Army took over our ship. Three Naval Reserve men came on board. They kept a watch at the gangway and warned all on board not to write anything that could be of use to the enemy, such as diaries that recorded the ship's position.

War news: The British ship *Tuscania* was torpedoed, 101 soldiers lost. The S.S. *Almanace* was also torpedoed, with six lost. The American steamer *Lake Moor* was sunk, forty-five lost, and the American steamer *Florence H* exploded in France, also forty-five lost. The American ship *William Rockefeller* was sunk by a submarine. On February 5, the *Philadelphia,* my old home, was sunk, with six lives lost.

On the eleventh, Captain Bennett and Mr. Mills, engineering superintendent for the owners, made an inspection, and then the *Californian* moved to an Army pier, and we started to load Army supplies–rails and sheet steel–for France. Later we shifted to a dock with a heavy crane and loaded partially disassembled railroad locomotives, Packard trucks, and boilers which alone weighed twenty-seven tons apiece. We coaled the ship and on Valentine's Day we went back to the Army pier where we loaded steel rails, railroad engine wheels, and canned vegetables. In the afternoon the wind was blowing a gale[12], and the vessel was surging. The stern lines parted and our gangway was damaged. I had more lines put out to secure the ship. The portholes were fitted with shutters, and the doors with electric current breakers, to be sure that no light showed during blackout hours. We had special crow's-nests fitted at both mastheads.

I sent Mother an extra $100 on February 15. While in town I picked up my repaired sextant and sent a package of papers and books home by American Express.

We finished loading on the twenty-second. Captain Curtis had been sent to England to take charge of the U.S. shipping board there. Captain Malman replaced him. A government photographer came on board with two clerks to check all personnel and prepare passports for us. An Army quartermaster officer joined the ship's roster. On February 27, 1918, we sailed in a convoy of fifty-four ships led by a Navy cruiser for an unknown European port. The ship was deep with heavy cargo, and the March gales began. By the third we were in a whole gale with mountainous seas, forcing the convoy to break up. With the crew living aft but working forward, they had to make the journey via the shaft alley[13] since it was impossible for them to walk the open decks. Once amidships to work or get meals, they stayed there and tried to sleep. We were too busy to think about submarines.

Although we were hove-to, the deck load of locomotives shifted. Soon a big sea went right over the raised poop deck and carried away the entire dangerous cargo stored there. The awning stanchions, pipe railing, and the hand steering gear were destroyed. This great sea also stove in several doors and tore the ash shoot away. The wind shifted, and we were in the dangerous semicircle of the storm. Snow and hail squalls were frequent. By March 7 the sea moderated and we were on course again, but from then on we encountered gales and winter weather. On the sixteenth we were back in the convoy. We zigzagged during daylight, being careful to keep clear of two ships in the convoy, one loaded with TNT, the other with gasoline.

My diary for this period was very abbreviated. Not only was it difficult to write in that heavy weather, but I took seriously the admonition to write down no sensitive material that might fall into the hands of the enemy.

On March 20, we were off Queenstown (now called Cobh), Ireland, where destroyers met the convoy. The convoy split, and half headed to the Irish Channel, half to the French coast. The Navy cruiser left us. (We heard later that it was sunk right after leaving our convoy.) We soon sighted convoys of ships headed west. On the twenty-first there was dense fog at daybreak and the convoy hove-to. After noon the fog lifted and we made full speed to destination. We found ourselves in Brest Harbor, where we anchored for the night. At daybreak we were underway down the French coast, single file, close in, under convoy led by small French patrol boats. We passed behind Belle Island where we saw the topmasts of our company's *Kansan* as she sat on the bottom, sunk by the enemy. Before dark we anchored in Quiberon Bay for the final destination, St. Nazaire, France, and were towed into the locked harbor. On March 24, French and American Army intelligence officers came aboard and examined the crew. The next day we moved to a pier under a large crane and started unloading railroad engine boilers.

The longshoremen were American soldiers. Those on the docks receiving the cargo were Negroes supervised by Army officers. They were getting poor results. These officers were then replaced with white petty officers from the South, and the work proceeded much more smoothly. These southerners were used to directing Negroes and knew how to get the best out of them. They also seemed to know more about unloading than did the commissioned officers.

April 2 we were discharging the locomotives. These weighed fifty tons each. We were using gear rated at forty-seven tons maximum capacity, a risky business. An Army captain and I were in the hold, supervising the inexperienced soldiers. This was challenging work for all concerned. The Army captain, in shirt sleeves and sweating, said to me, "Look what I'm doing down here while the second lieutenants are up parading the docks. That's the Army for you."

On April 4 we picked up a pilot and steamed up the Loire River, one of the prettiest sights I'd ever seen. The river curved through green farmland with the leaves on the trees just about halfway out. Cattle grazed along the banks. The land was cut into rectangular lots by drainage ditches and willows. Here and there we saw women scrubbing clothes along the rocky bank.

April 5 we were at the quay wall along the banks of the Loire at the city of Nantes. Just ahead of us was the American steamer *Munindage*, which had been taken over by the Navy and manned with a Navy crew. Mr. Stoltz, who had been a quartermaster with me on the *Montanan*, was now a Navy ensign on her. He paid me a call. That afternoon Captain Strong, with whom I had sailed, also visited. He had been on the run between France and England for the last six months in command of the *Montanan*. He wanted me to go on his ship as chief mate on his next run, Cardiff to France, but I thought I would be better off staying where I was.

Next day Stoltz and I went ashore together. We came to a river where women were washing clothes on the stones by the bank. Then we went through a cemetery where thousands of casualties of the war were buried. Next we visited a beautiful botanical garden, and then an art museum that had many fine paintings. The one that interested me most was of a beautiful naked maiden lying on a rock, looking into a still pool of water where she could see her reflection. I wished this scene could be real. We went to dinner at one of the swellest restaurants in town. The total bill for both of us was only twenty-two francs. The exchange with American money was such that it cost us only $4 plus a ten-franc tip.

We discharged flour day and night. Most of the laborers were women. Only a few were men, all of whom were disabled in some way, missing a leg, hand, or arm. These men ran the winches. They were a happy group. In the evening, when they had a few minutes' break, they danced and sang amongst themselves on the dock.

Across the street from the quay was a row of apartments. When I was on deck, a girl on the fourth floor waved to me repeatedly. Finally I got up courage and, at her bidding, I went over, climbed the four flights and found my little friend waiting for me at the top of the stairs. What a wonderful greeting it was for a lonesome sailor. We visited a while, and she told me about other American officers whom she had met. One was my classmate, Earle Hammond, who had been there when he was second officer on the *Kentuckian.* He had sent her money toward buying a piano and had given her a Bible. She also told me Stoltz had visited her. Hearing about my friends was interesting to a point, but I began to think that she was not especially interested in me after all. However, she begged me to come to see her before I sailed.

In the evenings I semaphored to a barmaid across the way. I was good at it and so was she. Where she learned how to do it I did not find out. It didn't occur to me at the time that I was obviously not the first male visitor to whom she had signaled. Of course, signaling this girl was not all that I had to do. I worked with the quartermasters on the bridge varnishing the brightwork. At every spare moment I semaphored to Marguerite, who seemed to be getting very affectionate. But rather than pursue this further, come evening I played pinochle with the two radio officers.

It was definitely understood that the captain wanted no women on board, but one day a well-dressed young woman came on, admitted by the chief mate. She was supposedly on business to collect laundry from the officers, but she was really in the business of selling herself. I was at my desk in my room with my door held open on the hook when the mate sent this woman to see me. When she was inside my room, he slammed the door and locked it, leaving the key in the lock so that I could not unlock it from the inside with my spare key. I was really mad. I finally got the outside key rattled loose so that I could get my key to work and got my unwelcome visitor out of my room. I hadn't given her so much as the time of day. I didn't have much respect for the mate after that. This joke of his was the final straw, since I had seen some of the other stunts he pulled. For instance, once he had sent a reel of steel wire ashore at a Brazilian port, an act I judged to be for personal profit. Another time he made a deal with stowaways, collected money from them, and then on sailing "discovered" them and had them put ashore on the pilot boat.

After supper that day I went ashore with Mr. Patton and other officers. We promenaded, as the French call it, through the residential section of the town. We stopped at the Grande Café where I had hot chocolate. Most of the others had wine or such and, as was usual there, we had plenty of female company. I did not stay long, as I found temptation getting the better of me. Later I met Jack Rylander, another classmate, and his French wife, to whom he introduced me. He was second mate of the Buena Ventura docked nearby.

On April 24 all ships left anchorage, passed out through the net, and formed a convoy. All hands were on lookout for enemy submarines, and we changed course frequently. At intervals we fired guns for practice, and our escorts dropped depth bombs. On the twenty-seventh the convoy split up into groups of three without escort. Bound for an undisclosed port in the U.S., we were now left to fend for ourselves.

On the twenty-ninth we checked radio reports of sub positions. I was busy navigating, making requisitions for stores to be acquired, and repairs to be performed on arrival, and we were teaching a Navy signal boy to steer. On the thirtieth we slowed to half-speed to conserve fuel. I had the quartermasters get the ship ready for our annual inspection: marking lead lines, cleaning lamps and lamp lockers, repairing signal flags, and the like. The weather varied from gale to calm and dense fog. When the fog cleared we sighted two transports eastbound. Each day brought radio reports of submarine positions and of ships sunk. We changed course often as a precaution.

We arrived at Cape Henry on the tenth. No sooner had we anchored off Newport News than we received orders to proceed to Baltimore. On arrival we were paid off. I sent Mother another money order in addition to the allotments sent her while I was away, and I tipped the messboy $3. This ended my first voyage to France.

## Notes to Chapter 3

1. Ship chandler: a seller of ship supplies.
2. Dunnage: lumber of all shapes used in the holds to secure cargo or raise it above the floors to preserve it from leakage and other damage.
3. Rose box: the strainer at the foot of the suction pipe of a bilge pump.
4. Draft: the depth of water necessary to float a vessel. Horizontal lines (the "marks") painted on the vessel indicate the depth to which the ship can be loaded.
5. Trim: level from side to side, forward and aft.
6. Bumboat: a small boat used to peddle provisions and small wares to ships anchored offshore.
7. Donkey boiler furnace: part of the ancillary steam engine used to operate deck gear.
8. Bent on: fastened.
9. Azimuth: bearing of a heavenly body, specifically the horizontal angular distance from a fixed reference as to a great circle intersecting a celestial body.
10. Deviation table: because the needle of a magnetic compass is affected by the magnetic attraction of the steel components of the ship, and because the magnetic compass indicates magnetic north rather than true north, the compass error for each heading must be determined and tabulated.
11. Jacob's ladder: a flexible ladder suspended from above, made of wire supporting iron rungs.
12. Gale: a wind from thirty-five to sixty-five mph, called in increasing degrees a moderate, fresh, strong, or whole gale.
13. Shaft alley: compartment at the bottom of a ship below the engine room where the shaft driving the propeller runs.

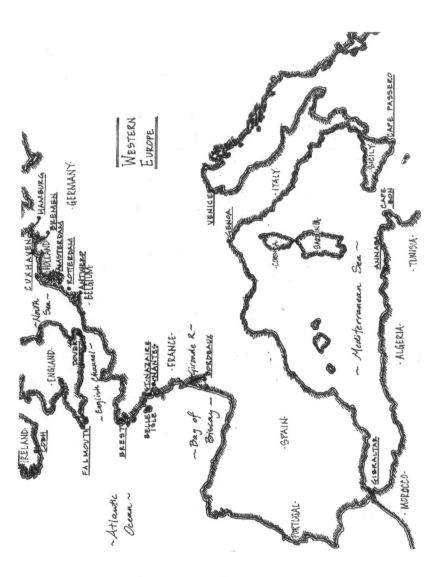

Western Europe

# CHAPTER 4

# STRESS AND DISTRESS

The Navy was taking over the *Californian.* An officer came aboard and encouraged us to join the Navy. Several did just that, but I sent a telegram asking American-Hawaiian to transfer me. I reasoned that not having joined the Navy earlier, joining now would mean that I would not get out in time to be first for the better jobs after the war was over. I also felt that in the Navy I would be doing the same work supporting the war effort that I was doing in the Merchant Service. I was lucky, too, in making that decision, because the *Californian* never made it to France on her first voyage as a Navy ship. She was sunk by torpedoes off the French coast.

I reported to the American-Hawaiian offices in New York and was told to report again in a couple of days. I bought a new suit and went to Irvington to visit the Wistrands. There I met Esther and Ethel, and probably other Wistrands, but my diary only mentions the girls. For me the day was a big success. While there I received a call from the company office directing me to report to the *West Eagle* at Newport News, Virginia.

## The S.S. *West Eagle*

I was busy immediately upon my arrival there. With no other officers on board, I stood the night watch. After the other officers reported on Sunday, I took the day off and went to Ocean View, Virginia, to see my father, Grace, Beatrice, and Albert. (Aunt Grace had written to Father that carpenters were needed in Norfolk, Virginia, so he had moved there and gotten established. Ralph was away in the Navy. Mother, Chester, and Clara were still in Massachusetts.) It was wonderful to be with family.

On May 21, 1918, the crew signed the articles. I was to get $130 a month and a 50 percent bonus for being assigned to the war zone. I also got life insurance, which gave $200 to my heirs if I were lost, or passage back to the U.S. if the vessel were lost and I survived.

That evening a pipe broke in the icebox while we were storing beef, and the repair delayed loading. It was midnight before all the beef was stowed. This was just the first of much that was to go wrong on this ship.

On the twenty-third Captain Maynard Young came onboard, and then went to New York to attend a convoy conference. Captain Lewis Green acted as master for the trip to New York. We sailed at six in the evening with a Navy gun crew aboard, taking the usual precautions by using extra lookouts and showing no lights. I had letters from Mother, Esther, and my cousin Miriam.

On the twenty-fifth Captain Young boarded with the pilot. Our convoy of thirty ships put to sea with everyone alert to danger. We knew we were bound for some French port, but no one knew which one. In the first hour we struck dense fog.

On June 2 we were forty miles south of the Grand Banks. Because we might encounter ice, the ships of the convoy opened out to 1,200 yards apart for the night. We had dense fog for thirteen hours, and when it cleared, the only ship in sight was the escorting British cruiser, which came alongside and signaled to us the position of the rest of the convoy. We joined the convoy again at seven the next morning. We zigzagged during the day. Weather alternated from haze to dense fog.

To maintain our position, our speed had to be changed constantly, but the engine couldn't tolerate these changes and it broke down. We had to stop to make repairs in spite of the convoy commodore's warning that we were making ourselves extremely vulnerable to submarine attack.

On June 5 we had caught up to the convoy, but to go easy on the engine we kept back more than the specified distance. The commodore gave us directions to rendezvous at two-day intervals since we couldn't keep position in the convoy. An English ship among us offered a hawser[1] to tow us, but we refused it.

It wasn't a pleasant feeling to see the escorting convoy continue on and leave us without protection. When we were in position, or nearly so, we were not a welcome member of the convoy because the *West Eagle* smoked badly all the time. When there was only a very slight wind from behind, our thick smoke rose straight up, making us visible to anyone in the vicinity, even those well beyond the horizon. Once the cruiser dropped back, it semaphored a message that we were doubling the visibility of the whole convoy with our heavy smoke. Unfortunately there didn't seem to be anything we could do to fix it. Several times our soot-filled stack caught fire, shooting a plume of smoke and sparks skyward, exposing our position in a spectacular manner to any submarines in the vicinity.

On at least one of those nights I had difficulty getting to sleep. I was thinking of the future and building castles in the air.

On June 11 six American destroyers approached. These were the largest and newest our country had. They relieved the British cruiser, which turned back toward the U.S. Next afternoon we were a hundred miles south of Ireland and two hundred miles west of Land's End, England, and Ushant Island (Ile d'Ouessant), France. All of us constantly scanned the sea for evidence of submarines. The gun crew was on watch in life preservers, ready to fight to the last. At noon we had to stop again for repairs. They took an hour and twenty-two minutes, long enough to have been sunk many times over, but one destroyer circled us until we were able to get back on station.

One dark night we met a big Red Cross hospital ship. She was well-lighted and headed in the opposite direction. Our destroyers were able to head her off so that she did not run right through our blacked-out convoy. (Running at night without lights of any kind, it was a wonder that the ships in the convoy were not sunk by colliding with each other.) At daybreak we found that the six American destroyers had been joined by six British men o' war. The British-bound ships and the French-bound ones parted company. At three in the afternoon our escort dropped ten or twelve depth bombs on suspected subs.

War news: The Norwegian steamer *Hendrick* was sunk off Cape Hatteras. Paris was being gunned from long distance.

We were now close to the rocky French coast near Cape Finistère. Overcast skies left our exact position in doubt. Each ship compared fixes. Because of the uneven bottom, we could not rely on sounding to aid in fixing our position. Darkness came on. At 9:00 A.M. we got a sudden signal, and all ships immediately changed course a full ninety degrees. There must have been great danger ahead for such a radical change to be ordered. We had many narrow escapes from colliding with our own convoy members during that maneuver.

On the fourteenth we made it into Brest without further incident. On arrival both French and American authorities boarded. No one was allowed ashore.

The landscape seemed to be cultivated in wheat. The fields were divided by green hedges, a sight for sore eyes.

When we were leaving the anchorage to join a convoy south, all at once our anchor chain started to run out. It ran through to the bitter end[2] and then carried away the shackle at the bottom of the chain locker. We had no other anchor and could not go to sea. A French Navy tug came to our assistance, and we tied up to a mooring buoy. A dragger came alongside. I boarded her and we set two buoys marking the chain's position at both ends. They put me back on the *West Eagle* and then dragged for the chain. On the second pass across they struck it, but the grapple slipped. At 1:30 they got a good hold on it and hove it aboard the dragger. They brought it under our bow, and by 5:00 we had it on board and secured. We then took a regular anchorage for the night.

On June 17 we joined another southbound convoy, escorted by French torpedo boats of the latest type. On the eighteenth we entered through the locks into the St. Nazaire basin. Next day the French authorities boarded, examined passports, and issued passes good from six to nine in the evening. We discharged the deck cargo of pilings to be used by American Army engineers.

War news: Eighteen more ships were sunk off the American coast.

On the twentieth I went ashore at St. Nazaire and strolled through the town, stopping at a barber shop and the YMCA. Along the Champs I saw many American nurses, always in twos. The public garden benches were full of couples, which made me feel homesick. I bought a French dictionary and grammar book.

As on my previous trip to France, we sailed thirty miles up the Loire River to Nantes to deliver flour. Along the river, tanned, barefoot women were making haystacks. They looked very attractive as I observed them from the bridge through the ship's glasses. The beautiful landscape with cattle and horses added to my homesickness. We discharged flour day and night using inexperienced French workers who managed to break much of the gear. This kept us busy directing and helping them and fixing equipment. Coming off duty from midnight to eight, I found myself dirty and sticky. The night air was damp, and the flour dust stuck to us like paste.

The women were very attentive to their duty, and the German prisoners of war did good work without being driven. There was one French soldier to guard every thirty or forty prisoners. No one was allowed to talk to them.

One evening one of our firemen on duty went down on the dock to talk with the women. He stayed so long that the steam went down, and the winches were without power. Before steam was up again, the cargo handling was delayed for several hours. Such were the contrasts and contradictions of life exaggerated by wartime conditions.

On June 26, after winding the chronometer at eight in the morning, I came off duty and studied my French books. Then, during the recess at midnight, I joined the men and women who had gathered between the piles of flour, and we danced while one of the soldiers played the accordion. We had a jolly good time. I got covered with flour dust again.

We finished discharging on the twenty-seventh, cleaned the holds, and then shifted the ship up the river nearer town and made fast to a steamer discharging coal. Next day while we waited for bunker coal, sixteen of our sailors and firemen refused to work because the law stated that they were to be advanced money every five days while in port. It was the sixth day since they had been offered any advance. They refused even to keep up steam. This was wartime, and we surely did not have the cream of the crop for crew. Captain Young had been unable to get money because his letter of credit had been delayed. He explained the conditions to the men. Still they refused to work, so the Army marched them to a camp where they were forced to cut firewood under the supervision of a tough Army sergeant. Their food consisted of nothing but plain bread and water, and they had to sleep on cold cement floors. Within twenty-four hours, they begged to go back to the ship to work.

June 29 we were bunkering a couple of miles below the town. At the coal plant there, coal dust was made into bricks for household use. I watched the French workers make the product by hand, pressing the soft, dusty material mixed with crude oil into egg-shaped balls which were then allowed to dry.

We continued to bunker with this dusty stuff. I had to keep my quarters closed tightly in spite of hot weather. Ashore, I walked about three quarters of a mile to town, took a train marked "Paris," and rode to the end of the line. Then I walked for about five miles in a straight line into the country, where I came upon attractive houses completely surrounded by rose bushes in full bloom. Many couples walked the footpaths, which were shaded by large maple trees. A pleasant breeze swept across the fields of grapes, hay, and peas.

On July 1 tugboats assisted us closer to the city of Nantes. We tied up to a quay two miles upriver, behind the S.S. *Buena Ventura*, Jack Rylander's ship. While waiting for ballast, we got the ship washed down with water from the river. Mr. Rylander came aboard to call. We walked over to see Marguerite, the barmaid I had semaphored on my previous trip. The time must have flown because when I looked up, I saw my ship being shifted across to the other side of the river. The third mate had taken my station in my absence. I had to walk about a mile to get back on board. I was embarrassed.

For the return voyage we loaded sand ballast, and in the between-decks[3] we loaded old French field cannon. In the States these would be distributed for display all over the country to assist in raising government loans. I went ashore with my friend Mr. Smith, the chief engineer, and two of his assistants. We dropped the mail at the YMCA, and then we all went to the Apollo Theater. The first part of the show was vaudeville, the second part a moving picture. The two assistant engineers then met their "fiancées" and departed for the night. Mr. Smith, a married man, and I returned to the ship at midnight.

On the Fourth of July, the four quartermasters and I started good and early getting the flags ready, and at eight in the morning had the ship fully dressed.[4] At the time there were fourteen ships in the harbor, ten American, three French, and one British ship, and all were dressed for the occasion. Flags were flown all over the city with the American flag predominating. By midnight many of our men boarded, showing the effects of the holiday, laughing and stumbling.

We got ready to sail. Most of the ship's crew and Navy gun crew had hangovers.

On July 7 we sailed on the 3:00 A.M. tide. Two miles down the river the helm failed to respond. Running with the tide at low speed gave us little or no steerage. The *West Eagle* did not make a turn in the river and we grounded. Tugs hauled us off and we proceeded downriver, but before we had traveled another eighteen miles, again the ship would not respond to the wheel. The pilot had us anchor and refused to take us further down the river without tugs alongside.

We arrived at the mouth of the Loire off St. Nazaire on the eighth. The tugs were dismissed and we proceeded to Quiberon Bay. We moved along the Gironde River in convoy and then anchored in Verdon Roads inside the submarine net, waiting for a U.S.-bound convoy.

On the ninth a French passenger ship steamed past with a full load of American troops bound for Bordeaux. We broke radio seals and received positions of latest contacts with enemy subs.

War news: The American ship *Westover* with forty-four on board was sunk, eight men lost.

On July 12 I signaled nearby ships in search of a doctor to treat our sick oiler. Vincent Astor's yacht *Norma* was on patrol duty nearby and sent a doctor, who found the oiler seriously ill. He was taken upriver to Bordeaux and put in a hospital there.

War news: An American hospital ship was bombed by German planes. Several on the ship were wounded and one man killed.

The fourteenth was Bastille Day, and all twenty American ships at anchor in the vicinity were at full dress. The following day a French ship came alongside and issued orders to have steam up and ready by noon the next day. Captain Young left to attend the convoy conference.

War news: A U.S. Navy cruiser was sunk by a mine, six lives lost.

Later a French boat came alongside, this time ordering us not to sail since the night before a ship had been sunk by torpedo just outside the harbor. That evening we had a violent wind and thunderstorm. Our anchor held, but many of the other ships' dragged. Having only one anchor, we were glad it held.

On July 16, 1918, we sailed single file through the opened gate in the net. Outside we formed two columns until clear of the mine fields, then joined four columns. There were twenty-four ships in this U.S.-bound convoy and another twenty-four bound for British ports. We were escorted by American Navy yachts, Vincent Astor's *Norma*, the *Aphrodite*, and the *Corsair*, together with two destroyers, one French dirigible, and several submarine chasers. As we proceeded, we sighted many barrels, bales, and other wreckage on the surface from some recently sunk ship. Later the convoy dispersed, and we were on our own. We zigzagged during daylight. Soon we met a convoy of eleven large American troopships headed for France.

We kept in company with the *West Shore* and the *West Point*. We could proceed no faster than the speed of the slowest ship. We communicated with each other by semaphore. Our ship carried no signalman, so I had that extra duty. We verified our navigational fixes, ship-to-ship, wagging our flags.

On the twenty-first we received a radio message that two enemy subs were ahead of us, a third behind us. I feared my luck would now change for the worse. *The West Point* dropped out of sight behind us. We were forced to reduce speed due to rough seas. When we came upon floating objects, we gave the general alarm and let the gun crew have target practice.

On the twenty-fifth the *West Point* overtook us at two o'clock, and the *West Shore* dropped behind so that she could practice shooting. Our gun crews were on duty continuously. On the afternoon of the twenty-eighth we had a wireless message warning us of the positions of four subs off the American coast, all ahead of us. We resumed zigzagging all the rest of that day.

We received regular warnings of enemy vessels and shaped our course to avoid them. At 1:00 P.M. on the twenty-ninth we sighted a convoy of troopships five miles to the south, escorted by one destroyer and one battleship. Next day we had more warnings and an SOS from a ship two hundred miles ahead of us. Ten minutes later we had another SOS from a different victim just ten miles to the north of the first. They were right on our course for New York, so we hauled further north. At 10:00 P.M. we heard of a third ship in distress one hundred miles to the north of the first.

Next morning at ten we received an SOS from the *West Point*. She was ahead of us and being pursued by a submarine. We encountered great swells that made our ship roll heavily. That made us lose suction to the circulator so we had to slow the engine. In danger of having to stop altogether, we altered course for smoother waters.

August 1 the wind and sea moderated, so we could set our course to Nantucket Shoals Light Vessel. We received the radio time signal from Washington and checked our chronometer. We found that it had lost four minutes and so we were in doubt of our position, but at eight in the evening we made landfall in sight of Nantucket Light Vessel and shaped our course for Shinnecock. We were keeping as near to the coast as possible to avoid the submarines that had just sunk a ship southeast of New York.

Next day we made the best possible speed, and at two in the afternoon we arrived at Ambrose Light Vessel. We tied up to a pylon, passed quarantine, and later anchored on Bay Ridge Flats to await orders, ending my second trip to France. The anchorage was crowded with ships. At three I called the captain, as we were swinging dangerously close to a tanker. We moved to a safer anchorage.

One of the deck engineers became seriously ill and required medical attention. The captain went ashore by boat and made necessary arrangements to care for him. That evening we made fast to the pier at the foot of Eighth Street, North River, and received much sought-after mail. Glad to be safely ashore, I went to visit my friends in Irvington.

War news: Thirty ships were sunk during that summer of 1918. Britain and America took over all Dutch shipping. The fishing trawler *Triumph* was captured by the Germans and was being used as a raider against Allied fishermen. Brazil declared war on Germany. In Russia the czar and his family were executed by the Bolsheviks.

I had now served my time as a licensed second mate and had been studying for promotion. I went to the customs house and applied for a raise in grade. I passed the eye examination and finished writing my examinations on August 8. Captain Green, assistant marine superintendent, advised me to stay by the *West Eagle* until I heard from his office. I got my upgraded license, having passed all the tests.

The *West Eagle* remained at the shipyard for several weeks. She was being made unsinkable by the addition of wooden bulkheads. There was little I had to do on board, so I headed home to Lincoln, visiting the Wistrands on the way. On Sunday, August 11, I had a good time with my family and then took the last train to Boston. I had six hours to kill before the midnight train left for New York, so I went to Everett to call on Dorothy Allan. Again, no one was at home. In Charlestown I stopped at the Sailors' Haven, which Dorothy's late father had run for the Episcopal City Mission. None of the family were there either, a big disappointment for me. On board in New York at eight in the morning, I received a package, a sweater knit for me by Lillian Danner, my Uncle John's younger sister.

It was prudent for us in the Merchant Service to learn all we could about the dangers to our ships. All officers were urged to attend Navy submarine and mine sweeping schools, which I did.

War news: The schooner *D.B. Barrett* was torpedoed off New Jersey, the *Madring Ada* and the *Magdrugorda* were sunk by shell fire. The S.S. *Joseph Cudahy* was torpedoed, with sixty-two missing, sixty-one eventually saved.

While bulkheads were installed on the *West Eagle*, the officers stood regular watches, but there was no other crew aboard. On the evening of the sixteenth, I went again to Irvington for a party. We gathered on a big rock on the banks of the Hudson River and planned a trip to the beach on Sunday. Esther Wistrand was my partner.

Next day I tried to get a good lunch put up for the Sunday beach party but was unable to do so. I bought a box of candy to take with me instead. On Sunday I took the train to Irvington where Esther, Ethan, and Eric met me at the station. We went on to Tarrytown and then by trolley to Rye Beach on Long Island Sound. There we went bathing and had the lunch that the girls had prepared. In the afternoon we swam, went on rides, and roller-skated. A perfect day it was and I hated to leave my friends.

> War news: August 20, the steamer *Frances J. O'Hara* was sunk by a sub. The S.S. *Lake Eden* was torpedoed, with sixteen lives lost. The American schooner *Sylvania* was sunk by a raider.

I received letters from Dorothy Allan and Bill Snelling. Bill, from Lincoln, was in the Army in France. I also had a letter from Dorothy's sister Margaret, who was in France in the Nurses Corps. I received a letter from Dorothy's other sister, Jean, who wrote to me from Amesbury, Massachusetts, where she was on vacation from her teaching job.

On the twenty-first I remained on board all day because the mate had to go to mine-sweeping school. The following day Captain Bennett and Mr. Green surveyed the work being done on board. After supper I took the train to Irvington, stopped to speak to Mrs. Wistrand, and then spent the evening with Esther. I was much smitten and saw her as often as possible.

> War news: The U.S. sub-chaser 209 was shelled by U.S. steamer *Felix Lansing* and sunk by mistake, four men missing. The schooner *F.L. Flaherty* was sunk by a sub, the U.S. steamer *Omega* torpedoed. All driving of automobiles on Sunday was stopped to conserve gasoline. The American steamer *Lake Owens* was sunk off England by gunfire, five men lost. Three American ships were sunk by gunfire in the mid-Atlantic.

## The S.S. *West Hampton*

On September 3, 1918, Captain Young took me on as chief mate to serve with him aboard the S.S. *West Hampton*, transporting war supplies to France. This would be my third trip to Europe. As chief mate I was just one step below captain. I would soon be master of my own vessel. I vowed to work and study hard to be worthy. Since this was just five months before my twenty-fourth birthday, I felt I was progressing to good purpose.

We could not forget the war. That evening a group of us read with interest several newspaper articles concerning the arrest of men without draft registration cards. We were glad we had ours and were serving our country.

I arrived on board the *West Hampton* at nine the next morning. For two weeks I was very busy as we loaded Army supplies.

War news: The American ship S.S. *Dora* was torpedoed off France, eighty-nine on board, all saved. The American ship *Mount Vernon* was sunk, thirty-five lost. A British transport with American troops was sunk, all lives saved.

I received a letter from Esther Wistrand asking me to forget the past. She must have found another beau. My heart sank. Even so I had to call her father about a package I was to take to his son Clifford, who was in the Army in France. Later I went ashore, bought hard white collars, new socks, and life went on.

War news: A Navy patrol boat was sunk off Tampa, Florida.

A new lifeboat arrived, an extra, because in addition to the regular crew we also took on a gun crew of twenty-eight men. A Navy chief petty officer was in charge of them. The ship had the usual five-and-a-half-inch guns fore and aft, plus antiaircraft guns.

War news: The American steamer *Berwind* was sunk by sub, four men lost.

I received pay, sent money to Mother, and paid my life insurance premium. I went to Irvington to pick up the packages the Wistrands wanted me to deliver to Clifford, and I said goodbye. Esther was not at home.

I went ashore the evening of the thirteenth and sent Mother more money, with a package of letters and pictures for her to keep for me.

We finished loading early on the fifteenth after securing the deck cargo (trucks, acids, and other chemicals). At noon we were assisted by tugs to the stream and anchored so close to the piers that when the ship swung with the tide I had to be on the bridge with the engine on standby.

War news: The *Buena Ventura* was torpedoed, fifteen lives lost.

My friend Jack Rylander had been second mate on the *Buena Ventura* the last time I saw him in Nantes.

We got well secured for sea and washed down. On September 18 we sailed for France after passing through the net. The gun crew was stationed and extra lookouts were posted. Lifeboats were swung out ready for lowering. We took our position in the convoy of fifty-four merchant ships, formed nine ships wide and six deep. The commodore in charge was in the middle ship in the first row. He managed and drilled the convoy by flag hoist and ship's whistle.

War news: The American steamship *Kingfisher* was torpedoed, crew safe.

Due to trouble with the steering gear, on the twenty-fifth we fell behind, a straggler and target for German submarines. We were blacked out and zigzagging. When we were able to adjust the gear, we rejoined the convoy in a few hours.

On the twenty-seventh sailors refused to coal the galley. I took them before Captain Young, who settled things with a warning.

The nights were very dark, and it was difficult to keep on station within the convoy. We got our position by dead reckoning only. Finally I got star and sun sights for position.

War news: The S.S. *Ticonderoga* was torpedoed, 217 lost in the mid-Atlantic. Only twenty-three were saved. The *Albert Treves* sank off the American coast with eight hundred men aboard, twenty-one missing. She had engaged a sub in a five-hour running battle. The American S.S. *Saba* struck a mine off the New Jersey coast, thirty lost.

We arrived at the French coast on October 8 after three weeks at sea. We entered the net at the mouth of the Gironde River and anchored at Verdon Roads. I signaled other ships but, unlike my last voyage to France, I found no one I knew.

We passed up the coast in a French convoy and anchored in La Pollice Roads. French authorities inspected our credentials. Then, with the pilot on the bridge and me at my station at the forward end with the carpenter and bos'n, we had an accident. We struck the stone breakwater and damaged the starboard bilge. The captain sent Mr. Cornell, the third mate, down to the deck to see if the ship was making water. Harry Cornell had been on several ships with me before. From the forward end I saw him getting the tarpaulin off the corner of the hatch. I ran back and asked what was the idea of doing such a thing. Mr. Cornell said that the captain told him to see if the number two hold was making water. I said, "You will find nothing that way with the hold full of cargo. Get a sounding rod and sound the bilge." Later we found six inches of water entering every hour.

We entered the locked harbor (a harbor which must be entered and exited through locks that maintain adequate water depths for ships). In docking, we damaged our stem railing slightly. We had touched the American steamer *Ida Moore* while attempting to tie up to the quay. We were not having a good day. After docking, we started discharging and continued to pump the starboard bilges. Green labor damaged a boom.

On the ninth I wrote a letter to Clifford and sent him the two boxes of candy from his family.

War news: On October 11 the Allies want to talk peace.

Saturday the twelfth, another boom was damaged. In the evening I went ashore for a haircut but couldn't get one as there were no lights in the town.

Two days later I tried again and was successful at the best shop in town, operated by a crippled father about forty years of age. He cut the hair. His boy, about nine, did the lathering. His daughter, age twelve, did the shaving.

War news: The American steamer *Lucia* was torpedoed, ninety on board, four lost in the mid-Atlantic.

On the sixteenth I had business in town with Captain Young. We were riding the narrow streetcar to town. The captain was well dressed, dignified but heavy. He weighed about 250 pounds. The two seats ran the full length of the car so that passengers on opposite seats faced each other across the aisle. Several young women were opposite us. They were giggling behind their hands. I didn't know what it was all about until I saw the captain take hold of his big belly and shake it up and down, making the girls laugh out loud.

Soon the *West Hampton* was empty. The Army engineers built a cement box inside the damaged bilge to stop leaks around the dent in the hull. The holds had been inspected, with special attention paid to the damaged section. Surveyors considered the concrete repair safe enough for us to get across the Atlantic until permanent repairs could be made in the States. We began loading red powdered pyrite ore as ballast. Pyrite ore is rich in copper and sulfur. When those are extracted, the residue of red powder is used for making red paint.

We overhauled the lifeboats and made ready for sea, taking on a thousand barrels of fuel. After dark, while we were still loading the oil, the tank ran over, making a big mess on deck. I mustered everyone I could to help clean it up.

We finished loading pyrite from barges on the twenty-eighth. With 2,100 tons aboard, we went outside the harbor to anchor and later joined a French convoy in which we crept down the coast to Verdon Roads. We anchored inside the net and waited for an outbound convoy of our speed.

On the thirty-first we sailed in a convoy for the U.S. The sea was rough. The ship pounded and labored in the Bay of Biscay, and soon we encountered moderate to whole gales. We had to keep headed into the wind to keep from being blown back on the rocky French coast. We could no longer keep position with the convoy. We were on our own.

Soundings made on November 1 showed that the bottom of the damaged number two hold was leaking badly. Eight hundred tons of pyrite were stowed there, above the bilges. On further investigation I discovered that the pounding from the gales had knocked out many three-quarter-inch rivets in the hull, and the water was pouring through these holes.[5] I went down into the hold on a lifeline. After repeated tries I managed to plug seven of the holes with wooden dowels, but with continued pounding in heavy seas, three days later the damaged bilge was again leaking in the seams. The water leaked faster than the pumps could remove it. The bilge was about three feet deep in sea water. Eventually the water rose above the flooring and washed the pyrite ore into the bilges. This pasty red mess plugged up the strainers, and we could no longer pump the water. The rising water leveled off the pyrite as the ship rolled, and she took a slight list.[6] With pyrite and free water all on one side, the list increased, as did the threat of capsizing.

Chief Engineer Smith had small holes drilled through the bulkhead to let the water drain into the fire room bilges, and then we pumped the water overboard from there. But soon the red water precipitated into those bilges also. We enlisted the gun crew to clean the fire room bilges. They had to carry buckets of the wet sediment up the long steel ladders and dump them over the side. This was the only way pumping could continue.

Meanwhile the list increased. The master ordered all hands, the stewards included, to go into the 'tween decks, where pyrite was stowed three feet high, and carry this dry ore in buckets from one extreme side to the other. Work began at one in the morning. It was very difficult since there was only four feet of headroom.

Soon after this process began, the water in the hold rushed to the other side, carrying ore with it. The ship then listed further to the opposite side. Since the ship now listed to starboard, the intakes to the condenser came out of the water. We lost vacuum and had to stop the engine. Then we had to carry dry ore back to where it came from in order to reduce the list and get our intake back under water.

Meanwhile, with all the ore now on one side, the flooring on the high side was free to float. Heavy planks, four inches thick, twelve wide, and twenty feet long, had started to come loose. As the water rose, the planks floated free. When the ship rolled, they pounded first one side of the hull, then shot across like battering rams to the opposite side.

Now hold number two held three feet of water above the normal level of the ore, and the bilge pipe lines were plugged solid. I ordered the hatch opened at number three, which was connected to number two. I had gear rigged to hoist the planks out. This was November 5, six days after leaving France, and we were all exhausted.

I asked the bos'n to send some men down to fasten lines onto the planks. Only one brave soul volunteered. He was knocked down on the first roll and bruised by a plank. He was helped out of the hold and to his bed, soaking wet, hurt, and weary. None of the others would consider venturing into the swirling madhouse. I myself went down, hoping to encourage others to join me. None did. I was by myself. The planks thundered from one side to the other, driving into the side of the ship with each roll of the vessel. I studied the moving and washing for a few moments. Then, having a fix on the rhythm of the planks' motion, I ordered, "Lower the falls."[7] I was dressed in my watch clothes, as I had just come off my 4:00 A.M. to 8:00 A.M. duty. I lowered myself into the cold water to my waist, then cautiously hooked the planks to the falls, one at a time. Three hardies in the crew offered to join me but hesitated. The crew hoisted the planks out on deck and sent them overboard. I made progress, though I got knocked down repeatedly.

My shoes filled with water and ore and then burst from my feet. My pants and underwear tore off too. Finally I had nothing on below the waist, but I still had my shirt and the sweater Lilly Danner had knit for me.

Shortly after noon, all of the planks were out. I came out of the hold covered with red pyrite, clothed only from the waist up. I was the color of a copper Indian. Captain Young met me at the top of the ladder. He gave orders for the steward to fill my tub with hot water. The captain was so pleased with what had been done that he came to thank me even as I bathed. He said he had been afraid the floating planks would tear the ship to pieces.

The weather, blessedly, was improving. In the afternoon we worked on getting the water out. The deck department hoisted water out in oil barrels and dumped it on the deck. The wind picked it up as spray and spattered it all over the camouflage-gray ship, covering it with red ore.

As the gun crew cleared the fire room bilges. Mr. Smith and his engineers made new attempts to get more water out, and together we seemed to be making progress.

War news: November 7, we heard that the crews of the German fleet had revolted.

On the ninth, exhausted, we were still at it. All hands were shifting ballast within the 'tween decks because the list kept the suction inlet out of the water. We had to stop the engine. This was when the captain called for assistance.

Chief Engineer Smith was afraid there was danger of losing the vessel, and he conveyed this message to the captain. He in turn radioed for a coastbound ship to stand by. A British steamer bound for New Orleans offered, but as her regular course was much different from ours, the captain called another, and the American steamer *Oseneke* came toward us.

Then the weather got worse again, with moderate gale winds and mountainous seas. The pounding was so severe that the captain had the *West Hampton* hove-to with the sea on the quarter continuously.

At 8:30 in the evening of the eleventh, the American steamer *Oseneke* arrived and stood by. This was the encouragement we needed. Some of our weary men actually smiled. We had forgotten all about submarines. Only those on the gun crew, not engaged in cleaning and bailing, watched for them. We did not know that the Armistice had been signed. We were all trying our best to keep the ship afloat.

Next day the wind and sea moderated, but now the vessel had a seven-degree port list. The fire room bilges were still plugged full of pyrite. This stopped the pumping and bailing until all hands were successful in clearing part of it. Half of the gun crew carried on with them, cleaning bilges day and night. Both the *Oseneke* and the *West Hampton* were now running short of fuel.

By the fifteenth the water wasn't gaining much. The *Oseneke* ran close to and abreast of us, still bucking a whole gale. Mr. Smith told the captain that he could do no more. "All my efforts have failed," he said in weary resignation. Smith was a fine man, but I knew it was his nature to be pessimistic.

After he made his report, I was summoned to the master's room for consultation. "Smith says no more can be done to save the ship," the captain said. "He says that water is in the largest hold and rising. I think we should abandon ship and get on board the *Oseneke* while we can, before the weather gets worse again. Stay, and we all drown."

I was thinking but made no reply. "Well," he said, "What do you think of it?"

"Captain, I will stay by the ship."

"Young man, tell me what you expect to accomplish by staying."

"I hope to get at least two men to stay with me and help to pull up a towline from the rescue vessel. There is no danger of this ship sinking, sir."

Convinced, Captain Young never mentioned abandoning the ship again.

The two vessels were in sight of one another and hove-to. Finally, in the afternoon of the sixteenth, the weather moderated further, and both vessels resumed course to Halifax.

The next day, at three in the morning, we got a radio message from a Canadian vessel calling for assistance. They wanted a tow, but owing to our condition, we could not assist. We offered to take on the crew but that was not wanted.

On the eighteenth both ships were very short of fuel, having used up so much while bucking headwinds and heavy seas. We heard that the vessel in distress had been abandoned and had sunk. The crew had been rescued by another vessel.

On the nineteenth it was overcast with an easterly gale blowing, no observations possible. We hove-to once more. We slowed and took soundings every hour. According to our reckoning, we passed south of notorious Sable Island, the site of hundreds of wrecked vessels, but we couldn't see it. We were approaching Halifax in dense fog. Each day we compared sightings by semaphore with the *Oseneke*. We heard that the American steamer *Montosa* was nearly out of fuel and trying, like us, to make it to Halifax. They were burning the ship's wooden fittings, hatches, and booms to make steam. She was in severe distress. All three ships ordered pilots. The first pilot to arrive took the *Montosa* in first.

At ten that night we began to have decent weather. The leaking was under control, but both ships were nearly out of fuel. As we arrived off the sea buoy marking Halifax Harbor, we found that the *Montosa* had gone in with the pilot that we had ordered. The *West Hampton* and the *Oseneke* had to wait until daylight for pilots. The masters of both vessels went to bed and left written orders to be called when the pilot was sighted approaching. Meanwhile, we had to keep position and in readiness by passing around a sea buoy, going back and forth to a position five miles to the northwest. We were running on fumes.

Upon arrival in Halifax, Captain Young, Mr. Smith, the carpenter, and I went before the American consul to extend protest legally.[8] Following these proceedings, I was free to go. I got a haircut and a shoeshine and soon had but a single thought in my head.

For years, I had been smitten quite seriously with Jeannette Smith, a girl from Halifax. We had met several times in Lincoln at my Aunt Grace's, and we had carried on a correspondence. Now I hoped to surprise her with my arrival in Halifax.

As soon as I got ashore, I called and found that the family had moved to Eastern Passage. I took a taxi there and on arrival found that I had been searching for the wrong Smiths. Returning to Halifax I found that the Smiths I wanted now lived in Moncton, New Brunswick, on the Bay of Fundy. I took the 3:10 train there, a distance of some two hundred miles, after sending a telegram saying that I was to arrive in Moncton 9:35 P.M. On arrival I called the home and got the right Mrs. Smith, Jeannette's mother. She told me that Jeannette and her husband were at the station to meet me. She had a *husband!*

Stunned but looking about, I found them. Jeannette was dressed in a long fur coat. Her husband was by her side. They greeted me, and I remember so well burying my face in the shoulder of Jeannette's fur coat. Just carried away, I was. I couldn't believe that she was married.

After a cordial reception, the three of us walked arm in arm to their home, which was only a couple of blocks from the railroad station. Mr. Gourley, Jeannette's husband, was an official of the railroad. They had a nice home, and we continued a pleasant visit. They had a baby, too, just a few months old.

Since I had come so far, and it was already late, they insisted I stay the night. I was given the guest room. I was preparing to retire when there came a knock at my door. I opened it and Jeannette entered. She threw her arms around me and said, "Oh, Charlie, say the word, and I will leave everything for you."

I was speechless. I thought, *I am the principal support of my mother and Clara and Chester.* From my point of view, the proposal was incredible and impossible. I just stood speechless. At last she left me. I could not sleep.

Next morning, Sunday, we had a nice visit and early breakfast. The two of them walked with me to the station. I boarded the 9:00 to Halifax. Mr. Gourley had me buy a third-class ticket and suggested that I walk forward to second class after it was collected. I was shocked by such a suggestion coming from an official of the railroad. At five I was back on the *West Hampton* to resume my duties. So much for love. I never saw Jeannette again.

The *West Hampton* sailed from Halifax to New York on November 27. In New York Captain Young went ashore and left me to look after the ship in the crowded harbor. We became shorthanded as crew members left. Our stern swung with the wind and tide and touched a tanker anchored nearby, slightly damaging it. I got the engine going and moved the anchor a few yards to a safer location, a huge effort for me with no crew aboard. I didn't hear from Captain Young for days. Though I never discussed this with anyone, I knew he was an alcoholic. I didn't know much about this condition. I tried to hide his liquor or dilute it to minimize his drinking whenever it seemed urgent to do so. I never discussed any of this with other officers although they must have been aware of the problem. It didn't occur to me that my actions and attitude might be helping to perpetuate his destructive behavior. Captain Young always treated me well. He was a gentleman and an able master, when sober.

The war was over. The Armistice had been signed while we were struggling to keep afloat. The Army began repairs to the ship on December 7. Guns, naval stores, ammunition, and the gun crew were removed, and the ship went to dry dock. I spent Christmas Day aboard as there was still no sign of the captain, though my family wanted me to come home.

The year 1918 had been an eventful one for me. I had served as second mate on the now lost *Californian* from January 1 to May 15, on the *West Eagle* from May 17 to September 4, and then on the *West Hampton* as chief mate from September 5 till the end of the year. I had two months to go until my twenty-fourth birthday.

## Notes to Chapter 4

1. Hawser: a heavy line used in towing or mooring a ship.
2. Bitter end; the inboard end of a rope or cable. The bitter end of an anchor chain is fastened to the bottom of the chain locker, the compartment below the main deck where the anchor chain is stowed.
3. Between-decks: space between decks in a ship's cargo hold; also called 'tween decks.
4. To dress a ship means to decorate it with pennants or flags in honor of a person or event.
5. The hull was built of overlapping plates fastened with rivets, which fell out with the pounding. The joints leaked once the rivets were gone. Since WWII, ship hulls are butt welded so that overlapping and riveting of plates is a thing of the past.
6. List: the leaning of a vessel due to greater weight on one side.
7. Falls: a rope and block, or pulley.
8. Extend protest: a document sworn to before a notary or consul, declaring that the weather conditions encountered on the voyage were such that if the ship or cargo reveals damage, it was caused by "wind and weather," and not through any fault of the ship, master, officers, or crew.

## CHAPTER 5

# COMMITTED TO THE SEA

In early January, 1919, I went home to Lincoln and saw my family. At a South School dance I found that all the small girls I had known there had now grown up. I hardly recognized them, but I had a fine time. I tried once again to visit Dorothy Allan on my trip through Boston but still could not find her. When I returned to New York, Captain Young was aboard.

In mid-January I went to visit my cousin Miriam, whom I had not seen for years. When I arrived at the train station in Springfield, I looked around to find her but hardly knew her when I saw her. She didn't recognize me at all. When I started to take her hand, she said, "Are you my cousin Charles?"

"Yes," I said, but she hesitated, not quite believing me. When I offered to kiss her, she drew back for fear that she had made a mistake. After stopping at a hotel for me to take a room for the night, we walked to her rooming house, where we found a place to ourselves and tried to get acquainted. Soon afterwards I returned to the hotel for the night after making plans with Miriam to meet for breakfast next morning.

I got up early and went to meet her. I had barely rung the bell when she opened the door to greet me. After breakfast we attended a service at the First Church of Springfield. Then I took her to a nice quiet spot in the hotel lobby and tried to have a heart-to-heart talk. We finally said what was on our minds and felt better for it. At two we went to lunch and then took the train to Northfield to visit her family. They were all glad to see me and I them. Miriam and I returned by train to Springfield and I walked with her to her rooms. At last I took my leave and boarded the 3:00 A.M. train back to New York. I really liked Miriam a whole lot.

93

I arrived on board a little after eight in the morning but, not having had any sleep and having had such a big day the day before, I felt funny all day. I couldn't seem to think of anything or anybody except Miriam. If she weren't my cousin, I would say that I had fallen in love with her. I went to bed early and tried to sleep it off. I was very uneasy.

On February 12 we sailed for Bordeaux, a typical rough winter passage. On March 14 we were on our way back home, loaded with eight thousand tons of freight, including heavy artillery, and twenty-one soldiers and four officers. Many of the soldiers were seasick. I also brought home three bottles of the best perfume made in France.

We arrived at Newport News on April 4. Captain Young went ashore, and once again I did not hear from him for days. I wrote to Miriam and sent her a bottle of perfume and four meters of blue crêpe de Chine fabric. I was becoming a bit anxious about Captain Young. At last he arrived on the tenth at eleven in the morning. The next day we sailed again for France where we loaded cargo—Army trucks, ordnance, steel, clothing, and airplane equipment—and another twenty-one soldiers and four officers. We departed for New York on June 11, and on our arrival there I went straight home to Lincoln. This time I was able to meet with Dorothy Allan on my return trip through Boston.

In early July I visited Miriam again. We walked to two springs on top of a hill, a pretty spot. As I was helping Miriam across a brook, I failed to reach the other side and went in up to my knees. We laughed until we cried. We returned in time for supper then went swimming. It was a perfect day. Next morning we had a splendid time together getting the chores done. I stayed with Miriam until it was time to leave. Departure was mighty difficult.

On the ninth I received letters from Mother, Miriam, and Dorothy. Dorothy's letter read,

> You are a most persistent person. I'm almost afraid to encourage you the least little bit. You seem to have a very high opinion of me. I'm grateful but should hate to prove to be a disappointment to you. You are a sailor and, no doubt, have lots of sweethearts. Now that I have written that—I'm only guessing. I don't know if I should take you seriously or not. For safety, I'll take it that you're a good friend. However, you must not write me affectionate letters even if you really mean what you write. Why?—Oh, just because!!

On the eleventh the crew went on strike. We were scheduled to sail to Newport News for cargo and then to Italy, but all ships, including ours, were tied up as crews struck all along the coast.

*Editor's note:*

*Unions affiliated with the International Seamen's Association, including firemen, oilers, water tenders, cooks, and stewards, demanded recognition of their unions by shipping companies, a $15 per month increase in wages, and eight-hour watches, as opposed to the twelve-hour watches common on most ships. (Deck officers served four-hour watches.) The strike tied up about half of American ships and especially affected shipping of food and raw materials to Europe for reconstruction following the war. Union leaders saw the companies' willingness to negotiate with them as a major victory in itself and were willing to concede on their demand for a closed shop. This demand, however, was to become the most significant issue in the unions' battle with shipping owners over the next two decades. In 1919 the unions settled for the $15 increase in wages and ultimately did not press for hiring preference for union labor. The strike was settled on July 26.*

I wrote to Miriam every day, and I heard frequently from Dorothy. Captain MacNamara relieved Captain Young, who was given command of the *Alaskan*. On July 23 I received a long-awaited letter from Miriam and got two more from her two days later.

On July 27 I was busy getting the vessel ready for sea and a crew signed on. Then, after all those days of waiting for the strike to be settled, the engineering officers refused to sign on. Their association had ordered them not to until all their demands were met. At last the unions were satisfied, and we sailed for Cape Henry. I was able to visit my family in Ocean View before we sailed for Europe.

While making our passage to Italy, I read over all my old letters. They brought back memories. To clear my mind again before going to sleep, I read *The Crisis* by the American novelist Winston Churchill, one of the books Miriam had given me.

On August 17 the ship stopped at anchor off Gibraltar, where the captain and "super cargo" went ashore together to do ship's business. (Near the end of the war, the U.S. Shipping Board trained supervisors of cargo to counteract thievery. Their duties were similar to those of a purser on a passenger ship. On merchant ships they acted as one of the officers to do the ship's paperwork, assist the master in his business dealings, and ensure that the government would have accurate numbers, weights, and records. Since the *West Hampton* belonged to the Shipping Board, she carried such an officer, whose nickname was "super cargo.")

On the eighteenth we sailed for Venice in excellent weather. Sighting many small sailing vessels, I thought of the days when Columbus was a seaman. How on earth could people have believed that the earth was anything but round? Seamen, at least, should have been able to see it as such.

On the twenty-sixth we arrived off the entrance to Venice and anchored. After passing quarantine, we tied up at a quay wall right in the city. The crew was pleased to be able to get ashore so easily and spend their time off in town rather than having to spend much of it traveling to get there.

With the ship in port for two whole weeks, we had good time for sightseeing. I also shopped for gifts to take home: a blue china tea set for twelve, costing 700 lire or $72 American, another tea set for eight costing 450 lire or $48 American, four hat pins with engraved initials for 12 lire, one mosaic picture for 15 lire, and two cameos, one 50 lire and the other 23 lire. Nearly every day I wrote to Mother and Miriam.

One day Mr. Cornell and I took a ferry to Lido di Venezia, a long, thin island separating the lagoon of Venice from the Adriatic. The beach, with clear white sand, was one of the most fashionable bathing beaches in Europe. At the bathhouse we received the customary suit, towel, and a large white sheet. We expected to get a place to change, but, to our surprise, others were changing on the open beach. After some careful observation, we awkwardly did the same under the sheet and had fun doing it.

Next day my mission ashore was a grim one. I had to visit the American consulate concerning one of my sailors, who had been reported drowned at Lido Beach. During the afternoon of September 2, I gathered Ordinary Seaman Maurice O'Keefe's clothing and other belongings, made a list, and locked them up for safekeeping. On September 6 Captain MacNamara woke me in the evening to say that a body had been discovered among the rocks about two miles from where O'Keefe was reported to have drowned. The captain had gone with the police, the American vice consul, and a doctor to the scene. Although the body was badly mutilated by fish and beginning to decompose, it was clearly O'Keefe.

On the seventh I met the captain and vice consul at St. Mark's Square. We took the launch to the city hall, where we secured a death certificate. Then we took another launch to Mallomocco Cemetery, where a Catholic priest held services. I took a picture of O'Keefe's final resting place, grave number thirty-nine, to be given to his folks back home. Later I had the carpenter make a nice wooden cross of oak and sent him to the grave to erect the cross and take another picture.

The captain had asked the Shipping Board for 1,500 tons of ballast, the minimum necessary to put the ship down in the water and get the rudder and propeller covered so that we could make headway and manage the ship in a seaway. The Shipping Board representative cut the quantity to 700 tons in spite of the captain's protest. The ballast was waste fill, such as coal ashes. I had been very careful to prepare the scuppers, drains, and bilges so that none of this material would plug up the drainage system. With the 700 tons in the bottom, all tanks full of fuel and fresh water, plus other tanks with water ballast, the ship's draft was only nine feet, ten inches forward and fifteen feet, two inches aft. I suspected that we didn't really have even close to 700 tons of ballast. The propeller and rudder were one-third out of the water. This was hardly a seaworthy condition for a low-powered vessel about to cross the Atlantic.

Before we left Venice, Captain MacNamara told me briefly of his difficulty in getting the required amount of ballast. He then telegraphed the agents in Gibraltar, ordering more ballast.

Approaching Gibraltar, I had hatches opened, booms up, and steam on the winches, ready to load the second 700 tons of ballast ordered. The captain and "super cargo" went ashore by launch.

At seven next morning a single lighter came alongside carrying beach sand and by 10:00 A.M. we had finished loading all of it. Neither the captain nor "super cargo" showed up. We kept waiting and wondering. Finally at three, the two approached the ship in a boat. I expected the captain to tell me when more lighters were to arrive. Instead, he asked me, "Mr. Mate, did you get your seven hundred tons of ballast?"

"Captain," I replied, "we haven't received more than seventy tons so far."

"It is your fault, Mr. Mate. The super cargo and I checked the quantity on the beach. It is up to you to check it on board. Up anchor and let's go to sea."

The whole performance seemed strange to me at the time. I couldn't understand the sarcastic "Mr. Mate" that the captain used to address me. I began to suspect that the provider of ballast was paid to deliver the full 700 tons. The money had no doubt been divided among the participants of the deal with only a small portion of the amount of ballast contracted for actually delivered.

It was fortunate that we had smooth weather, but with the vessel riding so far out of the water we could make only 220 miles for a day's run, even with the engine turning at top speed. On September 21 we began to encounter strong northerly swells. Not only was the ship riding much too high but, with all the ballast way down in the bottom, she also righted herself like a whip, making for a very uncomfortable ride.

When we arrived in Newport News, I received orders from our New York office to report there on Tuesday. I also had letters from Dorothy. Friday I visited Father, Grace, and Albert. I left a suitcase full of clothes with Grace and returned to the ship. Arriving aboard I paid off the crew, and later we were towed to dry dock for bottom cleaning and painting. The work was completed quickly and next day at noon the vessel was floated and towed to anchorage off the repair yard. I took my baggage ashore and went to Ocean View, arriving in time for supper with the folks.

The next day I packed the remainder of my belongings, wrote the log up to date, and left the *West Hampton* for good. At home I had a lively talk with Ralph, urging him to come with me to try his luck as a merchant sailor. He agreed. As we traveled to New York together, I had a rare chance to talk to my brother at length. I dropped him off at the customs house to obtain his

AB (able-bodied seaman) and lifeboat certificates, and I went on to the American-Hawaiian office to see Captain Bennett, who ordered me to the S.S. *Alaskan* at once. I relieved the mate and once more met Captain Young, who was to be master. Later we signed on the crew, which included Ralph as a quartermaster.

I visited Miriam that weekend. It was very difficult to say goodbye.

## The S.S. *Alaskan*

We sailed for Baltimore where we started loading utilizing the belt system, the most up-to-date method of the time. In only two days we were loaded with 10,000 tons of coal and 1,108 tons of coke.[1] Before we sailed, I went ashore with Ralph. I sent Mother a money order and bought rubber boots, socks, two sodas, a newspaper, haircut, and shoeshine. Then there was bus fare. All of this I accounted for in my ledger as was my habit. The next morning we sailed for Rotterdam. On November 11, 1919, a year after the Armistice, we encountered heavy northeast swells, and the vessel was unable to make headway. Discovering the rudder had broken below in two places, we called a nearby British ship, the S.S. *Pennyworth*, and she agreed to assist us.

We had no tow wire, but the *Pennyworth* had a four-and-a-half-inch wire two hundred fathoms long. With both vessels stopped, we lowered our work boat near the stern. I took charge with four volunteers. It was a risky procedure to get the boat into the water without hitting the ship, or capsizing and being crushed under the counter.[2] We did not have the quick-disconnect hooks modern ships have. However, with good luck and competent seamanship, we got the boat away and towed a Manila line toward the *Pennyworth*. When we were near enough, they threw us a heaving line. We made the heaving line fast to the Manila line. Now all we had to do was get back aboard the *Alaskan*.

Back near the stern and hooked on, the men above ran us up as quickly as they could, but as we were being hoisted, we found ourselves looking up at the ship one minute and a few seconds later looking down at her as we rode the crest of a wave. Once on board we ran the Manila line to the steam winch and hove it and the tow wire aboard. We made this fast, and when all was secure we reported ready to the two captains.

Slowly they got their ships in position two hundred fathoms apart. Almost immediately a big sea rose in between the vessels. The wire became as tight and straight as a solid bar and parted in the middle. It was useless.

Before sailing, I had received several two-and-half-inch mooring wires in sixty-fathom lengths, each with an eye spliced in both ends. These were still on wooden reels, stored temporarily on top of the coal in the forward hatch. To get hold of them meant opening the hatch, a risky proposition in a heavy sea. The captain turned the ship so that the hatch would be in the lee of the wind. We opened the hatch, hoisted out the lines, and then covered the hatch again as quickly as possible.

Although the ship was deep and awash, pitching and rolling, we managed to get the wires off the reels and shackled together, making a new line smaller than the *Pennyworth's* but twice as long. By the time we were ready to dispatch the new towline, it was getting dark. The captains agreed to suspend operations until daylight.

At daybreak on the morning of the twelfth, the *Pennyworth* lowered her boat and sent a line to us. We bent on the end of our wire line and, as soon as her boat was securely on board, we eased the line out to her. Great care was taken to handle this line slowly and cautiously to save it, and to be sure no one was injured. It was our last hope.

At 9:30, the towing hawser was connected, and we got underway very slowly, increasing the revolutions by just two at a time.

*In telling this story, Dad said, "We were taken in tow by a British ship."*
*We landlubbers assumed that British ship was ahead. Not so. The*
Pennyworth *was towed by the* Alaskan. The Pennyworth, *behind, did the*
*steering for both.*

It was agreed that it was best to proceed to Falmouth, England, for repairs. Captain Young radioed for tugs to meet us and kept the owners informed by relayed radio messages. Tugs assisted us into the harbor on November 14. Repairs began and we passed quarantine. Later that afternoon, customs officers came on board and placed a writ on the foremast, putting the ship under arrest. Repairs were stopped and a guard posted. This was to prevent incurring any further expense until the issue of salvage was settled. The owners of the *Pennyworth* had put in a claim for salvage, as was customary under British law.

The *Alaskan* was idle for a whole month. During this time Captain Young lived ashore in a hotel so as to be in contact with the agent, insurance underwriters, and American-Hawaiian. He was also close to sources of alcohol and was drinking heavily. A sailing sloop was hired to act as a running boat between ship and shore. This boat carried the mail and crew ashore and back. The captain came out to the ship frequently, but, being a heavy man, and in his cups, he seldom came on board. Instead I would meet him at the foot of the pilot ladder to conduct the ship's business. He was often too drunk to function effectively. On occasions when he had me ashore with him, he sometimes had difficulty standing. In court during salvage proceedings, I had to be by his side to keep him from falling down. Whenever the judge asked him a question, he would answer with slurred speech, "Your Honor, my mate will answer that question."

Bond was posted to cover the salvage claim. The writ was removed, the guard taken off, and repairs to the rudder resumed. Repair work continued on the rudder day and night whenever weather permitted, but the slightest chop to the water stopped the work, since the part they were attempting to weld was very close to the water's surface.

On December 16 temporary repairs were at last completed. Captain Young came on board with the local pilot and a North Sea mine field pilot, Captain Gay. Captain Young had cleared the ship and received a seaworthy certificate from Lloyds, permitting us to sail to Rotterdam provided we took a standby tug along with us. We raised the anchors quickly and sailed. Captain Gay directed us successfully through the mined channel of the North Sea, but we saw all sorts of vessels that had been wrecked in the war. On December 18 we anchored at the entrance to the Maas River, the approach to Rotterdam, but as a gale rose we had to head out to sea again to ride out the storm.

Two days later, we were at the entrance to the river once more. We had to wait for high tide before proceeding because of our deep draft. Two large tugs met us and each one took a towline, one forward and one aft, to assist in the steering. The local pilot knew the passage would be difficult because the ship's bottom was so near the riverbed.

It was good weather, the tide was rising in the river, and an experienced river pilot was directing the vessel. However, these factors did not help our steering ability. We bumped one bank and then the other in spite of the tugs. A mile inside the jetties, she stuck fast on the bottom, and we had to await the next tide. The after tug got her towline foul of our starboard propeller, so we cut it as close to the wheel as possible. For two more days, with the tugs assisting, she floated at every high tide but grounded when the tide dropped. If so much investment were not at stake, the situation might have been laughable. Sometimes she was headed up the river and sometimes down. Worse, at one low tide, she grounded crosswise in the river, blocking ships going in either direction. This was dangerous, for there was the likelihood of the vessel breaking in half since both ends were supported and not the middle. Besides that, sand being washed down the river banked up against the ship. This raised havoc with our main condenser, which needed water to cool the steam, which in turn was essential to boiler operation. We managed to swing her at last and let the wind hold her hard against the lee bank. During this whole dreadful passage upriver, Captain Young continued his heavy drinking. The ship chandlers supplied him with all he wanted.

The answer to our problem was to lighten the ship before trying to proceed further. Cranes and lighters were brought alongside. We discharged coal to the lighters and, on December 24, with 1,200 tons discharged and two strong tugs on the towlines forward and two others astern pushing, we steamed up the river.

At 5:30 in the afternoon, we came to a turn in the river. Being cautious, the pilot had her on half speed. The *Alaskan* kept going straight ahead. There were idle ships ahead of us. The pilot ordered full speed on the port screw and full astern on the starboard. She kept on a straight course. The forward tugs pulled to the right, the after tugs to the left. Nothing helped. We were on a collision course. The engines were reversed at maximum full astern. She kept on, aided by her mass and by the tide.

I was at my station forward. I let go both anchors. The forward tugs, to keep from being dragged into the collision, let go their towlines.

At 5:36 the *Alaskan* collided with the S.S. *Holland* with a glancing blow, and within four more minutes also hit the S.S. *Ups* obliquely. At last she stopped, just as she was to put her bow into an American four-masted schooner whose long bow sprit came right over my head as I was standing on deck.

Stopped among these vessels, we found our starboard propeller had become foul of the mooring chain of the S.S. *Holland*. The tide ebbed and we grounded once more, stranded until the next tide. The four large tugs were dismissed and four smaller ones engaged. These were handier in the confined quarters. Early Christmas morning we proceeded up the Maas and finally reached our destination.

On the day after Christmas, we started to discharge coal into canal boats. Rotterdam was a huge port. I spent time ashore sightseeing when I could. Captain Young lived ashore in a hotel away from the noise and coal dust. I had no opportunity to limit his drinking. When we had arrived in Rotterdam, I had taken his liquor away from him so that he would be fit to go to court. He said to me, "If you won't let me have it here, I will have to go to a hotel." He went. He came to the ship almost every day but seldom came aboard, preferring to send his taxi driver to fetch me while he waited in the cab. We would talk over the workings of the ship for a few minutes, and then he would return to town.

On December 29 the chief engineer, Captain Young, and I went to court to extend protest before the judge, declaring that the bad weather encountered on the voyage was the cause of our mishaps. We gave extracts from the log book to verify our claims.

On January 3, 1920, we started to load sand ballast since there was no return cargo available. The rudder was surveyed once more by a diver, who judged the rudder to be intact but not safe, so two knees were installed over the welded areas. These were bolted to the coupling. We also had the condenser cleaned and repaired because of the sand that had been taken in when the ship was crosswise in the river.

On January 7 we sailed. Captain Gay guided us through the channel made by the mine sweepers to Falmouth, where we left him. Captain Young told me that we would take the southern route home for better weather, and we proceeded with heavy southwest swells. At 2:30 we sighted a floating mine close on board. It unsettled us all.

The master was drinking heavily, as he had been ever since our long stay in Falmouth. On leaving Rotterdam, I knew he had a big stock of liquor in his room. As long as we were at sea, I could take care of the vessel and did so whether the master was fit or not. I did not, however, take advantage of the situation. I made my regular reports to him and daily presented the official logs. He always signed them. At noon each day I reported the ship's position. I would say, "I make the course for the next twenty-four hours such and such," and Captain Young would reply, "Make it so, sir." We had been through a lot together. I always treated him with respect, and he treated me the same.

On January 13 the second mate took sick and remained in bed for the rest of the voyage. From then on the third mate and I stood watch four hours on and four off, around the clock, every day.

The captain did not go to meals but had the steward bring a plate of soup or some simple food to his quarters. Most of this time he spent sitting at the roll-top desk in his office. When I went to his room or to the bridge to stand my watch, I took special precautions to see that his door was in the ventilating privacy position because I did not want the crew to see his condition when they passed his cabin. I saw to it that any mention of him was never unfavorable. Whenever he came on deck under the influence, either on this ship or on others on which I sailed with him, it was my custom to ask him to go back to his quarters. Usually he came out of it and sobered up. He never drank in American ports, since he had lost his job in another company for being drunk on duty.

On the eighteenth I stood the twelve-to-four morning watch, then the eight-to-noon watch. Coming on duty at eight, I noted that the captain's door was closed. I had my breakfast on the bridge, and shortly thereafter the steward went to the captain's room to offer him breakfast. He found him dressed but lying on his back on the deck as though he had been thrown out of his swivel chair when the vessel rolled. The steward reported this to me, but I thought nothing could be seriously wrong. I told the steward I would check on the captain. I went down and tried to move Captain Young to his bedroom next door, but without help I could only drag him by the shoulders. I could not budge his immense midsection onto his bed, so I left him sitting in the corner of his bedroom. I did not think that the situation was very unusual for him when he was drinking and said nothing to anyone about it. I went back to the bridge, stood my watch, did my navigation and log writing, and consulted with Bos'n Whitney regarding work being done. At noon I turned the watch over to the third mate and stopped to report to Captain Young. I found him dressed as before and sitting at his desk eating a bowl of soup. He signed the noon slip to the chief engineer and approved my suggested course. When I was called to go on duty again at four in the afternoon, I noted that his door was on the hook—no cause for alarm—and I proceeded to the bridge to stand watch until 8:00 P.M.

It was about an hour into my watch when the steward rushed to the bridge to inform me that he had found the captain lying on his office floor again, this time face down. I calmed the steward and asked him to accompany me. I thought that this time I would use him to help me get the captain up onto his bed. I straddled the shoulders and the steward straddled his feet, but as we attempted to lift, we found his body not limp but rigid. Captain Young was dead. We noted that he had bled some from his mouth and nose.

I immediately sent a wireless message to the owners in New York: "CAPTAIN MAYNARD YOUNG HAS DIED NATURALLY, 18 JAN, 1300 TO 1500 HOURS. ALL IS UNDER CONTROL. C.N. BAMFORTH, MATE."

I told the chief engineer I had found the captain on the floor at eight in the morning and that I had left him unconscious in the corner of his bedroom. The chief said, "That's funny, because at 8:10 while I was eating my breakfast in the saloon, the captain rushed in and headed toward the ship's medicine cabinet. He and I have the only keys, you know. In a little while he saw me at the table and came and sat down in his regular place and chatted a little. He drank three glasses of water, got up and returned above to his quarters. He didn't eat anything."

The chief and I went to the medicine locker and found that the pint bottles of Jamaica ginger and peppermint were empty, although they had been nearly full before. Then we went to the captain's quarters. We found no liquor but several empty bottles. Apparently he had run out of liquor and had gone for the alcohol in the medicines.

I called Bos'n Whitney, a man of long and faithful service. I said, "I am turning over my duties as mate to you. You are to supervise the crew and take full charge of the upkeep of the vessel." We talked about details, and he responded, "Aye, aye, sir." I told him to prepare Captain Young's body for burial at noon of the next day.

Next I questioned the third mate and the quartermasters to see if they had seen or heard anything of the captain during their watches. Henry Young, the captain's nephew, had been at the wheel, just one flight above the captain's office. He said, "I heard a thump at 3:30." The third mate and I decided that must have been when the captain had fallen, and we took it to be the time of his death.

Next morning the chief engineer and I went through the captain's belongings. We gathered and saved things of value while Bos'n Whitney was preparing the body for burial.

By noon all was ready. I stopped the vessel, and we all gathered at the stern near the ship's flag, which was hauled down. The captain's body was weighted and sewn up in clean, white canvas. It was placed on a hatch plank. Over it was a new American flag with the canvas edge secured to the ship.

All who were interested were invited to attend. With all hats off, I read the burial service from the Episcopal Book of Common Prayer. When I came to the end, I said, "I hereby commit his remains to the deep." Crew members did as directed and lifted the inboard end of the plank. The canvas casket slid over the side and sank into the sea. The American flag was hoisted to half-mast. Then all crew members returned to their duties. Entries were made in several logs and properly witnessed. I sent another radio message to the owners: "CAPTAIN M. A. YOUNG'S REMAINS WERE BURIED AT SEA NOON THE 19TH. BAMFORTH, MATE."

We were now bound to Baltimore. The second mate was confined to his sick bed. I had to see that he was cared for. He was elderly and so ill that he was unable to do the most basic things for himself. By regulation the ship was specified as a master and three-mate ship. Now it was a relief master and one-mate ship.

On January 25 the ship was very difficult to steer. By lying face down and looking over the stern at the rudder as the swell lifted it out of the water, we could see that it had broken in the welds. The knees added over the welded pieces were loose, and the rudder could only be made to move part way to port.

I had the sixteen-inch towing hawser brought on deck. The end was made secure and shoved out the center chock, aft. The other end was then secured to five-inch Manila lines and brought to the deck winches on either quarter. By hauling on the lines, the size of the big bight (loop) lying in the water could be controlled, thus giving us steerage by giving the ship a varying frictional drag in the water. Since the rudder would go halfway to port, we towed the bight on the starboard quarter. We were in good weather, so we could make a fairly straight course.

That evening I sent a third radio message to the owners in New York: "EXPERIENCING RUDDER TROUBLE POSITION 35 N BY 58 W. HAVE A MASTER, SECOND MATE, AND TOWBOAT MEET THE VESSEL AT SANDY POINT. ETA TO BE SENT LATER."[3]

We continued to have good weather, but when we were north of Bermuda we had to change the course to northwest to make for Cape Henry and the entrance to the Chesapeake. Strong headwinds came up and we had great difficulty keeping the ship headed in the proper direction. In fact, twice we made complete 360-degree turns before reaching the Cape.

On January 29 we took aboard a Baltimore pilot to whom I explained the situation. Immediately he wanted to get off, desiring no part of a rudderless, masterless vessel. I urged him to stay, noting that we had crossed the Atlantic in midwinter in this condition. I promised him that at daybreak I would have myself lowered over the stern to assess the extent of the rudder trouble in detail. He stayed.

With favorable weather and very light airs, we sailed the 130 miles from Cape Henry to where the Chesapeake Bay narrows and the dredged channel begins. There we met tugs as ordered. The new captain and second mate were both on the tug but could not board until the vessel had passed quarantine. After we passed, Captain Blackwell and Second Mate Davis came up the tug's ladder to the deck. Captain Blackwell handed me a sealed envelope from the owners and, with hardly a word, walked to the bridge to take command. He was not at all polite to me. I learned that he and others thought that I had killed the captain myself so that I could take command. They harbored these suspicions because I had buried him so soon after death. Of course, I didn't have a master's license and couldn't have assumed such rank even if I had wanted to. They realized this later.

On arrival in Baltimore, the first thing I had to do was to take care of the sick second mate. An ambulance met the ship and took him to the Seamen's Hospital. Next I had to obtain a death certificate. The log books were examined and the ship's company interviewed. I showed the authorities Captain Young's signature affixed each day in the log books, the night order book, and the reports to the chief engineer. These signatures revealed the captain's gradually decreasing dexterity. The testimony given by his nephew concerning his condition was also convincing, and a death certificate was issued.

I entered the vessel at the customs house and returned to the ship with a representative of the Shipping Commission and a local paymaster. We paid off the crew for the voyage. Then I turned everything over to Captain Blackwell. My letter from the owners directed me to report in person to the general manager of American-Hawaiian at the New York office.

I took a sleeper to New York. There I met officials who were anxious to hear the details that would form the legal story to be taken up with lawyers, charterers, and the insurance companies.

In the afternoon I called on Captain Young's brother, Walter, who was the chef at the Commodore Hotel. He was very understanding and he knew about his brother's weakness. He made arrangements for me to call on the captain's widow. He and I had lunch together, then I called on Mrs. Young. The meeting was a cold one and an unhappy way to conclude a nightmare of a voyage. I handed over her husband's valuables, which included his Masonic ring and a small amount of cash. Although she and the captain had been separated for several years, she was very distressed. I also sensed that she was angry because he had not left her more money. Mrs. Young openly blamed me for her husband's death. She was hateful to me and acted as though I had deliberately killed him. Fortunately, Walter had warned me of the kind of reception I was likely to receive. It was a sad affair.

At five that afternoon, I took a train to Springfield to call on Miriam. We were kindred souls and very much in love, cousins though we were. Following tearful goodbyes, I boarded the train for New York.

I was back at the American-Hawaiian offices at nine Monday morning. After settling for my expenses to New York, and with interviews completed, I was told to return to Baltimore and rejoin the *Alaskan*. Once there, I felt at home again as mate, making the ship ready to go on dry dock where a new rudder was constructed.

With repairs complete, we started loading coal on February 9 and sailed on the afternoon of the eleventh for Holland. We carried less cargo this time so that we would be able to get into the Maas River without grounding.

Before departing I received a letter from Dorothy.

Dear Charlie,

I don't know whether to let you go on writing me semi-love letters and letting yourself think you really care for me, or to cut you off at once. I truly don't see how you can know that you care a great deal for me because you don't really know me or I you. For myself, I don't know either. I am afraid you are in love with love. I know I am and always have been. . . . I don't know how I shall ever find out about you if I never see you to get really acquainted, and it isn't fair to encourage you at all under those conditions. I'd like nothing better than to carry on a "love" correspondence with you, but I shan't because when I do see you I shall, no doubt, feel self-conscious. If you could only "rush" me for a little while I'd soon find out where I stood, but the only way you can do it is by mail and that is not very satisfactory.

I'll tell you frankly I can flirt. . . . I'm giving you fair warning. I think I'm fickle and I demand a lot and only give what I want to. If you want to continue to let yourself think you care for me with that knowledge, you may go to it, but don't expect too much from me. I'd like to marry, but I don't know if I could ever trust a man to be true to me. . . . So, you are twenty-five. I am older, but unless you know how much, I'll not tell you, but my birthday is April 22. Can you remember it? You see I'm trying you out now. Little things sometimes mean such a lot! . . .

I'd like to get your letters, so write often, sailor man. Not that I expect you to do so, chiefly because you are a sailor. Can they ever be true to one girl?

Due to a strike at Rotterdam, we were directed to Antwerp, and on March 3 we anchored off Flushing to wait favorable tide to enter the Scheld River. On the fourth I wrote a letter to Dorothy and then tore it up. We finished discharging on March 11. Captain Blackwell decided we did not need ballast, reasoning that this ship with small screws and low power would handle all right without it. We departed and were soon clear of the locked harbor, standing down the Scheld River. Out in the broad Atlantic, we encountered a moderate westerly gale and rough seas. The engines, having no governors,[4] raced terribly when the propellers breached the surface as we plunged through the swells. The master ordered the vessel slowed to less than steerageway. Then the ship lay rolling in the trough of the seas.

For the next several days, we averaged only 113 miles a day because we were stopped for so much of the time. To get the propellers down in the water and improve thrust, the captain reluctantly had the lazaret (after storeroom) filled with seawater. We drifted ninety-five miles to the south as we were hove-to most of the day, and made no progress toward our westerly destination. On the twenty-sixth we made only eighty-one miles. Captain Blackwell, fearing that we would surely run out of fuel, ordered seawater put in number four cargo hold. This helped. Then the port propeller dropped a blade. This made for heavy vibration, and the propeller had to be slowed to prevent damage.

April 4 we arrived at Baltimore. On the seventh we received new crew members from New York to fill several vacancies. We had had such an uncomfortable passage that many in the crew decided not to sail on her again. We started loading coal at the B & O piers using new automatic mechanical trimmers, but they didn't work well on this ship. She was designed with many decks for general, not bulk, cargo. We shifted to the old pier where trimming was done by men using shovels.

We headed for Antwerp again, then received radio orders to proceed to Rotterdam. On May 2 we picked up the Maas River pilot and anchored to await favorable tide. Our draft was only thirty feet, six inches and more appropriate for the Maas. We finished discharging coal and taking ballast and sailed on the fourteenth for home. Not surprisingly, the insurance company objected to our having put seawater in the hold for ballast the previous trip. We used sand this time.

The strong winds made it difficult to stay on course. Captain Blackwell slowed the ship to prevent the engines from racing, but with too little headway, we couldn't steer, so he stopped the engines altogether. Soon she was in the trough and took a vicious roll to starboard, shifting the ballast. The lumber stowed on the after house went overboard, carrying the side railing with it. Eventually, with improving weather, we were able to resume full speed.

*Blackwell seems to have been less competent than others, though as a loyal mate, Dad would never have put it that way.*

We docked in Brooklyn May 29 and discharged ballast. I received much mail. Dorothy and I were getting closer of a mind in our letters, and I was, almost in spite of myself, starting to "rush" her.

On June 2, with a new crew signed on, we sailed for Norfolk. The ship had a new charter to take coal to Switzerland via Genoa. June 6 I showed

Father around the ship, and when free I went to Ocean View. The whole family was now together again. I loaned Grace $800 at 5 percent to build a cottage.

Next day we finished loading and sailed once more. On June 28 we reached Genoa. We moored just inside the breakwater with our bow held by both anchors and our stern tied to the quay wall. Many other vessels were moored in the same manner parallel to us so that barges could tie up on either side of the ship. Due to a shortage of barges, we could discharge only 665 tons a day.

One night I went ashore with three of our engineering officers. They tried to set me up with a pretty dame who joined us at the dinner table. She couldn't speak a word of English, nor I more than a few of Italian. In spite of this her message was perfectly clear. At one point she took my hand and somehow it touched her bare thigh. As it was my conviction to save myself for marriage, I returned aboard at nine.

We sailed for the States on July 28, and on August 17 we arrived in New York, stopped at quarantine, anchored, and fumigated the whole ship with cyanide gas for a period of three hours while we all had to stay on deck. After ventilating the ship, we tied up at Morse's Shipyard in Brooklyn. I found out that the ship would be in port for a few days, so I applied at the customs house for examination for a raise in grade on my license. All went well, and on August 24 I received my license as "master unlimited."

Since the charterers had made money on the last trip, I was presented with a check for $150, a gratuity for services rendered. I had received $611 in pay for the voyage, and a better than 20 percent bonus was mighty welcome.

On the twenty-seventh I received a call from Captain Bennett. He explained, "We had hopes of giving you the command of a ship, but we are getting back so few ships from the government that we can't take care of the masters we now have. Would you be willing to go as chief mate of the passenger ship *De Kalb* that we are acquiring?" I accepted. I made one more trip to Italy on the *Alaskan*, then reported to the American-Hawaiian offices. I was told to take a week's vacation and report back on October 8. (In those days, normally only captains and chief engineers got vacations.)

I took the midnight train for Boston. Monday, October 1, I met Dorothy at her office. We went to lunch on the top floor of Filene's department store. In Lincoln the next day, Bert Farrar and I packed Mother's belongings and sent them to her in Virginia. Now that Mother was once more with Father, I no longer had to support her and the twins, so I could get serious about a girl. I took Dorothy's suggestion to rush her. I met her after work. We went to Shepard's Restaurant for dinner and to the Wilbur Theater, where we saw *As You Were*. I went home with her to Swampscott and stayed overnight at the Allans' house on Outlook Road. Dorothy and I had lunch at Thompson's Spa. Next day I met her at her office again. We went to

Swampscott to the local football game. Sunday I went to church with Dorothy and Jean, Dorothy's sister, after which we had dinner at the Allans'. Jean then drove us to Lincoln, where Dorothy and I visited my relatives and friends.

I took the midnight train back to New York. It had been a very special week's vacation. Dorothy had accepted my proposal of marriage, and I was in seventh heaven.

## Notes on Chapter 5

1. Coke: hot-burning coal used as industrial fuel.
2. Counter: the after part of a vessel's hull where the lines converge towards the stern; the underside of the overhang.
3. ETA: estimated time of arrival.
4. Governor: device to limit maximum speed.

The S.S. *Mount Clay*

## CHAPTER 6

# A GIRL AND A SHIP

### The S.S. *Mount Clay*

Every ship has its own character and personality. The *De Kalb*, soon to be renamed the *Mount Clay*, had plenty of both. Built in Germany in 1904, she was originally the *Crown Prince Eitel Friederick*. Although out of date as a coal burner, she had twin reciprocating steam engines of eight thousand horsepower each and could maintain sixteen knots. During the war, the Germans had used her as a commerce destroyer operating with the German Naval fleet along the coast of South America until the United States seized her. With her name changed to *De Kalb*, the U.S. used her for transporting troops to Europe. After the war, she was laid up in the Hudson River, where she caught fire. In 1920, United American Lines, a branch of American-Hawaiian, bought her from the government to use as a cabin ship for runs between New York and Germany. Captain Malman became her master and I her chief officer. She was undergoing a $3,500,000 reconditioning.

On November 8, 1920, I boarded and relieved the previous mate. There was no heat or light on board, so I engaged a room in a private home near the shipyard. I cashed my bonus check and ordered the uniforms I would need for my duties as chief mate of a passenger ship.

I had to learn about the ship from bottom to top. When I joined her, there wasn't a single plan or statistic on board to study. Any that existed were in the hands of the architect. I was on board this cold ship from daylight to dark, learning all I could. She was to be fitted out to carry 1,600 passengers and thirty-eight lifeboats. She would carry an American chief steward, but the second

113

steward and all his assistants were to be Germans from the old German passenger ship fleets. Many of these men were available, since all the German ships had been destroyed or taken away during the war.

The postwar boom affected the quality of help available, and the shipyard staff consisted of less than the best craftsmen. Steel angle irons that had been twisted in the fire were being removed. The inexperienced workmen slid them to the dock through the brass-rimmed portholes. In the process they left deep grooves in the brass, causing leaks even when brand new gaskets were fitted. The ship was scheduled to load passengers a month after I boarded. Due to poor planning and organization, the work dragged on with one delay after another.

I bought two books on the German language and practiced in my spare time. Deeply in love, my head was frequently in the clouds, but I had a lot to do. I worked in my room on requisitions for stores and equipment. Dorothy and I wrote to each other daily, and I could hardly wait for her next letter. I traveled to Swampscott to see her as often as I could, and once she came to New York to visit me.

On November 16 I went to Tiffany's and ordered Dorothy's engagement ring. On the twenty-fourth I took the midnight train to Boston and on to Swampscott. I presented the ring to Dorothy. We were engaged to be married.

The *Mount Clay* underwent stability tests. Departure was now nearly three weeks late, and the passengers had to be continually consoled. With company officials on board, we sailed on a trial trip to Fire Island. We found the steering difficult and we adjusted the compasses. Next day we started loading cargo and passengers and signed on the rest of the crew.

On December 23 I took the train to Boston and met Dorothy for an evening together. It was hard to break the spell when I had to catch the midnight train to New York. I was in love with a girl and with a ship.

On the twenty-fourth I was busy getting the new crew signed on and uniformed. We took on stores, and I mustered the crew at emergency stations. The engineers could not get water on the fire line. This was terrible. It meant that we could not test for leaks.

While loading mail on Christmas Day, One-Eyed Charlie, who was in charge of the shore gang stowing the mail, found salt water leaking through holes in the bulkhead from the adjoining compartment. This compartment's scuppers[1] should have led to the bilges, but some of them must have been routed otherwise. All of the 'tween decks had been loaded with barrels of salt pork, and I had had the spare steerage class bunks stowed in the corners. The second officer and I climbed over the tops of the pork barrels and in and around the metal bunks to find and close valves. This was a slow, hard job. My arms were badly scratched from reaching through the stowed beds, and I developed blood poisoning in my left arm.

On the twenty-sixth we sailed. Next day the portholes in the passengers' quarters on the lower deck were leaking badly. Our two carpenters worked continuously, caulking up the leaks. The eight side coaling ports began to leak also. I sent the crew down in the coal shafts to caulk these doors from the inside, which was not the best method but the only practical one at sea. There were other leaks, the sources of which we were unable to determine for quite some time. The bilges were filling faster than the pumps could handle. The crew were working day and night trying to cope.

In number one shelter deck we had barrels of lard stowed. Water had flooded that compartment. Then the water ran down into barley stowed in burlap sacks in the deck below. This water in turn then ran to the number one bilge. Seawater was also coming into the chain locker. We found that a hole about an inch in diameter had been drilled in the hull. This must have been an intentional act of sabotage by the Germans just before the ship was interned.

On Tuesday, December 28, we were having trouble keeping the vessel afloat. She was listing badly. The water was so high it put out some of the fires in the boiler room. We made for Halifax in distress. By radio we ordered five new pumps sent to Halifax from New York and Boston via express delivery. Five days after sailing from New York, we were anchored in Halifax Harbor waiting for the new pumps, hoping they would arrive in time.

I had been up day and night without rest, and the blood poisoning in my arm was worse. The ship's doctor was determined to leave me in Halifax, but I insisted on staying with the ship.

New Year's Day, 1921, found us engaged in urgent searches for the sources of leaks. We had a gang of longshoremen on board, shifting cargo in number one hatch. The weather, typical for January in Nova Scotia, produced rain and snow alternately. We exercised the crew at fire and boat stations, lowering number one and number three boats to the water, and had the crews row them around the vessel. This provided a measure of entertainment for some of the passengers, most of whom had wet cabins.

After shifting cargo in number one hold, at last we found a major source of leakage. A saltwater toilet supply pipe had broken. By then several hundred bags of mail were soaking wet.

On the fourth day at anchor, we repaired a cracked plate through which water was getting into the chain locker, and then made another discovery. Hidden behind metal sheathing was a second hole, drilled in the hull near the water line. It had been filled with cement and painted over, another act of sabotage.

On January 6 repairs were completed and the water pumped out. We took on the local pilot but had to delay sailing until a heavy snow storm abated and visibility was restored. At 9:30 in the morning we raised the anchor and put to sea.

An hour later we left the pilot and almost immediately struck heavy snow, a fresh gale, and very poor visibility. In the afternoon, seeing better, we were able to increase speed somewhat in a very rough sea. Next day at 8:00 A.M. we were six hundred miles from New York, the position we had been in when we had first turned back for a harbor of refuge. We had lost nine days and fifteen hours and had used 204 tons of coal and 380 tons of fresh water without getting very far towards our destination. A claim would be made in due time to the insurance company.

South of Newfoundland we put extra lookouts on duty to look for icebergs. My arm was still being dressed twice a day but was improving wonderfully. We encountered gales of wind and high, rough seas with alternating heavy rain and hail squalls. By the eleventh it was a whole gale from the northwest with mountainous seas, many of which we shipped. Some of them did considerable damage. From then on things got better. Most of our trials were over.

On January 15 we entered the English Channel. The next day we sailed up the Elbe River, reaching Hamburg on the eighteenth. We discharged passengers and cargo and made repairs. We took on board a spare tail shaft that had been there since before the war.

On January 28, 1921, the *Mount Clay* departed for New York with one thousand passengers. Squally and hazy weather was the rule for the Atlantic in winter. As we were laboring along south of the Grand Banks on February 9, we received a radio SOS. The Belgian steamer *Bombardier* was in a sinking condition, her load of grain having shifted to one side. She was on her beam ends,[2] ready to capsize with each roll, and in danger of losing all hands. We headed toward her at maximum speed, but a few hours later we heard by radio that another steamer nearer to the endangered vessel had taken over the rescue. We resumed our course, but somehow we had not received the true position of the *Bombardier*, for in a few more hours, to our surprise, she loomed dead ahead of us. We proceeded with plans to rescue her crew.

Captain Mathews of the *Bombardier*, many years a master, with strong motivation to save his command at all costs, found new hope on seeing us and decided that, just maybe, his ship could be towed to port before it sank. He asked for a towline. Captain Malman could see that the *Bombardier* was indeed in imminent danger of sinking. He replied, "No tow. Dispatch your personnel promptly or I will leave you." That left Captain Mathews no option. He and his men quickly lowered their boats and boarded the *Mount Clay* by Jacob's ladders. They acted with considerable enthusiasm.

Safely on board the *Mount Clay*, the rescued crew were cared for and berthed in the best available places. I shared my room with Captain Mathews. In New York he handed me his telescope, his only rescued possession, as a token of appreciation for courtesies extended to him.

We had carried many immigrants among the passengers, and since the monthly quotas were exceeded at the Port of New York, we were diverted on February 11 to Boston. I telephoned my sweetheart at her place of work, and she met me at the pier at two.

We discharged the passengers, baggage, and mail. I had a wonderful visit in Boston with Dorothy. During the day she entertained herself in town, and then I joined her for dinner at Shepard's Restaurant, escorted her home to Swampscott, and returned to the ship by midnight.

February 13, we sailed for New York, where we landed the remaining passengers, baggage and mail. The crew was paid off. I received pay at $233.38 per month.

We took on fuel in preparation for the next trip. It was the custom in New York to put a foreman and one hundred laborers on board early on sailing day to clean the ship. There was a far better system in Hamburg, where the dirty bunkering of coal was stopped several days before sailing. There, I was given one head foreman and ten gangs of about ten men each. Each gang was specialized and experienced in a particular line of cleaning. There were men for the hull work, men for the stack work, and others assigned to decks or to houses. There was a group of locksmiths, a group of carpenters, etc. They worked slowly but well. By contrast, the gangs in New York seemed to go off in all directions at once and much work was poorly done or missed entirely.

On my second trip to Hamburg, we sailed with 706 passengers. It was an uneventful voyage, although we had typical winter weather. February 24 was a nice sunny day, and I urged all passengers to come on deck to get an airing. (I received 10 percent of the fee for renting steamer chairs to passengers.) While they were out, we held fire and boat drill. On March 4, we arrived at the mouth of the Elbe where we landed passengers, and the ship proceeded to Hamburg. On the tenth we sailed for New York with 1,075 passengers. On March 15 an elderly passenger died. At ten that evening, the master held a funeral, and the body was buried at sea. On March 22, we were once again diverted to Boston where we discharged 668 passengers and thousands of bags of mail. Dorothy met me that evening, and I took her to the Colonial for dinner and then to her home in Swampscott. Two days later Dorothy came to the ship from her office and joined me for lunch on board. I took her back to her office, and at 4:00 P.M. the *Mount Clay* sailed for New York with the remaining passengers.

From New York I took the midnight train to Boston, arriving in time to catch the first morning train to Swampscott. While there, I secured our marriage license and made plans with Dorothy for our May wedding, engaging the church and the organist. I took the midnight train back to New York. Once there I went uptown to price dress suits at Rogers Peet, and I bought our wedding rings. We finished loading cargo and mail and took on 670 passengers and sailed for Germany once more.

When we were nearly clear of the harbor, a passenger jumped overboard. We stopped the ship and lowered a lifeboat to search for the man, but there was a strong flood tide. The men in the boat searched until well after dark but were unable to find the body.

The master notified the company agents by radio and we prepared to resume our voyage, but, in raising the anchor, the chain came up anchorless. There had been no great strain on the anchor and we were puzzled until, on examining the end of the chain, we found that a saw cut had been made in the shackle connecting the anchor to the chain. Here we had clear evidence of another attempt at sabotage by the Germans. The saw cut had been filled with lead. The wonder is that the shackle had not parted before, during the war, when the ship had been in continuous service as a troop transport. Short one anchor, we proceeded to Hamburg and returned to New York on May 3, docking at Pier 86, North River. We discharged American citizens but kept all others on board because Ellis Island was overcrowded. The foreign passengers were told to stay aboard until there was room for them.

At five in the afternoon, as the passengers were sitting down to supper, the entire stewards' department walked out on strike. The company hired shore labor to clean the ship on the inside and to wait on the passengers and the rest of the crew. The 850 passengers remained on board until May 6, when they were landed between 7:00 and 9:00 A.M. Then the engineers also walked off on strike. This was the union's key act, which they thought was final.

All American ships in the harbor went on strike, with no engineers except the chief remaining on the job. The younger engineers insisted that the union call off the chiefs, too, and the union did just that.

A ship makes no money while laid up, so we made every effort to get moving. There was a very able chief engineer on a nearby freight ship who wanted to work in spite of the union order. He made arrangements with the United American Lines and signed a ten-year contract to sail as chief engineer on the *Mount Clay*. We also signed on a whole new crew. The owners had seven freight ships standing by, planning to have them and the *Mount Clay* all sail at the same time. Both the owners and the union had their delegates signed on in the same crews. One group's mission was to see that the ship sailed, and the other group's was to prevent it from sailing. Emotions on both sides ran strong.

On the designated sailing day, at ten in the morning, the union reported to the collector of customs for the Port of New York that the *Mount Clay* had a crew on board who would not be able to act in an emergency because they could not understand orders given in English. The customs service then examined the crew and found that this was a false allegation.

Finally the unions publicly acknowledged that if the *Mount Clay* were to sail, the strike would be broken. Preventing such an event became their last-ditch effort.

Just before the last passengers boarded the *Mount Clay*, the union plant-ed one of their militant members on board as a fireman in our engine room. This man tried to get the firemen on duty to strike, but they were in no mood to do so and rushed the union man up to the deck. The crew mauled him and were trying to throw him off the ship. Trying to go ashore and escape their wrath, he managed to get close to the gangway but was recog-nized by crew members on deck. I tried to stop them at first, thinking that they were attacking a passenger, since he was dressed as one, black derby hat and all. By now the man had a bloody nose. He got a full bum's rush with a cry, "He's a union delegate—off with him!"

We failed to make our sailing target hour of twelve noon, but at 2:00 we steamed out of the harbor with the other ships.

Outside the channel, the chief engineer prevailed on the captain to stop the ship in order to check all systems before proceeding. This prudent activ-ity was carried out successfully, but when the ship stopped, the passengers feared that the crew had rebelled. They offered to man the ship themselves. Once their fears were put to rest, and the ship finally sailed, she made an excellent voyage. She averaged close to sixteen knots, whereas before the strike, the best she had done was thirteen knots. The union-busting crew simply worked harder, especially at the miserable job of coal passing and fire tending.

Once the ship was ready to get underway, my duties for this voyage were complete. I got off on a launch that took me to shore. Relieved of terrible tension, I took the train to Boston to prepare for my wedding. I had my $91 dress suit from Rogers Peet with me. In Waltham and Concord I withdrew the little savings I had in banks there and bought a steamer trunk for our honeymoon trip.

Our wedding took place on May 18, 1921. On that day I made myself scarce, since the bridesmaids and others were to use my room in the Allans' house on Outlook Road for dressing. The Church of the Holy Name was beautifully decorated with apple blossoms. At eight in the evening, the big event of my life took place. Dorothy Anderson Allan and I were married by the Reverend Cornelius Tillotson. We had a reception in the parish hall, after which we returned to Outlook Road, where close friends joined us.

We planned to make our escape out the back door and meet a car on the street. I went to my room to change and, in pulling my suitcase from under the bed, I found it full of women's underthings. For a moment I had forgot-ten that the girls had used this room to dress in, and I was embarrassed and frustrated. I was sure a trick had been played on me. I cursed silently but then discovered that it was not my suitcase at all. Mine I found by search-ing further under the bed. What a relief!

I got dressed and went downstairs to meet the well-wishers. Dorothy had planned to stand on the back stairs and throw her bouquet to her brides-maids. Then we were to escape out the back door. We had not rehearsed this

part, and we were obsessed with leaving. We ran out the back door, thinking only of getting to the sedan waiting for us on the street. Hand in hand
in the darkness, we stumbled through several backyards, gardens, chicken
wire fences, and down a steep embankment to where the car was waiting.
We got in the back seat and were off before any could follow.

Once settled in the car by ourselves, Dorothy expressed her first of many
disappointments with me: "You failed to kiss me at the altar!" In my defense
I must say that much of what took place had not been rehearsed, and I had
only witnessed one wedding before, and that was when I was a small boy.
Then she looked down and found that she was still clutching her bouquet.
For this she blamed me also. Then, as though the whole day had been a disaster, her corsage was missing. Things eased a bit when we got to the station
in Boston and found the corsage on the running board, undamaged.

I had engaged a room on the train by phone and was told that the only
rooms available were in a "section." I didn't know what a section was, but I
engaged a room anyway. We went into the station, picked up our tickets,
saw our baggage taken care of, and went to the train to find our room. We
found ourselves in a strange car with no end staterooms, just a long alley on
one side of the car with many compartments. We got to the door with our
assigned room number, opened the door and were disappointed to find no
adjoining dressing room. It was embarrassing for both of us. There was no
toilet either. Dorothy said that she did not want to travel under such conditions. I went to find the porter and, when I told him of our predicament, he
was reassuring and hastened to explain. He accompanied me to the room
and, asking Dorothy to rise from where she was sitting, raised the corner of
the cushion. There was the toilet. I was relieved. There may have been
dressing rooms at either end of the car, but I simply stayed in the aisle until
Dorothy prepared for bed.

Our honeymoon trip took us through New York City, where we seemed
somehow alone, lost, and then to Virginia to visit my family. My wife saw
how my father had brought up his children. In the warm summer climate at
Ocean View, the dining table was on the screened porch. We were required
to speak only when spoken to and to tend to business with no turning
around to see passersby. My new wife watched to see if my father set the
example or not. At one point in the meal, my father turned to see the sights
as two young lady bathers strolled by the house. Not bound by his strict
rules, Dorothy pounced on my father, to the great pleasure of the whole
family.

From Ocean View we traveled to Washington, spending four days with
my Aunt Grace and Uncle John Danner and their daughter Anna. Our
money and time were running out, so instead of making our intended trip
to Niagara Falls, we bought train tickets to New York. There were no compartments or sections available, so I asked for an upper and lower berth,
which was the only other sleeping arrangements available that I knew of on

trains. The ticket agent, seeing my companion dressed in her pretty, broad-brimmed hat covered with flowers, and noting my obvious innocence, which assured him that we were newlyweds, said to me, "Why not get just one lower?"

I asked naively, "Can I do that?" Dorothy was so embarrassed that she tried to escape, and in so doing she brushed against the chalkboard listing arrivals and departures. Her blue taffeta dress was covered with several colors of chalk.

On June 8, we took the train to Northfield to visit my Aunt Lizzie. Miriam was not at home. On the eleventh we took the noon train to Swampscott via Boston. We had been gone twenty-five days. At Swampscott we had our pictures taken in our wedding clothes and took the midnight train again to New York. When we arrived there, I called the operating manager at American-Hawaiian, who was quite put out with me for not having left him a forwarding address. He had tried to contact me to give me a job as master, but since he couldn't find me, he had given the position to someone else.

The *Mount Clay* was arriving from Hamburg. We met the ship, then checked into the Judson Hotel in Washington Square, not the best hotel, but the best we could afford. It was dreadfully hot in the city, so in the evening we took a bus trip out to Coney Island just to cool off and returned without stopping. The next day I took out more life insurance, and after lunch we went to the baseball game between Chicago and New York. Babe Ruth got his usual home run.

June 16 we spent aboard the ship. The following day I resumed my duties as chief mate of the *Mount Clay*. Dorothy and I spent nights at the Judson until, on the twenty-second, I put Dorothy on the train for home. Saying goodbye was a day's work in itself.

Between June 23, 1921, and January 9, 1922, I made six more round trips, New York to Hamburg, as chief mate of the *Mount Clay*. Most evenings in Hamburg I read myself to sleep at night. Dorothy was still working and living with her mother in Swampscott. Each time I arrived in New York, she took the train from Boston to meet me. We spent as much time together as I could spare from the ship. We stayed in town and took in the theaters, opera, and beaches. We couldn't afford the better hotels, but we had a good time until I had to put her on the train for home on the night before sailing.

When we docked in New York, all the passengers would crowd to the rail, looking for their friends on the dock. The passengers were in such a state of emotion that they could not or would not hear the order to stand back from the rail. With all passengers on one side, if the ship listed dangerously, we had dock hands near the low rail turn on the fire hoses, directing the stream not at the passengers but parallel to the rail. Innocently and automatically, the passengers would step back rather than risk getting wet.

In July we had orders not to take Polish passengers for the U.S., since their immigration quota had already been filled for that month.

*The Johnson Act of 1921 had slowed the flow of immigrants from postwar Europe through a quota system based on national origins. Great Britain, Ireland, and Germany received the majority of allotted quotas, while immigration from southern and eastern Europe was severely restricted.*

By the end of 1921, the German mark had dropped in value to nearly nothing. Desperate men stole cargo, mostly lard and salt pork, to feed their families. The German authorities tried to stop the stealing by putting a soldier near the gangway, but then the men would not work at all. Our ship, however, was running well. Our organization of labor was efficient, and everyone appreciated the chance to have work and good food on an American ship.

On December 18, 1921, I was given my first brief assignment as master, sailing the United American Line's ship *Kermore* from Hamburg to Kiel. She had just been sold to an Austrian firm and had an all-German crew. I was the only American on board. In spite of language problems, engine troubles, gales, and a hard-to-control empty ship, we arrived safely at Kiel the day before Christmas. I turned the vessel over to the new owners and, after a walk around the small town, I took the train to Hamburg and rejoined the *Mount Clay*.

On route to New York in early January 1922, I led the usual search for contraband and liquor and this time found plenty. I was going through the coal bunkers with a metal hook and came upon two burlap bags containing a total of 131 quarts of liquor. Sixty-six of these Captain Malman had me turn over to the purser for sale at the ship's bars. The remaining sixty-five quarts we would hand over to customs on arrival.

On January 9 we reached New York and Dorothy boarded the night train from Boston in order to meet me. While I was eating supper with the other officers, the master-at-arms came rushing in from his gangway station to notify me that four suspicious men had come aboard, insisting that they were part of the engineering crew. The master-at-arms had checked with the first assistant engineer and found that they had lied. Mr. Staley and I went to our rooms for firearms and started rounding up the trespassers. I cornered one in the firemen's forecastle and sent him toward the gangway with a warning and a slap across the back of the ear. Positioned halfway between me and the gangway, Mr. Staley did the same. At the top of the gangway, the master-at-arms sent him on his way. We rounded up two more of the trespassers and got rid of them with a similar send-off.

I stood facing the gangway but farther back from it than the other two officers. A fourth man came from a passageway behind me, and as he passed swung at the back of my head with a solid iron bar. I was knocked out cold and fell to the deck. I hadn't seen him coming and didn't know what had happened to me for days afterwards.

As my assailant ran towards the head of the gangway, my colleagues tried to intercept him. The master-at-arms kicked him and he fell, but he rolled off the gangway and managed to escape, running to the sea end of the pier. These men had a boat there, into which they had hoped to stash the smuggled liquor.

Mr. Staley came to my aid where I lay unconscious on the deck. The ship's doctor summoned an ambulance and I was taken to the emergency room at City Hospital. My skull was fractured.

Even though the trespassers had left the ship, Mr. Staley and the master-at-arms were able to round up two of the first three, whom they held at gunpoint while city detectives were called. Though I had not seen my assailant, city law enforcement held the men locked up for two weeks waiting for me to attend a lineup of suspects. Mr. Staley and the master-at-arms were not able to make an identification.

I was transferred from City Hospital to Bellevue Hospital. Even though my condition was critical, I was placed in a ward since there were no private rooms available. I had round-the-clock nursing care, and as soon as it was free, I was put in a large soundproof room. This room was where they normally put screaming mental patients, of which there were many at Bellevue.

Dorothy visited me every day, with or without permission. She came in through the emergency entrance, and though challenged several times, she kept right on walking as though she were someone important. She was never stopped. Dorothy's sister Margaret, a registered nurse, came to New York and saw to it that I was properly cared for. Lucky as I was not to have been killed, there was still great concern about the longterm effects of my injury.

American-Hawaiian paid all my expenses and those of my family, including Margaret's. They also kept me on the payroll. Mary Ackimore, a New York friend of the Allans, took care of Dorothy at night. The company advanced money to her as she required it. I continued to have special nurses around the clock, and Dorothy gave me loving attention.

Many of the company officials visited me during the first several days of my confinement, but I was only conscious a few minutes at a time. As Dorothy told me later, I was terribly distressed during my conscious moments because, dressed in a hospital gown, I had no "bottoms to my pajamas" and kept calling for them each time I woke up.

On January 13, four days after I was assaulted, I felt a trifle better, and the next day the police called on me. By the seventeenth I was feeling better, but I tired easily and the following day became very depressed because I had been relieved as the *Mount Clay*'s chief officer.

I was discharged on January 24. Dorothy and I left the hospital in a taxi for the St. James Hotel, where we had dinner and spent the night. Next morning, as we were about to leave for the train, city detectives arrived and wanted to take me to the station to identify the suspects. Since I had never seen the man who hit me, I couldn't help them.

At the house on Outlook Road, I slowly recovered. By the twenty-ninth I was able to take short walks and rides. On my twenty-seventh birthday, February 3, I received lots of good wishes, presents, and a cake. By then I was recovering well and beginning to enjoy myself. On entering the doctor's office for a checkup, I said, "I'm having the time of my life." I was lucky to have only a minor disability as a result of my injury: I was without any sense of smell for the rest of my life. For years I would say to Dorothy, "I don't smell," and she would reply in jest, "How do you know you don't?"

Although I had been a regular churchgoer when I lived at home in Lincoln, I had never been confirmed in the Episcopal Church. On April 4, 1922, I was confirmed by Bishop William Lawrence at the Church of the Holy Name in Swampscott. On the following Sunday, at church with Dorothy and Margaret, I received communion and tasted wine for the first time in my life.

At last I was well enough to work, and I returned to New York on April 12, reassigned to my old station on the *Mount Clay*. Captain Malman had been assigned to the S.S. *Resolute*, and Captain Brown was the new master of the *Mount Clay*. On Tuesday, April 18, I sailed once more for Hamburg. I got terribly tired about noon each day, mainly in my legs, but I managed to carry on. As before, I usually read in the evenings, but at least a few times I got out and saw the sights in Germany. One evening I went ashore with Mr. Mabardi. We called on the Spaldings and took them to the Alster Fairhouse for dinner and then to the Trocodero, where we danced the night away. We kept Mrs. Spalding and her daughters, Peggy, Toltee, and Irma, busy dancing. Mr. Mabardi and I didn't get on board until nearly four in the morning. I was called at six but failed to waken until the steward brought my coffee forty minutes later. In a big rush, I mustered the crew with my shoelaces untied. On sailing day Mrs. Spalding and her three daughters had dinner on board. They gave us all kinds of flowers as they saw us off.

## Notes to Chapter 6

1. Scuppers: drains.
2. Beam ends: a vessel listed so far to one side as to be unable to right herself.

# CHAPTER 7

# MASTER AND FATHER

**The S.S. *Nevadan***

During my first year of marriage I became a Freemason, and in June of 1922 I obtained my second degree in Freemasonry. On June 27 I was made master of the American-Hawaiian Lines vessel S.S. *Nevadan*. Frankly I wasn't too happy leaving my wonderful home on the *Mount Clay*, but I couldn't turn down an advance in my profession.

The *Nevadan* was crewless, a dead ship. I reported to the office with my requisitions for charts and aids to navigation for her scheduled trip to Germany. Coal-burning and relatively small, the *Nevadan* was 395 feet long, 55 feet wide. Her gross tonnage was 5,284 or 3,325 tons net, with deadweight of 8,000 tons. Mr. Strasser arrived to be my chief officer. I went to the Shipping Commission for the articles, to the customs house to clear the ship, got charts and light lists, and then went back to the company offices to draw money. After loading cargo and fuel in Norfolk and Canton, we sailed for Bremerhaven, Germany, in early July.

While on the *Mount Clay*, I had taken advantage of my company discount privileges and booked passage for Dorothy and her mother to tour Europe. I had expected to be with them from time to time on my trips to Hamburg. My new job on the *Nevadan* would interfere with those plans, but I hoped to be able to spend at least a little time with them.

Mr. Strasser and other heads of departments kept the ship secured and running smoothly. July 29 we passed the English Channel and the North Sea, where the fog kept me up all night. At daybreak we were close aboard the Weser Light Vessel and I was on top of the wheelhouse, standing at the standard compass. I wanted to pick up a pilot near the entrance to the river, so I was gazing intently at the compass to note the slightest change in the ship's direction. Using the speaking tube, I ordered the wheelman to port the helm. I received verbal acknowledgment, but there was no movement of the compass. I ordered, "Helm, hard a-port." Still no movement of the compass. Mr. Strasser, bless him, called up to me, "Ship is swinging to port, sir." It was only then that I noticed the compass card was stuck in the bowl. I was distressed to think of what I had done—a new master in a strange port, doing something that could have been disastrous, especially in such fog. It was a good lesson. Thankfully we got the ship on course and made a good departure from the light vessel.

Soon we picked up the Weser River pilot and docked in Bremerhaven. I went to bed and slept for fifteen hours. Next day I entered the ship and drew $250 in equivalent German marks. Inflation was so severe that I had to borrow a telescoping suitcase to carry all the marks.

My wife and her mother were passengers on the S.S. *Resolute*, which was due to land at Cuxhaven August 5. I took the train there and at 5:00 A.M. met the *Resolute* at the pier as she was docking. I couldn't wait for the gangway so I shinnied aboard via the stern mooring lines. I found my family asleep in a first-class cabin. While waiting for them to dress, I paid my respects to Captain Malman.

The *Resolute* sailed at nine for Hamburg, and I had to return to my own ship at Bremerhaven. Once aboard the *Nevadan*, I too sailed for Hamburg, down the Weser and up the Elbe, hoping all the way that I would soon be with my wife. I was on the bridge all night. Docking in Hamburg at 5:00 A.M., I cleaned up and took the first ferry to town. At seven I arrived at the home of Mrs. Ketler, who let rooms to visitors, once more finding my womenfolk asleep and comfortably situated.

We had a late breakfast at Mrs. Ketler's, where butter was served only to those who paid extra. We were the only ones who had butter. Another peculiar thing was the bathtub, which was huge. If we wanted hot water, we paid extra for the gas to heat it. Apparently most of the others bathed in cold water, or perhaps not at all.

I took my family aboard my new command for lunch and a visit. Two days later, having accomplished my ship's business, I took the family to the Continental Hotel for dinner. Communists were holding a parade in the square outside. August 12 was my sailing day. I took Dorothy and Mrs. Allan to dinner and then I said goodbye, leaving them to tour Europe on their own.

Coming down the Elbe in close quarters, I had to be on the bridge with the pilot. The North Sea coast was foggy part of the time. All the way to the East Goodwin Light Vessel, we carefully followed the narrow channel, which had been cleared of mines. By the nineteenth we had passed East

Goodwin Sands, an immense graveyard of ships. Some ancient remains of grounded ships had been there for centuries, finally burying themselves in the sand.

In dense fog I cleared the North Sea and passed Dover at noon. I was tempted to anchor but considered it safer to keep going, depending on the steam whistle to avoid collision. I had visions of another ship cutting us in half if we were dead at anchor. So from my perch atop the wheelhouse, right under the deafening sound of the steam whistle, I piloted the ship down through the Dover Straits. Then in fine weather through the English Channel, I was able to get some sleep. On August 27 we made Boston Light and docked at noon, assisted by a pilot and a tug.

It was odd to be at my home port while my family was in Europe, and I missed them terribly. I had four letters from my wife, who wrote to me describing their stay in Hamburg adding,

> It is now 8:15 and Mother is enlarging a brassiere for me! I can't see that I'm any bigger. The bras must have shrunk.
> Just before breakfast I lost several quarts of bile. I felt better after it and enjoyed my breakfast. Aren't I funny?

Monday, August 28, I reported to the company office, did my ship's business, and advanced the crew money. Tuesday my sister-in-law Margaret visited the ship with me. We had lunch together at Filene's, and then I returned on board and sailed for Baltimore. We had thick fog all night over Nantucket Shoals. There was no radar then, of course, and with numerous fishermen around, we had to pay the closest attention to safety. I kept the whistle going, and we sounded with the lead regularly, comparing the depth and nature of the bottom to help fix our position. On August 31 the weather improved. At midnight we passed Cape Henry. The next day, at Baltimore we were boarded, inspected, and passed quarantine. I had four more letters from my wife.

In Baltimore, we loaded cargo. On September 13 I signed crew members on "for a voyage to the West Coast of the U.S. and return to port on the Atlantic Coast, north of Hatteras, for a time not to exceed three months." This was a disappointment, since I would have no further opportunity to be with my wife in Europe. I found out that my pay as master would be $320 per month, the rate for junior masters.

We had difficulty securing firemen since by 1922 most ships burned oil, a much easier fuel to handle than coal. We finished loading on the seventeenth. I cleared the ship and we sailed for Philadelphia, where we loaded more general cargo. I sent a draft of $300 to my wife in Europe and received a letter from her. She and Mrs. Allan were now in Munich. On the nineteenth I made out the payroll, advanced money to the crew, and bought tobacco for the slop chest.[1] I received a letter of instruction for the voyage from the owners and checked aids to navigation through to San Francisco. I had never been on the West Coast and was looking forward to a new experience.

With all the ship's business attended to, I took the train to Swampscott, where I took my third degree in Masonry at Wayfarers Lodge. Back in Philadelphia on September 22, I signed on new men to fill vacancies, and we sailed for the West Coast. I assigned the radio officer to manage the slop chest and attended several ill persons amongst the crew, besides doing the ship's writing, and for exercise I shoveled about six tons of coal off the deck into coal bunkers.

By the twenty-seventh I had caught up on my sleep. At daybreak I took star sights and worked out a fix, then shoveled about five tons of coal, bathed, ate breakfast, and read. At 8:00 P.M. we passed east of San Salvador, the first New World landfall made by Columbus. We were now in the northeast trade wind belt with the wind astern.

At the Panama Canal I received letters from Dorothy describing their trip to Paris. October 3 we had heavy rain squalls rounding Cape Mala. I put one fireman in irons for refusing duty and assaulting an officer. In a few minutes he agreed to go to work and was released. It was fiercely hot. I had tarpaulins spread over the after booms to make shelter so that the crew could sleep on deck. I washed and painted my quarters.

On the twelfth Cape San Lucas Lighthouse at the lower end of Baja California was abeam, ten miles off. I wired my ETA to the agents. At noon we were 725 miles south of San Pedro. Soon the wind hauled northwest and the air turned cooler.

The *Nevadan* reached Los Angeles mid-October. This gave me a chance to visit my brother Ralph, who now worked in Long Beach. We spent one evening at the Servicemen's Club. There we met Miss Upham, who was much admired by all who knew her. Years before, she had worked at the Sailors' Haven in Charlestown where Dorothy's father had been superintendent.

Sailing north from Los Angeles, we made good speed in smooth water. Visibility was good so I kept close inshore to avoid the heavy head seas. The land sloped abruptly from the mountains to the coast. We could easily see the coast road, farmhouses, villages, and hotels. At San Francisco I had more letters from Dorothy, who was now in Scotland. She wrote, "You will find me a bigger armful when I see you in December. I am missing you something fierce!"

On October 22 I got up at eight and was writing a letter to my wife when Mr. Eddey, the agent, and his staff came aboard. We talked ship's business, and then he advised me to take a trip out to Golden Gate Park. I was not disappointed. There were beautiful woods, shrubs, flowers, lakes, picnic benches, games, and a band playing. It was very refreshing to me. While there I wrote letters.

Monday the twenty-third we started discharging. A work-a-way passenger signed on next day, and one more man signed on in the crew. I discussed new cargo chain lashings for lumber with my mate. Lumber would be our return cargo, and I had never carried it before. After lunch I called on Captain Tucker of the *Panamanian*. He called me the "Boy Skipper."

On the twenty-fifth we sailed for Puget Sound. It was my first time up the rockbound coast. We passed Umatilla Light Vessel, rounded the cape, and entered the Straits of Juan de Fuca. We came upon the *Nebraskan*, with Captain Brown as master. We had been shipmates. He was bound, as were we, to Willapa for lumber.

We arrived in Seattle via Port Angeles on the twenty-ninth in dense fog, and we crept towards the dock, anchoring about one ship's length away. The fog cleared four hours later, and we steamed alongside the dock.

We finished discharging and sailed the twenty-five miles to Tacoma. There we tied up at the Tacoma Smelter Docks and loaded five hundred tons of copper pigs into the bottom of the ship. We then sailed to Baker Dock, three miles closer to the city. On Halloween, we loaded canned milk, canned fruits, tallow, and canned salmon. I thought about my wife and mother-in-law, who were scheduled to sail for home from Europe that very day.

November 1 I drew money to advance to the crew. The dock owner, Mr. Baker, gave me two wild ducks that he had just shot. They had been flying south after fattening up in the Canadian grain fields, and they were mighty good eating.

From Tacoma we sailed first for Seattle and then for Bellingham, where we were delayed by fog. At 9:00 A.M. we went alongside the lumber mill docks. I spent the afternoon going through the lumber mill and box factory, which I found very interesting. I walked around town and chatted with two Indian couples.

Captain Stream was the pilot to Willapa Bay, which we went around twice without seeing on account of fog. There is a dangerous bar to cross on entering Willapa. We put relieving tackles on the steering quadrant and took all precautions. We grounded getting in the channel at one place in low water, then steamed up the river to a mill at Raymond. The river was so narrow at a sharp bend to starboard that we had to put the bow against the bank and then work her stern around with the engine.

We loaded lumber for the next four days. The people in the lumber mill towns were well-heeled. They had the nicest cars and clothing, but no one wore neckties. Even the bank president had his collar open at the neck and a big diamond stickpin in his shirt front. I found everybody very friendly. I was introduced to a politician who gave me a ride to see the sights. We stopped at his office to drain a bottle. Since I was a teetotaler, I refrained, so he took me into another room and said, "Here, look these over." They were pictures of beautiful naked girls. A surprising alternative to liquor, they brought back visions of my loved one three thousand miles away by land, more than twice that by sea.

We sailed for Portland on the eleventh but it was getting dark and therefore unsafe to cross over the bar at Willapa. We anchored inside for the night and the next day made the crossing. Off the Columbia River Bar we changed pilots and soon docked at Portland.

I shifted the ship downriver on the fourteenth to a lumber mill at St. Johns. At noon Lloyds representatives made a survey regarding the grounding in the Willapa River. There was no significant damage evident, and they issued a seaworthy certificate.

At St. Johns we completed loading lumber at five and sailed for Astoria with fog threatening to close in entirely several times. Finally we were forced to anchor just twenty miles above Astoria at midnight.

While loading more lumber at Astoria, I signed on two crew members who had joined the ship in Portland, and I cleared the ship for New York. We completed our load with twelve-foot-high lumber stacks on deck, secured with chain lashings and turnbuckles. In the afternoon we took on the bar pilot and sailed for New York. It was terribly rough going over the bar. In the deep swells, as the bow or stern dipped, we were in danger of striking the bottom. Rough seas and overcast skies meant no sightings of heavenly bodies for a fix, but I did get several lines of position by radio direction finder.

Sunday, November 26, we had to stop the main engine for repairs due to a broken piston ring in the high pressure cylinder. On the twenty-ninth the cove boiler cut out. Next day it was repaired successfully.

On Thanksgiving Day the stewards and cooks served roast turkey with all the fixings. I passed around a box of cigars. On Friday I was up early as usual to get star sights and work out a position to compare with what the officer on watch got. I worked on abstracts, wrote letters, looked for land, and saw many turtles.

On Saturday I held safety drills. At 11:00 A.M. we entered the Panama Canal, where I received letters from my wife from Europe. Two of them were written during her passage home on the S.S. *Resolute.* I read them eagerly while passing through Gatun Locks.[2] Dorothy was grateful for the extra money I had sent her. She was also pleased to be expanding in her bustline.

We put to sea in the Caribbean and immediately hit heavy headwinds. I finished reading *The Everyday Life of Abraham Lincoln* by Francis Fisher Browne. I was greatly impressed by this super man. He was a wonderful character to the end.

December 9 we passed Cape Maisi at the eastern end of Cuba and could see the wrecks of two vessels on the beach. The wind and sea moderated, and we were able to increase our speed. The routines continued: safety drills and fumigating. Next day we stopped for two and a half hours while renewing the broken piston ring in the high pressure cylinder. We then passed Watlings Island (also known as San Salvador), the last of the West Indies.

The eleventh saw fine weather but heavy northerly swells that made the ship pitch, retarding our headway considerably. I pressed clothes and did paperwork, including payroll and discharges for all the crew, as it was customary to pay them off on arrival at the end of the voyage.

The weather grew cooler, the wind hauled northerly, and by the thirteenth we encountered overcast skies and drizzle. I put on heavy underwear. We got radio bearings and sounded regularly.

On the fifteenth we arrived at Ambrose Light Vessel, took the New York Sandy Hook pilot aboard, and passed quarantine. At nine we arrived at Brooklyn. By eleven I was at the company offices, did my ship's business, and met my beloved again, at last. She was, indeed, a lovely armful. I went back aboard to advance the crew money and met Dorothy again at six for dinner. I had to be on board for annual inspections on the eighteenth and otherwise did my business as master, but I spent as much time with my wife as possible.

On the day before Christmas I was with Dorothy at our friend Captain Drill's house. I telephoned, and finding that my ship would be ready to sail at three, I said goodbye to my loved one once more.

We had dense fog on Christmas Day. Visibility and weather remained poor, and we would move a few miles, then anchor. We managed to get within twenty-five miles of Philadelphia on the twenty-seventh. I had a lookout up in the crosstrees. At last we reached port.

On Friday the twenth-ninth Dorothy got me on the phone. She had been worried about me as she had not heard from me for several days. I tried to explain that I was stuck in fog. We arranged to meet again in Baltimore. My wages for the year were $2,671.

*These earnings, to which must be added his free room and board aboard ship, were above the average for 1922, when the average factory worker earned about $1,400 a year. In 1997 dollars, his salary would have been worth about $90,000.*

New Year's Day, 1923, with the cargo all out, we sailed for Baltimore to reload for the West Coast. I telegraphed Dorothy and looked forward anxiously to our meeting again.

We had a week together in Baltimore, and though I was often busy with ship's business, we visited friends, did errands together, and had lunch in a restaurant each day. I sailed for Los Angeles in the evening of the ninth. On this trip I built a settee in my office after surveying the lumber available on board. It was a satisfying use of my spare time. When the project was complete, and I had time to think, I was very homesick. More and more I missed my best girl.

We berthed at Los Angeles February 2. I received numerous letters and packages for my birthday, my twenty-eighth. I kept busy answering business letters, doing my own typing, the two-finger method. On the fourth I was up early reading my mail when Ralph popped in, all dolled up. We chewed the fat, had dinner, then drove to Pasadena. His car broke down, and we left it in a garage for repairs. Harry Snelling picked us up, and we went to supper with him and his wife, Enid. Then Harry drove us to Venice. On the way Enid said she was cold since she had no panties on. Ladylike she was not.

Venice, a sort of amusement park, had an attraction called the House of Many Angles. Ralph and I urged Harry and Enid to go first, but they insisted we men go first. So Ralph and I stepped inside of a sort of closet with a bench-like seat. We sat down, waiting for the surprise. All at once the seat rolled out flat, and still seated we rolled onto an endless belt, which sloped downward. At last the belt stopped. Ralph and I got off and waited for our companions. We looked up and saw Harry and Enid, seated, coming toward us feet first. When they got close to us the belt suddenly stopped, then started again with a jerk. Both Harry and Enid were knocked backwards, feet in the air. It was then clear that Enid, in fact, lacked her panties. Enid was angry that we had gone first and claimed it was a put-up job!

From Los Angeles we sailed for San Francisco, where, along with my usual ship's business, I bought supplies for the slop chest. Whereas most captains had agents stock theirs, I bought stores wholesale for my slop chest and made more money for my extra effort. I could sell cheaper by doing my own buying and my sales to crews were better since I made a special effort to stock what they wanted. From San Francisco we sailed to Seattle, and then returned down the coast again. The weather varied from moderate gale to calm and overcast. I hoped everything was all right at home as I worked hard on a dresser for our baby, due to be born soon.

On March 28 we passed our company ship S.S. *Ipswich.* While exchanging messages, Captain O'Brien said he had heard that my vessel might go in the Gulf Coast run. This was not encouraging to me. In fact, I wrote in my diary that I'd as soon go to jail.

We reached New York on April 7. I telephoned Captain Bennett and then called home. Dorothy was in the Lynn Hospital with a baby boy born March 27. I took the midnight train for Boston. Jean and her friend Alice Shaw met me and drove me to the hospital, where I found my family increased by one scabby-looking little fellow.

Later Jean and Alice drove me to see the new house Dorothy had bought for us. The mortgage had put me in debt. For the first time in my life I owed money, and lots of it. Then I returned to the hospital and was glad to find both my wife and the boy improving. I caught the midnight train back to New York and my job, happy and relieved of worry. Usually I am a light sleeper, but this time I slept like a log. I never knew when the train started or stopped, and I had to be wakened by the porter.

On April 11, I crated the baby cabinet and sent it home by Railway Express. I cleared the ship for Philadelphia, settled my accounts, and sent $800 home. We were delayed sailing due to a shortage of manpower. By the thirteenth I had secured most of the required crew and engaged a shore gang of eight men to work the ship to the next port. On April 14 we entered the Delaware and docked in Philadelphia. A week later I took the noon train, arriving in my new house at ten. I found Dorothy, Mother Allan, and Margaret still up but exhausted from the business of moving and the baby crying. We all went to bed, but little Allan woke us up at three. I slept very little all night with so much to think about.

I worked about the house, making the new place livable. There were electric extensions to arrange, plugs, curtain rods, and clotheslines to put up. I worked until nine and went to bed dead tired.

April 22, Dorothy's birthday, I was awake early and put up two pulley lines for drying clothes (there were many diapers already). After breakfast I managed to blow a fuse while doing my wiring. I put up shelves, a platform in front of the set tubs in the basement, and fixtures in the bathroom. At two in the afternoon I called a halt and spent the rest of the time with my family until 10:00 P.M., when I left for New York and Philadelphia by rail.

In Philadelphia I was busy all day. Uptown I happened to run into a Miss Glockner. She had been a passenger on the *Mount Clay* when I was chief officer. The next day I sent a messman with scarlet fever to the hospital. Then the crew struck and walked off. The officers did not join them.

We finished taking bunkers[3] on the twenty-seventh. I had a new set of firemen, but the *American*, which had none, was scheduled to sail first, and the company ordered me to send my firemen to the *American*. I sent them in two taxis. This added to my difficulties in assembling a crew. These days no one wanted a fireman's job on a coal-burning ship, but eventually the owners sent me new crewmen from New York, Baltimore, and Norfolk. Then the crew I had sent to the *American* quit, and I was once more ordered to transfer my crew so that the *American* could sail. I protested, but to no avail, so I hired two more cabs, and this time I accompanied them. I had the cabs stop at the head of the dock. I got out, went aboard the *American*, and met the captain and chief engineer. Both were indifferent to conditions on their ship and said they didn't intend to cater to any crew members. I went to the crew's quarters and found them dirty and unattractive. Returning to the men in the cabs, I explained the situation. They all wanted to return to my ship with me. We did just that and sailed next day with a full crew.

Many of the men who had signed on as firemen had never been to sea before on a coal-burning ship, but they thought they could do anything. Mr. Strasser and I tried to make the job as attractive as possible.

On April 29 we passed out of the Delaware. The new firemen had difficulty keeping up the steam. We arrived at Locust Point and were still having difficulties. Firemen who found the job difficult asked to get paid off, and then new men had to be secured. The company had several of its coal-burning ships on the East Coast at the same time, which multiplied the problem. If we happened to get an experienced fireman, he would do his best to discourage the new men, and though he didn't make direct trouble himself, the inexperienced men did. Many times the engineers on duty had to fire the boilers themselves to keep the ship active.

At that time lots of union literature was being distributed throughout the crew quarters and cargo holds. The bulkheads were plastered with it. The new crew members began to agitate after they had been aboard a day or two. I ordered the best of food served and the quarters kept clean. Some of the junior officers resented my giving the crew so much attention.

Each day a few men played sick or demanded to get paid off. I spent my time on the phone, trying to secure replacements for crew members who were leaving. Several times I met trains and carried the arriving men to the ship in taxis. At last on May 6, with a full crew, we got underway.

We had fine weather on our way to Jacksonville, but our average speed, which should have been ten and a half knots, was only seven. The new firemen were coached to work slowly and general discontent was being bred among them.

We reached Savannah and began loading fuller's earth.[4] I received five letters from my wife. That was the good part. I continued to lose men and was short in all departments, especially in the boiler room. Men continually asked to be paid off. The company kept replacements coming from Charleston when not available locally.

On May 12 loading was complete, and tugs towed the ship into the stream. I convinced the engineers to steam the vessel down the river to anchorage. We discharged the pilot at Mayport, and on Sunday I took the ship safely outside the St. Johns River where we anchored. At 1:00 A.M. the pilot boat from Mayport brought out the needed crew members.

I called the new men to my room before getting underway and read them the articles: route, time, and pay rates. They signed on agreeably for the voyage. I had complied with the law, I thought, and later, at the Panama Canal, I had the shipping commissioner verify this. However, when we arrived in Los Angeles, I was ruled to have shanghaied the men because they had no option or opportunity to go ashore from the anchorage. My contract with them was not considered a binding one.

Making only about seven knots' speed, our trip down the East Coast had been a slow one. Our company's ship *Pennsylvanian* passed us easily on the way. She burned oil, had no trouble keeping up steam, and no trouble with the crew. I envied her.

On May 17, coal passer Mahoney refused to work, claiming he had a sore back. I put him in irons and after a few hours he was glad to go to work, quickly forgetting his back trouble.

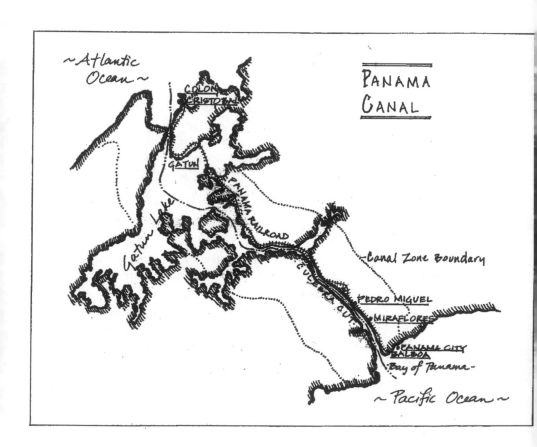

Panama Canal

When the ship was approaching Gatun Locks, Mahoney and Cannon, another crewman, jumped overboard and attempted to swim ashore. There was another American ship with us in Gatun Lake. Mahoney and Cannon, I suppose, had expected to get on it. We stopped the *Nevadan.* One of the escapees climbed up the bank of the canal. The other climbed onto a lighted buoy. We wired the Canal police, who sent a boat and a car to pick them up. After we anchored at the southern exit to the canal, the police brought the men on board. The police told me that the men were planning to jump overboard again, so I had them locked up until the ship was safely on her way from Balboa. I ordered Mahoney and Cannon brought before me. I tried to reason with them and explained that the laws of the Canal Zone allowed no one to land there. I told them that I would not fine them and that I would charge them only the police costs of $2.50 apiece if they would continue to work to the next port. They agreed and I released them.

May 22 we rounded Cape Mala and soon met our sister ship *Panamanian,* an oil-burner with no crew troubles. Next day the radio officer reported hearing the master of the *American* sending several reports of steaming troubles to the owners. Although the *American* had started the westbound voyage ahead of us, we were having less trouble, and we had overtaken her. I heard later that on the *American*'s return to New York, the captain gave up his command in frustration and went out on another ship, an oil-burner, as second mate.

In the afternoon, Mahoney was brought before me again, this time charged with hitting an engineer with a shovel. Through questioning of both victim and accused, I found that Mahoney had not struck the engineer on duty but had pushed him with his shovel. Either way, the engineer wanted the fireman downrated. We had no one to take his place, so I put Mahoney in irons until he agreed to work. In ten minutes he was released. I gave him a fatherly talk and promised to pay him off at the first port if he continued to do his best. I warned him not to be influenced by the troublemakers. Mahoney then proved to be a good man all the way to port, where I paid him off as promised.

Overall, however, we weren't getting enough steam, so on May 24, I stopped serving dessert to firemen. For the next three days, I had tarpaulins spread over the booms so that crew members could sleep on the cooler deck.

On June 1 moderate, cooler winds came to us as we left the tropics. Several firemen complained of rheumatism and colds. Steam was down a bit again, and the *Californian* overtook us.

Sunday the fourth was cool and comfortable, topside at least. We were steaming along fairly well, but I slowed her down during the night to make daylight arrival at quarantine in Los Angeles. We berthed at 10:00 A.M. All the firemen left the ship by climbing over the stern, not waiting for the gangway to be put down. All, that is, except Mahoney, who had given me the most trouble. I took Mahoney with me to the Shipping Commission and asked the commissioner to pay him off.

The commissioner asked, "Did you get the message to meet the crew at my office at eleven? They have brought charges against you for mistreating Mahoney."

I said, "Here is Mahoney. Ask him if he was mistreated."

Mahoney responded, "I only got what I deserved, sir." The commissioner dismissed the charges but advised me to pay off the firemen at their request, including those who claimed they had been shanghaied at Jacksonville. I paid them off.

On the eighth I had a telegram and letter from Dorothy. It was always good to get news from home. Next day I was busy with ship's business and had sat down to write to my wife when my brother Ralph popped in. I stayed two nights at his place and on Sunday we went to the First Christian Church together.

On the thirteenth I cleared the ship, signed on the new men, and left wages with the shipping commissioner for a man who had to be left in the hospital. I felt sick all day. It must have been Ralph's cooking. Not hearing a word from Dorothy didn't help. At 11:00 P.M. we sailed for San Francisco. On the fourteenth the officer in charge from midnight until four had trouble with the wheelman, probably an outgrowth of discontent among the firemen.

We arrived alongside the municipal pier at Richmond, across the bay from Frisco, and discharged fuller's earth. While on business in San Francisco, I met Captain Kane, the marine superintendent, and at last received mail from home. I brought my accounts up to date, as I thought I might be transferred to another vessel, and in the evening went to a movie. I still felt sick all day on the nineteenth, but a letter from Dorothy perked me up.

On June 20 I went uptown and paid off yet another two crewmen at their request. I asked American-Hawaiian's operating manager, Mr. T. G. Plant, for reassignment. He was sympathetic and agreed to have the company pay my way east by rail. Next morning I bought a steamer trunk.

Monday morning I left the *Nevadan* in a taxi, took the ferry to Oakland, and boarded the train to Chicago. The Overland Limited gave me a wonderful view of our great country. I finished reading *Successful Family Life* by M. H. Abel and slept well. I talked with passengers from San Francisco going to Germany on the S.S. *Bremen.* In Albany I got acquainted with a Miss Fischer of Long Beach. She asked me to call her the next time I was in San Pedro.

At four in the afternoon of the twenty-ninth, I arrived at my cozy home. All were well and happy. On Sunday, July 1, we went to church for the Baptism of our boy, Charles Allan. After dinner Jean took us for a drive in Alice Shaw's Franklin. On our way back, coming up steep and curving Greenwood Avenue, the axle shaft broke. Jean had difficulty checking our progress while backing down the hill with a full load of hysterical passengers and inadequate two-wheel brakes. She backed gently into a parked Model A Ford. With all of us pushing, we were able to get the Franklin off the Ford. I straightened the Ford's bent fender by hand, and it looked just fine.

For a whole week I worked around the house and yard. We made a diagram of the property and arranged for landscape grading. I trimmed trees, picked blueberries, and purchased a lawn mower, a wood plane, a saw, some canvas, and a fire extinguisher. Some afternoons I went swimming at Fisherman's Beach, just down the hill. Jean went with me while Dorothy took care of the baby and rested. I planed doors to fit properly, put up bookshelves and clotheslines, and staked the yard for grading. On July 9 the family persuaded me to stop puttering, and we drove with young Allan to Alice Shaw's summer place in Amesbury on a bluff overlooking the Merrimack River.

The company assigned me to the S.S. *Ohioan* for one east-west round trip. July 15 I said my goodbyes, and the *Ohioan* sailed for New York. I entered the ship, wrote Dorothy, and sent her $500. We sailed for Philadelphia and then for the Panama Canal. It was wonderful to be in command of a ship that burned oil instead of coal. The weather was fine, and I did a lot of reading between making out the Canal papers and figuring our fuel requirements. I was studying a book entitled *Etiquette*. It was a subject I had been scolded about by my wife.

On August 9 we arrived in Los Angeles where I spent any free time with Ralph, and Harry and Enid. In San Francisco I told Mr. Plant, the operating manager, that I would like to be on a ship that made Boston a regular port of call. I showed him pictures of my family and home. After two lonely days aboard, I walked to town and called on my friend Rolph Folsom. He invited me to his house for dinner and let me read two letters from Dorothy to his family.

At Seattle I received a long letter from home. Allan already weighed fourteen pounds, ten ounces. At Astoria we loaded canned salmon, and I bought a case of it for home use. I found out later that my wife gave away all of it because she did not care for any kind of canned fish.

On the return passage we had fine weather, and when not working on navigation, payrolls, writing, and odd jobs, I worked on a mat of braided strands of rope fiber for the front door in Swampscott. We reached New York on September 27, and I was relieved by the regular master of the *Ohioan*. Dorothy was waiting for me with baby Allan at the Hotel Belmont and we had a happy reunion. Two days later I saw my family off, got a haircut, and returned by train to San Francisco.

At the company offices in San Francisco, I reported to Mr. Plant and then to Captain Kane, the marine superintendent. I was assigned to the S.S. *Dakotan*. She was on dry dock for repairs, after having been beached. I was feeling very lonesome aboard a dead, cold ship. I was only aboard her for a couple of weeks, however, when I received hurry-up orders to relieve the master of the *Arizonan.*

## The S.S. *Arizonan*

On the *Arizonan's* previous voyage, the company had promoted a chief officer to master. Southbound along the coast of California, he had gotten caught in a fog among the Santa Barbara Islands and had to anchor until it cleared. Through carelessness he had received a reciprocal radio direction finder bearing from Point Conception instead of a direct bearing. He took it upon himself to write to the Navy to tell them how their destroyer fleet had grounded on Point Arguello a few months before by making the same error. The company would never have found out that their captain had put their vessel into such a dangerous situation, except that the Navy Department followed up by writing directly to the head of the company, asking for an official report. After they discovered what he had done, the company discharged the master promptly on his arrival in San Francisco, and I was given his command.

I was glad to be on an active vessel, my own command, and not a temporary job. The *Arizonan* was a big, slow ship built in 1905. She had in-turning twin screws, twin reciprocating engines, and made ten and a half knots' speed. October 26, 1923, we sailed for Seattle. She rode light with very little cargo, so to make the best speed, I had to keep her in close to shore in smooth water.

In Seattle, remembering my days as a market gardener, I enjoyed strolling through the public farmers market to see the marvelous produce competitively displayed. From Seattle we sailed to Tacoma, Portland, and on to San Francisco. I had five letters from home with snapshots of Allan. Saturday I visited the Folsoms in San Mateo, and on Sunday I had dinner with Miss Violet Marshall at the Women's Faculty Club in Berkely. The Marshalls were friends of the Allans back east.

On November 12 at 4:00 A.M., a big lighter filled with bailed hay came alongside as directed for loading to begin at eight. The barge captain asked the second mate to take a small line aboard so he could hold his barge steady alongside. The second mate replied, "Shove off and come back after eight." Disgusted, the barge captain complied, but he took his time returning. At eight sharp, the owners had men at two hatches to load hay, but there was no hay barge in sight. At ten the barge appeared. Hearing the details, our marine superintendent instructed me to carry the second mate back to the East Coast and replace him with a more interested and cooperative young officer.

On the fourteenth I went to department stores to buy paintbrushes to use in making toys, and that night we sailed for Los Angeles. On the sixteenth

Ralph met me, and we went with his baby daughter, Georgeanne, to a beach party where hot dogs were cooked with mushrooms on an open fire. Ralph stayed all night with me on the ship..

I started to make a kiddie car for my boy on our way to the Panama Canal. Off Acapulco I worked on a table for home and a game of ringtoss for a Christmas present. At Gatun Locks I received a letter from home with several snapshots of Allan.

On the trip north, through wintry winds and sea, I cleaned the varnish work in my room, painted my chairs, pipes, and radiators, and for the next few days made my room neat and ready to receive friends in port.

We arrived in Boston on December 12. In Swampscott I looked over my new home and put more things in working order. I had fewer than three days free and spent part of the time doing ship's business and Christmas shopping in Boston.

Back in New York on the seventeenth, I received a telephone call from Dorothy. She and Allan were coming for a visit. I was puzzled as to where to put them up. Captain Bennett gave me permission to bring them on board. When I met their train, they were both very tired.

I enjoyed having my family aboard with me. Allan seemed to get used to the noise of cargo being worked. While my family made do after a fashion, I often had to go to town. On the twentieth I opened a Christmas present from Dorothy. It was a half dozen pair of hole-proof hose. I had been in the habit of darning mine until they were ready to fall apart.

Sailing day came on the twenty-first and I had to send my family home. On Christmas Eve we were piloting through the West Indies. Before lying down, I opened the rest of my Christmas presents. I was happy. So many were so good to me. December 25 was a wonderful day. I dressed in whites and imagined my home surrounded by snow. I spent most of the day reading one of my gift books, *Duty As a Dad.*

On arrival in Seattle I had two letters from Swampscott. All were well and happy, and that cheered me. In Seattle and Tacoma I purchased lumber for the garage I planned to build at home. At Portland we loaded lumber and wood, and I received a dozen letters.

On our way to San Francisco, the starboard propeller hit a submerged object. On the thirty-first a survey of the propeller revealed no significant damage, and a seaworthy certificate was issued. In San Francisco on February 5, I had dinner with Miss Tosca Woehler. She was an educator and a good friend of my sister-in-law, Jean.

Between San Francisco and San Pedro, we developed an eccentric motion in the starboard propeller shaft near the stern tube and had to reduce rpm. Mr. Noland, the chief engineer, had me come to the shaft alley and observe. We decided to return to San Francisco for repairs. I was anxious to see the ship high and dry to discover what was wrong. We found that the stern tube bearing had frozen to the shaft and had been turning with it.

It had been a wise decision to return. The shipyard worked around the clock. A new bearing had to be made of lignum vitae, a very durable, oily wood. The wood was cut and placed so that the shaft would ride on the end of the grain of the wood.

I had another dinner with Tosca at the Pig and Whistle, and we went to a show at the California Theater.

> *The reader must be aware by now that my father, a man's man, loved women. I was witness on many occasions to his enthusiastic welcoming of each female who entered our home. He swept them into his arms, picked them up off their feet, swung them around, kissed them, and bellowed his welcome. Often their hats came off or something else went askew. Each lady squealed with delight while Mother screamed at him, "Put her down this minute. Honestly, Charlie, you are the limit and not to be trusted."*

Repairs were complete on the twelfth, and we sailed for Los Angeles. I began making a play yard for Allan in my spare time and later made him a highchair of oak. On March 7 we arrived at New York. I called home and found my wife down with the grippe but improving.

## Notes to Chapter 7

1. Slop chest: store run by the ship's master, selling tobacco, candy, shaving gear, oilskins, etc., to the crew.
2. Gatun Locks: section of Gatun Dam, which forms Gatun Lake; part of the route through the Panama Canal.
3. Bunkers: fuel; in this case, coal.
4. Fuller's earth; an absorbent clay.

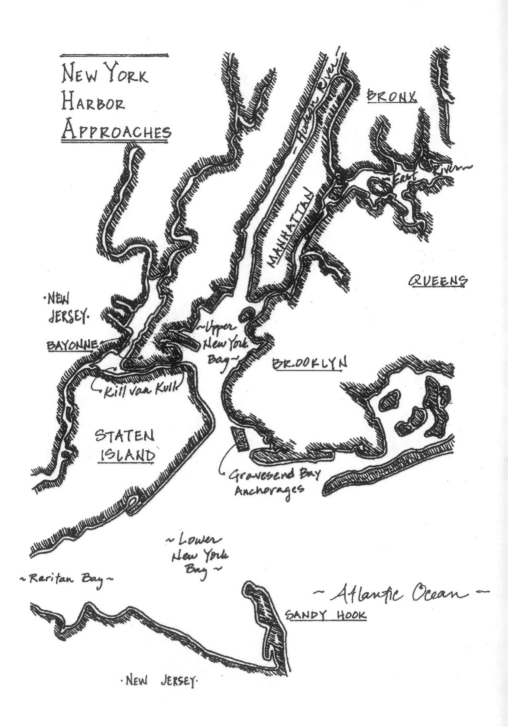

New York Harbor Approaches

# CHAPTER 8

# GOOD TIMES, HARD TIMES

Business was very bad in the spring of 1924 because the economy was depressed. American-Hawaiian took some of its ships out of service, and I was ordered to get the *Arizonan* ready to lay up. I was kept on the payroll to take care of the ship and Captain Bennett gave me permission to have my wife and son live aboard. To make the ship livable for my family, my quarters were fitted with a potbellied stove and kerosene lights. I got hold of an icebox, a kerosene stove, cooking utensils, and a gallon oil can to make a potty for Allan.

On April 4 tugs towed my dead ship from New York to Bayonne, New Jersey. Captain Bennett made the trip with me. As we crossed the bay, he had the shore gang throw several barrels of oily bilge water overboard. I was horrified and stopped it. Later he persuaded me not to have seen what I felt was a dirty deed. At Bayonne we tied up at the end of an abandoned railroad coal pier overlooking Staten Island.

Also aboard were Mr. Noland and other engineers, as well as one cook and one messman to feed and wait on the minimal crew. Dorothy and I made our meals in our own quarters. I was paid $331 a month and gave Dorothy her usual $250 allotment.

We were getting adjusted. We three could be together and relax for the first time, and I could get acquainted with my boy. We made daily trips to town with Allan in the stroller. The nearest post office was two miles away, a long walk along the pier, then a climb down, and a long walk through a meadow. Evenings we often took a walk on the upper level of the pier. In good weather these walks were not too unpleasant, but there wasn't much life to view. We could see several other ships and barges out of work. Most vessels had no keepers aboard. They were listing and rotting.

I made Allan a play yard on deck. He learned to walk during this time on board. When he went from one room to another, he had to sit on the high threshold and swing his legs to the other side. When he first got home to Swampscott, although there were no thresholds at all, he sat down at the doorways and swung his legs to the next room before standing up to walk again.

I was responsible for both my vessel and the nearby laid-up *Nevadan.* On weekdays I worked around the vessels all day long. I sounded the bilges regularly, checked over equipment, did some tarring to prevent rust, and the like. Evenings I made my usual rounds about the vessels, wrote the logs, and entertained Allan.

On April 25 Captain Bennett came to look into laying up three more vessels nearby. He talked to Dorothy. For my morale, he was anxious to keep her with me, making a home. May 12 the *Hawaiian,* another of our company's ships that were out of work, was tied up outside the *Nevadan.* Now I had three ships to take care of. On the fourteenth I put new glass in my bathroom window and collected dry stores from the *Hawaiian.* That day Dorothy had her hair bobbed, losing her long, curly tresses for the first time. It made her look very different. After supper she helped me make new window curtains.

By May 23, with the addition of the *Nebraskan,* I was in charge of four vessels and had a crew of two chief engineers, one assistant engineer, one steward, one messman, one bos'n, eight ABs, and two night watchmen. My chores included setting up water barrels for fire protection, repairing locks on doors, checking the radio equipment, sorting linen, and making written reports. On sunny days I had all the ships opened up to dry out. I often took Allan with me on my errands to town. He couldn't have behaved better.

On the first of June, a fine day, Dorothy, Allan, and I crossed the Kill van Kull in a rowboat and took a walk on Staten Island. Often on Sundays that summer, we three took the ferry there. On a farm belonging to Snug Harbor, a retirement home for sailors, we sat on a blanket on the grass.

On August 20 I went by bus with Dorothy to New York, where I bought her a muskrat coat. Then we met my mother and my brother Albert, now thirteen years old. They had traveled to New York from Norfolk and stayed for a week's visit. I put them up in the captain's quarters on the *Nebraskan,* abeam of us. Albert went on errands with me in the forenoon. I bought him sneakers and overalls. Then he helped me lay canvas decking on top of the wheelhouse. One day I took him with me to New York, where I took care of the payroll and then showed him the big city, including the Statue of Liberty and the aquarium.

On Friday, December 5, I got a letter ordering me to send my family home. The company was suffering huge losses. Dot had a bad cold and didn't want to go. Nevertheless we packed the trunk and suitcases, and the next day I put Dorothy and Allan on the train for Boston. After eight months it was a sad ending to the most extended period we had ever had as a family together. I then dutifully notified the company that their orders had been carried out.

I kept busy about the ship, made my weekly reports to Captain Bennett, and had Mr. Noland up to meals with me often for company. I had to shift the fire extinguishers to my room to keep them from freezing. They took up a lot of space.

December 10 Captain Bennett came aboard to see that the vessels were ready for winter and to discuss cutting down on the crew. Prospects for business seemed no better. He was very apologetic about having to send my family home. Within a few days I shortened the crew to six men, and then I sent Allan's carriage home by Railway Express. Letters from home said that all were sick with colds. The bos'n bought a Kiddie Kar for Allan for Christmas. He had enjoyed Allan a lot and missed having him around. Mr. Sullivan, the watchman, got a letter from Allan written by his mom, but I had none.

Captain Bennett provided me a relief captain so that I could go home for the holidays. In Swampscott, Dot and I attended the Christmas Eve midnight service at the Church of the Holy Name. During the next two days I did chores about the house and wrapped the steam pipes.

*About sixty years later, my wife and I were back visiting in Swampscott. We drove by the old place to take a look at the house and especially at Dad's rock garden. We were happy to see that the current owners, the fourth since I had sold the house in 1979, were keeping things up. The man of the house was working in the yard and I spoke to him, saying that I had been reared at his place. He invited us to tour the inside. In the basement I was fascinated to find the same old single-line vapor heating system, including the asbestos-wrapped pipes with Dad's neatly stitched canvas coverings. Apparently the asbestos, so beautifully confined, had met environmental safety standards.*

I repaired Allan's bed, put up a new clothesline, and hung a gate at the top of the stairs. Dorothy and I went to the movies in the evening, and then I took the midnight train back to New York. All the ship's toilets were frozen, so I got busy and thawed them out.

On the last day of 1924, I made the regular trip to town for milk, bread, mail, and newspaper. I was lonesome and longed to get back to sea.

I continued on full salary despite little or no work for shipping. In January, 1925, I had the crew clearing fire hoses and electric cables. We had to spread sand on the slippery decks to prevent falls. It was mighty cold.

I was kept informed of the shipping business by regular letters from Captain Bennett and an occasional one from Mr. Plant at company headquarters in California. Letters from home came nearly every day. One day

I received a telegram rather than a letter from Dorothy. Worried, I telephoned. It was just the midwinter blues. Allan was sick and Dorothy was tired. It was difficult for her to write when she felt depressed.

On January 24 the temperature was near zero, and the galley fresh water froze. It took two hours to get it thawed out. We kept busy trying to keep the fresh water to the toilets thawed. For the crew's toilet, we had built a wooden house located over the space between two ships. With that old-fashioned arrangement we had no plumbing problems.

Word from home told of difficulties burning coal in the furnace, so I ordered a heat regulator to work the dampers. On board the crew kept busy shoveling snow. I had trouble getting heat in my quarters and found my stovepipe frozen.

I had to let the bos'n go. The company couldn't afford to keep him. The lack of shipping was hurting all around. Although I received lots of mail, I often felt blue.

I made out a will and mailed it to my wife to put in the bank vault. I sent Dorothy her monthly allotment with an extra $27 still due on the heat regulator. I bought a guide book by Krans on piloting in New York Harbor and studied at the public library for two hours.

After nearly twelve months on board my laid-up ship, I was called to the New York office and given orders to make the *Arizonan* ready for sea. On March 16, 1925, I was fully relieved of the laid-up fleet. Four tugs towed the *Arizonan* to Brooklyn, where she was put on dry dock. To prepare for sea duty, the whole bottom was given a coat of anti-corrosive and a coat of anti-fouling paint. She was floated and hauled to a service pier in the yard for annual inspection. I had a chance to go home, but only long enough for a physical examination, a discussion with a carpenter about house repairs, and a visit with Dorothy to friends in Everett. The following day I took the midnight train back to New York, where I signed on a crew and bought presents for Allan, who was soon to be two.

Repairs and crew were complete on April 1. We went to anchor and took on five hundred barrels of oil from a barge. We swung the ship outside Ambrose Channel to adjust the compasses. It was wonderful to be back in commission. Dorothy and Allan arrived by train, and we had a few evenings together. From their hotel it was a short walk to a park, which Dorothy and Allan enjoyed during the day when I was busy. On Sunday the fifth we took a tour of the city and then went back to the ship for dinner on board. I put my family on the train for home on the eighth and cleared the ship for the West Coast. A partial strike by longshoremen delayed us but, at last on April 11, we finished loading and sailed. It was good to be back in business once more. It had been over a year since I had been at sea.

I continued as master of the steamer *Arizonan* until September 1926, carrying cargo on the intercoastal route via the Panama Canal. When in Los Angeles, I always visited my brother Ralph and sometimes his wife and family as well. While we were docked in San Francisco, I liked to call on Tosca Woehler in San Jose and Violet Marshall in Berkeley, as well as my friends the Folsoms. In Seattle I visited my friends the Harlings and Miss Bergen, friend of my chief mate, Mr. Gaidsick. On the East Coast, I visited my family in Norfolk. Whenever we docked in Boston, I went home to Swampscott if I could. As always, I kept busy cleaning and improving my quarters and building furniture for the house.

Dorothy wished I had a shore job but was happy to follow me by train to New York, Philadelphia, Baltimore, and Norfolk. Even though she was a poor sailor, she traveled by coastal passenger steamer once or twice. She usually brought Allan with her.

As we proceeded up the Central American coast on my first trip back in service, I did extra amounts of navigation using star sights. I was getting back into the groove. In San Francisco I walked all over town looking for a present for Dorothy but found none. She had sent me a watch chain. I had been using a black shoestring.

At home I was convinced that my women could not cope with burning coal for winter heat, so I made arrangements to have an oil burner installed by fall. It was a big investment, $594, as it was not common to heat houses with oil at that time.

October 31, 1925, we sailed with the largest cargo ever taken out of San Francisco. We had a deep draft—thirty feet, three inches forward and thirty-one feet, seven inches aft. The advertising of this ship and her demonstrated efficiency helped boost the company common stock $5 a share to $18. On our way south to the Canal we passed many ships heading north. Business was surely better this year than last.

During this time I received a letter from Dot that included snapshots of Allan, but her daily letter writing seemed to be a thing of the past. I guess the honeymoon was over. Perhaps she had some reason to be envious of my West Coast friends who received such enthusiastic attention from a sailor far from home. No doubt she knew that I was attractive to a number of lovely women. She and I were festering in our loneliness. My whole life was spent at sea, and I longed for home and hearth. She who loved to travel was cooped up with the demanding tasks of childrearing while fending off her mother on the one hand and her two sisters, who had compelling vocations of their own, on the other. Ours was not a storybook marriage but a dream held tenuously together by the U.S. Postal Service.

I studied piloting, took examinations, and obtained endorsements on my license to pilot in New York Harbor to Yonkers and the East River to Blackwell's Island. Pilots who seldom used tugboats to assist were inspirations to me, and I planned to be as good as they were.

The S.S. *Pennsylvanian* at sea

While we were docked in Seattle in late June and July, I took driving lessons from Mr. Thompson, my second mate, in his Ford coupe. I worked on the Ford myself, changing the oil and greasing it.

*Father got a driver's license in Washington. He was a terrible driver. His ability to judge speed and distance aboard ships was superb, but in a car he was hopelessly inept. Following one or two narrow escapes from disaster when we had our first car, he left all the driving to Mother.*

At the end of July, I was given a vacation followed by a transfer. I squared my accounts, left all in order, and at 8:00 P.M. on July 28, 1926, I left the *Arizonan* and trained home. My week of vacation was a busy time, what with all the odd jobs around the house, visits to relatives in Lincoln, and going to the movies and the lodge meetings, which meant so much to me.

## The S.S. *Pennsylvanian*

On Monday, September 13, 1926, my vacation ended, and I took command of the S.S. *Pennsylvanian.* This was the ship whose mate had refused to take me as a quartermaster back in 1915 when I was first starting out. Like my previous command, the *Pennsylvanian* worked the intercoastal route.

On arrival at Commonwealth Pier in Boston, we hit the end of the dock, even though we had the assistance of a tug. Captain Johnson, the pilot, was doing the docking. I was disgusted with his sloppy performance, especially since as the master I had to take the blame. I made up my mind that I would do it myself from then on. The ship had a slight dent in the port quarter. No excuse!

At home on a short visit, I repaired and painted the baby crib because Dorothy was expecting another child. Dorothy wanted to see more of me and urged me to take a shore job.

My brother Albert joined my ship as a sailor. Evenings I talked with him while he was on lookout duty. I had him at the wheel once in a while and gave him lessons in tying knots and splicing rope yarns. A captain never fraternized with crew or even petty officers to any great extent; a kid brother was different.

On June 2, I noted the West Venus above the new moon as cradle with the brothers Castor and Pollux nearby. It made me wonder how big my own family was that day. When we arrived at Los Angeles, I heard the grand news from Dorothy that our second child, John Rodman, had been born on May 27, 1927. Once more it was awkward being so far away.

The ship had to be laid up in San Francisco for ten days, which gave Albert and me some time for sightseeing. We went to Golden Gate Park and listened to the band play. With Tosca, we saw the movie *Old Ironsides* and played cards. In San Jose we visited Tosca at her school and took in the movie *Naughty but Nice.* I wrote to Dorothy telling all about it.

I was temporarily assigned to the *Ohioan* from the end of June till July 12, when I returned to the *Pennsylvanian,* which was still undergoing repairs and in need of my supervision. I finally heard from Dorothy after an anxious and suspense-filled delay. John Rodman, a sickly baby, was having serious feeding problems. I wrote to her and sympathized. While the *Pennsylvanian* was in dry dock, Albert and I prepared meals together in my room. We had fun sharing letters from home, sorting snapshots, visiting friends, and taking in the latest movies. One day my portable front teeth broke, and I had to go to town for repairs. That was one thing they couldn't do in a dry dock.

Dorothy's letters told of her having an awful time with the baby. At the Panama Canal I received her letter reporting that John Rodman was not improving.

In Baltimore on August 23, I told Captain Bennett about my son's sickness. He had Captain McAvoy relieve me so that I could go home. Dorothy met me in Boston, and we went to Children's Hospital and stayed while John Rodman was operated on for stenosis of the esophagus.

On the twenty-seventh Malcolm McLean, one of Jean's former students, drove us to Boston to see the baby. He drove us in again on Sunday after church. Then a telephone call from the hospital on August 30 told us that our child was desperately sick. We rushed to the hospital. I gave blood for my baby. Next day he was a little better. But on September 1 the hospital told us that he was failing. I gave more blood for a transfusion and he rallied a bit but was hanging on by a thread. At eleven at night another call from the hospital said he was critical. We arrived at the hospital just after midnight. At quarter to three, he passed quietly away. An autopsy showed he had had pneumonia, an ear infection, and an underdeveloped liver. Alice Shaw and her sister, Floss Preston, came home with us, answered the phone, and helped us arrange for our baby's burial.

On September 3, 1927, at eleven in the morning, at Woodlawn Cemetery in Everett, we buried John Rodman beside his grandfather, John Allan.

> *This is a fine example of how Dad wrote down facts but no feelings. I know firsthand, however, that he had them. I remember riding in a car on the way to the funeral. My father wept so desperately and helplessly that I was afraid he might suffocate. It was the first time I remember seeing him cry, but not the last.*

One day while I was home, I pulled Allan in his wagon down to the town square and then we sat on the beach, just the two of us. Dorothy needed some quiet time at home.

On my last day of vacation I waxed floors, cleaned the cellar, poisoned rats, and sharpened knives. Alice drove me to the train, and I called from Boston for a last farewell, then boarded the midnight train to New York. Back on board the *Pennsylvanian*, I had Albert visit in my rooms.

Sailing south in mid-October, there was fog but so much wind that I could not hear other vessels blowing their whistles. I had to head close to the lighthouse. We managed to get out and clear without mishap. I heard later that in these dangerous conditions, the *San Juan* had hit the rocks hard with great damage, and on the West Coast the S.S. *Coos Bay* had crashed on Mile Rock and was a total loss.

I began studying piloting for Los Angeles Harbor and pursued this at every opportunity. November 21, 1927, I sat for pilot examination and received my license for Los Angeles.

In the spring of 1928, while docked at Boston, I had our neighbors come aboard for dinner while the ship was shifted from one terminal to another. They all enjoyed it. (Our neighborhood at the top of Fuller Avenue was a fine one. Our houses had all been built about the same time. Those who came to live there were mostly young families like ours, and we were all very compatible.) At home early one morning Allan and I installed battery-powered headlights and taillights on his pedal car.

*My big pedal car with lots of nickel trim looked vaguely like a Buick. I loved it. None of my pals in the neighborhood had one. I pedaled it hard enough to break the crank axle twice.*

We had our usual bad weather at sea during the winter months. On April 6, 1928, we encountered heavy weather on our way up the Florida coast. The *Pennsylvanian* had a raised forecastle that made the short, choppy seas particularly dangerous, so I kept a careful lookout from the bridge. At 2:00 P.M. I sent for Mr. Haggett, chief officer, to warn him of the possibility of shipping heavy seas forward. He assured me that the forward booby hatch was secured and that he was prepared. Only a few minutes later, however, from my station on the port wing of the open bridge, I saw Bos'n Smith on the forecastle, battening down the small hatch with his back to the sea. Before I could alter course to give him a lee,[1] the ship buried her forward end. A huge wall of water carried him to the rail and smashed his face into the chain pipes.

Mr. Haggett rescued him and gave him first aid. Smith was bleeding heavily about the nose and mouth. I had to look after the safety of the vessel, but I sent several requests for medical advice to the Public Health Officers ashore. Before we could receive an answer, Smith came close to suffocating from clotting blood flowing down his throat. Trying desperately to clear Smith's windpipe, Mr. Haggett wrapped a towel around his finger and thrust it down his throat as far as he could reach. It did the trick and ended the agony. The bos'n rested quietly until we docked at Charleston, where we had an ambulance take him to the hospital.

Our deck load of shingles had taken a beating also. It hung over the side, tethered there by what was left of the chains with which it had been secured.

In 1928 I arranged to serve as port captain in San Francisco for a couple of months. Dorothy and Allan came west by train to be with me after I moved ashore to a fifth-floor apartment on Post Street. The rent was $50 a month. We tried living like normal people with shore jobs.

As it turned out, we didn't spend as much time together as I would have liked. My job was very demanding. It involved supervising the loading and discharging of cargo and piloting company ships here and there all day long, but without the satisfaction of commanding my own vessel. Many nights I found myself working late and sleeping in some ship's chart room. We had a few evenings together, but often Dorothy and Allan were off at the Folsoms in San Mateo or visiting elsewhere, and I would come home to an empty domicile. A shore job didn't seem to be all I had thought it would be.

We did have some good times together. On Sunday, July 1, we three were joined by Mr. Brown, the company agent, and Mr. Ted Herbert, also a member of the firm. We all took a train ride up Mount Tamalpais and to Muir Woods. It was a wonderful trip. At the summit I was recognized by other tourists who had been passengers on the *Mount Clay* when I was her chief officer. We watched the fog roll in through the Golden Gate. Another day we went to the Legion of Honor Building, and from that elevated location we watched the ships *Zale* and *Emma Alexander* pass out through the Golden Gate. While walking around the high cliffs at Land's End, we could view the ship *Coos Bay* as she lay stranded and broken on the reef.

Dorothy and Allan shipped down the coast to San Diego to visit the Danners. While my family was away, I ate my meals on ships. At the apartment alone on Sunday, July 15, I washed clothes and then took a streetcar out to the shore for a hike. During the week, I cleaned house to be ready for Dorothy, and after work on the twenty-fifth I went home eagerly to meet my family, who had returned from San Diego on the S.S. *Yale.*

Three days later I was busy on the *Hawaiian* until 10:30 at night. I had tickets to go to a show with Dorothy, but since I couldn't make it, I had Mr. Herbert go with her to the theater and to a coffee dance afterward, on me. I was getting tired of difficult shifting, docking, and supervising cargo, especially when the tide was unfavorable.

August 18 I saw Dorothy and Allan off to Seattle on the *Ruth Alexander.* I shifted more ships around the bay, had a visit with Captain Keene and Albert, then moved back aboard the *Pennsylvanian,* my old ship and home. Before sailing for Seattle, I asked Mr. Plant for a vacation on the East Coast.

Dorothy and Allan were down at the docks to meet me when the ship arrived at Seattle. We took Grey Line Bus Tours of the area and went through a lumber mill and door factory. I went to the Harlings to be with Dorothy and Allan for our last night together. Next morning I put them on the train for home, and I sailed for San Francisco.

Back aboard the *Pennsylvanian*, Albert and I studied together evenings. On the eastbound trip I studied piloting and penmanship. We arrived at last in Brooklyn, and my vacation was granted. I was relieved by Captain Hersey and arrived in Swampscott at midnight, taking Dorothy by surprise.

In reviewing the year in November, I made myself sick by noting how extravagant I had been. To save money on Christmas gifts, I spent a lot of time in the carpenter's shop making toys for Allan.

At Christmas, Albert headed by train for Norfolk where he would spend the holidays. In Philadelphia I spent Christmas Eve at Wanamaker's, listening to the season's music played on the great organ. The next day, with the ship idle, I played checkers and pinochle with Captain Johannsen.

The year 1929, the year of the big stock market crash, began for me at sea between Boston and Philadelphia. Arriving in Philadelphia on January 3, I had a letter from Dorothy telling me that our friend and neighbor, Norman LeGalle, had died and that his wife was very sick. Mrs. LeGalle died shortly after that, orphaning their children. It was a bad year for pneumonia.

On the eighth, Dorothy called to say that we had received an offer to buy our corner lot. Having spent so much in the previous year, I had put it up for sale. She didn't want to sell it, and I guess I really didn't, either. We turned down the offer. That same day I enrolled in a salesmanship course with LaSalle Extension University. We sailed for the West Coast, and in every spare moment I studied piloting for the Delaware River.

Evelyn Bergen called as soon as we arrived in Seattle, and together we celebrated my birthday at the Hotel Bowin. While in port I bought ten shares of American-Hawaiian stock with money I had earned from the operation of my slop chest.

Rudder repairs were completed on February 19 and on that day I had practice driving the company car. Then we sailed for the Canal. On the way, I studied piloting. In a westerly gale we lost part of the deck load of shingles.

A month later at Philadelphia, I went before the local inspectors and took examination for pilot's license for the Delaware Bay and River up to Philadelphia. That evening Albert and I studied our lessons and played checkers.

On March 17 we had such rough seas that one end of the gangway carried away. We stopped to recover it and, with considerable excitement, almost lost the bos'n overboard.

At home I was busy as usual. I painted screens and worked on a playhouse for Allan in the backyard where I got a good case of poison ivy while clearing brush. Evenings we played bridge with the neighbors. March 27 was Allan's sixth birthday, and his mother took him to the Metropolitan

Theater in Boston while I stayed home cleaning and shellacking floors. On one of my trips to the ship, I had the rear axle and crank for Allan's miniature car welded.

One Sunday, cousin Miriam, my old heartthrob, called on us with her husband, Bob Fuller. It was an awkward visit, and when they left I went for a long hike with Allan.

I set sail once more for the West Coast. The new radio operator was unable to get bearings and couldn't work the direction finder, but we did hear that Babe Ruth had hit his first homer of the season. Off Scotland Light Vessel, in rough seas, we witnessed a tug lose its stack and two mud scows overturn. I spent my time studying salesmanship, for my sake, and etiquette, for Dorothy's.

## Notes to Chapter 8

1. Give him a lee: to position the ship so that the bos'n is away from the force of wind and sea.

## CHAPTER 9

# ORIENTAL JAMBOLI

In late April, 1929, while we were docked at Los Angeles, Aunt Grace and Uncle John had supper with me on board my ship. We were sitting on deck when the S.S. *Golden Tide* passed by. I pointed out to my guests that she was one of American-Hawaiian's new Oriental Line ships. Little did I know that in a matter of hours I would be commanding her. She had been so plagued with discipline problems that her master had been relieved of his duties. Mr. Plant, the operating manager, and Captain Kane, the marine superintendent, ordered me to the *Golden Tide* to straighten things out. Mr. Plant told me he had found conditions on board out of control—liquor on the mate's breath, the chief engineer eating breakfast at ten in the morning, and other lax behavior. I assured him I would handle these problems in due time.

Mr. Plant and Captain Kane expressed their concern that in foreign ports the crewmen sometimes failed to be on board to perform their duty. As a work inducement, they wanted to stock beer on board to be sold at cost to the crew in limited amounts under the supervision of the master. Until then, beer had never been allowed on any of our company's ships. They tried to persuade me to start the practice. I objected. I was asked to try it, and nearly fell for the suggestion, but finally I told them, "No. If you insist, please get another master." They dropped the plan.

Next Mr. Plant suggested I let the chief officer go, but since he knew the ship and the route, I was reluctant to do so. He certainly could not be so bad that I couldn't handle him.

May 5, 1929, I turned the *Pennsylvanian* over to Captain Nash and called on Captain Peterson of the *Golden Horn* for information about the Oriental run on which I was about to embark. Next day I boarded the *Golden Tide*. She began to load cases of gasoline and kerosene, and I studied the intended route. On May 12 we sailed for San Pablo, where I received five letters from Dorothy. She was feeling anxious about my going to the Orient.

During the first few days on the *Golden Tide*, I was careful to see that company and government regulations were prominently displayed over my signature: no liquor allowed on the vessel, no women, no smoking, meal hours specified, smuggling forbidden, and stowaways not allowed.

It was overcast, the ship rolled, and decks were awash. I had the crew secure the ship, and we held fire and boat drill. I had planned to take a fairly northerly course, but since the deck cargo was awash with the ship fully loaded, I decided to take the longer southerly route, likely to have better weather. I headed the ship west-southwest toward the Hawaiian Islands, down to the 30th parallel, then I ran a rhumb line course.[1]

I kept busy both mentally and physically. I had brought along a boxing bag and, following the lessons I'd found in a magazine, I boxed regularly after supper. I studied salesmanship each day and did daily inspections with the chiefs of departments every morning at ten. I wrote to Dorothy,

At sea, May 22, 1929
My dearest,

The eighteenth was the eighth anniversary of the day we became one happy one. I'm glad I got you before anyone else did. I've been happier each year. . . .

Please don't expect fur coats or big extras as I am taxed to the limit. By paying you the maximum regularly I deprive myself of the opportunity to bring you gifts and extras as I'd like to do. In fact I *hope* to be able to leave your allotment at $260 a month.

I spend as little as possible myself and yet it's surprising how much is necessary. I know it is the same with you and I appreciate your cooperation. It's with *your* help that we are able to make a home and are paying for it. Another six years it will be paid for, and then I suppose we will be planning for Allan's education.

*I picture Mother fuming as she read this, wondering why he thought he had to pay off the mortgage so quickly.*

I left Albert on the *Pennsylvanian* as he is far better off there. Although I have perfect confidence in him, I hate to lead him into temptations. Good liquor is cheap and commonly used by all on this route. Men like to ship out on this run since girls are so available and very cheap. In fact it's nearly impossible to keep them off the ships. They are poor and in need of a little money to buy food. The girls are quite filthy and one of our principal troubles is to make the men take precautions to guard against disease. The company has adopted the Army and Navy method of supplying the men with prophylactic tubes free of charge. I have a supply of twenty dozen on board for a total crew of thirty-six. The company has proven it pays to take all precautions. Even then there are always several sick ones to care for. This problem is not nearly as common on the intercoastal run. I'd rather have Albert associate with the best men and women possible, and that's where he is now.

Your last letter was written on the tenth, after a nice day with Miriam. It makes me laugh every time I read it and yet I don't get your point. I certainly do hope I have improved socially, in dress, education, and so forth. However, I know of only one incident where Miriam could have found fault with me. That was when I failed to let her know promptly that I was staying with you and not visiting her.

*A portion of a letter from Mother is pasted here: "We [Miriam and I] talked you over in grand style. It will be good for your conceit to know she thinks you have improved a lot. Think that over!"*

It's a mighty good thing that I never did get to Northfield that time. I had only just been relieved of the support of my parents and I felt freer than ever. It was the first time in my life that I no longer felt compelled to support my family.

*In other words, if he had gone to Northfield, he might have proposed to Miriam instead of Dorothy!*

May 26 I spent most of the day reading about the route and the countries I was about to visit. I played three games of checkers with Mr. Colbert, my freight clerk, and held fire and boat drill again as most of the cargo consisted of kerosene and gasoline. I gave much attention to ventilation. There were twenty-six cowl ventilators on deck which had to be trimmed continually. I had not been aboard long when I discovered that there was no wire on the deep sea sounding machine. Apparently it had not been used at all in the Pacific. I had the wire installed and used it frequently to advantage as an aid to navigation.

The officers and crew were confronted with a great many regulations since I had joined their vessel. They knew that I had never been on this Pacific run and my "East Coast system" was not to their liking. I found that smoking had been allowed on deck. I forbade it at all times because we were carrying such flammable cargo. The officers and men resented this and retaliated by refusing at first to buy anything from my slop chest.

I also ran across the chief engineer being served breakfast at 9:30 in spite of my instructions to the contrary. This had to be stopped because the men serving him at this time should have been cleaning their respective stations. I saw to it that it did not happen again.

During the night of May 30, we crossed the 180th meridian, the International Date Line, so we had to skip that day. My reading included *What is Wrong With China.*

On June 8 our small, heavy vessel pitched and labored and made only about seven knots in a confused swell. June 9 we passed close to Lot's Wife, an island 326 feet high and only 100 feet across at the base. It is known to have no bottom at twenty fathoms, thirty feet from its sides. Quite a wonder! I used a whole roll of film trying to get some pictures. Nearby we sighted several Japanese fishing sampans following schools of fish.

Approaching Shanghai on June 13, we sighted the reflection of North Saddles Light, then caught a glimpse of the light itself. An American pilot, Captain Ball, guided us to the dangerous cargo area eight miles above the entrance to the Wampoo River. As soon as we were in our berth, bumboats were alongside with their services and wares to sell. There were barbers, dentists of a sort, pimps who took orders for girls, and many merchants with fancy silks and other items for sale. They did not wait for the gangway. Instead they passed a hook up with a pole from their boats to our gunwale and shinnied up ropes to our deck. In anticipation of all these people coming aboard, the chief mate had had the carpenter build a temporary toilet at the aft end of the ship for the natives to use. By the time the ship was secured and the crew could relax, these businesses were already set up for them. There was noisy competition among them for the sailors' attention. I was uneasy having so many strangers aboard. That night, bothered by mosquitoes, I slept little, if any.

When we arrived at each port, I handed out prophylactic tubes when I advanced money to the crew. All crew members took advantage but one, the messboy who waited on me and the other officers. Not surprisingly, this man was the only one on the entire trip to develop a venereal disease. I had to pay him off in Manila and send him to the hospital.

We discharged cases of gasoline and kerosene. I allowed no smoking on deck. Each frail wooden case contained two five-gallon cans. As the sling loads of cases were hoisted out of the cargo hold, streams of liquid poured out. The continual motion of the vessel all across the Pacific had worked open many of the cans' lead and tin seams. The holds and deck were wet with leakage. I was horrified, fearing fire and explosion. Then my heart came into my throat when I discovered that at each of the five hatches there was a burning charcoal pot heating a soldering iron. Workmen were soldering the cans even as the gasoline leaked out. They ran the hot iron over the soldered seams and did stop most of the leaks. I could easily visualize a bit of rope yarn or paper settling on one of these charcoal stoves, catching on fire, and sending the vessel to kingdom come. I ordered the charcoal pots hung over the side; even then I worried.

We discharged into lighters eight miles below Shanghai. I went ashore with the agent and took a guide through the native city.

Since it was my first trip to Shanghai, I had to learn the customs of the port. I was much concerned about pilferage. The agent put several watchmen aboard, but I got up at night in my pajamas to check on things myself. I regularly found two or three watchmen asleep under lifeboats, and I kicked them to wake them up. Later, discussing this situation with the agent, I found that I was wrong to do so. The agent had contracted with a company to watch the ship during her entire stay in port. The watchmen had to take turns sleeping. It was also the practice for the men who worked the cargo to take turns sleeping. I had much to learn.

I made it a practice to get up in the wee hours to look about and hear what was going on. With the clock under my pillow so no one else could hear it, I set the alarm for 2:00 A.M. Then I walked out on the upper boat deck and quietly looked about the lighters tied up alongside. The weather was hot and the workmen, when not on duty, slept on the tops of lighters in the river in a swarm of mosquitoes.

I was experiencing no trouble with the crew, contrary to what Mr. Plant had led me to expect. My men were always on duty as required. However, while I was watching the cargo operations from the boat deck at 3:00 one morning, I saw a woman dressed in black come to the galley door aft of the crew's quarters. When she saw me she ducked inside. I went to see what was going on. Suspecting that she might be stealing cargo or the crew's belongings, I was surprised to find her to be quite elderly and busily scrubbing the crew's clothing.

Next I looked in the forecastle where the sailors slept in bunks. The lights were on, but all the sailors apparently were fast asleep. In each of the narrow bunks with a sleeping sailor was a native girl. Without speaking, I roused each of the girls and motioned to them with my flashlight to get off the vessel. All the girls got out of the bunks, but they gathered in a corner where they ate from platters of food that the crew must have provided for them. Then they got dressed, not in native attire but in American dresses and stockings. I urged them to hurry. Finally the girls got together at the other end of the vessel and climbed down a side ladder to a sailboat moored in the dark that I had failed to spot before. They appeared reluctant to leave. Apparently there were more girls still aboard. I let two go after them. They went immediately to the midships quarters. I was afraid they might find others in the officers' quarters located there, but instead they went to the stewards' quarters and roused two more girls who had been sleeping with the messboys. Finally they seemed satisfied that their whole group was intact and they left.

I mentioned my discoveries to no one. However, on a subsequent nightly investigation, surveying the crew's quarters, I went to turn on the light in the forecastle. The button had been removed from the switch, so I relied on my flashlight. In each bunk, once more, was a native girl. I decided that I had not seen them; it was none of my business. Each night in China it was the same. The crew were all present for their work each day. There was no absenteeism. Obviously my nighttime prowling was well known, although no officer mentioned it to me, nor I to them. I judged that the men acknowledged that their master was interested in enforcing his rules. They, in turn, offered their respect by doing their duty.

Shanghai,

June 16, 1929
My dearest,

I have been aboard all day looking after the discharging and loading. We sail at daylight for Amoy, a distance of six hundred miles, a three-day run.

Don't worry about conditions in China, dear. The trouble is all in the interior where the battleships of the world cannot penetrate. From what I see, Europe and America control China as much as possible with their navies and armies. . . .

It's Sunday, although they have no "Sunday" in this country as far as shipping is concerned . . . I've yet to see a lazy Chinaman. One sees them as "horses" everywhere. Nearly all hauling is done by manpower, even the cargo boats. The harbor is full of them being sculled, and there is always one woman, the captain's wife, pushing an oar on each boat. . . .

Smoking opium is against the law, and there are heavy penalties for doing so in China, but there are public opium dens in the French Concession where the Chinese have no authority. There are a few barrooms in the English and French concessions but none in the native city. They have hardly enough money to buy rice, but they do drink tea. There is no plain water fit to drink. Boiled, it makes good tea.

No one will be allowed ashore in Amoy due to the unhealthy conditions there, so next place we see is Hong Kong.

June 17 we sailed for Amoy and passed through the Bonham Straits. There were many Chinese fishermen under sail. We saw a fleet of them ahead of us, several hundred strong. The light reflected from their sails changed as they parted to leave us a passage.

Amoy was noted for thievery, so on our way there the chief mate had all the brass flanges on the deck gathered up for safekeeping, replacing them with temporary iron ones or wooden plugs. On the twenty-first we sailed from Amoy to Hong Kong. I used no pilot sailing, but I suppose we paid for him just the same. That was not the only loss. While in port, the longshoremen had crawled over the cargo destined for future ports, pilfering much of it.

163

On June 22 we arrived at Lin Mun and anchored north of Stone Cutters Island. Bumboats ran alongside and hooked lines over the gunwale. Up these lines shinnied dozens of Chinese who fastened painters from their boats up and down both sides. Getting aboard while the ship was still moving gave these traders an edge over others who were not so courageous. They attached themselves to the side of the ship in spite of our speed and repeated warnings from the officers.

We experienced another peculiar and hazardous practice on the way. Several boats, with two persons rowing, deliberately raced across our stem as we proceeded at full speed. It was said that they were trying to cut off the devil that was following them. The fact that they did this repeatedly indicated that their efforts were not successful. It was a very dangerous practice, but miraculously we ran down none of them.

Hong Kong,
June 22
My dearest,

I'm sorry to hear that all of you have been so ill. I do hope that you have long since recovered. I hardly expect you to be as comfortable as normal, but, dear, you are on the way toward making our family more complete and we are all (including yourself) going to be happier than ever. And that is what you want, is it not, dear?

Hong Kong,
June 23
My dearest,

So far I have been wearing that old Palm Beach suit ashore as well as aboard since it is too warm to wear even my light gray suit. It is soiled and ragged and worn out. There are several even warmer ports ahead for me for the next month, so I went ashore after supper to a tailor's and got measured for two Saigon unbleached linen suits. They are to be ready tomorrow afternoon. The material and tailoring cost $26 Hong Kong, or $12.75 American for the two suits!

Although I rode ashore with the agent, I had to pay my way back to the ship and that cost me $1.75 American, so really the suits cost me $14.50. Not bad if I can get by without paying duty. I had planned to get another Palm Beach suit in New York since this other one had been so satisfactory, but I just couldn't wait.

Hong Kong,
June 24, 1929
My dearest,

. . . I've been in three or four department stores looking around this morning. Only thing I bought was a can of black Shinola [shoe polish] that came from the States. It cost me less than I would have paid where it is made!

I expect the general agent and a passenger, a colonel, to join me for the next eleven days. The fare will be $77. I can't understand why passengers like to travel on freight ships, as we have comparatively poor accommodations and it is no pleasure for me having to share my quarters.

Next port is Haiphong in French Indochina, a 619-mile trip, three days' run.

Heaps of love,
Charlie.

After discharging cases of kerosene and gasoline to lighters and sampans, we sailed for Haiphong. On our way we steamed by the southern side of Hainan Island, which had many outlying reefs marked by kelp. I was kept busy checking our position by sights and bearings of rocks and mountains.

June 27 we moored between two buoys just above the city in the dangerous cargo area and immediately began to discharge to barges in the river. I had a nice letter from Dorothy and I stayed aboard to write to her.

Haiphong,

June 27

My dearest sweetheart,

. . . I am enjoying my two passengers, but they are just about melted by the heat, while I am about the most comfortable I have been in some time. The temperature is about the same, eighty-seven. It is nice and dry today. I guess if my passengers had more work to do they would leave the firewater alone and feel better!

On arrival here I received the nicest letter from you, dear, thanking me for arranging the allotment and increasing it. . . . Don't worry, dear. Although I never see my paycheck or the biggest part of it, I still work hard for it. It surprised me also that I was able to increase your allotment. I thought that I might be able to send you more but somehow, so far, that has not been the case. I have had to buy a lot of little things that I hadn't planned on, and then there were those two light suits I had to have. Oh, I'll make out, dear, that's my job, but you do make it heaps easier when you appreciate my trying.

The river landscape here is very pretty. It's made up of delta land with, here and there, an odd-shaped mountain. . . .

The approach to the city was by boat up a crooked river and via roads, one vehicle wide, on ridges between vast rice paddies or swampland. I could see rugged mountains in the distance. We discharged barrels of asphalt and loaded tile from Hanoi, a short distance inland from Haiphong. It was a pleasant little city, quite modern and French.

June 29, 1929

My dearest,

. . . I took a sampan to go ashore. A sampan is a small boat on which sail is used when there is a favorable breeze. Otherwise they are sculled with an oar or rowed as is typical in North China. Whole families live aboard these boats. The men may work off their boat by the day, but the women are born, brought up, married, and die right on these boats. It is the women who do the rowing or sculling, with the assistance of a daughter or a small boy. The women will take you ashore for a few cents.

When I landed on the dock, there were twenty-five or more ricksha drivers, all trying to get someone to hire them. With only a half a block to the office, I walked, yet they all followed, trying to get me to ride with them. It seems that the Europeans here never walk a step outside of their gates. Every street has hundreds of rickshas parked, waiting for a chance to make a few cents. There is practically no trucking done here. If a cellar is to be dug or a mountain moved, hand labor does it, and in each city it seems to me that all heavy tasks are performed by women over forty years of age. . . .

Women wear pants and dress like the men. The laboring men or women wear black, loose-fitting pajamas, but the office people wear white pajamas. On top of these pajamas, the wealthy merchants wear a silk dress that comes down to their ankles.

I've seen a farmer coming to town with his produce hung from the ends of an eight-foot piece of bamboo and moving at a near run. I never see any Chinaman work, or even walk, lazily . . . .

The native women carry their babies in a sack on their backs and do the work of men all day. I've yet to hear a baby cry. Much of the time the babies sleep right on their mothers' backs. The agent and officers tell me that in Japan they have quite often seen a woman loading the ship with two babies on her back at the same time.

There are 15,000 foreigners in this city, practically all of whom are French. The foreign section of the city is very modern, with wide, shaded streets and granite or masonry buildings built on a plain, formerly delta land, but now well drained. Electricity and modern conveniences are common in this section. There are nice stores and lots of fine-looking French women everywhere. All of them want to do so much for you. These are the first women who seemed at all feminine to me since I left the States. The native part of the city, where the coolies or poor Chinamen live, consists of bamboo huts as in the rest of China.

June 30

Dear Mother Allan,

I have been seeing lots of new and interesting people, things, and parts of countries. I feel that this trip is a valuable part of my education. I try to pick up as many viewpoints as possible and to see the native people in their own sections, as well as Europeans in their provinces or concessions. . . .

Parents who are too poor to send their boys to school nevertheless are farsighted enough to have the child prepared for a future. They let their boys out to some merchant or manufacturer for a term of three to four years where they serve as apprentices, receive food but no pay. When their term is up, these boys hire out for whatever they can earn, probably a few cents a day, depending on their skill.

A majority of these boys are skilled workmen when they are ten or twelve years old, and it is surprising what remarkable workmanship they produce with antiquated tools. Labor is so cheap and plentiful in this country that modern machinery is not required. Where it would cost us $2 gold to load a ton of cargo in Boston or New York, it would cost 12 cents in Shanghai or Hong Kong!

Although there are millions of poor Chinese, there are some very wealthy merchants. These can always be identified by their dress. There are many well-educated Chinese as well, although over 95 per cent of the population is illiterate. The Chinese are understood to be peaceful, with no interest in national affairs. Therefore, because there is no unity, they have no strength as a nation and are readily influenced by outside powers. I've read several books on China and have learned a lot.

Foreigners here treat the natives as inferior and are able to pay for every kind of service. But irrespective of the price, I am not comfortable riding on another man's back, such as riding in rickshas or chairs carried on men's shoulders.

All in all I think we Americans have the best country in the world for a home.

Do wish I could be home and give you sixteen kisses on your birthday.

On July 2 we moored at Nabe, seven miles below Saigon. Once more we discharged cased kerosene and gasoline to barges. A small leak was found in the side of the hull. The chief engineer had a cement box made over the opening on the inside so that the hull was intact for the rest of the voyage. Then the empty compartments were carefully cleaned and made ready to receive 500 tons of general cargo and 1,300 tons of rice for Cebu in the Philippines.

Saigon,

July 2

My dearest,

After a fairly good trip down the coast, a distance of 802 miles, we entered the river this morning and picked up a French pilot, Monsieur Paste. We came up a very crooked river for thirty-six miles through low delta land planted with rice on both sides as far as the eye could see. We are now anchored in a regular berth seven miles down the river from the city in a fine open roadstead.

My passengers went ashore at nine. The agent and customs officers were here before noon. I wanted to go to the consul's but there was no boat available until three, and as it takes an hour to get ashore, I am waiting until tomorrow. I don't want to be ashore evenings and have to wait until the next morning to get a launch since we are continually working cargo. I haven't even had a glimpse of the city yet.

Heaps of love to my own little girl and son. Your Charlie.


July 4, 1929

My dearest,

Yesterday morning the agent met me by appointment and drove me to town in a big Italian Fiat. We must have been driving for nearly an hour to the town through miles of low delta land, awash as this is the beginning of the wet season. The ground is soft and everywhere it is being plowed and made ready for planting rice. The plowing is all done by water buffalo. They are black and halfway between a big hog and an ox. Work on the farms is done from daylight 'til dark. The road we drove over most of the way was only wide enough for one car. In fact, I didn't think there was sufficient space for one. We crossed a narrow steel bridge wide enough for one car and several other bridges just barely wide enough for two. We passed many natives walking as we drew near the city, and the streets became wider and the buildings more modern, contrasted with the country architecture of bamboo huts with thatched tops and sides. The city buildings were of concrete and the transportation varied from rickshas to Australian ponies to foreign cars, some of which were electric powered. There were very few Fords, contrary to most cities of the world.

Everything is French here. There are four Americans in town: the consul, two vice consuls, and one other. There are eight Britishers but little English is spoken. Our agent is a Chinaman, K. D. Hoh, a graduate of Columbia and one year at Harvard. He is forty-three years of age. I did my business with him then took a ricksha to the

Continental Hotel to meet Mr. Thompson, the general agent, whom I had brought here as a passenger from Hong Kong. I visited with him while he finished his drink, gin and bitters. Then we both took rickshas to the consul's residence, where we were served cognac and whiskey sodas. I had plain soda. Mr. Waterman, the consul, arrived there at 11:30. They were just closing the office to go to "tiffin," a French breakfast and siesta. Everything—department stores, drug-stores, offices, and all—closes between 11:30 and 2:00 P.M. So I had to postpone my meeting at the consulate until after two. Meanwhile we returned to the Continental Hotel for tiffin. I was the guest of the general agent from Hong Kong.

I had to order *Water, Plain!!* There were seven courses:

1. Very nice soup (possibly pea or tapioca).
2. Choice assortment: shrimp, fish, lentils, salads of various kinds. We helped ourselves from a large tray that also included ripe olives and several things with which I had no familiarity.
3. Bread, which was one inch in diameter and eighteen inches long, and two fried eggs.
4. A sort of chicken stew.
5. Creamed spinach.
6. Assortment of fresh fruits. (I ate a delicious mangosteen.)
7. A sort of fancy rice cake pudding.

My meal cost the agent $2.50, plus $1 for the outside table, for a total equivalent to $1.75 gold. Each course was served with clean dishes and silver.

After this noonday meal we went to rooms in the hotel annex. Mr. Thompson and my passenger from Hong Kong had separate rooms with baths. Their bathrooms were larger than our dining room at home. I stayed with them until 2:00 P.M., when I took a ricksha to the consul's and was there on business until 4:00. Then I ricksha'd through town, stopping for Kodak films for one of my officers, mail, and postcards. Next I went to agent Hoh's office, where we talked over business at a nearby café. He had bottled beer and I had orangeade. I turned down an invitation to a Chinese dinner with him, our general agent, the American consul and his wife, and a few other friends. This was to take place at Cholon. The customary time to start dinner here is 9:00 or later and continues for hours. I would have had to stay at the hotel until this morning, sailing day, and I had no means of communicating with the ship. . . . I returned after driving throughout Cholon, where I saw the many big rice mills. I got aboard at 7:00, in time to sign all bills for the port. We finished loading at 8:30, then awaited daylight for a pilot. In spite of my place being well screened, I was forced to engage in numerous hunts for mosquitoes.

169

We left Indochina for the Philippines on July 4, proceeding down the Saigon River through low delta land and tropical thicket. While turning around to head downriver, the engineer below failed to put the engine astern, although that was the position of the telegraph. We had plenty of headway on, right toward the river bank. The telegraph was positioned repeatedly in desperation. The ship continued to forge ahead. Finally the engine was reversed, but momentum brought us closer and closer to the bank. The chief mate at his regular station on the bow was close enough to see the imminent danger. He frantically waved his arms and yelled, "*Back her, back her!*" She stopped just inches from the bank and we were able to get her turned around. What a relief that no damage was done!

We sailed for Manila in heavy rain squalls with no sightings of any heavenly bodies for three days. We had only the magnetic compass to guide us. I judged the distance traveled by our engine revolutions, but this didn't take the wind or currents into account. We had no sonic depth sounder, only the deep sea sounding lead. At the device's limit of six hundred fathoms, we could not touch the bottom. The afternoon of the third day was dark due to low-lying nimbus clouds. It rained so hard that visibility was only from a half to one mile. I estimated I could make landfall before dark, if lucky. If not, I would have to head west and heave-to until daylight.

I kept especially good lookouts for cliffs or breakers ahead. When I could see a mile ahead, I had her on full speed; and when the visibility shortened, as it did every few minutes, I would again put the telegraph on half speed. At 4:00 P.M. I was about to call it quits for the night when we sighted breakers close on the starboard bow. We were right smack in the entrance to Manila Bay. I couldn't have made a better course for those three days under the best of conditions. With the anchor down, we relaxed and felt secure for the night.

In Manila, thrilled to receive five letters from Dorothy, I wrote:

Manila,

July 8

My Dearest,

Are you drinking lots of milk? It seems funny that Allan is suspecting anything as early as this.

After an adventurous voyage across the South China Sea, I went ashore this morning in a small launch and then to the office in a two-wheeled gig with a little horse drawing it. There are no human-powered vehicles here as there are in Hong Kong. There are American-looking streetcars and many automobiles, practically all American makes.

The wind is so strong and has been blowing into the bay for so long that the surface of the water in the harbor is level with the streets and in many places is over the curb. The harbor water is so high that the rainwater can not drain off. I saw very little in town but what I did see was a nicely laid out American city. I returned for lunch, read my mail, rested for about an hour, and now I am with you. I didn't accomplish much this morning, as the customs house, post office, Shipping Commission, and marine surveyor's offices, as well as the banks, were closed in celebration of the arrival of the American Governor General. I had hopes of sailing from here tonight, but with the several delays, I think that we will now be here until the night of the tenth. Our itinerary for the rest of the voyage is as follows:

Manila to Iloilo, 361 miles.
Cebu, 222 miles.
Panabutan, 203 miles.
Zamboanga, 52 miles.
Davao, 320 miles.
Lamit Bay, 630 miles.
Manila, 680 miles.
San Francisco, 6,049 miles.

It is encouraging, dear, that so far at least, you are not suffering as you did with John Rodman. Guess it's just as well your mother knows. You certainly deserve credit keeping it to yourself as long as this. It might be different if you had me at home to confide in.

Manila,
July 10

My dearest, I received the picture of my little man today. How he seems to have grown and how proud I am of him. Makes me feel that I don't see him nearly enough. I'm glad I am not on this run continually. . . .

We left Manila on the tenth and had nice weather all the way to Iloilo on the southeastern side of Panay Island, a distance of 361 miles. Early July 13 we sailed for Cebu without a pilot. I held fire and boat drills, advanced money and prophylactics. Passing Opon Light we slowed down to make a daylight arrival. In Cebu we discharged the rice we had brought from Saigon. It had paid to have the hull carefully cleaned and the compartment ventilated to prevent tainting. We had also placed wooden vents throughout the bags so the rice wouldn't heat. The rice came out in fine shape, as well as the three hundred tons of gypsum we had shipped from Los Angeles.

Cebu,
July 16

My dearest,

We are working night and day discharging general cargo and loading copra. Copra is dried coconut in bulk, which is used in making oil and oil products such as hairdressing and soap.

The picture you sent me of my little man gives me many a thrill, dear. I just had to get up and have another look at him. He has a personality all his own. You could not have made me any more pleased, dear. . . .

We are nearing the point where we will be homeward bound. What a pleasant feeling! We are scheduled to leave Hong Kong on August 3. With good weather we ought to make Frisco in twenty-seven days.

I cannot get home too soon, dear. I love you both, Charlie.

On July 17 we shifted the ship to Opon to a narrow dock extending from the shore. It was only fifteen feet wide at the end. We ran lines to the trees onshore to make fast. Normally ships tied up there and worked cargo from one hatch at a time because the end of the dock was so short along the ship's side. In our case the cargo to be landed was in number one and number two hatches. The mast was in between these hatches, and the stays prevented the booms from being swung abeam. I asked the chief mate, "How about letting the port stays to the mast go? In that way we can work two gangs at a time."

My mate said, "It can't be done. It's been years since the stays have been let go." I insisted that he take them down. Once done, both hatches discharged to the dock at once, saving the ship a day's time. The natives carried the cases on their heads to the warehouse. We sailed at 5:30 P.M. for Panabutan on Mindanao Island.

On arrival we docked at a small, rickety wooden dock loaded with lumber. This was the only dock or industry at this port, just one small mill that cut mahogany. When the dock was full, a ship came and took the lumber. The mill hands did the loading. A little shortwave radio in a shack on a hill was the only communication to the outside world.

We loaded 263,000 board feet of mahogany lumber. By loading all night, we finished and cleaned up the dock at noon on the nineteenth. Then we sailed for Zamboanga, a short run. We docked portside to a fine dock, a well-constructed, T-shaped concrete pier. It was at the foot of the main street of the town. Many cruise ships tied up there, the water being deep right up to the pier. There was no freight on the dock, nor were there any warehouses there or in the town. The pier had been designed to accommodate passengers. We loaded copra with two gangs of twenty men each, cased coconut with a third gang, and gasoline with two more gangs. All cargo was loaded and discharged directly to and from motor trucks.

At 9:00 A.M. I went swimming alongside in deep water. In climbing back up the ladder I felt my wedding ring slip off. It had always been a little large, and when my hands were cold it was likely to slip off. I had lost it several times at home in Swampscott washing windows, but I had always found it again in the leaves at the base of the foundation. This time it was down at the bottom of the Pacific Ocean. What could I tell Dorothy? Could I buy a new one to replace it? Certainly not with a clear conscience.

Well, it was a nice day and I went uptown. The island was covered with coconut palms. During the day I drove out to the prison farm at San Ramon and then visited the Overseas Club, where I had a haircut.

The ship was two days behind schedule since leaving San Francisco. Copra was not often loaded after dark because it was difficult to keep the local labor awake and working. Nevertheless, I told my chief officer we were going to continue loading until midnight. "Impossible!" he said. "The men won't work. They will just sleep on the job."

I said, "They will work!" I ordered all officers to duty and told them, "*We* will keep the men awake. I'll do my part." I then went up and down the cargo holds to see that the copra, carried in bags on the head of each worker and poured into the holds, was properly trimmed to the wings with shovels by those below. To receive this cargo, the holds had been carefully cleaned and lined with straw mats to assure ventilation.

While uptown the next afternoon, I met the ship chandler, who had been pestering me to buy stores that I did not need. He wanted to do anything he could for me. By so doing, he thought he could break me down to buy some stores. He asked where I was going, and I said that I intended to take a walk straight out into the country. He wanted to give me a ride and at last I accepted. I only wanted to see the countryside. However, he assumed otherwise, hircd an ox cart, and we drove for about an hour. The country houses were one-room affairs built on stilts six feet off the ground. The owner's pigs, hens, ponies, and water buffalo were housed under the family's living quarters.

We drove for miles, where to I had no idea, since my host spoke very little English. Most of the country was planted in tall palm and coconut trees. The weather was fair, the sky clear. With the bright moon, the view skyward was glorious. Finally we came to three long, one-story buildings radiating from a central garden. At the end of each building nearest the hub was a screened-in verandah. We left the ox cart, and my guide escorted me in and introduced me to several young women. The chandler was sure this was what I was looking for. From the verandah I could see a central alley that ran down through the building with rooms on either side.

The women were all of dark complexion, apparently Filipinos. They didn't speak much English but tried to be hospitable. After a few minutes the ship chandler saw that I was not particularly interested and said, "We go see number two." I was no more interested there, so he said, "You no like. We go to number three." In this lounge there were several well-dressed men facing away from us. This was obviously the most expensive of the houses. Finally my escort became convinced of my disinterest. As we moved to go, the men all turned to face me, giggled, and greeted me, "Hello, Captain." They were all members of my crew. I'm sure they got a big kick out of the incident. We had a pleasant exchange, and I left with my guide. He was quite discouraged that he had not pleased me, and as we were riding back to the ship he expressed his disappointment. I tried to explain that I had enjoyed the trip. He asked what more he could do. So I told him the big problem of my wedding ring at the bottom of the sea and asked him if he could get me a diver to try to recover it. Many of the natives in the southern end of the Philippines were pearl divers, and I had them in mind when I asked him for help. The ship chandler said he would indeed arrange to have a diver come on the following day. He gave a price of three pesos.

Zamboanga,

July 19

My dearest,

No pilots or tugs were used at either of these ports. When I have navigated successfully like this, never having seen the place before, I record the event and feel that there is another page finished and that I am ready for the next challenge.

I walked right through the city in a straight line for one hour, and this took me pretty well into the country. This is by far the nicest city I've seen in these islands, with paved, well-lighted streets and fine buildings. The natives seem far more prosperous than elsewhere. Coconut growing is one of the principal occupations here and it must be a profitable one.

Tonight, toward the end of my walk, it was a beautiful sight to look up through the trees and see the moonlit sky. I wish you could have been with me to see it, dear.

I hope you are getting along nicely, dear, and that you are enjoying the nicest place I know of to live, the U.S. of A!

We started to load copra with three gangs. At 9:00 in the morning, the ship chandler arrived with his diver, who was dressed in ordinary work clothes. I really did not think it possible ever to get the ring back, but I invited the diver on board. He asked me for a description of my ring. I asked, "How much?" and he replied, "Three pesos. No find, no pay." I quickly engaged him. He went onto the pier, stripped, and dove in. Surfacing and treading water he put on a pair of goggles, then headed down again. He was gone so long I gave up waiting and walked away. Almost immediately he surfaced, with no sign of the ring. He got dressed, came on board, and, as he approached, surprised me by removing a ring from his finger. It looked to me a bit green, as would happen to a piece of brass. I was sure it was a fake. But inside it read "D. A. to C. N. B. 1921." It was my ring. Delighted, I handed him five pesos rather than three and thanked him. The ship chandler seemed pleased also. I was so happy I gave him an order for some fruit and greens in spite of myself.

Rain delayed us some, but we finished loading 660 tons of copra, 22 tons of rubber, and 200 tons of desiccated coconut, having caught up by working during the night.

We were at sea on July 22, between Zamboanga and Davao in fine weather with occasional heavy rain squalls. In Davao next day, I had lunch ashore with the agent and the stevedore. Then, at my request, the agent drove me to the country to Mr. Firakawa's hemp plantation, where I saw the product growing and being stripped, dried, sorted, classed, and bailed. I was shown the hand-stripping method and the modern way by machine. It was very interesting to me, since hemp was used to make most of the rope used in our business of seafaring.

At Davao we discharged gasoline and lubricating oil and loaded hemp and copra. I pressed everyone to get the ship away as soon as possible in order to get back on schedule. We finished loading on the twenty-fifth and sailed for Lamit Bay. With all the dangerous cargo out and the holds cleaned, I announced that smoking would now be allowed on deck, provided the smokers kept clear of the open cargo compartments and ventilators. Pleased at this, the crewmen increased their purchases of cigarettes and other supplies from my slop chest.

At sea,

July 26
My dearest,
    All over the Philippines it seems to me that all the big business people are Japanese. There is very little American money invested here, and most of the stores are run by Chinese. The Filipinos seem to be very irresponsible. In China the laboring class eat rice with chopsticks while the Filipinos eat rice with their fingers, although the wages are much higher here.

We had good visibility to Lamit Bay, but an unfavorable current cut our speed to nine knots. The sun was about to set. There was a wider entrance farther north, but using it would mean arriving after dark. Since there would be no lighted aids to navigation, I would have to delay entrance to the harbor until the following day, so I chose a less safe but quicker route. I pushed and cut off a mile or so by going in a narrow cut between two high, rocky islands with a low "whaleback" or round rock on the port side, barely awash. I could see black clouds well on the starboard bow several miles away. Otherwise the visibility looked favorable for entering this passage, so I continued at full speed. I got the vessel lined up for the center of the opening and the course well checked on the compass. We were just entering this treacherous cut when a gust of wind hit us and the heavy nimbus clouds overhead opened. The rain was so heavy it was impossible to see even halfway to the bow of the vessel. I did not want to proceed, but the water was too deep and the passage too narrow to anchor. It was unsafe to stop and I dared not slow down for fear of losing course to the wind. Realizing the urgent necessity of keeping a steady course, the chief mate took the wheel himself. I put my faith in the magnetic compass. Once beyond this shortcut we would be able to anchor. Now with the bow through the opening, the stern would surely follow. It seemed like an eternity, but soon we were safely inside the narrow passage and the rain let up.

At 5:30, just as it was getting dark, we arrived inside the rock-bound harbor and were safely anchored. In no time the ship was surrounded by lighters loaded high with mahogany lumber destined for San Francisco. Loading started immediately and continued throughout the night. We had gained another half day by trying hard.

Lamit Bay,

July 27
My dearest,
. . . The man in charge of all the harbor work for the lumber company introduced himself to me as Seechts, and I'll be hanged if it wasn't Mr. Albert Seechts' brother.

*Albert Seechts had been an officer aboard the* Ranger *and had been determined to make a sailor out of Dad.*

He is a man about fifty or more and about ten years younger than the man you met. . . . It turned out that the brothers had not seen each other for many years but, having made this connection, I became Frank's friend right off, and he couldn't do enough for me. Imagine, I met a neighbor's brother on the other side of the world, and I never even knew before that Albert Seechts had a brother. . . .

I rode on one of the tugs to the lumber camp twelve miles up a creek. We passed through low, wooded land to the mill situated on higher land at the foot of the mountains. Here I found a well laid-out mill, a little village in itself. There was a canteen, general store, and hospital. The population consisted of twelve white men and about three hundred natives. I had a sick fireman with me and he was treated at the hospital by a native doctor. There was no charge. The doctor took great pleasure in treating the man. I was considered a dignitary and given "the key to the village." The white men were thrilled to talk with me and hear about the rest of the world from which they were cut off except for the visit of a ship now and then. The mill *was* the town, many miles from the nearest village. There were no connecting roads and no vehicles except those used at the mill itself. The only connection to the outside world was by a steamer that brought supplies as it came for lumber once a month. There must have been some form of radio communication but it was not in evidence. There were no white women present. Mill houses, of bungalow type set on stilts, surrounded a small, cleared valley. These houses were connected by high wooden walkways. The white men who ran the mill ate at a dining room in the main plant. Each of these men lived in one of the company houses. In these houses lived the man's family, a Filipino wife and several children. I was shown inside one and was introduced to the family, who spoke only Spanish. I saw no evidence of a school or church.

The men were anxious to buy things from my slop chest, especially oilskin coats and rubber boots. I opened my store up to them. They wanted to return the favor, so when I left the plant they gave me a burlap bag full of bottled beer. I gave it all to the men on my ship. My crew had enjoyed no liberty. Besides, there was nowhere to go, so I thought the beer might help morale and do little harm.

At sea,

July 29

My dearest,

We left Lamit Bay yesterday noon and expect to arrive in Manila at daybreak.

I haven't had any mail from anyone since leaving Manila on the tenth, so we are all looking for word from our sweethearts in the morning.

I have three married officers on this ship. The second mate has a wife and four children, two in high school in Maine. He sends most of his money home and doesn't have enough left to get home himself. Then I have two married engineers, and they send practically every cent they get home. These three officers don't have enough for themselves even to look respectable. All the others are single men and are very careful about their dress, with clean white uniforms every day. Their laundry bills are enormous. This tends to draw a sharp line between the married and single men, more so than on any ship I have been on before. It's not very pleasant for the married officers.

Well, I wonder how you are making out this summer, dear. I do hope it is not too terribly hot.

Are you planning to send Allan to school this fall, or does he have to wait another year? I'd like to have him in school as soon as possible, but of course you know best.

He looks like a little man in this last picture you sent me. I suppose he has had lots of fun this summer in the camp I built. Has it really kept him at home a great deal? I hope a heavy gale of wind did not tear the top off. Wasn't it nice I was home long enough to build it? Heaps of love, Charlie.

We returned to Manila on our way back to San Francisco on the morning of July 20. On the way from Davao, one seaman acted listless and didn't feel like working. I prescribed a dose of salts since his bowels were not working. I had another seaman with an infected belly button. I had had him operated on in Davao and he was healing satisfactorily, but I had a doctor in Manila check him to be sure I could care for him on the return trip to the U.S.

The man to whom I had given the dose of salts wasn't much better, so I decided to have him see a doctor half a mile away. We walked across a field to a big warehouse that housed the agent, the shipping commissioner, and the public health officer. I directed my sailor to the doctor's office while I went upstairs to see the agent. As I was sitting with him, discussing my business, all of a sudden we heard an ambulance clanging below. We looked down from the verandah and saw my seaman being taken away to the hospital in a great rush. He needed emergency surgery for a ruptured appendix. Fortunately nature had walled off the rupture temporarily, but I never again prescribed a dose of salts for a stomachache.

I left the officers' messboy in the hospital in Manila also. He was the one who had always refused prophylactic tubes every time they were offered. He had a bad case of venereal disease.

Manila,

July 30

My dearest,

At 5:00 P.M. we shipped two passengers, an ex-chief engineer who had been left in a hospital out here, and a college professor of English. Both are going to San Francisco with us via Hong Kong. The fare is $221 apiece. The minimum on the passenger boats, second class, is $250. First class is $350. So you see they travel with us, two in a room, because it is cheaper.

Say, dear, don't let me prevent you from getting a car. Buy one tomorrow. No doubt you can rent part of a neighbor's garage. I cannot see where I prevent you from having one. I stay aboard the ship, steer clear of parties, and buying drinks and smokes for others. I do my own laundry and in the last two years have increased my savings deposits by $5 and have had fun doing it so that you might have that car, dear. Can you suggest how I can increase your allotment? I'd be glad to do it so you could have that car you want and that I want you to have. I'm very sorry I cannot plan any better. I still have hopes of your having one yet. I'll build the garage the first opportunity. I love you, dear. Charlie.

We loaded hemp and plywood and on the thirty-first sailed for Hong Kong. Heavy rain squalls continued, so heavy it seemed that the clouds were bursting. On the morning of August 3 we anchored at the eastern entrance to Hong Kong to discharge and load cargo to and from flat-bottomed sailing junks.[2] We witnessed the family institution of junk operation. The whole family lived in the high stern and all looked after the ship and cargo. A little girl no older than ten carried her baby brother strapped to her back so that even she could work with both hands.

On August 4 I searched the ship for contraband and stowaways. I had all the gear tested and checked and saw that all hands were on board and the ship was secured for sea. At 5:30 we sailed for San Francisco. It was fine weather and we were all happy to be homeward bound.

The ship was loaded with empty steel drums, hemp, wood paneling, brown crepe rubber, and furniture from Manila; copra, scrap rubber, raw rubber, and hemp from Zamboanga; hemp and copra from Davao; lumber from Panabutan; more lumber from Lamit Bay; and raw rubber, cinnamon, and tea from Hong Kong. We also carried general cargo from various stops: black woodenware, leather products, rattan furniture, chinaware, rice starch, yellow beans, raw silk, and silk products, along with some decorative brassware.

Due to the failure of the previous master to impose discipline, this ship had had a reputation for sloppiness, and the owners had expected me to correct it. Apparently I was successful because all during the trip, the officers and crew did a marvelous job and were always ready to do their duty. There had been no drinking that interfered with their responsibilities. The chief officer worked admirably, although he must have had a hard time under this "East Coast master." Leaving Hong Kong, he stood his four-to-eight morning and evening watches faithfully, though I could see that he was suffering the aftereffects of his farewell partying.

I planned to return on the shorter or great circle course, taking advantage of the Japanese current and prevailing westerly winds. On the tenth we were off Yokohama and passed through the last set of islands before reaching home. All clear for the U.S.A.!

I finished reading *Philippine Islands* by W. C. Forbes. It had been lent to me by one of the passengers, Dr. Shannon of the University of the Philippines.

I held a complete and thorough search of the vessel for contraband. None was found. I had been told a story about the chief engineer. It seems that on the previous voyage, when he went ashore on arrival at San Francisco, the customs officer had searched him at the gangway and found an empty box in his pocket. "What's this?" he asked.

"Oh, that's nothing. Just an empty box for my boys to play with."

Suspicious, the customs officer invited him to his office at the head of the pier. He sat down casually and said, "Now, Mr. Engineer, have you got any contraband on you?"

The chief replied, "None." The customs officer ordered him to remove his hat. As he did so, green gems fell to the floor. The chief had to pay a fine and his emeralds were confiscated. Such incidents put the owners in bad with customs, so it was prudent for me to be diligent in preventing smuggling by having several thorough searches.

We had been away from the States since the middle of May, over three months. The crew was anxious to get home. Our fresh supplies were no longer worthy of the term. The tomatoes in the salad could hardly hold together and such things irritated the men. I tried to keep up spirits by setting a cheerful example. Finally, at the officers' mess table, the dissatisfaction was expressed at supper time. I asked, "What's the matter? Name one thing I can correct."

The chief engineer spoke up and said, "I have a complaint."

"Let's have it," I said.

"We need more variety. We haven't had ham jamboli for a long time." Ham jamboli was made from leftover breakfast ham and bacon chopped up and mixed with boiled rice. That was the only specific suggestion. I said that personally I could think of a lot more to complain about than that. Then I called the chief steward in and said to him with unsuppressed annoyance. "Have ham jamboli frequently or until it sticks out their ears." That stopped the growling somewhat.

After the crews had made out their purchase manifests to be shown to the customs officers on arrival in the States, I held surprise searches of the ship. I found a few little things, and I saw to it that they were added to the manifests. Once I surprised the crew by having the heads of competing departments perform the searches.

The *Golden Tide* approached the Golden Gate on August 28, 1929. We had been away for three months and three days. It was a trip I had dutifully made to satisfy the needs of American-Hawaiian's management. Now I was ready to go home, both to the *Pennsylvanian* and to the East Coast.

As we pulled into the slip in San Francisco, I was surprised to find Captain Wilson on the dock. He was there to relieve me as master of the *Golden Tide*. I was disturbed. What had I done wrong? Had I been fired? Thoughts about my past performance and my future career raced around my head. I just hoped I wouldn't be ordered back to sea in a hurry before I had a chance to go home.

Once on board, Captain Wilson quickly allayed my fears. He announced that Mr. Plant had made plans for me to travel east by train, have two weeks' vacation at home, and rejoin the *Pennsylvanian* there. Such was the way our company took care of its officers!

In no time I packed my duds, sent a night letter to Dorothy, paid customs duty on the gifts I had purchased in the Orient, and boarded the train for Boston by way of Chicago. Almost five months had passed since I had seen my wife and child, and I could hardly wait for our reunion.

At home on September 2, I found Dorothy and Allan and my youngest sister, Clara. Mother Allan was visiting friends in Nova Scotia. Young

Allan had grown considerably. Dorothy had grown, too. She was a lovely big armful.

It was a relief and a joy to be home again. My two weeks were quickly filled with a round of visits to relatives and neighbors in addition to my seasonal chores and home repairs. I shellacked floors, extended the dining room china closet to the kitchen, and played a lot of cards. Albert came for a visit. Allan, now six, went to school for the first time. The days flew by.

Back aboard the *Penn*, I painted my bedroom and resumed the study of salesmanship as we made the trip to the West Coast.

## Notes to Chapter 9

1. Rhumb line course: method of magnetic course changes that accomplishes the objective of covering a space between two points on a sphere with the least distance traveled.
2. Junk: a Chinese flat-bottomed ship with battened sails and a high poop.

The "Boy Skipper," Captain of the *Pennsylvanian*, 1928

# CHAPTER 10

# SAFETY FIRST

During the 1930s, I continued as master of the *Pennsylvanian* on the inter-coastal route, carrying manufactured goods west and raw materials east. Occasionally, due to lack of business, we had to bypass a regular port of call or we laid up in port for a day or more. Business remained poor throughout the country. In 1931, American-Hawaiian announced a five percent person-nel cut. I tried my best to support my company and save it money by run-ning a safe and efficient ship. I secured licenses to do my own piloting and avoided using tugs whenever I could. I relied instead on my knowledge of how my ship behaved in wind and current, whether deeply laden or riding light. The usual practice among American-Hawaiian captains was to use tugs when sailing to help the ship turn, but I went even further. My turning technique involved the use of a four-and-a-half-inch spring line[1] with a loop end over a capstan[2] on the dock and the other end fastened to the wheel of a steam winch on deck. I had the crew working with me 100 percent, and I was proud of this team effort.

I felt I was lucky to have a job, but my duty to my ship didn't make for close family harmony. I was busy every minute with my responsibilities to the owners, the crew, the agents, and the ship, as well as providing the means for my family to live. My work supported us in the midst of the Depression but at the same time made it difficult for me to be a father.

January 7, 1930, I was at Portland, Oregon, supervising the loading of six hundred tons of paper boxboard. In the afternoon I received a telegram from my sister-in-law, Jean: 'SON BORN NOON BOTH MOTHER AND

CHILD FINE." Our family was now complete in number, but distance and separation made us a fragmented whole.

At home Dorothy was captain, and she carried the responsibility well. Of course, she always wanted more, especially a car. She didn't like having to depend on Jean, who so often drove us around in her friend Alice's car. Dorothy took driving lessons, got her license, and borrowed her sister Margaret's Ford as often as she could. She bought the car for $50 when Margaret realized that paying to keep it in a garage was expensive and inconvenient. She had only been driving it in summer anyway, because of its loose-fitting, portable isinglass side curtains and lack of a heater.

February 5, 1930, when we docked in Brooklyn, I got Albert started in the Navigation School at the Seamen's Church Institute at 25 South Street. That evening I instructed him in navigation by dead reckoning. Arriving in Boston on the thirteenth, I met my son Richard, now five weeks old. He and his mother were doing fine, and Allan seemed to be weathering the competition for time and attention.

In March I received a letter from Albert announcing that he had received his third mate's license. I was proud of him. He had served for three years on my ship starting as an ordinary seaman, then as able-bodied seaman, then as quartermaster. Now he was ready for a job as an officer. Captain Brown of the *Texan* hired him. Brown had told me he hoped to get Albert as an officer on his ship because he knew I had trained him well. Brown himself had sailed under me several years before.

In November, 1930, arriving at San Francisco from Astoria with Captain Norberg piloting, we had clear weather to the harbor, and then dense fog set in. We were near the *Oakland*, a passenger ferry owned by the Southern Pacific Railroad. On approach to the docks, both vessels were blowing the single blast fog signal. When the vessels were in sight of one another, the *Pennsylvanian* continued to blow the one blast. When this occurs, the single blast becomes a passing signal, meaning that we had the right of way. But the *Oakland* failed to stop until it was too late. Though the *Pennsylvanian*'s engine was on full astern, we could not stop her headway soon enough. At 10:35 A.M. we collided with the *Oakland*. The *Penn*'s bow had made a hole in the side of the ferry just behind the starboard side-wheel. I kept the ship coming ahead slowly with our bow still in the hole until we could determine that the ferry wasn't leaking. Meanwhile forty-six passengers boarded the *Penn* over ladders at the bow. How Johnston, my chief officer, got them aboard so quickly I couldn't understand. The ferry made its own berth without difficulty. I anchored until the weather cleared.

While we were at anchor with the ferry passengers still on board, a launch came alongside carrying a newspaper reporter who wanted to come aboard. I refused him permission. The reporter told me, "I'll get you for this." He took some pictures of the ship and persuaded a woman passenger to come down the Jacob's ladder to tell him her story.

The collision had strained the plates and loosened a few of the rivets on our fore peak tank, which was full of water for ballast. Pictures of a small stream leaking from the tank were printed in the newspaper over a caption stating that the *Pennsylvanian* was leaking. This normally describes a vessel taking in water, not water coming out of it high above the water line. One can't always believe what one reads in the papers. There had been four other ship collisions in San Francisco Harbor that same day, all more serious than ours, but it was ours that got all the publicity, partly because passengers had been involved and partly because the public had been campaigning for a bridge to be built across the bay. The Southern Pacific Railroad, whose ferries controlled all traffic across the bay, opposed the bridge proposal.

When the weather cleared, I docked my ship without assistance at our regular berth. Thousands of civilian onlookers were on the dock to meet us. We had to warn them to keep back so as not to get hurt by our lines. Mr. Plant came on board and spent the afternoon investigating the accident. I allowed no one else aboard until Mr. Stow, our assistant operating manager, permitted reporters to come aboard, provided they printed nothing derogatory about me.

According to law, Captain Norberg and I were required to file our written reports in person at the offices of the U.S. Steamboat Inspection Service. The day after the accident, we called on the hull inspector to file our reports. Mr. Stow came with us. The hull inspector was out of the office, so we were directed to report to the boiler inspector instead.

As soon as the boiler inspector saw us, he began to bawl out Captain Norberg. Mr. Stow interrupted his tirade and had us exit as quickly as possible. Apparently, years before, when Captain Norberg had been master of a steam schooner, the boiler inspector had been his chief engineer. Norberg had allegedly stolen a bushel of the chief's clams, beginning a feud between them.

We still had to deliver our reports. So Mr. Plant went with me to present them to the supervising inspector, Captain Turner. This meeting also had strong potential for angry confrontation. Years before, Captain Turner had been a chief mate on American-Hawaiian ships and was sore because he had never made master. Each time an American-Hawaiian affair came before him, he insisted on expressing his displeasure with the company. Mr. Plant, ever the diplomat, and knowing that Turner had applied for retirement, was very cordial and offered to help in getting his request accepted. It worked. Captain Turner was downright gracious and accepted the reports as written. True to his word, Mr. Plant followed through on his promise. Turner was soon retired, a thorn removed from our sides.

The ferry's damage was estimated at $5,000. The damage to the *Penn* was $300. Neither the ferry's hull below the water line nor her side-wheel were damaged. The ferry claim was settled out of court, the accident determined to be unavoidable, with the captain of the ferry getting much of the blame. I was not fined, nor was my license suspended. Nevertheless, my safety consciousness had been sharpened. I double-checked all bulletin boards on the *Penn* to see that all precautionary notices were visible, and I started a "Safety First" letter on its rounds. In my Alexander Hamilton correspondence course, I studied the section on safety engineering, and I faithfully held safety drills, including man overboard. Without warning, I'd throw a life preserver overboard and yell, "Man overboard!" The officers and crew were required to recover the "man" in an integrated team effort. On each occasion a different deck officer was in charge of maneuvering the ship, lowering the boat, and directing the boat crew. When a drill was unsatisfactory, I had them repeat it until they got it right.

In 1931, in New York, I had what turned out to be my last meeting with my mother. I invited her on board for a visit, and together we visited Albert aboard his ship. We toured the Woolworth Tower, the tallest building in the city at the time. At Saks Fifth Avenue I bought her a cloth bouquet for her coat. Then I put her on the train for Irvington where she was to visit our old friends, the Wistrands. We had a pleasant time together, for which I was to be forever grateful.

Then while I was far away, the bad news of 1931 really hit me hard. I was in San Francisco when I received a telegram from my sister Grace saying that Father had died of a cerebral hemorrhage. I notified Dorothy, Albert, Ralph, and the Danners by wire, and sent flowers and money to Grace to help with funeral expenses. Soon afterward I talked to Albert via ship's radio, and he told me that Mother had had another nervous breakdown and had been sent to the hospital in Williamsburg, Virginia.

On May 17 I had a radio message from the owners: "Deeply regret to inform you of your mother's death. . . . Advice received from Grace Ward of Norfolk." Within a month of one another, both my parents had passed on. Father was only fifty-three and Mother fifty-four years of age. In spite of all the hardship my father often put her through, my mother could not live without him.

I was living two very distinct lives three thousand miles apart. My West Coast friends became my alternate family away from home. With them I saw the sights, went to movies, played cards, ate many a dinner, danced, and sang songs. During my Swampscott vacations, maintaining the house and yard kept me busy. Seldom did I get to bed before midnight. Today they would call me a workaholic, but my days at home were limited, and there was much that had to be done.

Dorothy Bamforth with Allan and Dick

One wintry March, I was home long enough to go coasting with Allan and his friends down the hill in front of our house. There wasn't much motor traffic in those days, and, on request, the town put "Caution Coasting" signs up at both ends of the hill. One summer day I rented a dory and took Allen out fishing. We caught enough for supper—three rock cod and twenty yellow perch.

> *Dad tried to make me a man of the sea by rocking the dory enough to ship a little water. I was very frightened but tried desperately not to show it. At one point I grabbed for the gunwale, and somehow my treasured Ingersol wristwatch came off and went straight to the bottom. This overshadowed any memory I might have had that fishing could be fun. When we got home, Dad began to clean the fish in the pantry soapstone sink till Mother told him, "Get that mess out of my sink." He finished the job outdoors.*

On Allan's eighth birthday, March 27, 1931, we held a party for him on board the *Penn* with games and supper. There were twelve children and seven mothers present. I was also coming to enjoy my son Dick, a happy child at fourteen months. I was glad to call him "my boy." Once, when Dick was two, the ship docked in Charlestown at Pier 48, where there was hardly any apron on the dock for a companion way. We had a straight carpenter's ladder stretched to the boat deck. One afternoon my wife arrived with the boys. All three climbed up the long ladder and boarded near one of the lifeboats. Dick pointed to the lifeboat and said, "Mama, Mama, is that Daddy's boat?"

Dorothy came to meet me each time I arrived in New York, and we had a grand time, just the two of us. We did sightseeing, dined in restaurants, and went to the theater. We spent nights in hotels for the most part. Sundays we usually went to one of the fine churches. Some trips Dorothy would leave New York by train or bus and rejoin me once more in Philadelphia. We were lucky to have Mrs. Allan at home to look after the house and the boys. When we were together at home, we frequently entertained friends or went with them to the theater. Neighborhood gatherings became regular events. It was a good life.

Once the boys came down to New York with Dorothy, and we did the aquarium and the Empire State Building. We rode the Fifth Avenue bus and took the boys to Radio City Music Hall. Dorothy and Dick went home on the train, leaving Allan with me to stay aboard for the trip to Philadelphia, where I showed him the town. He then stayed aboard for the trip to Boston.

At sea I kept busy, as always, in my spare time. Nearly every time before making landfall, I worked the stars for a position fix to keep my hand in. I climbed both masts to the trunk to inspect all running and standing rigging. I often took the wheel myself to allow all hands to complete oiling the wooden decks. I was studying cost accounting and corporate finance, in addition to the sections on safety in my correspondence course material.

One day I cleaned four guns and did target practice over the stern with Mr. Smith, a passenger who had been a captain in the Marines during the war. Another day I played shuffleboard with him. Although I had mixed feelings about passengers on freighters, they did provide stimulating diversion, since the role of captain is basically a lonely one.

I also kept busy making furniture. Since the lumber for these projects was rough sawn, I ripped and planed it to size by hand for the exercise. I built a mahogany bureau and a youth chair, and window boxes for Albert's wife, Betty, whom he had married in 1931. I made a French door for the porch and a pair of garage doors. Almost forty years later those doors were still in good shape, whereas the factory-made pair on the second stall had to be replaced, long since having rotted in the joints. I worked on a sickbed tray with folding legs, a shinnying rope and a seesaw, a pair of stilts, and a desk for Allan. I visited a boatyard to study the methods of building small boats with the intention of making a sailboat for my boys.

I used Dorothy's car to transport the furniture I had made from the ship to home, all tied on securely, of course. Dorothy sputtered a lot about abusing the car with such cumbersome loads, and berated me for not paying for trucking, but I couldn't be dissuaded from the practice. I knew how to secure things and always took precautions to protect the car's painted surfaces.

While we were docked at Norfolk one trip, I showed Clara and Chester around the ship. In spite of losing both their parents during the school year, they each had graduated from high school with honors. In Philadelphia I went to see the lawyers about Mother's will. I had been appointed executor and guardian of Chester and Clara. The estate amounted to about $1,000. Because of the nature of my work, I appointed Grace as executrix and guardian in my stead. She was now head of the family in Norfolk and its principal financial support, working every day at the Naval shipyard as she had for years. Alone now without her husband, she ran the home. While raising her two daughters, she had buried both our parents and arranged for our twin brother and sister's college education. I felt blessed to have such a sister.

At the Panama Canal in December 1931, there were eight ships southbound and fourteen northbound, which was encouraging for those depressed times. The last day of 1931, we loaded armor plate to be junked, and I tallied up my financial records. My net profit for the year on my slop chest was $708.13, and my stock had turned over three times. Pretty good! I used most of my profits to buy American-Hawaiian shares. I was also able to deposit $383 in my savings account. Our property taxes at home were less than $200 a year, and I paid no federal income tax at the time because I could claim to have been out of the U.S. for more than half of the year (an exemption long since changed). My Massachusetts state income tax amounted to $18.18. My pay for the year was $4,303.58, darned good in those times.

In 1932 the Great Depression continued, but I was one of the lucky ones. I continued to have steady work. I tried to improve myself through my reading and study, through physical exercise, and by not eating too much.

At the end of June I listened on my radio to the Democratic National Convention in Chicago. It was a lively one and helped me decide how to vote on my absentee ballot.

*Dad did not say in his notes for whom he voted. Unlike Mother, who was strongly prejudiced in her politics, Father made a point of reading and listening to all sides of every issue. As a "loyal American," he supported whichever president was in power.*

On my last trip of 1932, we were to stop at New London on our way from Philadelphia to Boston. I was aching to see my wife and sent a telegram asking her to meet me there. We spent the night together in New London and next afternoon I put her on the train for Boston as I sailed for the same destination. I had a few days at home before sailing once more for Philadelphia and points south.

On December 17 we sailed from New York in a blizzard. Although I was now a qualified pilot, I was extra cautious and took on a Sandy Hook pilot to help get us out through the blinding snow. It was cold, about eleven degrees, and windy. We sailed with the snow pouring down on the ship. It took us three hours to travel the twenty miles out of the harbor. Next day we hosed several feet of snow off the decks. I had a large cardboard box filled with snow and stowed it in the icebox. At the Panama Canal I had the box of snow brought onto the bridge. The canal pilot delighted in pelting the canal employees with snowballs, and they in turn managed to return a few. I then arranged for the box of snow to be sent to the Boys' Club in Balboa.

As 1933 began I was still on the West Coast. In Seattle I took Albert's wife, Betty, and her mother to the Roxy theater one evening. Another time I bought a turkey to take to them. It had been raining for days, and when I arrived I found Betty and her mother in a panic that the house would slide down the saturated banking as a neighbor's had done. I joined them in bailing out the cellar until one in the morning. Fortunately the house did not slide.

June 18, 1933, was a bright sunny day in San Francisco. The ship was idle. After supper I took a long walk with Trixie, my fox terrier, who lived with me on board. Returning, I found four families with children admiring my ship. They had been out for a Sunday drive, and this was one of their stops. (On the West Coast, ships in the Merchant Service were much admired, whereas on the East Coast, the merchant ship docks were not considered a place where nice people should be seen.) With Trixie on her leash,

I stopped to talk with the visitors, who had lots of questions about my ship. Then I showed them some of Trixie's tricks. I had her roll over, then jump over my extended foot, over and back.

Another car drove up with a lone young woman at the wheel. She beckoned to me, and after I had answered a few questions, she said, "Get in." She told me her name and said she was a dental aide. I introduced myself as the skipper of the ship. As though to make me prove it, she asked me to invite her on board. This was really against the rules, but I was challenged and intrigued. *I will see that she doesn't get hurt,* I thought to myself, which was the owner's principal concern in these matters. We spent a few minutes in my quarters, but when I failed to offer her a drink and told her that I was a teetotaler, she started looking in the closets and medicine cabinet, apparently hoping to find liquor. Finding none, she suggested we go for a drive.

*Things are pretty dead around here,* I told myself, *so why not?* Though I knew that riding with a stranger was risky business, I felt equal to the adventure. She drove up a hill and stopped where we could look down over the city. The land sloped gradually down to the river, and with the sun getting low, it was a beautiful sight.

She mentioned that the car needed gasoline, so we drove to a gas station and got a dollar's worth, about five gallons in those days. I was on my guard as usual. I had the habit of always carrying a billfold plus a big change purse, which I kept full of quarters. I paid for the gasoline out of my change purse to avoid showing my bills. Then she asked suggestively, "How far would you like to go?" I made no reply, so she drove me to a lounge. She wanted a drink. After I ordered hers and a ginger ale for myself, I'm sure she must have thought, *What a funny man!* From there we drove to an isolated spot in a park. The sun had set. Trixie was asleep on the back seat. In the dark I cuddled up, our bodies touching, but I managed to keep my hands to myself.

"Are you sick or something?" she asked. "Any normal man would have taken me for a walk in the woods." The next thing I knew she was driving me back to the ship. She stopped two blocks away from the dock. "It's not good for me to get closer. I might be recognized," she said. I didn't understand what she meant. We were there at the curb only a moment or so when, looking in her rearview mirror, she exclaimed, "Here comes a police car! Get out quick and give me some money." Although I felt no reason to fear the police, I jumped out, not wanting her to get in trouble. From the curb, I quickly dumped the remains of my change purse into her hand. The police car followed as she drove off.

*What an adventure,* I said to myself, walking to the ship, *and how smart of me to avoid being cleaned out.* Instinctively I grabbed for my wallet just to be sure, pulled it out, and was relieved to see that all was as it should have been. Only then did it come to me that Trixie was asleep on the back seat of the woman's car.

It was now close to eleven, and my ship would be sailing at six next morning. I thought, *I must get Trixie back tonight or give up ever seeing her again.* I went to a telephone and called the police. I was referred to several different stations, but after an hour it became obvious that the police could not help me. I gave up and went aboard.

Next morning at 5:45 I was on the bridge with the pilot. The seaman was at the wheel, and the engine telegraph was on standby. The officers and men were at their "let go" stations at each end of the ship, and the bos'n was about to hoist the gangway. I looked down on the pier. There at the gate was my beautifully dressed acquaintance approaching the ship with my Trixie in her arms.

I didn't want her to come aboard and delay our sailing. I was embarrassed and hesitated to go down on the dock to get the dog myself. Instead I sent a junior officer. Then I was more ashamed of myself than ever for not expressing my appreciation to the woman in some better way. All I did in my chagrin was to call down to her, "Thank you. Thank you very much." We sailed away with Trixie at my side.

I have had many narrow escapes in my lifetime. This was one of them. I was a married man and didn't write much of this in my diary for obvious reasons. If I were to tell my wife, she would never believe that I had had such control of myself.


My youngest brother, Chester, had decided to follow Albert's lead. He signed up with American-Hawaiian as an ordinary seaman and joined the crew of the *Pennsylvanian.* On one arrival in San Francisco, Captain Kane said to me, "I understand that you have another brother with you."

I responded, "Yes, my third. If you object I will make a change."

Captain Kane replied, "No, you seem to manage well enough with kin aboard. Nobody else seems to be able to."

After he had made two intercoastal trips with me, Chester was transferred to our steamer *Minnesotan,* while the *Penn* was laid up on the West Coast for the month of November 1933. Business throughout the country remained poor. I paid off the crew, and in the evenings that followed I listened to the radio and sewed on my rag rug. Although it was good weather in San Francisco, it got cold on a dead ship. When we finally got power from the dock, electric heaters made it better, but I had little to do.

During the *Penn*'s lay up, I was given various temporary jobs on several ships. For a while I was assigned to the *Missourian,* one of our newest ships, which had a gyro compass. It was the rule to check the gyro course with the magnetic one at half-hour intervals. We had thick fog going up the West Coast until midnight. I stayed on the bridge until the visibility improved and then I turned in. At 2:00 A.M. the officer on watch called me. He had found the ship to be twenty degrees off course because the gyro compass had failed. Knowing nothing about gyros, I had it shut off, set the course on the magnetic compass, and turned in once more. We rounded La Push, picked up the company pilot at Port Angeles, and docked at Seattle. I didn't have the gyro repaired there but left everything as it was to be seen by the owners in San Francisco on arrival. I felt the ship was safe to run on the magnetic compass alone. On December 5 we docked at San Francisco. Mr. Plant had me meet in his office with the gyro company's sales representatives. They, of course, wanted to sell the company more gyros for our ships. They were obviously disappointed that I had found the device superfluous.

On January 29, 1934, after selling fifty shares of American-Hawaiian common stock at nineteen and a half, shares that I had bought previously for eight and a half, I paid off the home mortgage. It was the only loan I ever took out, and I couldn't wait to pay it off. It was a great relief to me to be rid of it. We celebrated by taking the family to the Russian Bear Restaurant on Newbury Street in Boston. I burned the document in a bowl at the table. After dinner we went to a hockey game at the Boston Garden.

*I remember the burning of the mortgage very well. It was bizarre to have a fire at the table. The restaurant was very swank and an unusual occasion all around.*

In the spring of 1934 the West Coast was tied up by a longshoremen's strike. On May 11, docked in San Francisco, we worked cargo with strike-breakers. By the fifteenth many ships were idle, including the *Pennsylvanian.* On May 23, after feeding the strikebreakers and checkers, I took the ship to anchor to await orders. Later that day we went to a covered pier, port side to. No tugs were working, but somehow during the night the strikers towed in a big empty barge and tied up astern of us, intending to block our departure.

It was a tricky and dangerous job to maneuver the ship out around that barge, but I was primed for the challenge. As we proceeded, longshoremen on the pier threw egg-sized stones at the bridge, but we got clear safely and docked temporarily at the pier's end. I picked up our mail and at 10:00 A.M. anchored off Yerba Buena Island (then known as Goat Island). All my crew and officers remained aboard, safely out of the reach of strikers. I worked in the ship's carpenter shop getting materials together for making a bookcase.

By May 25, the strike had the whole port tied up. Of the twenty-five other ships idle and at anchor nearby, five were American-Hawaiian ships manned by officers and skeleton crews. Still at anchor, I held safety drills. The news told of terrible strikes in Minneapolis and Toledo. We had been without contact with shore for five days and of course had no mail. At 9:00 A.M. I ordered a lifeboat lowered and sent it under oars to our company pier to get stores and mail.

On the twenty-eighth there was considerable rioting along the water-front. On June 2 at 10:00 A.M., I steamed close to our company's ship *Golden Hind,* just in from Manila. I called over to my brother Chester, who was one of her quartermasters. Then we docked alongside Pier 26, and I went uptown through the picket lines. I always went alone and made no attempt to avoid the strikers. I'd simply walk right through the lines, which were four and five men deep. I attempted no conversation, just walked straight ahead. I drew my paycheck and $2,000 on the ship's account to pay my men. I ordered stores and had them sent to the ship via parcel post to avoid interference by strikers.

*I asked Dad, "How did you manage to walk through these lines without fear of opposition? Didn't the hair stand up on the back of your neck?" He replied simply, "I was known."*

I kept myself busy working in the carpenter shop on my bookcase. The strike continued, but we were able to get some cargo aboard, a thousand tons a day, from closed freight cars. On the sixth I shifted the ship to Howard's Terminal, Oakland, and discharged forty autos and two hundred tons of other cargo. Police kept the strikers two blocks from the waterfront. Forty-two policemen were on duty at Howard's alone, and the docks were being fenced off with barbed wire.

On June 7 I worked my way up through the picket line and bought candy and tobacco for my men. We were able to load only one hundred tons of cargo and sailed for San Francisco at noon. Docking once more at Pier 26, we took on stores, then shifted to Pier 45.

The longshoremen's strike was spreading to New York and the Great Lakes. On the eighth of June we had to discharge Seattle-bound cargo into freight cars to be forwarded by rail. There was no chance to ship it by water. We stopped work at dusk, since after dark the men would have been exposed to the striker's wrath. I stood by the vessel.

None of my men had been ashore during the strike and all were anxious to go. They noted that I had made it through the picket lines, and since the strikers were now being kept across the street from the piers, all ten decided to leave the ship together. They were led by Mr. Martin, chief engineer, and Paddy Ward, chief mate. They did not try to cross the picket line directly. Instead they walked in a group up toward the Ferry Building hoping to merge with the arriving passengers. Four streetcar lines met the ferries at the foot of Market Street. My men hoped to get through the picket lines there, but the strikers also moved toward the Ferry Building to head them off. As a result, the police riot squad escorted all ten of them back to the ship, and the police announced that they would no longer offer protection to any ship's crews. Thwarted in their attempt at freedom, my men stayed safely on board.

One day I made a trip in a boat to our *Golden Hind* and paid a visit to her captain and Chester. That afternoon I went uptown through the picket lines on errands. I got $2,000 cash uptown, walked back through the lines, and was able to pay my crew in full to date.

On June 15 women pickets had to be dispersed several times by police for unruly behavior. Strikers were weary, and J. P. Ryan, president of the Longshoremen's Union, at last promised them they all would be back at work the first of the week. The longshoremen in Los Angeles voted to return to work, but all those up north voted to continue the strike. On the eighteenth we waited until noon for longshoremen to return to work. None showed up, so we resumed loading with nonunion people. The passenger ship *Mariposa* arrived nearby and all three hundred in the crew walked off to join the strikers. Mr. Plant met the union representatives at Mayor Rossi's office but, as there was no progress in settling the issues, Mr. Plant walked out of the negotiations.

On the nineteenth we sailed for Norfolk with nearly a full load. After such a trying time on the West Coast, it was a welcome relief to get home to Swampscott for my vacation and the inevitable household chores. I enjoyed painting the garage.

July 28 I went to Boston to pay off a disgruntled crewman who wanted to leave the ship. In the afternoon I went swimming with the boys, and in the evening we all went to the Paramount Theater in Lynn to see William Powell and Myrna Loy in *The Thin Man*. We took Allan to Eastham on Cape Cod to spend a couple of weeks of his summer vacation with the Johnson family. I sailed once more from Boston on August 4. Sailing past Eastham, I tried to attract my boy's attention by blowing the whistle.

*I didn't notice. I was probably watching Mrs. Johnson fry up an eel that her husband had caught.*

August 19, off the coast of California, I held a surprise man overboard drill. The buoy was recovered in fourteen minutes, a satisfactory rescue.

Next day fog set in at midnight. We were going up the Santa Barbara channel, which is only a few miles wide. I was walking the bridge about midnight. Mr. McPhee was the officer on duty. At twenty minutes after midnight, he noticed that the sailor at the wheel was either steering a very steady course or no course at all. He seemed not to be moving the wheel in the slightest. McPhee took a look at the compass and saw that the ship was ninety degrees from the intended course, headed full speed for the mountainous shore. McPhee and I both shoved the helmsman aside, swung the wheel hard over, and kept her swinging to the right for a full 180-degree turn. We steamed away from the shore until we figured we had gone about a mile. We then stopped her to get a bearing by radio direction finder off Point Conception. Checking the depth, we concluded that we were only one mile offshore. We must have been very close to the beach when we had grabbed the wheel. It was another of my narrow escapes from disaster, probably the narrowest until then. The wheelman had been stupid with drink.

On September 8, 1934, we learned that the S.S. *Morro Castle* had burned just off the New Jersey coast, with two hundred lives lost. The *Morro Castle* was a four-year-old deluxe passenger ship in the New York to Havana run, considered state of the art for the time. Fire of undetermined origin spread rapidly through the ship. Passengers were unable to reach the decks and the chief officer in charge delayed the sending of an SOS for half an hour. The captain had died just seven hours before the fire was discovered at about 3:00 A.M. on the very morning the ship was due to arrive back in New York. It was, at the time, America's most scandalous sea disaster. As a result, many reforms concerning safety and equipment and procedures were made throughout the industry.

In January, 1935, headed for the West Coast, we heard by radio that the Teamsters Union had joined the longshoremen on strike in New York. January 30 we arrived in Los Angeles. There were no men available to discharge our cargo. February 6 the union forced crews to join the union under threat of bodily harm.

On February 11 I gave Trixie to the night watchman. She had been a good companion and had adapted to shipboard life as well as could be expected, but at sea she got too fat and her toenails grew much faster than wooden decks could wear them down. I had to trim them, and once I had made her bleed before I got hold of some special trimmers. She had to have a box, cat-like, for her bathroom duty, which she didn't like either. Though we loved each other, she and the watchman were good friends, and I decided it was better for her to have a shore existence.

On the fourteenth we docked at San Francisco once more. I talked on the phone to Rolph Folsom. His wife had been hospitalized for an operation so I asked him to bring Rolph Junior, who was eleven, to the ship for the weekend. Next day we saw *The Little Minister* with Kate Hepburn. On the sixteenth he and I went for a long hike that took us onto Carguenons Strait Bridge. At four we sailed for Oakland. Young Rolph wrote to his mother and we played catch together on board. At noon we sailed for Alameda, where we took the ferry to San Francisco, then a Johnson speedboat to the aircraft carrier *Saratoga*, which was at anchor in the bay. At five we were back at San Francisco, where I delivered the lad to his father. I took the ferry back to Alameda to rejoin my ship.

On February 18 the longshoremen refused to load. Ten days later we were finally on our way and a whole northwest gale and heavy seas engulfed us. We were running before the sea. I was eating my breakfast in the saloon when Mr. Dearborn, my chief mate, came in. As he sat down he said, "It's real rough out there."

"It could be worse," I said. I had no more than uttered those words when a big sea hit the portside amidships. Instantly we were waist deep in water. The sea bent the side of the steel house and drove in the portside light and the heavy door to the saloon. It lifted the boat deck, damaged number two port lifeboat, and shifted the deck load of lumber. Breakfast was halted and all hands turned to, securing the ship. Luckily the only injury was to one messman, who suffered a sprained ankle.

March 1, with the sea moderating, we resumed course and speed. We were busy for the next few days making temporary repairs. The stewards had wet stores, linen, cushions, and bedding to take care of. Engineers had to contend with water in the fuel and in the electric lines. The chief mate had a demolished lifeboat to work on, along with shifted deck cargo and broken ports. I helped remove the salt from my quarters, which also had been flooded. With work well underway, I resumed my studies and worked on a knot board for Allan.

*I took the knot board to a Sea Scouts meeting in Swampscott after Dad brought the finished product home. It was very grand. Arranged on a varnished mahogany board with beveled edges, it had sixty-eight knots symmetrically arranged. The knots were mostly made from small-diameter cotton line.*

On March 13 in Norfolk, my sister Grace and Captain Bill Corrao called on me. Bill's title came from his work in the rail yards where he oversaw the makeup of trains. He was a widower with two daughters who were older than Grace's girls, but they were all close friends. As a good neighbor, Bill had helped Grace through the hardest times, as when our parents died. It was a sure thing that they would marry, but they had to wait until a divorce was granted from Grace's husband, who had been institutionalized since early in their marriage. She and Captain Bill later traveled to Reno for the decree and were married there on December 13, 1935.

At Port Richmond, Pennsylvania, we loaded eight pieces of structural steel for the Golden Gate Bridge, then under construction. These pieces weighed from twenty-two to fifty-six tons apiece. At the Ford plant we loaded sixty-five cars destined for Portland, Oregon. Then we shifted the ship to Pier 48, where we were unable to get men to load during the night, so we were held over.

In Portland on April 29, two of our oilers shut off the steam and called a strike, but union patrolmen (the rank and file's delegates) found no cause for a strike and sent the men back to work. However, since there were no long-shoremen to load, we sailed for Astoria for lumber.

I received ballots for the officers to vote either for the company's proposal or for the Masters, Mates, and Pilots' Union to represent our interests.

On May 8 the crew tried several times to force nonunion men off the ship by demanding that I pay them off. They threatened to strike if I failed to do so, as the crew had done on our *Golden Peak*. Finally three union men claimed that they had been hurt and left the vessel. In this way they collected their pay.

In June I wrote a long letter to our San Francisco office regarding the stewards' department functions. It had been the custom for years for the stewards to bring coffee to the bridge at six in the morning. They declared they would discontinue the practice since it was not written in their contract. With each new contract, the unions gained additional concessions. During the morning of July 13, 1935, I discussed this and other matters with the Stewards Union delegate from shore. I observed that the ship's personnel had lost their spirit and seemed less happy now that they were spending all their energies figuring out how to do the least amount of work.

Once that summer as I sailed from Boston, I watched the excursion steamer *Dorothy Bradford* as she sailed for Provincetown. Among the passengers was my son Allan and a friend on a holiday. I steamed close by and gave three blasts on the whistle.

> *This time I saw, heard, and was very excited. I had a hard time, however, making my companion believe it was really my dad's ship saluting us.*

In September, my son Dick entered the first grade. Allan was now in junior high school.

Labor conditions continued to trouble us throughout that fall. On the morning of December 5 we were at Pier 26, San Francisco. None of my crew would go on the pier to take lines, so I had the ship lay there. Finally at midnight two men volunteered. They went down and tied up the ship, and we all turned in. Otherwise we would have been up all night keeping the ship positioned until linesmen arrived at seven in the morning. Apparently my men wished to go ashore.

On the morning of December 29 my crew threatened to strike because our fresh stores were not to their liking, but I stood pat and they dropped their threat. I found out that Able Seaman Taylor was the instigator. Next day the crew refused to sail as they had ten minutes more for their noon hour. The officers and quartermasters handled the lines, and we sailed in spite of them. On January 1, 1936, I gave a little lecture to Taylor when he came to my slop chest to buy cigarettes. I said to him, "So, you are the one who made the trouble in L.A." I warned him that to disobey like that again could bring him a four-day fine.

On January 24 in Philadelphia, a Seamen's Union patrolman from shore tried me before the crew. They claimed that I had discriminated against one seaman by making him stand a watch that I had not required of another, that I had sent men over the side during man overboard drills, and that I had refused to sell cigarettes. I volunteered to stand trial and was able to clear myself of all charges.

On the twenty-sixth I got home to Swampscott in time for supper, after which Dot, the boys, and I went to the movies and saw *Mutiny on the Bounty*, based on the novel by Nordhoff and Hall.

Having told Allan to inform his friend Ted Husler, the Ford dealer in Lynn, that I was ready to buy a car, I talked with Husler next day on price and particulars. Then I went to town to clear the ship with the local inspectors. In the evening we contracted to buy a new four-door, standard 1936 Ford V-8 sedan for $699. The next morning I made the old car ready to turn in. I was allowed $85 for the 1930 Model A roadster that Dorothy had bought from Margaret. It had not been much fun to drive in cold or rainy weather, since the side curtains, windshield, and floorboards leaked rain and air. The new car had roll-up windows and a hot air heater!

I cleaned the in-ground garbage can, installed a new light switch in the front hall, adjusted two doors so they would close properly, and cleaned the kitchen sink drain and the boiler firebox. Then I drained the boiler, cleaned the gauge glasses, put my tools away, and sailed for Philadelphia.

There had been an unusually high number of maritime accidents in recent years, and American ships had been accused of not taking proper precautions when performing safety drills. To make sure we were prepared in event of an emergency, I held a surprise man overboard drill. Seamen and quartermasters refused to man the boat. I called on each man individually to give his reason. They thought the drill was unnecessary and believed they did not have to participate. I did not press the issue but made all entries in the official log book. During the drill, Mr. Harwell, third officer, was in charge of the boat. Mr. McPhee, second officer, gave the orders for the quartermasters and seamen to man number four boat. None obeyed. Chief Mate Butman charged each man individually. I took their statements, then asked the men to volunteer. All refused. Mr. McNeil, quartermaster, was at the wheel. When asked if he would volunteer, he said, "I am in a tight spot."

I entered the case in the log book with a report to the owners and the U.S. Local Inspectors of Steam Vessels. I made no charge in the log book against any of the men. The purpose of man overboard drill was to enable the effective rescue of a man who could be one of their own. Was I wrong and everyone else right? By taking their statements individually and documenting the incident carefully, I could take the issue up with the legal department. I opted to do this rather than force the issue with the men. Government authorities were much in sympathy with the unions at that time.

In reviewing the logs, I found that I had held eleven boat drills during the previous seventy-five days. The law required one every seven days. This was proof that I had not overplayed my role.

It later developed that the crew's refusal was a union project to check the master's authority. When I was paying him off, Mr. McNeil, who had been on the ship a long time, told me that the union was forcing him off the ship for being a good company man. I asked him what he thought of the crew's refusal to take part in the boat drill. He told me that the men had orders from the Seamen's Union to refuse to man the boat. I asked him if he would go with me and tell that to the U.S. Local Inspector. He agreed and did just that. After we told McNeil's story, I decided not to press mutiny charges.

Later Chief Mate Butman reported to me that the crew had been instructed by their patrolman to refuse to store cargo or to use the steam washing machine. In addition an ordinary seaman had refused to go into the chain locker. I took this up with Captain Kane. He instructed me to make them do as I ordered. I also took this up with Mr. Brown, who dealt directly with the union patrolmen. He ordered Patrolman Stewart to instruct his men properly.

On the way to Los Angeles, the crew complained that no butter was being left out for night lunches. I made sure that the steward left out both butter and jam. There was no need to have trouble over such an insignificant item.

West of Cape San Antonio, Cuba, I again held safety drills, this time changing the regular officer rotation for these drills. This caught the men by surprise, and they failed to respond. A good lesson.

Late in April, 1936, the stewards' department threatened to walk off because I had fined one of their men for refusing duty. I stuck to it and explained that final settlement would be made before the U.S. Shipping Commission in San Francisco. They went back to work.

In San Francisco on May 12, I had a conference about labor relations with Mr. Brown, Mr. McPherson, and Captains Gleason and Kane. Next day I went to the U.S. Shipping Commission and canceled the day's fine against my recalcitrant steward. He and the rest of the stewards' department had redeemed themselves.

I received a letter from the office of the operating manager.

Dear Captain Bamforth:
Acknowledging your letter of May 28, I am glad that you are taking an absolutely definite stand in refusing to allow the union men to get away with any violations of their Agreement. For the security of all of the men on the ships, including the officers, it is absolutely essential that no violations be permitted.

As you probably have heard, the *Iowan* was tied up on the Sound for fifteen days by a strike of the union in an endeavor to force the Filipinos off. The ship finally sailed with the Filipino crew intact.

The *Hawaiian* lost a day eastbound at San Pedro over a similar demand, but she also sailed with no concession made by us.

I simply want to repeat: Do not permit any violations of the Agreement to occur.
With best regards, I am,

Yours faithfully,
T. G. Plant
Vice President

## Notes to Chapter 10

1. Spring line: a line leading from the forward part of a vessel aft to the pier, used particularly to aid in maneuvering a vessel around a dock.
2. Capstan: a steam-powered rotating drum used to haul in a line.

## CHAPTER 11

# PARENTING ROUND TRIP

On July 9, 1936, Allan, then thirteen years old, went to sea with me for one round trip from Boston during his summer vacation from school. It was hot and sultry. Allan rigged an antenna for his radio.

We docked on the Delaware River on the tenth. It was a record hot day, 104 degrees. On the eleventh I left Allan on board while I went to town on business.

> *There was a nauseating stench from the Delaware River. The gasses were so strong that the white paint on the ship turned various colors. I remember gasping for air as midday approached. Sewage, including my first view of used condoms, was floating on the surface. Three boys were diving into this mess from a rotting wooden vessel. As I watched the men loading, one of them vomited into the hold, and I felt a bit sick myself.*

In town I bought a kayak kit and paddles. Next day in Bayonne, New Jersey, it was fortunately a bit cooler, and in the evening Allan and I played Monopoly with the officers. Allan wrote to his mother on my typewriter. Then he signed on officially as a member of the crew at the rate of one cent a month. Anyone going to sea had to be either a passenger or part of the crew.

July 16 Allan went about the decks, getting acquainted. I was moved to keep him studying. He was not an enthusiastic student, and I felt it my duty to help him. He was a poor speller, even worse than I. I provided him with my dictionary and almanac for reference and gave him a list of words and questions to look up. In the evenings after doing his lessons, he and I took turns reading aloud from his favorite book, *Arctic Adventures*, by Peter Freuchen.

Allan started to make a birdhouse while we passed through the Spanish Main. Later I showed him how to make rope knots. In the Caribbean, he steered for three quarters of an hour.

> *Steering the ship was fun for me, but before I could get the hang of it by waiting for the ship to respond to the wheel, I overcorrected. The chief engineer noted the corkscrew wake that I produced and complained to the bridge.*

On July 21 I was up early to work stars and make landfall. The next day we anchored at Cristobal. The agent brought our mail, including several letters for Allan.

During our passage through the Canal, I washed, starched, and ironed clothes for both of us. We met our company's ships close aboard and saluted as usual with three blasts of the whistle and dipping of the flag.

> *I was thrilled with the sights while passing through the Panama Canal. I watched intently as the water and ship rose and fell in the locks. I was crazy about vehicles with wheels, and the most fascinating ones at the Canal were the mechanical donkeys that dragged the ship from lock to lock. Each one had a huge General Electric logo on the side. When we were in Gatun Lake, we saw speedboats in the distance. I took pictures with my Kodak box camera. Several are of the deep channels cut through the high jungle, and there are two of aircraft overhead.*

Afternoons Allan went aft with Quartermaster McCray to learn knot tying. Evenings he and I read aloud to each other. After supper we often watched the schools of porpoise playing about the bow. Allan really enjoyed that, and I felt wonderful being there so close to him. Almost every evening we played ringtoss, and he practiced knot tying. He was pleased as could be when he finally mastered the bowline. He got so he could tie one quicker than the eye could follow, or so he thought.

We also argued. He had never before been in conversation with me alone for any meaningful length of time. Some things I said seemed out of place to him. He was particularly sensitive if my views varied from his mother's, and he would assert himself in a way I had never witnessed before. He was growing up. Sometimes the discussion got really heated. It was bad enough to be contradicted by my wife at home, but I was taken aback when challenged on my ship where I was in full command. In spite of this, we were having a good time with each other, although he hated the rigidity of the written schedule I provided him for daily study.

We worked well together on the kayak, and Allan looked forward to each step in its construction. He liked working on the kayak better than studying, but I persisted. We read about the Hebrews, the Phoenicians—the first seamen to trade—and the introduction of the alphabet to Europe. Toward the end of these sessions, I could tell his concentration, weak at best, had vanished, so we read or reread a chapter in *Arctic Adventures*, to close the study sessions.

On July 31 we fired the Lyle gun.[1]

> *The firing of the Lyle gun proved to be a rather dangerous exercise because the chief engineer put too much gunpowder in the old muzzle loader. The gun was tied down to the roof of the linen house. I was to pull the lanyard attached to the cap, which was meant to ignite the gunpowder. I stood behind a railing to port of the gun. I pulled. Not hard enough. I gave it a good yank. This time the cap, a dud, simply broke. It was replaced. With the new cap in place, I gave the lanyard a smart jerk and all hell broke loose. The little overcharged cannon kicked back with such force that it leapt from its perch, breaking its tethers. This considerable mass of iron flew over the rail, just missing Mr. McPhee, who was standing in front of me. It would have gone right through lifeboat number two had not a railing stopped it. The railing was badly bent out of shape. The projectile with line attached was long gone, probably well over the horizon, and the line, whose end had been spliced to a large octagonal box, was nowhere to be seen. There was not so much as a strand of hemp left in the box.*
>
> *This was an exciting experience for me. I believe that Dad and others present were a bit shaken also but tried hard not to show it. While putting the gun and other equipment back in place, Chief Engineer Martin asked me to get some "red oil for the port light." I felt I had become a real participant in the operation of the ship and was anxious to please on my assignment. I went to the engine room and asked the engineer on duty for some red oil for the port light. With a straight face, he said he had none. I sought out the first assistant engineer. He was resting in his room, eating a banana from a large bunch hanging overhead. He told me that he had given some red oil to the carpenter, who was building an awning at the stern of the vessel. The carpenter leaned over the edge of the roof he was building. In response to my query, he kindly allowed, "I used the last of it yesterday." That seemed pretty final, and I reported this information to Mr. Martin, who reluctantly accepted my report.*
>
> *Two days later I was standing in the doorway of a young assistant engineer's room, passing the time of day. He made reference to my quest for red oil, and it was only then that I realized that I had been had. I made out as though I had known all along. Later I mentioned the incident to Dad, who confessed that it had been his idea to send me on that wild goose chase. Then he told me about sending other novices for buckets of steam, left-handed monkey wrenches, and the like. My initiation was well underway.*

Allan and I read in *Reader's Digest* about the rise and fall of Greece. August 1 we arrived and docked at Wilmington, California. At dawn we put the kayak in the water and paddled across the bay and back before breakfast. Aunt Grace and Uncle John came from San Diego for a visit. At noon Allan and I took them to dinner at the yacht club. In the evening, after the Danners had left for home, Ralph called on us, and we had ice cream.

After breakfast on Sunday, August 2, Allan and I paddled the kayak to Long Beach and back, a six-mile trip. Later Ralph and his daughter, Georgeanne, called for us and we had dinner at their home. Then they drove us through Los Angeles and Hollywood. We stopped at a movie studio for a brief tour.

*Dad and I enjoyed this tour thoroughly. In those days before television, movies were big in most people's lives. We wanted to know all about the stars and about how movies were made.*

In San Francisco Allan and I took a bus tour of the city. We visited the Ferry Building and saw the big relief map of California and samples of wire used in the building of the Golden Gate Bridge.

On August 3 we shifted the ship to Oakland. Off Yerba Buena Island, dense fog set in and caused us some delay, but at 8:00 A.M. we docked at Alameda to discharge oil and potash.

At two in the afternoon, using a car borrowed from the ship's runner, Mr. McPhee drove Allan and me to Alameda Airport where we saw the *China Clipper* take off and a Russian plane arrive. We also saw the *Philippine Clipper* in the hangar. Following a visit to the Alameda bathing pool, we went to bed early after a full day.

August 6 we sailed again for San Francisco. With dense fog all the way, I didn't go to sleep until morning and then slept until two in the afternoon. Later I helped Allan with his spelling. After supper I read to Allan from a book about the founding of Rome by Romulus, and the next day Allan read aloud about early religions.

In the days that followed we passed many commercial salmon fishermen trawling. At the mouth of the Columbia River, we saw at close hand a seine fishermen hoisting his net aboard. In Tacoma we bought fishing gear, and by 10:00 A.M. Allan and I were out in the kayak, trolling. We caught four nice salmon trout for supper and afterwards went out in the kayak once more. We caught two more salmon and were back on board by three as the ship was ready to sail for Bellingham. I was sunburned on my face and arms and very tired. I had done nearly all the heavy paddling. Allan had kept protected with a brimmed hat and long sleeves.

Labor news was that the Dollar Line ship, *President Hayes*, was strike-bound by her crew in Singapore because her master had demoted an oiler to firemen.

In Bellingham, Allan and I went through a lumber mill on a guided tour. Then we shopped uptown and got haircuts and milkshakes. In the afternoon we went aboard a five-masted schooner, which was loading lumber nearby.

Mr. Walter Dyke was an official of the Seattle Towboat Company. Ever the perfect gentleman, he called on me nearly every trip and always wanted to do something for me. Of course, he was selling towboat services. Though he knew about my techniques to avoid using tugs, he never stopped offering me favors. On this trip I broke my rule of refusing them and let him drive Allan around Seattle and take him to lunch. Mr. Dyke took him to see the Washington University grounds, Lake Washington, and Mount Baker Park, and then returned him to the ship. At three that afternoon, Albert called for Allan and me to join Betty at their house for dinner. Afterwards we saw *Charlie Chan at the Horse Races.* The next day, Albert called for Allan while I went to town on business.

We sailed for San Francisco on the fourteenth. Allan wrote letters and postcards. On the fifteenth we had safety drills, and in the evening I read to Allan about the Crusades.

In San Francisco I bought shoes and clothing wholesale for the slop chest. That evening the whole crew walked off on strike because Mr. Martin had fired the deck engineer, Mr. O'Neill. When a man "signs on" or "signs the articles," he and the company contract to live up to the conditions stated but, by mid-1936, crews often thought it was their right to break the agreement. When in an American port, it was my habit to pay the men off whenever they requested it, in spite of the contract. This meant that we were continually trying to fill vacancies and often ran shorthanded. It had been a pleasure for me to go to sea when the law was complied with and esprit de corps existed. Alas, no more.

On the eighteenth we had no crew, only officers and engineers. The strike was arbitrated, and we agreed to rehire the full crew. They were ordered aboard at 5:00 P.M. but very few returned. With no dinner being served, Allan and I went to town for supper and a double feature movie.

We loaded eight hundred tons of perilla oil[2] in bulk at San Pablo. I read to Allan about the Renaissance. On the afternoon of the twentieth, Allan and I walked to town.

Although we had enough stewards' department personnel to feed us, the firing of boilers, handling of lines, steering, and other essential work was being done by officers and engineers. It was a wonder we could get any officers willing to serve when crews had become so belligerent and drunk with union power. It was becoming a miserable business with such delays and financial loss for the owners.

Friday, August 23, at 10:00 A.M., I paid off the whole crew and tried to sign on a new one. Only the officers would sign. the crew would not sign until requested changes in their quarters were completed.

Finally, at 3:00 P.M., the crew signed the articles, but it was too late to sail. I conferred with Mr. Plant and Captain Rylander, the shipping commissioner. After supper Allan and I went to the Golden Gate Theater and saw *Sing, Baby, Sing.*

We left San Francisco for Los Angeles the next day, short one fireman. From Los Angeles, Captain Kelton drove Allan and me to Long Beach, where we enjoyed a tour through the ice and cold storage plant where my former chief engineer was in charge. Allan was fascinated with the ice-making machinery and the huge number of whole frozen steers hanging on hooks. That was Allan's last West Coast attraction before we sailed for New York.

On our return trip I insisted that Allan do his studying and gave him most of my day. I read to him the story of England in his scout book. He said for the first time since leaving home that he would like to get back, "even if I have to go to school." I read to him about Germany, helped him get ready for school, and together we made an instructional rope for teaching knots to his scout troop.

I corrected Allan's papers and in the evening read to him about Italy. We made a lamp base of a lasso rope together and read aloud to one another about the Scandinavian countries.

A good trouble-shooter, Allan repaired a short circuit in my radio antenna lead, resulting in much better reception. I showed him how to make napkin rings by fashioning Turk's-heads from rope. We painted his kayak with two coats of aluminum paint, and I played Canfield with him. I read to him about the country of Japan, and together we made a wooden cradle to be used for carrying the kayak home on top of the car.

Back at the Canal for our return trip across the Isthmus, I arranged with the ship's agent to take Allan ashore at the Pacific end, show him things of interest, put him on the train for Cristobal, and return him to the ship at the Atlantic end by pilot boat.

*I enjoyed this trip very much—so many banana trees, and the excitement of being driven around Old Panama City along LEFThand bends on the LEFThand side of the road in an American car with LEFThand drive.*

Allan and I studied books on electricity and diesel engines. One evening he and I figured the cost of operating the Ford for a year at six cents a mile.

*One warm afternoon while steaming through the hot Caribbean, Dad and I rested on our beds, stripped to our underwear. The door from his office was hooked open at the side of his bed so that from my bunk opposite, I could see him only from the waist down. He was reading a magazine and came upon an advertisement featuring the image of a comely woman. He held the magazine forward so that I could see the picture and asked, "Doesn't she look like Mother?" I didn't think so but said, "I guess so, a little." He withdrew the magazine from my view and apparently continued to study it, then he deliberately revealed his erect member. He made no comment. I was impressed or, perhaps, disturbed. I certainly remember the incident vividly. It added confusion to the great anxiety I was experiencing going through puberty. I suppose this was another lesson Dad felt I should learn. It was the closest thing to sex education that I can remember my father ever giving me.*

In the Caribbean we experimented with a wooden target for shooting over the stern. The first one carried away, but with a change in design of the vanes, the second one held. The officers, Allan, and I had target practice. Allan had his first experience with handguns.

*Following World War I, Mother had taken on the popular role of pacifist. As a result I was not allowed even to point a finger, to say nothing of pointing a stick or having a toy gun to play with. It was a new and exciting experience for me to hold a real gun. I remember being handed a .45. It dropped to the deck, my hand still clutching it. I had no idea it would be so heavy.*

Two afternoons, Allan and Quartermaster McCray signaled to me on the bridge from aft using semaphore. Evenings I read to him about romantic Spain.

One day we received a radio message transmitted in Morse code from the master of one of our ships. I had Allan decode it: "Captain Bamforth, S.S. *Pennsylvanian.* Fine weather since leaving New York. Have full cargo. Left about 1,000 tons on the dock. Best Regards, Gaidsick."

*Gaidsick had sailed with Dad and had soon become master of his own vessel. There was great mutual respect between the two men.*

Allan and I discussed the ships in my marine scrapbook, and we compared the French *Normandy* with the British *Queen Mary.* He was intrigued by the great transatlantic liners.

I was, of course, busy running the ship but spent as much time as possible with my son. It was a wonderful feeling to be so close to him and be involved in his education. One morning Allan wrote a letter to one of his schoolteachers on the typewriter. Then we climbed the foremast and, from the crosstrees, took pictures of the ship below.

*Dad was right behind me, and I was able to continue up, rung by rung, confident that I was safe. The ship below seemed very small. It felt as if I were on a pin in a cork stopper, bobbing around in the ocean.*

September 9, a fine calm day, Allan wrote about the trip to his Aunt Jean, who was to be his English teacher. After supper he and I were shown about the ship's engine room by Mr. Davitt, the engineer on duty.

Approaching New York, I advanced the crew money that I had secured at the Canal so that they could leave the ship immediately. I wired the owners and Allan's mother regarding our ETA.

With my permission the quartermasters gave Allan a formal initiation and presented him with a diploma.

*Quartermaster McCray, a fine fellow, worked hard to make the proceeding a fun occasion. He must have spent hours on the diploma, my favorite souvenir of the trip. He and the other quartermasters "initiated" me with things like having me remove my shirt in order to receive a "branding" on the back. (It was really ice shavings.) I tried to be very much in control and managed to refrain from reacting. I was, I'm sure, a disappointment to them. I wish I had known how to be one of them. Alas, I was only thirteen, with little prior experience in the company of males. Be that as it may, I treasure my diploma, which is framed and hangs even now in my shop. It is topped by a sketch of a sailor and a girl on a desert island. The sailor is speaking to her. She says, "No." Then it reads:*

*This is to certify that the culprit in the above photo, christened as C. Allan Bamforth, known among seamen as KAYAK, today, SEPT. 11, 1936, graduates from this ship with honors upon completing a round trip which included the ports: BOSTON-PHILADELPHIA-NEW YORK-PANAMA-LOS ANGELES-SAN FRANCISCO and SEATTLE. He has proven to us that he can spit seven feet into a northwest gale, take his liquor STANDING UP, leave his women where he finds them, and swear like a SEA DOG.*

WITNESSES
  C. N. Bamforth, Master
  N. G. Butman, Mate
  H. R. McPhee, 2nd Mate
  J. L. Harwell, 3rd Mate
  W. R. Millington, Junior 3rd Mate
  Chas. B. Davis, Quartermaster
  Charles McCray, Quartermaster
  Robert Miller, Quartermaster
  Andrew Malvio, Carpenter
  Thomas Morris, Bos'n

*Alfred R. Martin, Chief Engineer*
*Edward S. Rosenbluett, 1st asst. Engineer*
*L. C. Perkins, Radio Operator*
*Edward Carrol, Steward*
*F. M. Peterson, Fireman Del.*
*J. G. S. Powell, I.S.I. Del.*
*James N. Davitt, 2nd asst.*

*Each of the signatories played a part in the voyage. All of these men impressed me as having good spirit and were at ease under my father's rule.*

On September 11, 1936, we docked at Brooklyn at seven in the morning and I called Dorothy, who was at the Bristol Hotel. I was supposed to go on vacation. The plan was for me to drive home with my family, but due to unsettled labor conditions, the marine super asked me to stay close by the ship for a while. The labor problems were settled by three that afternoon, and I went home by train. I arrived there a half-hour before Dorothy and Allan drove in.

September 21 we voted in the national presidential primaries. In the evening, I went with Allan to a Boy Scout meeting, where we told the group about our trip. During the rest of my vacation, I painted Dick's room, installed the birdhouse Allan had made aboard ship, and cut off two pine trees near the garage and fixed a plank between them, about twelve feet high, to support two swings and a trapeze.

*We had the nicest playground in the neighborhood. Our friends used it as much as Dick and I, and Dad kept the equipment in first-class order for use by the next generation of children on the hill. He loved to have them come to play and talk to "Skipper."*

## Notes to Chapter 11

1. Lyle gun: a lifesaving device designed to shoot a projectile with a line attached.
2. Perilla oil: oil used in the manufacture of paint, varnish, and artificial leather.

# CHAPTER 12

# STRIKEBOUND

September 28, 1936, on board the *Pennsylvanian*, I listened to campaign speeches by Knox, Roosevelt, Alf Landon, Al Smith, and Norman Thomas.

> *Though a stalwart Republican, Dad always listened to both sides and kept up with the candidates' positions. He could discuss the pros and cons rationally. Mother, on the other hand, was a rabid partisan, and, in abject frustration, would demand, "How could you possibly say anything good about that bum Roosevelt?"*

An oiler had shipped on in New York at the last minute without signing the articles, so he signed on before the U.S. Customs officer at the Canal. After signing, he wanted to go ashore, claiming he was suffering from venereal disease. I had him examined by the boarding doctor, who found no such evidence. Then the oiler said, "I refuse to work if you keep me on board," so I let him go ashore, and we sailed shorthanded. As the saying goes, "What a way to run a railroad!" Short one oiler, the chief engineer managed by breaking in a wiper.

We heard by radio that our *Ohioan* was stranded in dense fog on Point Lobos, at the entrance to San Francisco Bay. The crew were rescued by breeches buoy[1] and hauled ashore from high ground, one at a time, as the ship began to break up on the rocks. It seemed a good time to hold abandon ship drill and we lowered two boats. All hands cooperated pretty well. The fate of the *Ohioan* had had a positive effect.

214

At Los Angeles I received a letter from my wife. She wrote, "You are arriving out there in time for labor trouble, aren't you? Please take care of yourself and the ship." Her warning was to prove to be an understatement.

I piloted my ship into Seattle, as all company pilots were busy. Betty came for me, and we had supper together and went to see a double feature.

I got orders to proceed to Bellingham. We docked at Bloedell-Donovan Lumber Company, berthing ahead of our *Floridian,* and the next day loaded lumber. After shifting to City Pier, we loaded pulp in bales, then sailed for Seattle with a full moon shining, a beautiful night. This day was the deadline for settling disputes with the unions. The union and companies failed to agree.

We entered Seattle Harbor at four in the morning on October 29. We hove out the anchor in preparation for stopping, but since the seas were calm, giving us good control at slow speed, we kept going, arriving at the Fisher's Flour Mill dock at 5 A.M. At eight we started loading, in spite of labor's threat to strike. Rumor had it the union had informed the men that they wanted Roosevelt elected and that a strike at that time would embarrass him. Next day, however, ships' crews did go on strike, together with the longshoremen. The *Pennsylvanian* was strikebound. My role and career as a captain was once more put to the test.

*An estimated thirty-nine thousand Pacific Coast maritime workers went on strike, and all shipping on the Pacific Coast was halted. The striking unions, all affiliated with the Maritime Federation of the Pacific, were the International Longshoremen's Association; the Sailors Union of the Pacific; the Masters, Mates, and Pilots Association; the Marine Firemen, Oilers, Watertenders, and Wipers Association; the Cooks and Stewards Association; and the American Radio Telegraphists Association. Atlantic Coast unions also struck in sympathy.*

*Negotiations between the unions and the shipowners were carried on throughout the strike, but a number of issues delayed resolution. The shipowners wanted to bargain with each union individually, while the unions insisted on a unified agreement through the Maritime Federation. The unions demanded higher wages, increased overtime pay, a shorter workday, and the right to preferential hiring, which was ultimately the most divisive issue.*

*Each side engaged in rhetoric: Harry Bridges, president of the San Francisco division of the International Longshoremen's Association and leader of the strikers, called for public support of "this struggle of forty thousand men, their wives, and families against the greed of employers representing but thirty-nine stockholders," and Mr. Plant, chief negotiator for the shipowners, accused Bridges of blocking a settlement.*

When I returned to the ship from shore about midnight, the stevedore and two supervisors were attempting to cover the open hatches. I helped

215

them complete the job and collected the keys to all storerooms from the heads of each department. I went to bed but was up again at 5:30. The stewards' department made no attempt to prepare breakfast. I set to work making out payrolls and by seven had paid off all crew members who were left aboard. There was one oiler ashore to be paid. His buddies took his belongings to the dock for him. Meanwhile, we arranged for a shore watchman, a former policeman, to be stationed at the gangway.

By six in the evening the officers and engineers also asked for their money, and I paid them off. Mr. McPhee, second mate, was the last. He did not want to strike but was persuaded by the rest, and at last he too asked for his money. Chief engineer Martin and I were the only souls aboard. Then next day, October 31, Martin asked for his money and left. I went through all quarters, storerooms, and the engine room, removed all fire hazards, and locked the rooms. I kept in regular communication with Mr. Plant in San Francisco by wire.

The flour mill ran twenty-four hours a day. It was completely fenced in, with a gate on the opposite side of the grounds, out of sight of the ship. Thirty to fifty picketers guarded the gate around the clock to prevent men or stores going to the ship. The mill hands were affiliated with the longshoremen's union, so they were sympathetic to the strike.

As of November 1, I was alone with the company watchman. I cleaned the chill room and iceboxes. At ten in the morning a patrolman from the Masters, Mates, and Pilots Association tried to persuade me to leave my ship. I stayed, and he left.

The temperature was between twenty-eight and thirty-eight outside. I had no electric power and my rooms were cold, as low as forty degrees at night and reaching only forty-nine by day. I tried without success to obtain an electric line for heat and light, and dry ice for the food lockers. Each day I sounded the bilges.

American-Hawaiian had two other strikebound ships in the Sound. Captain Bain was alone on the *Mexican* at anchor in Port Angeles Harbor, and Captain Foster on the *Wilzipo* was at the company's own dock in Seattle, well protected. From the mill I talked by phone with each of these captains and told them I was determined to stay aboard my ship.

I had given the watchman at the gangway orders to allow no one aboard. At eleven in the morning on the fourth, six big men, all strangers to me, attempted to board. I ordered the guard to forbid them entrance and block their path. I stood nearby. They stood single file on the gangway with the watchman at the head with his arms outstretched. When they asked for me, I stepped up to the head of the gangway and faced them close to. I introduced myself, then asked them their names, addressing each in turn. None would reply. They claimed to represent the officers' union. The spokesman in the lead said, "We came down to get you off the ship." I refused, ordered them off the gangway, and chastised them for not being men enough to give their names. They left reluctantly. To make it more difficult for others to approach the main deck, I disconnected the gangway and lowered it to the dock. The watchman and I lowered a straight ladder to the dock each time we needed it.

When the owners' pier superintendent made his regular rounds that day, I gave him a brief account of the six men who had tried to get me off the ship. I told him to make it public or to wire the story to President Roosevelt. I handed him my draft of a message. I didn't know if he would actually send it to the President of the United States, but next day Mr. Martin called me on the phone via the mill, and, speaking for the unions, told me that they would not be bothering me again, since their attempt to get me off the ship had caused bad publicity. The pier superintendent brought me a copy of the wire he had sent. My remarks had been wired verbatim:

SEATTLE NOV 3, 1936
TO THE HONORABLE FRANKLIN D. ROOSEVELT, PRESIDENT OF THE UNITED STATES, WASHINGTON D.C.
FROM MASTER AMERICAN MERCHANT VESSEL PENNSYLVANIAN STRIKEBOUND SEATTLE STOP I AM ALONE ABOARD TRYING TO CARE FOR VESSEL STOP PERISHABLE GOODS ABOARD AND SPOILING STOP YESTERDAY I WAS ASKED TO LEAVE MY COMMAND BY REPRESENTATIVES OF THE MASTERS MATES AND PILOTS ASSOCIATION STOP TODAY I HAVE BEEN INTIMIDATED BY SIX MEN CLAIMING TO REPRESENT SAME ASSOCIATION BUT REFUSED TO GIVE THEIR NAMES STOP IS IT YOUR WISH THAT I SURRENDER ALL RIGHTS UNDER THE AMERICAN FLAG OF MYSELF OWNERS AND THE GOVERNMENT TO THAT OF MIGHT

C. N. BAMFORTH

I received no reply from the White House.

*National radio network commentator Boake Carter had something to say. Carter described the episode on the air, naming my father, and indicated that President Roosevelt had been notified. Strongly conservative politically, Carter had no kind words for either the unions or the president. Mother was thrilled to hear the broadcast.*

I had enough food on board to feed forty men for three months. My challenge now was to keep it from spoiling. With no steam up and therefore no electricity to operate the ice machine, it would be a big job. The temperature in the icebox rose to thirty-two degrees. Completely cut off from shore, I couldn't secure any dry ice, let alone an electric heater for my quarters. I couldn't even get the telephone company to connect a phone. To contact the police, should there be an emergency, I was to set off lifeboat rockets. I had one kerosene lantern for the watchman at his post and another in my quarters.

The mill hands threatened to strike in sympathy. The mill manager called on me and explained that he could not get any fixtures from his electrician for fear of retaliation. I finally did get pieces of electrical equipment smuggled to me, a little at a time, by various visitors.

On November 5, after dark, I ran an electric cable under the railroad tracks and connected it to a mill light socket, which was quite concealed. This gave me light in my quarters and enough energy to heat small amounts of water in an electric coffee percolator. More than once I put too big a load on the line and blew a fuse.

At last I got a telephone on board. The telephone company would not install it, but American-Hawaiian engaged an independent technician to do the work. I had an unlisted number.

I was managing to get my own meals. Once a week I gave the guard two chickens or two ducks to take home, one to keep for his family, the other for his wife to cook and send back for me. His wife did a fine job, stuffing and roasting them nicely.

I turned over all the cases of eggs in the refrigerator to keep the yolks from adhering to the shells. Everything in the icebox froze solid after I smuggled in some dry ice. After midnight, under the cover of darkness, I was able to smuggle 250 pounds of dry ice aboard from the flour mill. I carried it up the ladder by myself, making several trips, unbeknownst to the picketers. The mill was still working around the clock.

I now had two guards working twelve-hour shifts. It was reported to me that Mr. Engstrom, district secretary of the Maritime Federation, had tried to have them removed by threatening to close down the flour mill. I heard that he made the statement several times to Seattle city detective Lieutenant O'Brien, insisting on "getting that captain off."

The evening of the sixth Evelyn Bergen and her brother braved the picket line and paid me a visit. November 7 I aired and cleaned the ship's midship quarters. That day I had a letter of commendation from Mr. Lapham, the president of the company. Lieutenant O'Brien, who called on me frequently, told me that the Masters, Mates, and Pilots Association members were bothering Albert's family. He speculated that they were trying to learn about me from Betty.

*A car with two men in it was often seen spying on the Albert Bamforth residence. Albert, a union member, was away and required to do picket duty in another city. This left Betty, her mother, and the baby alone at home. They were frightened and called Dad by phone. He notified the police. When the police approached the suspicious vehicle, it left the area with the squad car in pursuit. It was assumed that the union wanted to find out if Dad was visiting Albert's family.*

Lieutenant O'Brien offered to take me ashore and bring me back to the ship in safety. I refused. I was taking no chances. I wanted to look after the ship 100 percent. I would have made a prime target for the union if they had found me ashore. I didn't fancy being tarred and feathered and exposed to the public.

Mr. Martin had been looking at my ship from the West Seattle Bridge, where one could easily look down on her. He noted that she had a three-degree list to starboard, which worried him. He called me to inquire and asked me to close the condenser discharge valve, which I did.

I also connected up the jacking engine to the main shaft, put a long pipe on the end of a big Stillson wrench, and after lifting out the necessary floor plates jacked the main engine a tiny bit at a time. The engine was a big quadruple expansion reciprocating steam engine. I did a little jacking each day. It took me a long time to make the slightest movement of the pistons and valve rods, but it was enough to keep the packings from seizing. Otherwise the ship would be delayed while the seals were replaced once the strike was over.

We had plenty of dry wood dunnage aboard. I cut the boards up to burn for heat. I had cut the head out of a barrel to make a fire pot so that the guards, of whom there were now three, working eight-hour shifts, could keep warm.

I did not receive all the information that was discussed at company head-quarters but got the gist bit by bit. The flour mill was under threat of a strike if I was allowed to stay on the ship, so the American-Hawaiian local agent tried to hire towboats to shift the ship to the company docks at Stacy Street. The towboats would only do so if they took me off first. They couldn't get me off, so they agreed to shift the ship if I was locked in my room. The local agent agreed to this condition, but in seeking the owners' approval in San Francisco, Mr. Plant replied, "If that ship shifts, Captain Bamforth will be in charge." The towboats would not shift her under those conditions, so the *Pennsylvanian* stayed where she was.

November 11 I managed to get power for lights back on, but I still did not have enough power for radio or regular cooking. I had been boiling eggs and making coffee and oxtail stew alternately in my coffee percolator. I ordered a wood stove but couldn't get it delivered. So I had my friends bring small parts of it each time they visited. Finally the stove was complete and I set it up in my office. Then, after cutting dunnage on deck, I was all set for both heat and cooking.

The pier superintendent called regularly and took care of my errands for things like stationery and mail. I wrote and heard from my wife back home almost every day. I hadn't been there long when I wrote her to send me some old work clothes. Evidently she forgot all about it—at least she never sent any—so I sewed some conspicuous patches on a pair of blue trousers I was wearing. Once when Mr. Gaidsick, who was serving as assistant port superintendent for the company, was on board for his daily rounds, I had him take pictures of me. The picture I sent Dot was to remind her that the trousers I had were nearly worn out. She did not catch on.

*She probably ignored his request because she couldn't stand the sight of him in shabby work clothes. At home when he wore them to do errands, he had to hitchhike because she wouldn't be seen with him in such dress.*

Since I did not have enough electricity to work my radio, I found a smaller one, belonging to one of my officers, that worked on less power, and moved it to my room. Nearly every day I jacked the engines as well as the main, steering, and deck winches. I also sorted soiled linen.

November 12 I continued sorting and packing soiled linen and got my weekly report off to the owners. My day guard, Lieutenant McGee, brought me a squash pie that his wife had made. In addition to chicken and duck, I enjoyed baked ham after sending two to his wife. Now with a wood fire, radio, and good eats, life was just about grand.

I continued on board the strikebound ship, alone except for the watchmen and occasional visitors, and I worked hard every day to keep the ship secure. The winter weather grew colder with each passing day, and there was danger of things freezing. I closed up all the vents and doors to prevent air circulation and relied on the seawater to keep the engine room warm enough. I assembled canvas, wood, and tackle, and after dark hoisted all to the top of the smokestack. I covered the stack with wood and then a tarpaulin and lashed it around the sides. By daylight, this was conspicuous and caused the union to charge that the ship must have workmen on board. However, from the mill roof anyone could look directly down on the ship, so the suspicion that there were workmen aboard was never confirmed.

On the thirteenth the icebox read thirty-one degrees. I secured four hundred pounds of dry ice that day, carrying it all up the ladder in small loads. At 11:00 P.M. I went to the icebox to get two chickens and nearly passed out for lack of air. Carbon dioxide from the evaporating dry ice had displaced all the oxygen. I felt myself growing faint, so I leaped up the ladder and rested on the deck to regain my senses and composure.

When the strike had started, the ship was being loaded in the rain, and the canvas tents used to prevent water getting into the holds had been dropped, wet, onto the deck. They weighed about a ton apiece. I hoisted them in the air to dry using the deck winches, which I turned a little at a time using the big Stillson wrench. I had them elevated for several days, and when they were dry, I lowered them to cover the hatches. This also appeared to others as though a crew were working on board. With time and persistence, I managed to secure all five hatches by myself.

On the fifteenth Evelyn Bergen and her mother paid me a visit, climbing up the ladder like good sports. I served them chicken dinner and we played bridge.

On the sixteenth we had heavy rains. I had letters from home and one from the Masters, Mates, and Pilots Association, asking me to vote in their favor. Between rain showers I cleaned the decks. I wrote to Mr. Plant, and at 10:00 P.M. I smuggled seven bags of soiled linen out through the mill. I ducked in the alleyway as the mill jitney drove by and managed to get the bags into our agent's car without being seen.

On the seventeenth I washed dishes in the mess room and cleaned and aired the crew's quarters. I turned the engines, greased all bare steel in the engine room, and got the rest of the soiled linen ashore.

November 18 was a beautiful day. I aired out all quarters, went down in number one hold to examine the cargo, turned the engines, and sounded the bilges.

I had the pier superintendent bring me fifty feet of rubber garden hose for me to breathe through when I went into the icebox. I rigged it up to an Army mouthpiece and strapped it to my head so both hands could be free to work. Working for an hour at a time using this breathing equipment, I was able to sort fruit and turn eggs. In the evening I smuggled aboard another four hundred pounds of dry ice.

Next day the guard, Lieutenant McGee, brought me a roasted chicken and a quart jar of fresh applesauce. I cooked two oxtails in one percolator and vegetables in another. There were frozen whole hindquarters of beef in the icebox. I had not figured out how to cut them, so I had my beef by tails.

November 20 there were cold winds. I spent the day searching out and sounding the double bottoms. I received word that the deck officers from our *Mexican* at Port Angeles wanted to go back to work, and the owners gave them a chance, but nothing came of it.

Albert returned home to Seattle from Los Angeles where he had been doing strike duty. I talked with him over the phone.

*Dad never let Albert come aboard the Pennsylvanian during the strike, thereby treating all strikers the same, whether family or not.*

I washed, mended, and ironed clothes. Our pier super told me that all officers from our *Mexican* had asked to go back to work because they were afraid they would lose their licenses if they did not return. I called Albert at home and learned that he was being required to do picket duty from noon to 6:00 P.M. daily.

On Monday the twenty-third I had a letter from my wife that took the starch out of me. Since she realized I had had other women on board as guests, she saw no reason why she couldn't join me. She was envious but unrealistic.

On the twenty-fourth I washed down the decks, filled up vessels with fresh water, and flushed out all toilets. I had to get water by the bucketful from the mill garage, the nearest spigot. Carrying it up the straight ladder was a challenge.

Next day I had Mrs. Harold Gaidsick down to dinner. Neighborhood friends from Swampscott sent me a long letter of encouragement. That day I ordered a turkey sent from a store to Albert and Betty for the holidays since Albert was off pay.

Thanksgiving Day, Evelyn and her friend Mr. Archer joined me on board for dinner. We had turkey, dressing, pickles, cranberry sauce, white and sweet potatoes, onions, carrots, coffee, and mince pie, some of which I prepared myself.

*On December 9, Harry Bridges and Roger D. Lapham, president of American-Hawaiian, spoke before an audience of fifteen thousand people at the San Francisco Civic Auditorium. Neither side was willing to concede anything in its demand for control of employment. Mr. Lapham insisted that shipping must have the right to select its personnel, and Mr. Bridges said union control was a fundamental claim of the strikers.*

*As a result, a compromise proposal was made to President Roosevelt to create federally controlled hiring halls, but the unions rejected this measure, responding, "We will fight the system if it is the last thing we do. A fundamental of this strike is our demand for union control of the assignment of workmen. Without it we would return to a system under which employers blacklist union men at will and ruin any hope of keeping high the standards of seamen."*

December 11 was the first fine day in a week. I got tents dried and stowed below. Mr. Gaidsick brought me a lemon pie and I made him a nice lunch.

On the fourteenth, with cold weather predicted, I covered cowl and mushroom vents, covered mooring lines, opened up joints in fire lines, and turned over the engines. At 5:00 P.M. I went for my dry ice and ran into one of the mill men. He didn't know who I was, and I managed to get my four hundred pounds aboard without interference. I talked with Captain Foster on the strikebound *Wilzipo*. He was all alone at his post, like me.

Mr. Ritches and Mr. McIntyre, American-Hawaiian company officials, inspected the ship. Ritches remarked, "Should take only twelve hours to get this ship in service."

On the nineteenth I listened to Mr. Lapham, president of American-Hawaiian, talk on the radio. His message was followed by one from James Curran, president of the East Coast Seamen's Union.

I arranged for the police to watch my home in Swampscott. I didn't tell the family for fear it would upset them to know that there was a risk of union harassment.

The ship had 200,000 board feet of lumber aboard. I took the dampers out of the fire room vent and started to cut the twelve-foot pieces in half. I dropped them to the fire room to be used to start the boilers off when the strike ended.

Captain Foster brought me pork chops and beef steaks. I painted the galley, then broke out turkeys to be roasted for Christmas. I aired all quarters. To Albert and Betty I sent vegetables that were about to freeze and spoil.

On Christmas Eve I received many more cards, letters, and telegrams. I had a turkey brought ashore and sent to Albert. Through Alice Shaw I also arranged for a turkey to be sent to the chief of police in Swampscott for his courtesy in looking after my home.

Christmas Day was fair. I opened presents, which aroused warm but lonesome thoughts of all those at home. The next day I cut a thousand board feet of lumber with a handsaw and shoved it down a ventilator to the fire room.

The twenty-eighth was sunny and pleasant. I scraped and washed paint in the petty officers' mess room and later in the day smuggled aboard another load of dry ice.

Harry Bridges, Pacific Coast president of the longshoremen's union, was threatening to tie up the entire East Coast within two weeks.

The last day of 1936 was cold. I made my dinner of pork chops, fried apple rings, warmed-over mashed potato, toast, and cocoa. Mr. Plant offered the officers everything except preferential hiring. I wrote in my diary, "The *Pennsylvanian* and all other ships on the West Coast, strikebound. I have been on this ship alone for sixty-two days. I have kept well, and have been on the payroll, and have had fun preserving the ship and cargo for the owners and jobs for the men when they want to return."

January 2, 1937, I covered the skylights with canvas, opened pipe joints, oiled tools in the engine room, and sent off the weekly reports to the owners.

Monday, January 4, it snowed. Captain Bain, master of the *Mexican*, strikebound at Port Angeles, came to visit. I would not let him on board until he convinced me that we were working together. He denied all the charges that had been made against him. It appeared that he had acted in favor of the unions on his way to Seattle. The crew had struck, and he had directed the ship via inland waters so that the Coast Guard could not board and arrest the crew. After hearing his explanation, I invited him aboard. This was the day that the Masters, Mates, and Pilots were voting on whether to accept Mr. Plant's offer.

January 5 brought a northwest gale and snow which turned to ice, with temperatures twenty-five to thirty-one degrees. The wind made it hard to heat my room. The results of the Masters, Mates, and Pilots coastwise vote on the company proposal indicated a majority in favor, 329 for, 279 against.

Next day I got busy breaking radiator joints in the quarters in order to drain and prevent freeze damage. It took me until midnight. I failed to drain all of them in time and some pipes burst. The next day it was still very cold. I was trying to keep the pipes from freezing. I also worried about the eggs freezing in the chill room at night, so I put an electric heater there. That day I had several letters from the owners and from home. My son Dick was celebrating his seventh birthday.

January 8 was cold, with temperatures sixteen to twenty. I drained the refrigeration machine after calling Mr. Oaks, a chief engineer who had been a shipmate of mine in 1919, for advice. On the ninth it snowed. I checked the temperature in the engine room. It had remained above freezing thanks to my having eliminated all ventilation. I thawed drains, heated the chill room, checked and added water to the radio batteries, and painted the overhead in the saloon.

On January 14 I had a letter from my wife that had come, ironically, via the Battleship *Pennsylvania*. I cut up a pork roast and sent two ducks ashore to be cooked. Mr. McIntyre brought dry ice in the back of his car. He had two city detectives with him. He had been getting ice at the ice plant, but picketers stopped that. Henceforth the owner of the ice plant had the dry ice put in the back of his car. In the evening he drove it to his home and from there it was transferred to our company car, and finally it got to the mill warehouse. From there I smuggled it aboard.

I tested the fire line by filling my bathtub and draining the water through the fire line. I started reconnecting pipe lines that I had loosened to drain, after calling the fourth engineer, Mr. McLaughlin, for information on what to do.

On Sunday, January 17, I started to make a false beard for myself from rope yarns, dyed red with iodine. The following day was clear and pleasant. I put new piping on the radiator to the crew's mess room.

Tuesday I worked on my beard. In the evening Mr. and Mrs. McIntyre boarded for supper. We had steak, mashed potatoes, carrots, onions, custard pudding, and cake. Then we played bridge. I had letters from my wife, including the amount of interest on our savings account. Banks had paid only 2 percent in 1936.

January 20 Mr. McGill, one of my guards, was at home, sick, and did not report for the twelve-to-eight watch. I turned the main engine, made an order for hardware, and ripped, or rather broke, holes in radiators in those quarters where I hadn't been able to break threaded joints. I wrote home and heard part of President Roosevelt's inaugural address. After calling Albert and Captain Foster in the evening, I clipped two items from the newspaper. One was about three tanker crewmen being beaten by seven strikers on the waterfront. The second was about the S.S. *Lancaster* having sailed. She was the first ship to do so since the strike began. She was manned wholly by officers.

My Swampscott friends sent me a roll letter. Each friend had glued a new message on the end of the previous person's contribution. They included jokes and cutouts from magazines pasted in humorous arrangements. All of the Fuller Avenue neighbors had worked on it. When unrolled it was over eight feet long.

January 22 I heard that the S.S. *Lillian Luckenback* had gone to dry dock, moved there by tugs, and with the captain removed. The S.S. *Latouche* of the Alaska Steamship Company was allowed by the union to go to dry dock, provided the owners spent about $8,000 on crew's quarters, making improvements to their satisfaction. The S.S. *Victoria* was denied permission by the union to go to dry dock because she was old and had less comfortable crew's facilities than most newer ships.

I finished my piping work and then cleaned all cargo lights. I repainted fourteen portable cluster lights. In the afternoon, Mr. McIntyre brought Mr. Oaks over to call on me. They found me playing drunk for a joke. I served coffee, bread, jam, and cake. After they left, I made out the week's report to the owners and sent the Red Cross a $5 donation from my crew of one. I wrote a strong recommendation to Captain Topp, chairman of the Offshore Officers Association: "Accept the owners' offer and return to work at once." Then I made applesauce and wrote home.

On January 26 rumor had it that the strike was about to end. For the next couple of days I cleaned up and stowed gear away, all the while continuing my daily routines and making various repairs.

On January 28 Dorothy sent newspaper clippings about the strikes and gave me the news that Dick was down with chicken pox. On the radio I heard "Town Hall of the Air" presenting a discussion about industry and labor, the subject on everyone's mind.

Within the next twenty-four hours, there were more signs that the strike was coming to an end. American-Hawaiian stock jumped a full point.

I sent Yale locks from officers' quarters ashore to have keys made where they were missing. I corrected charts according to the latest bulletins. On January 30 I listened to President Roosevelt over the air. I wrote to Mr. Butman, my chief mate, "Be here Wednesday. We expect to resume service then."

Sunday the thirty-first, Albert phoned in the morning to say he was leaving for Los Angeles to attempt to rejoin his ship. I had a night letter from Mr. Butman. He wrote, "I will be there before Wednesday."

Monday, February 1, eight inches of snow fell. I received seventeen birthday cards. Mr. Gaidsick and Mr. Frazier came to lunch.

Engstrom, head of the strikers, made it public that the *Pennsylvanian* would get no crew. He was carrying out his old threat because I would not strike. Mr. Davis, my junior third mate, was told to join our S.S. *Iowan*.

Though he declared that he would rather sail with me, I sent him to Los Angeles as directed by our San Francisco office.

Tuesday, I cleared the snow off the hatches and cargo gear, and at noon Mr. Butman arrived in town from the East Coast. A pot of tulips arrived from the McIntyres for my birthday, and by phone I talked with my chief mate and chief steward. I distributed linen to all quarters.

Union members began to vote. Four of my officers were now in town. At 8:00 A.M. on February 5, the strike ended. The shipping companies conceded on every major point, including preferential hiring for union members. The unions had won.

Crews were ordered to ships. Although the union had my ship blacklisted, the officers notified me that they would be on board by eight the next morning, regardless. That morning there was a southerly gale, but otherwise it was regular warm spring day. At 6:00 A.M. I uncovered the stack, and at 7:30 deck officers came aboard. All during the day the crew gradually drifted on board, in spite of the boycott.

By using the wood I had stowed in the fire room, we had steam up at 3:00 P.M. By four we had lights and water. Several small pipes had been frozen and were leaking. These were repaired during the night. Heat was on in all quarters, and the ship was comfortable for the new crew. I wrote to my wife and turned in, happy and relieved. The ship was suddenly transformed from an icebox to a comfortable home. The *Penn* had been out of service for ninety-eight days. The crew had lost over three months' pay and were glad to get back. The company had all the food on board examined and found it fit for consumption. My efforts with the iceboxes had paid off. The eggs were hardly fresh, but the men were so pleased to be back on the job that there was not a single complaint.

For the duration of the strike I had kept busy and stayed in good health. The days had passed rapidly, and I had had hardly enough time each day to do what I wanted to do. In my letters to Dorothy and my boys, I had written each week how my beard was getting longer and longer, so long in fact, that I had to tuck it inside the waistband of my trousers. After the strike was over, newspaper reporters were eager to take pictures of me and how I had lived during the strike. Among those pictures was one of me in my fake red beard, cooking with a frying pan and a coffee percolator. Everyone loves survival stories and the comical things that make endurance possible.

Of course, in my letter writing, I had told Dorothy of my having visitors on board. She could not see why I didn't have her there too. I don't think she has ever forgiven me.

On February 7, 1937, we shifted the ship under her own power to Smith Cove and loaded canned goods. At 6:00 P.M. we sailed for Port Townsend. Next morning we loaded two hundred tons of newsprint in big rolls. At midnight we sailed for Tacoma, where we docked at the smelter. I went to town to clear the ship and met Mr. Adair, our new chief engineer, who had just arrived from San Francisco to join the ship. He had been delayed as trains were snowbound in the mountains. I signed him on the articles. Fireman McNamara failed to join the ship. I left his clothes and an account of his wages with the agent, and we sailed for Frisco without him.

February 9 we steamed down the straits of Juan de Fuca and rounded La Push to sea. At ten in the morning I made inspections and had the deck crew clear my quarters of my strike-time paraphernalia. All was shipshape by evening. I relaxed for the first time in months; nevertheless, I held the usual safety drills.

On the sixteenth I secured a seaman's discharge book, although the union forbade me to have one.

> *The law had been passed requiring the maintenance of these books. They were a record of hirings and discharges for each sailor. The unions thought that they would be used by the ship owners to blackball individuals, so they were strongly opposed to the implementation of this law. Since it was the practice to pay off everyone at the end of a voyage, constituting a discharge, it is difficult to understand their paranoia. On the other hand, such a book could reveal a pattern should an individual habitually seek payoff before the end of contracted voyages. The employers must have wanted these records to maintain the slightest semblance of control over those they hired. It wouldn't have been much, since the strike settlement included union control of hiring.*

The company had to give up its traditional practice of carrying four quartermasters on each ship because the unions no longer allowed them to be officer material. Unions dictated what work they could and could not do and would not let the owners select the individuals they wanted.

We sailed with a full load for Charleston, South Carolina. During this trip, I took the messman, who was the crew's elected union delegate, along with me on inspection tours. I asked him why the stewards had failed to do their work. "The union made you responsible," I said. This ploy turned out to be very effective, since he himself had made a lot of trouble regarding a leak in the mess room. Thereafter, the stewards did their work well. The messman was feeling the pressure and wanted to resign. His chums refused to accept his resignation.

On the way north from the Canal, we had strong winds and rough seas. I painted my office, but it was difficult working overhead with the ship continually rolling and pitching. On March 10, 1937, we arrived in New York. My faithful wife was on the chilly dock to meet me. Although it was below freezing, I had my sweetheart to keep me warm! It had been more than four months of enforced separation. On Friday we took the noon train for Boston.

# Note to Chapter 12

1. Breeches buoy: a ring buoy fitted with "pants."

# CHAPTER 13

# CAPTAIN COURAGEOUS

During my stay at home, I gave a talk at the Kiwanis Club in Salem about my strikebound days. I also arranged with Ted Husler to secure an old car for Allan to work on. Only fourteen years old, Allan couldn't keep his hands off the family car. He kept taking it apart and didn't always get it reassembled in time for Dorothy's shopping trips.

March 22, 1937, Captain Bennett passed away. He had been the Atlantic Coast operating manager for American-Hawaiian for ten years following a fascinating career at sea that began when he was just a boy. A native of Hancock, Maine, he had once served on schooners carrying lumber and stone from Maine to major construction sites on the East Coast. He had hired me as a quartermaster, and I was always "one of his boys." Bennett was one of the finest men I'd ever known.

Back on board ship, our New York office instructed me by telephone to have the crew get lifeboat certificates. They refused. Spanish longshoremen would not work until night, when they could receive overtime pay. We kept the ship in Brooklyn, where the loading was finally done by Polish laborers.

April 4, after departing the Canal and heading west from Balboa, I held a surprise man overboard drill and lowered number four boat. The dummy was rescued in seventeen minutes. The news that day was about five hundred Hershey Chocolate workers on strike and holding the plant. They were driven out by farmers who supplied the plant with milk. John L. Lewis, head of the CIO, threatened to close down Ford's auto works.

I had a long letter from my cousin Miriam, the first correspondence from her in years. Although she made no direct reference to our former relationship, I was haunted with memories and couldn't get her out of my mind.

In San Francisco I applied for relief from a $2,700 fine imposed on me because the crew had not secured lifeboat certificates on the East Coast. I pleaded that I had tried, but they had refused. The fine was dropped.

July 3 Peterson and Shilts, a wiper and a fireman, were under the influence of liquor and demanded to be paid off. When I refused, they started trouble. While I was at dinner with the officers in the saloon, they entered and offered to fight. They passed the junior officers' table and continued toward me. Others at my table stopped them and tried to force them out of the saloon but were unable to do so or to control their flailing arms. I got up and put a hammer lock on Peterson. We laid both men face down on the saloon floor, helpless and cursing. The officers sat on them while I sent for the police. That finished our dinner.

As the police were leading them away from the foot of the gangway, Peterson turned and called out, "Charlie, I will get you yet!" I was in the habit of being addressed as "Captain," never by my first name. Not suspecting that he meant me, I asked the officers, "Which one of you is Charlie?" They were confident Peterson meant me. The police led them away and locked them up. I had them returned to the ship once they had sobered up. I wrote up the official log, entering the incident, and gave them each a typed copy.

(Years later when I was serving as a pilot, I was sitting at the dinner table alongside the first assistant engineer. I did not recognize him, but he told me that he was the Peterson who had caused the trouble years before in my saloon. We had a good laugh together.)

More trouble occurred. On Monday, July 5, Mr. Harwell, the officer on duty, called me because Waite, an AB who was at the wheel steering, was failing to keep the ship on course. I ordered him relieved of duty. He was angry at Mr. Harwell for having reported him. I tried to reason with him, then sent him below. Waite called back to Mr. Harwell, a gentleman if ever there was one, "Come down on deck and I'll knock your friggin' block off. I'll get the Coast Guard to have your license suspended for this!" It was yet another example of how things had deteriorated in our business.

July 7, in San Francisco, I spent most of the day with lawyers preparing charges against the three seaman for misconduct and insubordination. In the afternoon I presented their cases to the U.S. Local Inspectors.

On our way to Seattle, several seamen had to learn to steer. I missed having quartermasters. In Tacoma I fined three men for failing to report for duty.

July 31 we tied up at Wilmington and loaded 1,600 tons of cargo. Our *Montanan* arrived and docked astern of us with booms still down because the crew had refused to raise them. My brother Albert, her chief mate, was having his problems, too. Next day we loaded potash. At 4:30 A.M. we were ready to sail, but the crew refused until the booms were down and secure in their cradles on deck. The delay amounted to thirty minutes.

To keep my frustrations in check, I started to build a Pullman-style berth for the spare room to make it more comfortable for the pilot or guest passengers. Then I made a stability curve for the ship and constructed a curve of metrocentric heights from which to judge loading procedures, which would maximize the vessel's ability to withstand heavy seas without capsizing.

As we arrived at New York, the tug captain handed me a sealed envelope on one corner of which was written "Ten dollars." When he was leaving and shaking hands, I slipped the folded envelope back into his hand. Did he ever look surprised! I rarely used tugs, but when I did, I never accepted kickbacks.

Once more I had to fine three men for being absent from duty. Labor difficulties were becoming more common.

I had a kind letter from Simondson, an eighteen-year-old guest passenger I had left at the Canal. He thanked me for my hospitality and wrote, "I admire you both as a captain and as a man." There were some true gentlemen among the young.

On September 8 we sailed once more from New York. The news that day: European nations had formed an armada to combat Italian submarines that were sinking merchant vessels. The crew of a Norwegian steamer held a sit-down strike; they refused to go to the Sino-Japanese war zone. The Japanese were repulsed in China. The League of Nations was to patrol the Mediterranean.

On September 23, 1937, we arrived at Wilmington, the port of Los Angeles. Since the ship was to be in port for the weekend, I left for San Diego via railroad and bus to call on my Aunt Grace and Uncle John Danner. He was then a retired lieutenant commander, regular Navy. After dinner we went to the movies and saw *Captains Courageous*, based on the novel by Rudyard Kipling.

On return to the ship, I found one of my men had been put in jail. I bailed him out. In San Francisco on the twenty-ninth, I went to the shipping commissioners and local inspectors, where I preferred charges against two of my men. They each lost their certificates for thirty days.

I insisted that an experienced man do the steering while both leaving and coming alongside the dock at Tacoma. The deck crew objected and refused to steer at all. I told them to cut out their foolishness, and they finally steered as directed. This showed how the men were drunk with power after the strike and would take over if you let them. The crew's belligerence required us to take extra precautions. I was growing very tired. We wasted an hour waiting for a crewman to come aboard. The delay was frustrating, but we on the bridge were elated because the night was exceptionally beautiful as we came through Bellingham Channel. The northern lights were more wondrous than the pilot or I had ever seen.

When I finally got a chance to rest, I began making plans to build a sailing sloop for my boys. In Los Angeles I bailed a man out of jail and bought gear to build the sailboat. I used a Wrigley tug to get away from the dock, and we headed for the East Coast. There was some question as to whether my crew would handle the lines to the tug, as the crew on the *Arkansan* had refused to do, because the towboat men belonged to a different union.

On the trip back to the East Coast, I worked on the sailboat. I kept at it even in stormy weather when the seas reached the boat deck. Then I wore hip boots. In my spare time I read Kenneth Roberts' *Northwest Passage*, just off the press.

I went home on vacation when we reached New York. The family visited my ship while it was in Boston in order to see the sailboat under construction. I cut out a sail for the boat from number six canvas. I pinned the strips and had Mother Allan stitch it together on her foot-pedaled sewing machine. On November 26, after a wonderful time with my family, I was back on my ship in Newark.

Next day in Brooklyn we had the crew secure the forward end of the ship and the regular shore gang secure the aft end. At 7:00 P.M. my crew stopped the shore gang from securing the ship. At 7:15 I intervened and got the shore gang back to work. Then the deck crew refused to work. I gave them ten minutes to think it over, suggesting that the problem be settled on our arrival in San Francisco. They bought my proposition and went back to work, but we were delayed. Fog shut in. I managed without tugs, doing my own piloting, to get the ship safely out of the harbor. At sea she pounded so hard in a heavy gale that I had to slow down to avoid damage. In spite of all our efforts, it was going to be impossible to make it through the Canal on the intended day of arrival, so we slowed down a bit to save fuel.

I had to spend all my spare time getting the ship's papers up to date, as only the minimum had been done while I was on vacation. I wrote to Mr. Plant about charging the deck crew with delaying the sailing of the vessel in New York.

We proceeded through the Canal on December 5. After being raised eighty-seven feet to Gatun Lake, we were delayed in heavy rains. We slowed down to avoid meeting a gasoline tanker in Calebra Cut and risking a collision. I had several letters from home and from one I cut out several lines to save. It was one of the few times my wife warmly expressed appreciation for me. At the Pacific locks, Captain Kane and his wife came aboard for the trip to Los Angeles. I made my shuffleboard and ringtoss equipment ready for the passengers to use, then I worked on the sailboat. I hadn't intended to do so while Captain Kane was on board, but he wanted to help me. He and I worked all one afternoon driving rivets in the boat frame, and then we fastened the ribs.

In Los Angeles, while I was advancing money to the bos'n, a stranger stepped into my office and said, "I am the seamen's delegate. I am taking Smith off and I want him paid off." I made no reply. "How about it?" he demanded in a rough voice.

"I do not want to pay him off," I said. "He has a contract to the end of the voyage in San Francisco."

Again the delegate said, "I am taking him off and I want him paid."

"I don't want to pay him off," I repeated.

"You are a hell of a hard guy," he said. "Come off that stuff."

"How about you?" I said. "Who asked you in my quarters?" We stepped outside, where he repeated his demand and left. This was another example of how the union was exerting pressure.

Next day I stayed away from the ship to avoid contact with the dictatorial delegate and any possible labor troubles. I went to boatyards in Wilmington and in San Pedro to see how they built boats. I thoroughly enjoyed learning these things.

Next day at midnight we arrived at San Francisco. In the past an ordinary seaman would have volunteered to go on the dock and tie up the vessel. Getting tied up quickly was a benefit to many of the officers and crew who lived in the area. However, as a way of showing union spirit and strength, no one volunteered. So I went to anchor at two in the morning and returned to the dock at six when line handlers were available. I paid off the crew which previously had been a simple task, but with the crew contesting everything and making unreasonable demands, it had become a wearisome procedure.

On December 23 I was invited to Captain Ludlow's but excused myself from attending dinner and a show since my ship was ready to sail. Alas, we were delayed two hours waiting for two cooks and the chief steward to return to the ship. I could have enjoyed myself ashore after all.

On the twenty-ninth two cooks were so drunk they could not get supper. For years the crew members had been a happy lot. They had tended their business and very seldom did they miss the ship or cause delay. In 1937, however, working with the crew was a continual battle. "Crews nowadays are a burden for all officers and not a help as in the past." So says my diary.

My pay for 1937 was $5,006.91.

*This was good money for the Depression years. In 1937, a crewman, for example, would have made around $1,000 a year, not counting overtime. But one must remember that in 1937 a new Ford cost only $650, or about half of a sailor's total pay. By comparison, at $22,000, the average price of a new car in 1997 took 73% of an annual salary of $30,000.*

January 31, 1938, an ordinary seaman was disorderly. I had him arrested. He was sentenced to fifteen days in the workhouse. February 2 a messman failed to join. I put his effects on the dock and left his account with the agent. February 12 I was notified that four of my men were in jail. I went to town and bailed them out. I had them sign for the money before they were let out of jail.

Sunday, February 13, we took on fuel oil. In spite of dense fog, I sailed from the dock because the crew threatened to hold the ship because we were short one AB. The troublemakers were dead drunk. We anchored off the pier until the weather cleared, then sailed for Seattle.

March 5, uptown, I met Captain Rogers. He didn't refer to me as the "Boy Skipper" anymore. I had just had my forty-third birthday.

The news on March 13 was about the German Army occupying Austria.

April 23 in Philadelphia, we were ready to sail at 1:00 P.M., but one crew-man was missing. The sailing board was posted for a 3:00 departure. We waited until three. Then, just as the clock struck, a deck engineer and an oiler deserted. Then we were *three* men short. Labor troubles were taking the fun and profit out of this business.

On April 24, as we approached Boston, we came upon the wreck of the *City of Salisbury*, a British ship stranded on Graves Reef. A total loss, broken in half and sunk, she had been carrying a cargo of zoo animals. Her crew had managed to put many animals onto a lighter, but most of them died from exposure. Her cargo floated about for weeks, and some was picked up on the Swampscott beaches. It became a heyday for scavengers. Customs officers finding foreign cargo in private residences charged the possessors import duty.

After a day at home replacing storm windows with screens in early antic-ipation of summer, I shifted the ship, with the family on board, to Commonwealth Pier, South Boston. There we got my sloop, named the *Sea Jack*, into the water by lowering it on lifeboat falls. My boys and I set sail for Swampscott.

There was a strong wind from the northwest. The sea was rough and forced water up through the centerboard box. We had to keep bailing. Dick complained that he wanted to go home to his mother. Apparently he didn't trust his father. Allan asked several times, "Do you think we will make it, Dad?" After passing Deer Island, there was too much wind for the mainsail. The boat would not run before the wind but kept broaching to.[1] I finally let go the sea anchor. I did not fear any danger but dreaded the thought of wor-rying the family at home by keeping the boys out all night, waiting for the wind to moderate.

I had the little jib sail aboard. It was only twenty square feet. I never dreamed that this alone could get us home, but I tried it with the mainsail furled, and we went flying home. After the jib was rigged and we were able to move more steadily, the boys relaxed somewhat and enjoyed the rest of the trip. When we passed floating cases of cargo from the wrecked *City of Salisbury*, Allan wanted to stop and investigate. I had arranged for a whale-boat to meet us off the Swampscott beach, and since we were already late, I pressed on.

At 1:00 P.M. we anchored off Swampscott. I know that most people thought I was crazy to be out in a sailboat in that gale of wind. We had come fourteen nautical miles on the small jib alone.

*Allan's account of the adventure: When the boat was lowered to the water, I looked at it straight down from the rail of the Penn. It looked no larger than a postage stamp. It was a bit scary climbing down to it by the rope ladder. I was fifteen, with some experience sailing as crew on an eighteen-foot Swampscott Dory class sailboat, but I doubt if eight-year-old Dick had had any experience in small boats. Needless to say, neither of us had been in a twelve-foot one on a maiden voyage in the open Atlantic in cold early spring. It took a bit of doing to sail her, filled as she was with lines, life preservers, a sea anchor, a pair of oars, and three passengers, two of whom knew not what to do.*

*All too soon we found ourselves in the open sea. I was at the helm. The boat wanted to head into the wind, a desirable trait normally, but she seemed much too determined. Heading her off just a few points took all my strength at the tiller. She heeled heavily, shipped water over the gunwale, and water came out of the uncovered centerboard box in a heavy gush. Dad pointed out a land feature for me to head for, making our course run parallel to a seagoing tug pulling a garbage scow. Since I couldn't keep her headed off without shipping water, it appeared that we were going right for the cable between the tug and the garbage scow. We were close enough to see the taught steel cable, which was ready to de-mast us. It was at this point that Dad got out the sea anchor, a hoop with a canvas bag attached. In my mind, it was a life preserver.*

*Dick's memory of the episode: I was in the third grade and age eight when Allan and I were taken out of school to sail the Sea Jack home to Swampscott from Commonwealth Pier. It was a chill, gray April day with abundant squally winds. The crew lowered the boat over the side and dropped a rope ladder. My father scampered down and my brother followed somewhat more gingerly. My heart came up into my mouth. I couldn't speak but wasn't far from crying or vomiting. The crew, more empathetic than Dad, rigged a bos'n's chair* [2] *and lowered me down gently.*

*The rest was hell. The sail was raised, and we zipped out into the harbor. Dad and Allan, who was fifteen and had been sailing before, managed the ropes, tiller, and swinging boom. I had never sailed in my life, and the vast quantities of cold salt water that poured in over the sides kept me in a state of unmitigated terror. I was handed a bucket and ordered to bail. It gave me a creative, if desperate, role to play.*

*Looming ships, tugs, and barges zoomed by as we sped toward the outer harbor. It was a foretaste of the Arthur Ransome book, We Didn't Mean to Go to Sea, which I was soon to read. I began to ponder the possibility of death by drowning. The cold, the wet, the wind, and the terror kept me bailing. Somewhere approaching Graves Lighthouse (what an ominous name!), Dad threw out a sea anchor. It was a great metal ring slung with a canvas bag that looked more like a trap for catching big fish, but it did what it was supposed to do, and immediately the little boat headed up into the wind, and life was steady, level, and calm again. We passed around the hefty lunches packed by the galley crew, perhaps as if they were to be our last meal, and I was actually able to get something down. I also tried hard to swallow my feelings of fright and rage.*

*Dad decided a simple jib sail was enough for the rest of the trip (a not-too-subtle recognition that there was something inappropriate about the way he had been handling this voyage) and we headed for Swampscott's Fisherman's Beach. It was just after noon when we approached the shore. Mother, who had long since called the Coast Guard, was watching with binoculars, and I was soon hoisted home to a warm bath and dry clothes. I don't remember the words Mother and Dad exchanged, but I have no trouble imagining their ferocity.*

*Not until long after our ordeal was over did I learn that my father and brother were also afraid that we might lose control. They well realized that this was not the weather for small craft and inexperienced crews. It was not a felicitous introduction to sailing, and it did not make me closer to my father. It was an adventure I didn't wish to repeat, and I was glad when the captain went back to sea.*

On my next round trip, I studied piloting every available minute. When I returned to the East Coast I went on an extended vacation, from July 7 to September 21.

*Dad received a trip off as a reward for outstanding service to American-Hawaiian. Mother received a complimentary letter from Mr. Plant, the chief operating manager, who was sensitive to the plight of captains' wives. This vacation put Mother and Dad in the same house for a far longer period than ever before. It proved to be a strain on the marriage. "Good-time Charlie" became a daily challenge for Mother to deal with "in my house."*

I went to Boston on July 7 to sit for pilot's examinations. Next day I went back again and worked on the examinations right through the meal hour. I finished at 1:30 and secured another endorsement on my license, "First-Class Pilot, Nantucket and Vineyard Sounds."

I spent my vacation visiting and receiving friends and relatives and taking care of chores. I tore the wooden bulkhead out of the cellar (it had formerly been a coal bin) and checked for termites, and then I built a closet in the cellar as a photographic darkroom for Allan. I also built a locker under the stairs for storage. I contracted with a plumber to replace the old soapstone sink in the pantry with a porcelain one and to install an aquistat on the boiler to provide hot water. I went to work tearing out the woodwork in the pantry so that the plumber could install the new sink. Then I stopped the stair treads from squeaking by driving in wedges and re-nailing them. After that I removed and rebuilt the pantry cabinets. I also covered the pantry counters with linoleum.

I moved the electric refrigerator, which had replaced our old icebox, from the back hall into the pantry. Then I installed a forty-gallon copper hot water tank in the cellar and had the old gas-fired stack heater from the kitchen moved down there beside it for heating hot water in the summertime when the furnace was shut down. I put a concrete base under the back porch to get the wood posts off the ground and installed water faucets to make a shower there. After these chores were complete, I began to paint the house. My sister Beatrice's husband, Bill Snelling, who was visiting, helped me with the painting, and together we put up sheet rock in the cellar.

I also spent time with my boys. One afternoon I took Dick onto the U.S. Naval destroyer *J. C. Jones*, which was anchored off Swampscott. Afternoons the boys and I often sailed out to Egg Rock and back. One Sunday Allan and I set sail in the *Sea Jack* for Marblehead. We had a good sail with a fine breeze. On the way back we had little air and were late. In haste we unrove the jib halyards by mistake. I sent Allan up the mast and the boat capsized. Rowing the dinghy, we towed her to the beach to right her and bail her out. We got home at 8:30. Dorothy was fit to be tied.

> *Expecting to be met by a wild wife, Dad (not "we") unrove the halyards in haste. I knew something about the instability of this boat, having handled it a few times myself, and I didn't want to climb the mast, especially since Dad insisted on sitting to one side of the centerboard box rather than strad-dling it. With no enthusiasm to motivate me, I was having difficulty shinny-ing up the mast. Dad fixed that by making a loop around the mast and anoth-er for my foot. He hauled on the main halyards as I stepped in the rising loop. I came to within inches of grasping the jib halyard at the block when over she went. Dad jumped clear. The boat lay on her side with me struggling to free my foot from the mast, which lay deep in a sea full of jellyfish.*

On September 7 I painted in the forenoon. It rained later in the day so I spent some time freeing paint-stuck windows. That evening Dot and I had it out with each other about the way I was spending my time. I was beginning to feel that I had been home too long.

The boys started back to school, and I gave the house a second coat of paint. Evenings when Dorothy was out, I visited the neighbors and one time helped Allan with his studies. Dorothy and the boys drove to Cape Cod for a day. I made my own supper and walked to the beach to look over the *Sea Jack.*

At last on Tuesday, September 20, I took the midnight train for New York and my job. I had been home for one full round-trip, two months and fourteen days. How the time had flown!

Arriving in New York I found the ship had been delayed by a hurricane. I bought an umbrella and checked into the Bristol Hotel. I went to a movie in the evening and when I came out it was blowing hard and pouring. As I came onto the street, I could hear breaking glass high up amongst the buildings. I said to myself, "This must be some storm!" It turned out to be the infamous hurricane of 1938.

The *Penn* sailed to New London. I walked all over the town to see the hurricane's destruction. The Merrit, Chapman and Scott Company had a lot of salvage equipment tied up at the docks. Their tugs and barges were all sunk. Cars parked on the docks in the face of the wind had all their paint blasted off as the pea sized stones from the harbor were driven against them. A lighthouse tender, a ship of substantial dimensions, was left lying across the railroad tracks. Many magnificent elm trees had toppled over and crushed houses. As these great trees came down, their root systems rose high in the air, taking huge areas of sidewalk and pavement aloft with them.

At Baldwin Locomotive Works, Eddystone, fifteen miles below Philadelphia, we loaded three hundred tons of heavy lifts to be part of the new Palomar telescope near San Diego. Captain Schermerhorn, who had replaced Captain Bennett as American-Hawaiian's Atlantic Coast operating manager, came to the ship with Mr. Plant's reorganization plan. In it I was asked to become a coast pilot. I accepted with the provision that if I didn't like the job, I could rejoin my ship.

On October 6, in Port Newark, Captain Johnson relieved me officially as master. I moved out of the quarters I had called my home for the past twelve years and went down below to the pilot's room.

# Notes to Chapter 13

1. Broaching to: swinging to the wind (a dangerous situation), broadside to the wind and sea.
2. Bos'n's chair: a narrow board suspended from above, used to hoist a man aloft for painting, etc.

# CHAPTER 14

# COMPANY PILOT

On October 10, 1938, I piloted the *Virginian* down the Delaware River, my first trip as a pilot. It was hazy. We could see a mile at the most. At the narrowest part of the lower bay, twenty-six miles from the entrance, I was making the elbow of the Cross Ledge Light on a shoal. On the opposite side of the channel was an unlighted can buoy. It was slack water[1] and I was making about ten knots when out of the mist loomed a vessel lying across the channel at right angles to my path. I couldn't stop and had no room to go ahead of her. I went as close under her stern as possible. When we got abeam, I could see that she was a U. S. Navy cruiser at least six hundred feet long, at anchor. We passed her safely, but it was a warning to me to be less aggressive and more defensive in my approaches in a foggy river. I was lucky.

In New York I found Albert on the *Montanan*, and I loaded my sea chest and other personal gear from the *Pennsylvanian* onto his ship, bound for Boston. That night I sailed as pilot out of Newark on the *Alabaman*. On arrival in Philadelphia, I had orders to go to Newark and join the *Montanan* at Erie Basin. A threatened tug strike became a reality, and I was forced to employ both my expertise and my nerve in piloting without tugs. I had to pass the S.S. *American* in the outer berth. She was crowded with barges all around her, but I was confident, and we made it out.

I sailed for Philadelphia, piloting the *Montanan* without tug assistance. I took her through Newark Bay, the Central New Jersey Bridge, around the sharp turn at Bergen Point and through the Kill van Kull, out through New York Harbor and to sea—successfully! We had fog going down the coast, and the whistle blew every minute or so. It was a strange ship for me, a strange job, and I got hardly any sleep. At 2:00 A.M. I was called to take her up the Delaware. It was foggy. We cautiously felt our way along the ninety-mile stretch until forced to anchor halfway up on Baker Range, waiting for fog to clear so we could see the buoys marking the channel. Finally, 10:30, we docked at Philadelphia and I went to bed. Then at nine that night I piloted her back down the river in clear weather.

The next morning I was on duty once more, piloting the *Montanan* across Vineyard Sound. Clearing Pollock Rip Shoals was another first for me as pilot. When I brought the ship into Boston, Dorothy was there, expecting to meet me on the *Pennsylvanian* en route to the West Coast. She was surprised to find me as pilot on the *Montanan*. I took my gear from the *Montanan*, and Albert came with us to Swampscott for supper and overnight.

And so it went. As a pilot, I lost a lot of sleep but enjoyed the challenges. When other vessels anchored due to poor visibility, I frequently kept moving cautiously in order to save the owners time and money; this was in spite of some close calls and potential danger, which I minimized by keeping alert.

When I got to Boston with time to go home, I took the Narrow Gauge Railroad to Lynn. Dot would meet me at the station, or I could take the streetcar to the bottom of Greenwood Avenue and walk up the hill. Sometimes when a ship had been delayed, I had extra time at home for chores and improvements. Otherwise I rode passenger ships and ferries in order to get the required number of trips as an observer to be eligible to take written examination for additional pilot's licenses.

On December 30, back in Philadelphia, I transferred to the *Alabaman* after having been up most of the night piloting the *Ohioan*. At 9:00 P.M. we sailed for Boston. It was an exceptionally clear night, but at 2:15 A.M. I got the vessel stranded on Brandywine Shoal. I had mistaken it for Cape May Light.

We took soundings about the vessel to see if she were taking on any water. Luckily we were stuck in sand and the integrity of her bottom had not been violated. On high water at 3:00 P.M., with assistance from the anchors and winches, she floated and we anchored in deeper water. Mr. Roberts of the American Bureau of Surveyors came aboard to investigate and, I'm glad to say, issued a seaworthy certificate.

I went to the captain's room and asked the surveyor to send a telegram to San Francisco. I had it written out and read it aloud in front of the captain. "To Mr. T. G. Plant, Operating Manager, San Francisco. I am sorry that I got the ship ashore on Brandywine Shoal. Apparently no damage. Survey completed. Sailing for Boston. Bamforth, Pilot."

*He wanted to relieve the* Alabaman*'s master of all negligence, contributory or otherwise. Dad found no need to consult his attorney first.*

We sailed for Boston. On dry dock no damage was found. It wasn't even evident that she had been aground, fully relieving me of serious concern, but there would be plenty of paperwork yet.

On January 6, 1939, in Philadelphia, I went to town and *reported* in person to the U.S. Local Inspectors of Steam Vessels about my grounding of the *Alabaman*, as was required by law. They had my written report. Next day they wanted to interview the crew before any other hearings took place. On the tenth Captain Schermerhorn interviewed me, and later, back in Philly on the sixteenth, I attended a hearing before the Marine Investigation Board. I sent Mr. Plant and Captain Schermerhorn an account of it all. On the twentieth I had a telephone call from Captain Schermerhorn in New York. He told me not to worry about having to go back to sea again or about losing my job. If I did lose my license, he said, the company might even put me to work on the pier. This was a great relief.

At this point in my diary I had copied these ten rules for personal success, which I had found to be essential in my work:

|     |                |     |                |
| --- | -------------- | --- | -------------- |
| 1.  | Be yourself.   | 6.  | Be a worker.   |
| 2.  | Be alert.      | 7.  | Be a student.  |
| 3.  | Be positive.   | 8.  | Be fair.       |
| 4.  | Be systematic. | 9.  | Be temperate.  |
| 5.  | Be persistent  | 10. | Be confident   |

I hadn't married until I was able to give my wife an allotment on the first of every month, and I had continued this practice since the beginning or our marriage. Now Dorothy told me she needed more money because she had been buying on the installment plan and had had to draw on the emergency fund, hoping to repay it before I found out. I knew it was impossible to catch up once we fell behind in payments, so I had her give me all the bills to the first of the year. It cost me $400 to pay them. I started her off on a clean slate with orders not to buy anything unless she had money to pay for it. That way required no bookkeeping.

*This marked a definite turn for the worse in my parents' relationship. In tears, Mother had confessed, knowing it might be worse for Dad to find out some other way about her overextended finances. She did not feel guilty because she believed she deserved more than what she got in the monthly allowance. Such humiliation of confessing she vowed would never be necessary again, but she could not forgive him for his rigidity concerning "the allotment." From then on she browbeat him to get extra money, saying hateful things, putting him down unmercifully, and rejecting his amorous advances. More than once I discovered him weeping. He refused to tell me why, but I knew that Mother must have given him one of her famous tongue-lashings. I felt sorry for him but did not know how to show it.*

On March 15, 1939, we heard that Germany had seized Czechoslovakia.

At home again on the twentieth I made a fold-up seat for Allan's basement darkroom. Photography was a creative hobby for him and both boys were to make good use of the equipment. I held a supper for fathers and sons in the neighborhood, followed by a scavenger hunt in celebration of Allan's upcoming sixteenth birthday. Just before this momentous occasion Ted Husler sold us our third new car, a Ford Deluxe V-8 four-door sedan, for $856. We received a trade-in allowance of $405 on the 1937 model. I sailed for Philadelphia on the *Mexican* and, while crossing the shoals at five in the morning, we heard Mussolini speak by radio.

War news: March 8, Italy took Albania. On the twenty-eighth Hitler rebuffed FDR's peace plea in the Polish quarrel.

May 3 I took examination as pilot for Wilmington, Delaware, and received the endorsement on my master's license. I was at home on May 10. Dick helped me in the garden. In the evening Allan was at a high school dance. I was proud of my boys.

In Newark on the twenty-third, I spent the morning looking over the new Esso tanker *Mapay*. She had just completed her trial trip under the command of Captain Gainard. He, a master for the shipbuilders, was a big, good-looking man, and he knew it. I overheard him say loudly to his wife on the telephone, "This is your handsome husband." I was impressed with his bravado but had reason to think that such an approach might backfire in Swampscott.

May 31 I had a "few words" with Dorothy and the encounter left me as weak as a rag. She had accumulated a whole list of complaints to dump on me.

On July 7 I received written notice that my license was being suspended for fifteen days, the penalty for grounding the *Alabaman* in December. I handed my license over to the U.S. Local Inspectors and reported to Captain Schermerhorn that I would not be able to act as a pilot or in any other capacity for that period of time. He asked, "What are you going to do now?"

"I'll ride ships to accumulate trips," I said, "so that I will be eligible for piloting licenses."

"Continue, and let me know when you get your license back," he said. That meant that I stayed on the payroll.

While my license was suspended, I sailed as an observer to get in my trips toward pilot's licenses for Long Island Sound and Narragansett Bay. The *Comet* and the *Arrow* ran every night in opposite directions between New York and Providence. They were twelve-knot, triple-screw passenger vessels. The officers on these ships were experts at their profession. Their ships had no modern navigational equipment like radar or gyro compass. Their tools were a timepiece, a magnetic compass, and a taffrail log, plus the log book, which was laid out so that pages two weeks apart, when the tides were the same, could be referred to. There were no chart rooms or any charts. Pilots and quartermasters had been on the same run for years and knew the route by heart. I learned a lot about piloting on these ships.

My license finally restored, I piloted the *Californian* up the Delaware on July 26. On August 1 I went to Port Newark with the port captain. Aided by two launches, we dragged the harbor for snags that had been damaging our ships' propellers. We found several. I was back on the *Californian* at 7:00 P.M. Then I took the midnight train for Boston and began my annual two weeks' vacation. The big event was our family trip to the 1939 New York World's Fair.

*I remember the trip as lots of fun. I, of course, liked both the General Motors and Ford exhibits. We all liked Chrysler's Frozen Forest. It was a huge automobile showroom. The adjacent lounge was set about with artificial palm trees whose trunks were refrigerated and covered with frost. Whenever we got too hot, we headed for the Frozen Forest. The place was always crowded. Finding seats, we "people-watched." Our favorite lounge area was raised a few steps. The wall behind was completely mirrored. People looking for seats would see the reflection and try to get to "the other side," only to run up against the mirrors, say, "Excuse me," step to the side and go through the routine once more.*

On the fourth day we were all pretty tired. I wanted to go one way, my wife and the boys the other. We parted, annoyed, and didn't expect to see each other again that day. Dorothy had the keys to the car, and I figured I would get back to our rooms using public transportation. I headed for the Russian Building. Halfway around, who should I meet coming in the opposite direction but my family. Having cooled down, we had a happy reunion, although it had been only a half-hour before that we had parted. We talked it over amicably and decided that we had seen enough of the Fair.

On August 16 my family drove to Norfolk to visit my kin, and I returned to duty in New York. I had three days to study before I got a ship to pilot.

War news: August 24, Germany and the Soviet Union signed a ten-year nonaggression pact. Americans were warned by their ambassadors to leave Europe. September 1 Germany invaded Poland. Britain and France declared war on Germany two days later. Germany began sinking British ships, and Britain bombarded the German fleet. September 6 President Roosevelt proclaimed our country's neutrality. American flags were being painted on the sides of all our merchant ships.

Back on the job I found that the company had ordered crews to paint out the flags that had just been put on the sides of our company's ships. There had been controversy over the wisdom of having our ships so clearly identified.

In early October I took Allan to my lodge for Fathers and Sons Night. We had dinner together in the banquet hall. I was always disappointed my boys didn't become Masons.

I received another piloting endorsement on my license, New London and Block Island Sound. On October 20 I went to Providence, sat for the pilot's examination, and received the endorsement "First-Class Pilot, Block Island Outside Narragansett Bay, Newport, Providence, Mt. Hope Bay and Tributaries to Fall River."

I was assigned to the *Texan* for a trip to the west to relieve the master, who was getting a trip off. I did my own piloting out of New York, down to Barnegat Light, then shaped the course for the Windward Passage. I gave the job of operating the slop chest to the radio operator. I didn't have him post the daily news as I had done on the *Pennsylvanian*. That kind of thing had been outlawed unless the company paid extra for the service. Of course, there was less need because by then many of the crew had their own radios.

The *Texan* had been built in 1902 and showed her age. When I had been pilot on this ship and had attended boat drill, I had noticed that the crew never swung the boats more than halfway out. On November 4, I conducted boat drill and ordered number one boat swung *"all the way out,"* and the boat to be made ready for lowering. This was at last accomplished with great difficulty, quite embarrassing the chief mate. He followed up by working the whole deck crew in correcting the condition on all four boats. We were delayed in Gatun Lake by traffic, so I held fire and boat drill again. We swung out and made ready for lowering number four boat. Now we could all be confident that the boats could be lowered in case of an emergency.

At Los Angeles we discharged all cargo destined for San Francisco because of strikes there. The cargo would have to be shipped by truck or rail. I held drills again, including watertight door drill, and I had the crew man the boats and set sails. In Oakland I secured our secret code for communication, necessitated by war conditions.

December 7 we loaded lumber at Prescott. After dinner the engine room crew announced that they required the afternoon off or else they would not assist in moving the vessel in the evening. I asked for their demands in writing, whereupon they canceled them. At 4:00 P.M. I advanced money to the crew and let them off, since everything in that small town could be seen in an hour. On December 19 in Wilmington, there was some dispute by the stewards over the washroom in that department being used by both whites and coloreds.

At home on January 22, I opened my delayed Christmas presents, did home business, and visited Mr. Mansur, Superintendent of Schools, about Allan.

*I showed no signs of being college material. As my high school graduation approached, Dad was looking for advice. Mr. Mansur was hardly diplomatic when he told Dad that I would never amount to anything without college. Dad, a self-made man, greatly resented this.*

Back to piloting again, I had the usual problems in East Coast waters during winter weather with many buoys off location and lighted ones often extinguished by ice.

At home I started making an office for myself in the cellar where I could study my charts instead of using the kitchen table where, when mealtime came, I had to scram. I built a high, oversized desk under a cellar window, room for books, stationery, a tall stool, couch, Morris chair, radio, rugs on the floor, a typewriter, and my own pictures and relics. *My home!* Even the telephone, on a long cord, could be brought into that room. Over the door was a sign that read "Master's Rm." I found it a pleasure to have my own study. I was never interrupted, and when I returned from piloting a ship, I was sure to find my things just as I had left them. My wife often talked of my office being full of junk. More than once she asked if she and Lena, our faithful helper, could go in and clean it out. I refused. Everything she had no use for was junk to Dorothy.

In February 1940 I was in New York. The S.S. *Queen Mary* and the S.S. *Queen Elizabeth* were both docked nearby. I walked over to see them but found that no one was allowed even on the dock side of the street due to wartime security. So I went back to the ship and wrote a letter to my sweetheart as I stood by the *Oregonian,* anxiously awaiting orders. At noon I was told to go home and standby there. At Springfield I left the train and looked up Bob Fuller, Miriam's husband, who was now traffic solicitor for New York Central Railroad. He drove me to his home and I stayed to dinner. It was good to see Miriam once more. I continued my journey on a later train. At home Allan and I drove to town to look at a trade school for him.

I spent the rest of 1940 piloting, studying for further pilot's endorsements, and taking temporary command of our company's ships. Meanwhile, the war in Europe kept escalating.

June 20 in Philadelphia, we discharged two thousand tons of sugar from the *Missourian* and several secondhand ships' anchors and chains bound for Britain to be used as weights to secure submarine nets.

June 27 I relieved Captain Olive of the *Virginian.* I went to the customs house, intending to pay off five men before the U.S. Shipping Commission at their request. Only one man showed up sober enough to sign his name. I left their pay account with the owners. Then I had my master's license renewed following a physical examination, as was required every five years. Later that summer, at the U.S. Navy Yard in Boston, I had my quadrennial physical examination as a Naval Reserve officer.

July 31 I was working in my study when Jean arrived home unexpectedly from Canada. She had discovered a lump in her breast, and she and Alice had cut short their vacation.

August 6 I relieved Captain Scorah on the *Floridian.* In the afternoon Maritime officers questioned me about discipline and Communist activities on board, among both crew and officers. I later found out these questioners were agents of the FBI. This was the day that Jean was operated on, a radical mastectomy.

In Norfolk on October 18, I reported to the *Carolinian,* then had lunch with my sister Clara. We passed the American steamer *Washington* on our way to New York. She was loaded with troops and war supplies headed for the Pacific and would return with refugees from the Orient.

On Halloween I went out with Dick and other younger children. We secretly attached rapping tacks[2] on windows of half a dozen neighboring houses. Florence Seed caught me hiding under her front window and, to get me out, she took the kettle off the stove and poured water down on me. The children all escaped dry. By bedtime I was terribly tired.

On December 29, 1940, President Roosevelt spoke to the people by radio about our government's policy: "Support England with everything short of war." Soon I too would be closely involved in that effort.

## Notes to Chapter 14

1. Slack water: still water at the turn of the tide, neither flood nor ebb tide.
2. Rapping tacks: a string with a weight attached and tacked to a window stile. When pulled and released from across the street, the weight strikes the glass, making a racket inside that cannot be identified.

# CHAPTER 15

# FEATHERED FRIENDS, MOUNTING TENSIONS

In 1941 Allan graduated from Swampscott High School. He passed the entrance examination for General Electric's Machinist and Toolmaker Apprenticeship and was hired. I bought him ten shares of G. E. stock, thinking this would give him more than a workingman's interest.

> *My physics and chemistry teacher was tutoring other boys on the examination subjects. My father decided that I should join those boys, and he paid the fee. It turned out to be a stroke of genius. G.E. was selling for $32 a share. Dad put up $300 toward the stock he bought for me and required me to contribute the $20 balance from my savings. The transaction completed, Dad said, "There, you are going to be a company man." It turned out that I loved my work. My father's choice of a career was perfect, and I am grateful to him for directing me as he did.*

### The S.S. *Illinoisan*

On July 1, 1941, I was assigned to the *Illinoisan* as master for a trip to India with war supplies for the British armed forces as part of FDR's effort to support Britain with all measures "short of war." I took over from a captain who had just returned from a voyage in the Pacific. The ship had barely survived a storm that had put the vessel on her beam ends. They had just made it to Honolulu. Following that experience, her captain never went to sea again.

The *Illinoisan* had old-style lifeboat davits that couldn't be left swung out for quick lowering of the boats without the addition of special booms. I had the chief mate, Mr. Overland, order timbers so that we could make our own. These came aboard with the rest of the stores.

We loaded down to the marks with an immense deck load of heavy machinery in great wooden cases. The carpenters strapped, chained, and shored them to the deck to prevent shifting in heavy seas. With all the huge cases on deck, it was difficult to get from one end of the ship to the other, so we had gangways built over the tops of the cargo. Mr. Overland and I made every effort to get things secured and safe for the crew.

On July 13 we sailed for India. The next day it was overcast, with heavy rain squalls. I had been on the bridge most of the time since sailing, and when I went below to my quarters I found they had leaked badly. Tired though I was, I had to clean up and save my possessions.

Mr. Overland seemed to be a good, experienced seaman. He had been on this vessel for some time and knew the ship well. We had what looked like a good crew. I relaxed and let the officers look after things.

I had Navy Department orders to keep the use of radios to a minimum, since radio receivers could generate signals of their own that might be picked up by the enemy, revealing our position.

*While the U.S. was still officially neutral, Axis vessels were attacking U.S. merchant ships, like the* Illinoisan, *thought to be carrying war supplies to the Allies.*

I collected all the crew's radios until we were clear of the designated submarine areas. The radio officer received the broadcast news and placed a typed copy in each mess room once a day.

I had instructed Mr. Overland to build the boat booms and to get the lifeboats swung out ready for lowering as soon as the ship was otherwise secured for sea. The boat booms had to be shaped from the big rectangular timbers in lieu of ready-made ones. On inspection I noted that the securing of the ship had been completed, but I saw no effort being made to get the boats swung out. I called Mr. Overland and questioned him. "I see no progress toward getting the boats swung out. Why not?"

"Sir, I don't see the need," he answered

"Make the boats ready for lowering," I said. "That's an order!"

Next day the mate and the ship's carpenter worked together all day, but at day's end they hadn't completed even one boom. At that rate, it would take more than a week to finish the job. The safety of the crew depended upon being able to get the boats in the water, fast. I decided to pitch in myself the next day after breakfast. I had no tools, so I got one of the engineers to sharpen a fire axe. Without saying a word to the mate, I lined off the taper required on a second timber and went to work with the axe. By four I had completed one boom by myself. The mate and the carpenter were still working on their first. When they saw what I had accomplished, they picked up the pace. With the three of us working, in three days we had all booms completed and the boats swung out and ready for lowering. Mr. Overland never again gave me a chance to challenge him. After those three days of hard work I was sore and stiff, but I told no one that I was hurting. From that point on, the crew knew that I meant business.

I made out new boat station lists and had them posted under glass in all mess rooms so that each individual knew where to go in an emergency. I had new falls and new water breakers[1] installed in each lifeboat so that they would be in the best shape possible should we be required to use them.

In fine weather it was a pleasure to be at sea again. In the evening with the officer on watch, I worked four heavenly bodies: Venus, Antares, Spica, and Vega. This gave us an excellent cross on the chart for the ship's position. I exercised daily by walking to and fro briskly and played catch with the officers, using a handmade ball. Men worked in shifts around the clock, making it necessary to serve three full dinners each twenty-four hours. I had to restrain myself from eating too much.

Not permitted to plot the shortest route to Cape Town, I followed the Navy routing to avoid German submarines. I set the course for the east end of Cuba. We went down through the Windward Passage, then toward Trinidad, and followed along the northeast coast of South America. We then headed for Cape Town, passing ten miles off Ascension Island.

Sunday, July 20, I took the day off to myself. I washed clothes and started to make a rag rug, but I had one bad mess to straighten out first. It was customary and, to me, essential that the ship's carpenter sound all holds twice a day to detect any leakage. He was to report his findings in writing to the mate and to chalk them on a blackboard in the engine room. I found this had not been done, not even once a day. I saw to it that it was done. This was the second experience I had had on ships used in foreign travel where this essential routine was thought to be unnecessary and only required for coastwise vessels.

July 23 the trades were dying out and we were entering the doldrums. I held fire and boat drills, insisting that the crew board the boats in the chalks and set sails.

By August 3 we had cooler, drier air. I spent most of the day decoding messages from the Navy Department with Mr. Geary. Geary, my purser, was experiencing his first trip to sea, but he proved to be a great help and a good shipmate. I also worked on my rug.

We sighted numerous whales and albatross. In order to ventilate the cargo with dry air, we opened the corners of the hatches, but we had to be very careful to avoid getting seawater into the holds, the ship being so deeply laden.

Nearing Cape Town on August 11, I advanced the crew the amount of their earned money that they requested. It was overcast, high fog, and hard to see the mountainous coastline and landfall. No sights of heavenly bodies were possible, but I did secure a radio direction finder bearing from Robins Island Beacon. We were ahead of schedule. We arrived at 1:26 A.M. and were boarded and inspected by the Navy and immigration. One German in the crew was detained for more questioning. While we were at anchor, I wanted to show colors in respect to the country we were visiting. The ship had no South African flag to hoist forward, so I had the British flag hoisted to the foremast. Immediately we were signaled from shore to take it down. I could only speculate as to the reason. Perhaps it was the spirit of independence among those who were then still British Colonials.

We docked, took on oil bunkers, water, and fresh stores. In Cape Town it was quite a sight to see flat Table Mountain behind the city with fog drooping down over the sides as if it were a white tablecloth.

I rose early next morning to get off the required reports, pay for supplies, and sign papers for the agent regarding water and fuel. At 7:00 A.M. we sailed outside the harbor, then anchored to wait for missing crewmen to return. They arrived via launch at 9:36, and we sailed for Bombay. I fined these men a day's pay each for having delayed the vessel. Gulls, gooneys, cape pigeons, and albatross accompanied us. We met rough seas and heavy swells.

We sailed south off the Cape of Good Hope in compliance with British Admiralty safe routing instructions. At noon we were circled by five Allied airplanes with whom we exchanged signals, giving them the secret code. On this day the Atlantic Charter was signed, with FDR and Churchill agreeing on war aims.

Many birds came about the vessel, and I took snapshots of them. At 7:00 P.M. there was one vessel ahead of us and a suspicious one following, which added to the tension of the trip. At last the latter changed course and disappeared below the horizon.

On the fifteenth we rounded the Cape and set course for Mozambique Channel between the African coast and Madagascar. I made regular daily inspections for cleanliness, including the proper sterilization of dishes, and repeatedly checked the condition of safety gear. I had lookouts on duty day and night. I was unable to get radio messages to New York by relaying them through other vessels because no ship would accept messages for fear of revealing themselves to enemy craft.

The sea birds were still with us. I marveled at their flight patterns. I felt they were my friends, and their presence gave me comfort in the midst of uncertain times and unknown waters.

August 19 was a fine day, the first in several. All day I worked with the officers practicing with both flags and Morse code. Morse signaling in U.S. ports was no longer commonly practiced on merchant ships but was employed in all foreign ports during the war. In the evening I studied the charts for approaches to Bombay.

August 25 we were crossing the Arabian Sea in squally weather. Mr. Geary took pictures of a whale that came alongside, and several others were sighted farther off, but my friends the birds were no longer with us. We were too far from land.

Approaching Bombay September 1, we found that the specified lightship was missing, and in the mine-swept channel, buoys were out of place. This was not entirely unexpected in those times but unsettling nonetheless. Soon we were relieved to find a guard vessel stationed at the outer end of the channel. Using coded flag signals, those aboard the guard vessel advised us of the course. The pilot boarded from a launch, and at 6:00 P.M. we entered the harbor of Bombay. We signaled to shore with flags and received a coded reply ordering us to anchor.

Our docking orders arrived on the fifth of September. The Indian pilot wore freshly starched whites: short breeches, white leggings, low white shoes, and a white cork hat. The temperature was one hundred degrees, with stifling humidity. After the work of the ship was well underway, I hired a horse-drawn carriage with a guide and rode about the city to see the sights. Bombay seemed a well-regulated city, but the buildings had no glass in their windows, only shutters that were closed at night. During daylight crows often flew in one window of the bank and out the other. Police directed all traffic on the streets, but cows were allowed to roam at will. If a cow decided to lie down in the middle of the street, traffic was diverted around it. With such freedom, the cows were very bold. In the park certain religious groups left their dead for the vultures to pick the bones clean. I shopped for cards and saw the high caste district and public laundry, which was quite a sight. In the open, it covered many acres, all in concrete and cut up into stalls. An open culvert ran through it from which each user could divert water.

On Saturday, September 6, the nightmare started: I found that Lewin, an ordinary seaman, had been driven off the ship by the deck crew in some kind of dispute. I discussed the affair with the consul but it was difficult to understand. I had thought I had an excellent deck crew—at least they had worked exceptionally well.

The next day the discharging of cargo continued while I wrote up the Lewin case. I spent most of the eighth at the consul's office on the case. At four the consul boarded to investigate further. I interviewed the watchman from number one hatch and Seaman Medlock in my room. The watchman identified Medlock as the man he had seen throw Lewin's baggage into the harbor. The consul advised me to pay off Lewin for his own safety.

At eleven that night, I was in the saloon pantry getting a cup of coffee before turning in when Bos'n Barr came stumbling through the saloon, in one door and heading out the other, stammering heatedly, "I'm going to get that bastard second cook." As he evidently had been drinking, I helped him on his way by removing myself from the passage, but I kept an eye on him. Twenty minutes later I observed him at the gangway, apparently in a peaceful mood. I turned in.

The night was hot and muggy without a breath of moving air. There were many native cargo handlers about the deck, discharging the cargo in full force. The crew slept on deck, aft, where it was likely to be cooler than below decks. There was the usual amount of drinking going on after a long trip at sea.

At 12:13 I was called from my bed by the officer on watch: "Fighting amongst the crew, sir." I ran on deck in my pajamas, where I found Seaman McManus bleeding heavily from a knife wound on his right arm. I left him in the care of the officer of the watch and went to investigate further. I was told that another man in the crew was badly cut as he lay on his cot, aft. As I came on the main deck, I ran into Barr chasing Second Cook Gonzales from aft, yelling threats at him. Gonzales managed to keep ahead and locked himself safely in the chief steward's room. I climbed over the big crates of machinery to the poop deck and made it to the second knifing victim. Messman Mosner was lying on his cot, injured and suffering. I tried to stem the flow of blood from his midsection while I called to the deck officer on duty to send for an ambulance and for the police. At 12:47 an ambulance arrived, and I sent the two injured crew members to St. George's Hospital with a junior officer accompanying them. When the police arrived I had Barr and Gonzales arrested, and they were taken to the police station.

When my junior officer returned and told me that Mosner had died on the way to the hospital, I summoned the purser and all officers. Some had to be wakened. I instructed them to get busy immediately interviewing crew members individually and to secure signed statements attesting where they had been and what they'd been doing all night. I wanted the process completed before the crew could get together and manufacture stories. It was well after daylight before we completed the procedure.

The local police investigated. A butcher knife from the crew's pantry was missing. Divers were employed to look for it on the bottom of the harbor near the ship, but it wasn't found. Shortly after daylight, I was surprised to find Barr back on board, after being released by the police. Gonzales was still being held. It seems that several of my men had gone as a group to the police station and had sworn out a statement that cleared Barr but condemned Gonzales. I kept feeling that it should have been the other way around. Gonzales was being held on a charge of first-degree murder.

With help from the consul and ship's agent, we hired the best criminal lawyer in Bombay. The immediate result, as soon as the lawyer got on the case, was to change the charge from first to second-degree murder. A continuing search for the murder weapon revealed nothing, but before Mosner was buried I consented to an autopsy, which ended the search. The eleven-and-a-half-inch butcher knife was found wholly within the victim's abdominal cavity. Mosner, a peaceful man who apparently had been sleeping innocently on his cot, was buried in Surrie Cemetery, Bombay. I spent the evening writing up the case.

Meanwhile, the ship continued discharging day and night. I paid off Gonzales. With Mosner deceased and McManus still in the hospital, we were three men short. Because we needed heavy lifts to remove the cargo, we had to move to a berth fitted with heavier cranes. We went to anchor to wait for an open berth. Thursday, September 11, still at anchor, I was trying to complete the crew with the help of the agent and the consul. I called on McManus in the hospital and Gonzales in jail. At noon we shifted to Victoria Dock under a hundred-ton crane.

Next day the authorities held three men as witnesses to the crime. We were now short six men. The ship had had barely enough personnel to operate effectively even before these shortages. These were long, hot, tiring days to be sure, but eventually, with the consul's help, I managed to secure four Scandinavian seamen, mere boys, who had missed their ships. The arrangement was that they would sail only as far as Calcutta, the next port.

I finished the ship's business, then shopped for myself. I bought the locally customary shorts and long hose to wear and a present for my wife, a native sari and petticoat.

September 13 at half past midnight, the cargo was all out, and we left the dock on high water when the submarine gate could be opened. We anchored in the outer harbor to secure the ship for sea. Next morning we set sail for Calcutta. As soon as we were clear of the mine-swept channel, I held fire and boat drill. Still short one bos'n and one AB, I put the carpenter, who had an AB certificate, in the vacant AB's watch, to comply with the law.

The fourteenth was hot with fair wind and current. I was sick all night and day. By 8:00 P.M. I was improved but weak. After a good night's rest I felt like a new man.

The weather was fine on the sixteenth. The ringtoss game I'd made was giving the officers a lot of fun. With fair wind and current, we averaged better than twelve knots. One of my new men, just a boy, and an OS were down with venereal disease, not able to work.

Soon we rounded the lower end of Ceylon, present-day Sri Lanka, and headed up through the Bay of Bengal to Calcutta. At one point we were hailed by a British man-of-war: "N–N–J," show your signals. Then "L–L–O", proceed. Finally, "W–A–Y", bon voyage.

Cautiously, we were approaching the mouth of the Hooghli River to the pilot station. The pilot was British and was accompanied by his own Indian servant who carried bedding, cooking utensils, and personal items, for both himself and his master. The ship was allowed to drift for three hours until 4:00 P.M. when the tide made up. We then steamed in and anchored for the night.

On the twenty-first we tied up at a berth. Next day the agent had us shift inside the locks of the harbor so as to avoid the heavy bore[2] in the river. We were assisted by two tugs to a berth where discharging resumed. I had a pleasant surprise, an airmail letter from home, assuring me that all was well.

September 22 I went to town on business. It was dreadfully hot and muggy. With the slightest physical activity, my clothes became soaked with sweat and I broke out with prickly heat all over my body. The port doctor, who called at the ship each day, recommended several baths a day and the use of a certain kind of soap. Mr. Overland was now in bed with chills and fever, probably malaria.

While discharging at Kidderpor docks, I contracted to have chipping and painting done by shore labor. Since Mr. Overland was sick, I supervised the work myself while the other officers looked after the cargo. The ship was so hot that I was the only one who slept on board. I had the only quarters with ventilation on all four sides. When the officers and men were off duty, they lived ashore at the Seamen's Church Home, which was much cooler than the steel ship. There they were waited on by the staff. Each morning they were served tea in bed. Since the crew's quarters aboard were vacant, I had the shore labor paint them, the stewards' storeroom, and passages as well. Alas, the crew demanded room money even though they had voluntarily vacated their quarters and were being pampered ashore for just pennies a day.

The men I had left in Bombay to serve as witnesses at the murder trial arrived by rail. Now I had to get rid of their replacements, but the police would not give me a permit to land them, another problem to be solved. At least Mr. Overland was back at work. Discharging cargo, chipping, and painting continued under his supervision, but this did not last for long. While he was looking after cargo, he got pinned between a sling load of lumber and number one hatch combing. Luckily he was not knocked down the hatch, but his leg was broken, and off to the hospital he went.

September 27 we were required to shift to another pier. The second mate was on duty aboard, but the third mate failed to show up. With the chief mate in the hospital, my ability to innovate and get the job done was well taxed. We were using towboats and the main engines in the crowded harbor. I put the second mate aft to make sure the line from the towboat didn't foul our propeller. I relied on native labor to do much of the work, supervised by a stevedore foreman. We had an Indian at the wheel. It took some luck, but we made the shift successfully. I tipped the foreman five rupees and the man at the wheel one rupee. Our loading of ore, cotton, and jute bagging resumed.

We had nineteen gangs trimming the ore to the edges of all five hatches, another gang under contract painting number four hold, and another forty-five men on deck, chipping rust. There was another gang chipping and painting over the side. To pay the laborers, the crew contributed a dollar a day from their wages for the privilege of being ashore and relieved of this work.

On September 30, besides the heat rash, I had a cold, due no doubt to the electric fan blowing on my bare body all night.

October 1 I called on Mr. Overland in the hospital. Then I went to the consul, the agent, and to the harbor police. I received permission to transport the four crewmen who had signed on in Bombay to the train that would return them there, but they could not leave the train while in the city of Calcutta because three of them had VD. I was required to conduct them personally to the railroad station and see that they got out of town.

The agent tried to get me to carry five hundred monkeys to the States. I turned down that opportunity, thinking I had enough to handle already.

October 2 I signed on five new crew members. In the evening, accompanied by the police, I saw the men off on the train to Bombay. Later I found another of my men had checked himself into the hospital with a bad case of VD.

We finished loading on the third. Mr. Overland returned from the hospital with his leg in a cast. At 8:00 P.M. we sailed for Colombo on the island of Ceylon.

October 6 we shipped seas, the main deck awash. The ship was not yet washed down, so rubbish got in the scuppers and restricted the free flow of water off the ship. As a result the chief steward reported that there was oil and water awash in his storeroom.

We were still two men short, one OS and one messman. I had another messman replacing Gonzales, the second cook, who was still in jail in Bombay. Later we got word he had been acquitted of criminal charges while we were gone.

My slumbers were interrupted at midnight on the eighth when the officer of the watch woke me to report that Chief Mate Overland was in a state of panic. He thought he was terribly sick and about to die. I examined him but could find no elevation of temperature or other symptoms. By ten next morning he was up and around. I thought that his fright might have been some reaction to liquor.

October 10 we arrived at Colombo, Ceylon, and we tied up at the outer oil crib on the north breakwater for fuel oil and fresh water. I met the agent and called on the consul, the Naval Control, and British Naval Routing officers. Free from duty, I went with Mr. Cruz from the agent's office to the "Elephant Factory." The manufacture of miniature elephants from rosewood and ebony was the principal industry for the tourist trade. I bought a few for Christmas presents. Then at noon we sailed for Cape Town.

A seaman I had signed on in Calcutta to fill a vacancy came before me to complain that he couldn't work any more. I told him, "Don't start anything like that. Do your best. That is all we ask." He went to work.

I could relax somewhat now because Mr. Overland had resumed his normal duties to the fullest.

Our cargo consisted of hessian cloth, jute cuttings, talc, manganese ore, kyanite ore, and cotton bagging. This totaled 9,280 tons, with a value of close to a quarter of a million dollars.

War news: Odessa fell to combined German and Romanian troops. Moscow's outer defenses fell to the Germans. The Portuguese gave Japan a landing field on Timor Island off the Australian Coast. The U.S. destroyer *Kearney* was hit by a torpedo off Iceland. U.S. public sentiment was growing to repeal the Neutrality Act.

Southwest of Madagascar it grew much cooler, and I ordered steam heat put on in all quarters. We had cape pigeons with us again. Toward evening we encountered a southerly gale and rough seas, and the ship was well under water. The safety of the crew was now our main concern, and we stretched lifelines for them to hold on to in getting about the decks. I reassigned the lookout from the forward deck to a position on the wing of the bridge and reduced speed to ease the vessel in the rough sea. As was usual in rough weather, the steward wet the tablecloths and put racks on the tables so dishes couldn't slide off.

It was a pleasure once again for me to watch the pigeons and gliding albatross. Mr. Overland caught a large albacore tuna on a towline. I took a snapshot of the men hauling it in. Spirits were high.

Approaching Cape Town, we were ordered to anchor and soon we were under quarantine and immigration examination. The sick men were seen by a doctor, then we were allowed to proceed provided we could sail by 2:00 P.M. to make room for an arriving convoy. Otherwise we would have had to wait several days, an unpleasant prospect. We entered, cleared, took fuel and water and fresh stores as quickly as possible, and I rounded up the crew who had gone ashore. Although many were drunk, we managed to take departure by 4:40 and shortly we held boat drill.

For the first time I had a good look at the city of Cape Town in daylight. It was a spectacular contrast to the Indian ports and a beautiful sight from the sea, with the city backdropped by Table Mountain and its falling white streams of fog. I doubt that any in the crew had been able to view the city except from the inside of barrooms.

On our way out we met a convoy of British troopships on their way to the Near East.

War news: On October 31 a second U.S. destroyer was sunk in the North Atlantic, with all 120 officers and men lost.

We encountered heavy weather once more. I tried to do some writing, but the ship's motion was so extreme I couldn't keep pen to paper. On November 3, with the swell moderating, it was more comfortable, and I ordered the heads of departments to bring four crew members before me for illicit actions in Cape Town. I gave them each a warning. The men with VD had their pay stopped when they quit working.

We intercepted an SOS from a torpedoed steamer, the *Braef.* There was nothing we could do to help. We were too far away. It was too dangerous to change our course. As we steamed toward Trinidad, the men who had been idle due to illness were returning to work.

War News: S.S. *Alwen* was attacked by a German raider, and the steamer *Bradford City* had been sunk. With boats adrift, her men were rowing for the mainland.

November 5, an AB, who had appeared to have been cured of VD a few days before, suffered severe symptoms again and stopped working. On the eighth all the sick men were well and back at work.

The U.S. Senate annulled the Neutrality Act. This allowed American merchant ships to be armed and sent into combat zones. I wasn't sure that arming merchant ships was a good idea. The Germans would no longer bother to allow men to get into the boats before sinking their vessel. Often a Nazi sub would surface, stop a merchant ship, order the crews into the boats, then sink the vessel. With the merchant ships armed, the U-boats would be foolish to expose themselves beforehand.

November 6 at Trinidad, I went ashore by launch with one of my crewmen to get him medical attention and to clear the vessel. The agent drove me to the suburbs for lunch, a pleasant diversion. After taking on fresh water, we sailed for New Orleans and I searched the ship once more for contraband.

War news: November 16 the American Navy captured an Axis vessel loaded with rubber from the Orient. She had been flying the American flag for disguise, claiming to be the *Willmoto*, and had crossed the Pacific, rounded Cape Horn, and come up the Windward Passage, where she was finally detected. Then her crew tried unsuccessfully to scuttle her.[3] She was, in fact, the German ship *Oldenwald.* A former merchant officer on the Navy ship had previously served on the *Willmoto* and had recognized the deception.

Messman Medlock, a regular bully, one of those involved in running Lewin off the ship in Bombay, had the crew turn on him. He was beaten up and came running to me. I gave him first aid but no sympathy.

November 27 we celebrated Thanksgiving with more gratitude than ever before. We were south of Cape San Antonio at the west end of Cuba. Two days later we enjoyed hearing the Army-Navy game by radio. Our problems seemed slight compared with crews on so many ships that had been torpedoed.

November 30 we made the entrance to the Mississippi River, docked at First Street, New Orleans, and started discharging jute. American-Hawaiian agents, insurance agents, a Naval officer, and a representative of the charterer came aboard.

December 1 I reported to the U.S. Local Inspectors, in writing and in person, regarding Mosner's death. For four hours the FBI investigated on board and continued the investigation the next day. Bos'n Barr was called to testify but refused to speak in my presence, so I left. Later I was told that he claimed that the murder was my fault for having failed to maintain discipline. I was the one who had called for his arrest in the first place, and he must have had it in for me. Three crewmen took off to avoid the inquiry. FBI agents told me that they would not get out of town before being picked up. At 7:00 P.M. I got the ship cleared at the customs house, and at 9:00 we sailed for Baltimore, three seamen short.

We were steaming down the Mississippi River on December 3, just after midnight. Thick fog shut in so fast and so dense it was as though a curtain had dropped before our eyes. We could see nothing. I ordered, "Drop anchor–full astern." The chief mate was standing by the anchor forward for such an emergency and did his duty. As the ship swung to the anchor, he reported that the bow was brushing the overhanging trees on the bank. It was a close call, but the maneuver was a success. The fog cleared, and we raised the anchor and proceeded. At 6:30 A.M. we were off Pilot Town, still in the river. Dense fog once more set in and we anchored again. At 10:00 it cleared a bit. We proceeded and soon discharged the pilot. At 1:30 P.M., with the visibility good, I rested. I was so tired I couldn't see straight.

December 5 we rounded the Florida Keys. In the full strength of the Gulf Stream we made 150 miles in ten hours, remarkable. Even so, this last leg of our trip home seemed interminable.

War news, December 7: Japan bombed the U.S. Pacific fleet at Pearl Harbor. The next day, the U.S. and Britain declared war on Japan.

On the ninth we docked at Baltimore. Even before we were tied up, FBI agents came aboard to seize three more of my deck crew, including Bos'n Barr, and took them back to New Orleans to complete trial. Barr was now the principal suspect, as I had believed all along.

I telephoned home and learned how upset and excited all citizens were over the air raids on our forces at Pearl Harbor.

December 10, at last I finished up my work as master of the *Illinoisan*. At noon I was relieved by Captain Massey. The charterer tipped me $250.

War news: Germany and Italy declared war on the U.S., and Congress declared war on them.

On the eleventh I was up at 6:00, left the vessel, and checked my baggage at the train station. I was with the FBI until 1:30, when I eagerly boarded the train to New York. My diary says that I went to the Music Hall. My wife must have been with me or I never would have gone to the theater. All I can remember about that day was being more tired than ever before in my life. December 12 I finished my business with the charterers and the Navy and headed home. I had been gone five months.

## Notes to Chapter 15

1. Breakers: small water casks used on lifeboats.
2. Bore: a sudden rise of tide that rolls up certain rivers and bays in the form of a breaker.
3. Scuttle: to sink a ship deliberately by opening holes in the hull.

## CHAPTER 16

# EXPLOSION!

Home on vacation, I accepted an invitation to speak at a Rotary Club luncheon, where I told of my grueling trip to India. With the family I went to see the movie *Sergeant York* and helped decorate the church for Christmas. We invited a British seaman from a man-of-war in port to join us for Christmas dinner, but he failed to keep his appointment.

On December 29, 1941, I received orders to report for duty in Philadelphia and supervise the loading of ships with war supplies. American-Hawaiian paid a dividend of $5 a share. I collected an unbelievable $600 for my 120 shares. In January 1942 I was assigned as American-Hawaiian's port captain in New York. I looked after the loading of all of our ships on the East Coast, piloted them, shifted them, and supervised annual inspections. I traveled by train to other ports on a moment's notice to relieve a captain here and another there. I was so busy I didn't get a chance for anything but work. Because of the war, manpower was in such demand that I had difficulty obtaining shore labor, let alone crew or officers. I had to direct the inexperienced shore help for every little detail. It was exhausting work and made me wish I were back at sea. Everybody's problems became mine and I had to make decisions for every situation. There was also a big rush for everything. For instance, the *American* was ready for sea but lacked a full crew. I had only partial success hiring, and when it was time for her to sail, no tugs were available. There was great pressure to sail, so I decided to take a chance and let her proceed without tugs. The ship struck the pier, bending the gunwale near the gangway, so she had to anchor while

I arranged for a survey and tried again to get the crew roster filled. At last she sailed, missing part of her intended cargo.

German submarines were active up and down the East Coast and mine fields were everywhere. Many aids to navigation were out of normal location. All this added to the tension of the job. It was a frigid January, too, and I caught a bad cold.

## The S.S. *Honolulan*

At the American-Hawaiian office on February 7, I met Captain Sutton, master of the *Honolulan.* He had an injured leg and could just barely get around. At that moment I was readying to meet the next ship in Boston and solve whatever problems might arise there. Captain Schermerhorn, the company's operating manager, came to my side and asked me how long it would take me to get ready to go to sea. Having had my fill of the job of port captain, I said, "Ten minutes." The *Honolulan* was ready to sail for the Middle East, but Captain Schermerhorn was not ready to send Captain Sutton on a long voyage with an injured leg, even though Sutton was eager to stay with his ship. Schermerhorn insisted that Sutton be examined. It turned out he had a fractured fibula. Since that made Sutton unfit to go to sea, Schermerhorn relieved him and put me in his place.

With the *Honolulan* already at anchor and ready to sail, I had some mighty fancy rushing around to do. In the ten minutes that I had given myself, I called Dorothy and told her that I was going on a long trip. I couldn't say where, but assured her she would be told later.

The suitcase I had with me was full of winter clothing. By phone I ordered a Palm Beach suit and some lightweight underwear from Rogers-Peet to be delivered immediately to the office. Then I concentrated on ship's business. There were officials to see and papers to file. That evening at 7:45, I boarded the *Honolulan* with my routing instructions. We sailed at 9:30.

The *Honolulan* had been built in Los Angeles in 1924. She was 446 feet long with a breadth of 54.3 feet, and her dead weight rating was 10,970 tons. She was designed to cruise at ten knots. We were headed for Basra in the Persian Gulf via Cape Town. We ran blacked out at night and zigzagged all day with lookouts stationed around the clock. Since radios were considered an aid to the enemy, I had them collected and locked up. I used one at certain hours to get the news, which I posted each day for everyone to see. I explained to the crew that it was for the safety of all that we keep the ship fully blacked out at night.

February 10, 1942, we crossed the Gulf Stream during the night. The sky was clear for the first time since sailing. I collected voluntary contributions for the Red Cross Annual Appeal, then spent a good part of the day on communications by code. The codes were kept in a weighted case for quick dispatch to the bottom of the sea in case of capture. I hemmed the trouser legs of my new suit.

War news: Singapore fell to the Japanese.

On February 16 we made landfall outside Port of Spain, Trinidad. We heard that submarines had attacked ships near Aruba and Curaçao. Next day we passed from the Caribbean into the Atlantic.

War news: The enemy sank three tankers and damaged another off Aruba and shelled the oil installations there. The German naval fleet left Brest in occupied France for the Mediterranean. MacArthur's forces were bombarded by the Japanese at Bataan. The British abandoned Rangoon.

On the nineteenth I was busy on ship's papers. In the evening we decoded a warning to all ships: "Enter and leave port by daylight only."

War news: A ship was torpedoed off Cape Canaveral, Florida. German subs were active off Martinique. Another ship was torpedoed at 13–24 longitude and 49–36 latitude.

Our position was 8–25, 52–37, not that far away.

February 25 we were off the coast of Brazil, running blacked out except for dimmed running lights. We held safety drills, a daily routine.

War news: The Japanese were advancing on Burma.

March 8 we enjoyed fine weather. The albatross joined us as we got nearer to Africa. On March 10 we saw something on the horizon after having seen no other craft for days. It was dangerous to investigate, but the object looked like a boat. Movement in and about it made me think that it might be people in need of help. I hauled up toward it. The nearer we got, the more it seemed like a rescue job. Most of the crew were on deck for the excitement. When we got within a half-mile, we saw something none of us had ever seen before—a dead whale, belly up. It looked white in the sun, or nearly so. The splashing in the water turned out to be sharks attacking the whale from below. There was nothing to rescue, and we resumed our course.

March 12 we sighted the first ship in three weeks. Next day I worked on ship's papers, getting ready for arrival at Cape Town. At 5:00 A.M. an albatross alighted on deck. I estimated its wing spread at seven feet.

On the fourteenth we passed the guard boat, arrived at quarantine, and then docked at Cape Town, where I met with the agent and the British Naval Routing officer. We took on stores, fuel, and water. As expected, I had no mail, but sent several letters off. The next day at six in the morning we were ready to sail, and to my surprise all crew members were on board, ready to go.

March 20 we were approaching the Mozambique Channel. The ice machine broke down, and the engineers worked diligently to get it operating. From one of my officers I borrowed the book *Mission to Moscow*, by Ambassador Davis, which I read with intense interest. We managed to get the ice machine running once again on the twenty-second, before any food was spoiled. Via German radio we heard about the sinking of our *Texan* on the Brazilian coast. It was like losing a close friend.

War news: The Japanese pounded our fortress at Corregidor in the Philippines and took the Andaman Islands in the Bay of Bengal south of Burma. The Italians were pounding Malta, the British battering Germany by air.

March 27 was Allan's nineteenth birthday, and again I was far from home and family. March 30, with the crew doing repairs to the running rigging aloft, one of them accidentally dropped a marlin spike,[1] and it went through one of the nine partially-assembled Boston Bombers on deck. We were now passing from the Indian Ocean to the Arabian Sea.

April 4 we entered the Persian Gulf through the Strait of Hormuz. Our instructions were indefinite, so we steamed carefully for forty miles, sounding continuously, and at last came upon the pilot boat and Naval Control. At 7:00 P.M., with the pilot aboard, we proceeded and anchored eight miles below Basra, Iraq, for the night. The port, situated on the Shatt-al-Arab River at the mouth of the Tigris and Euphrates Rivers, had been in the hands of the Germans but had recently been seized by the British Navy. The natives much preferred the Germans, which posed some problems.

On the seventh we docked and started discharging the nine Boston Bombers via a floating crane and then discharged grain to the dock. When I went to meet Mr. Munn, the British quartermaster receiving the cargo, he pointed to the sides of the planes, which were stenciled "Britain Delivers the Goods." On each of them, the word "Britain" had been crossed out and "Uncle Sam" written in with chalk. I laughed and said, "Must have been some member of my crew." He smiled. Munn hated Basra and called it "the asshole of the world." I found the labor, laundry, and stores services very unsatisfactory.

The terminal was a fine one, with docks built of hardwood, but the village was simply a clump of one-story buildings made of timber, mud, or corrugated steel. We could see fertile land on the banks of the river extending from the shore up five hundred feet to the tableland of desert. There was nothing green or growing anywhere else. Small sailing vessels traveled down the river with the current, but when headed upstream, they were hauled by hand from a path close to the banks. The women wore black and none had shoes. We often saw them walking from the docks up a path to the village and sitting down on the desert sand to rest. The main street in town was decked over to keep out the sun's heat. Sandstorms were common. They seemed like fog, with the air full of very fine particles. The entire port was blacked out at night.

April 8 Captain Truxton from the American Military Mission brought on board two passengers to be returned to the States. I was not keen on taking them, but after much discussion with the agent and the consul, I realized that when they are put aboard by the government, "That's it." April 9 we shifted to the stream off Ashur and were moored to buoys. I went ashore by boat.

War news: U.S. forces on the Bataan peninsula in the Philippines surrendered to the Japanese.

April 10 my chief mate, Mr. Coas, was sick with a temperature of 100.4, pulse 102, face flushed. Seaman Corsetti had the itch, for which I gave him a sulfur ointment. Messboy Lander was sick, possibly from drink, and AB Thompson also had the itch. I got Dr. Thornton to the ship by boat. Mr. Coas's condition was diagnosed as malaria. I was to see that he took quinine three times a day. The doctor prescribed medicine for Mr. Bowles's sore eyes. Those with the itch and several with diarrhea were prescribed castor oil.

April 15 at Magil, I had much to do about the passengers. On the seventeenth we discharged oil pipe. The weather was fine but very hot. In the evening I was suffering from the heat. I called on a British ship close by. She was a former German vessel seized by the British the previous September at Bandar e Shapur, Iran. Captain Streets was the master, and he turned out to be a friend of Ivan Sutherland, my next-door neighbor at home.

On the eighteenth we had an air raid alert and I held fire and boat drill. Next day we moored at Abadan, Iran. The following day we passed quarantine and began to discharge pipe. The mate informed me that we were short one lighter and that we needed more wire slings. I ordered more. It was dreadfully slow work using but a single sling.

April 20 I was sick with diarrhea myself and very weak. We were discharging inefficiently, with only one gang and too few wire slings. Next day I sent the chief steward ashore to see about obtaining vegetables and having the laundry done. No results. The agent advised against sending laundry ashore. He told me that the *Charles Carroll* had lost a quarter of hers. Before noon an additional lighter came alongside so we could work a second gang. I stayed on board, half sick and weak.

April 24 I was feeling better and that night slept well until 1:30 A.M., when I was wakened by Seaman Brown, who was standing on the lighter alongside and calling for a ladder to get aboard. The gangway was down, but being in his cups, he either couldn't find it or chose not to. I had a pilot ladder lowered for him, hoping he would then go to bed and be quiet. He did. April 25 I sent Seaman Reeves to the hospital for venereal disease treatment. During the day the crew cleaned and painted the lifeboats. I finished reading *The Seven Wonders of Africa.*

On the twenty-seventh, four crew members were in the hospital with VD. That night one of the native longshoremen suffered a broken leg while discharging pipe. He was taken ashore to the oil plant's hospital, but because of his religion he would not allow treatment of any kind, a sad thing because his leg was severely deformed, and he would never have use of it again.

On the twenty-ninth we sailed back to Basra and resumed discharging. In desperate need of clean linen for the crew, I sent the ship's laundry ashore. By May 2 work on the lifeboats was complete, and on the fourth we were on our way to Bombay. As we steamed along the sandy Persian (Iranian) coast, we could occasionally see a man riding a camel. The routing officer told me that Japanese submarines were known to be in the vicinity, since some Japanese had purchased fish from a local fisherman a few nights before. Brown was sick with a temperature of 103. He was taking quinine and aspirin. I ordered my messboy to wait on him at meal hours. Between meals I gave him fruit juice, and by 8:00 P.M. his temperature was down to 99. Asking a seaman to check on him every two hours during the night, I worked on ship's accounts, washed and ironed clothes, and tended the other sick crew members.

War news: U.S. and Filipino troops on Corregidor surrendered to the Japanese.

May 7 we zigzagged in smooth water. I checked overtime sheets and tended the sick. Brown was much improved.

War news: In order to protect maritime trade routes and to avert Japanese invasion, the British took over Madagascar from its Vichy French rule, after three and a half months of fighting the Nazi collaborators. The Japanese advanced east up the Burma road into China but lost heavily in a naval battle off the northeast coast of Australia.

May 9 we were blacked out and zigzagging, navigating with much care. I held fire and boat drill and secured boats inboard. May 11 we lay at anchor off Bombay. I took a boat for shore, where the agents advised me regarding medical services, stores, and laundry.

On May 12 I contracted to have the top of the engine room tank chipped. I sent Seaman Small, who was suffering with VD, to the doctor. I sent the chief steward ashore to look at stores and to get laundry taken care of.

I was ordered to keep the ship alert and ready to go to sea at a moment's notice in case the port was attacked by the Japanese, as the port of Colombo, Ceylon, had been. For that reason I ordered the crew to remain on board. This was not a popular decision. At noon Brown complained of a sore foot and asked to go ashore for treatment. I refused to give him permission, since he had seen the doctor for treatment that morning. While I was at supper, four seaman sneaked into the shore boat. The officer on watch reported this to me, and I ordered them back on board. They returned sheepishly.

On May 16 we had about a hundred shore laborers on board chipping rusted plates. Brown and Small insisted on going ashore, with or without a pass, for medical treatment. I did not consider their cases legitimate. Small came on the bridge and foulmouthed me. I warned him that his attitude could persuade me to use irons. At 3:00 P.M. Brown again begged for medical attention. I gave him a pass and permission to go at his own expense. Next day at noon he returned from the shore boat and started up the pilot ladder. He was so drunk he couldn't make it. Officers were afraid he would fall overboard, so they hoisted him up. Wiper Shark failed to return until 5:30 P.M. He had no excuse. I fined him two days' pay.

That did it. The crew held a meeting and gave me an account of their deliberations. As a result, I gave three delegates liberty to go to the consul to discuss their grievances. I wrote a letter to the consul explaining that my order was for the safety of ship and crew. I noted that in the case of the Japanese air attack on Colombo, ships that were ready had gone to sea, and those that were not ready were sunk.

At 9:00 A.M. on Monday the eighteenth, McMasters, Brown, and Racomonte, the three elected union delegates, went to the consul's office to see if shore leave could be extended to all the crew. While ashore they met men from other ships who claimed they were not restricted, which convinced them I was being much too severe. The consul told them that he was not going to tell any captain how to run his ship. The next day Brown asked if a few men at a time might have leave. I said I would consider such a compromise and I granted liberty to a few men in each department, subject to the department head's approval. All were happy. I still kept the ship ready to go to sea, if need be, even if we had to leave without part of the crew.

On the twenty-sixth we were still anchored off Bombay. Small went to the clinic once more, having allegedly been there all day long the day before. He claimed to be too sick to work. Brown was ill but went ashore with my permission. Seaman Corsetti was missing all day. He returned at five in the evening, and I fined him one day's pay for absence without permission.

Small returned to the ship at noon the next day with a verbal message from Lander, who was in the hospital. He had been missing without permission since Saturday but was reported to have been seen in a bar on Monday. Brown reported for duty only for two hours. At last, 2,687 pieces of clean ship's linen were returned. Passengers Kelley and Holmes left the vessel with all their personal effects to report for work on the passenger ship *Brazil,* which was returning to the U.S.

We had ninety-five men from shore chipping and painting on deck, in the engine room, and over the side. The noise was painful. Lander was still missing. Brown reported for duty for a full day.

Most of my officers, engineers, and crew faithfully performed their duties as they were supposed to, for which they earned my undying gratitude. There were just a certain few who worked every angle to be off, using illness as an excuse. I had to give them the benefit of the doubt.

May 30 I went ashore, found that cargo was ready to load, and I made a trip to the hospital to see Lander, who was then suffering from heart trouble. The following day we shifted to the Alexandria docks, where we started loading manganese ore from two strings of wagons abreast the ship, each string containing about seven hundred tons of ore. After being at anchor for three weeks, it was good to get the ship back in service again. While the loading of manganese proceeded, the shore gang continued chipping and painting.

June 2 I went to the hospital and saw Lander. The doctor said that he was fit for work. At three he reported on board and told me that he would start work in the morning. At 4:30 P.M., Mr. Coas came to my door. He had Seaman Brown with him and complained to me that Brown was trying to take over the mate's duties. Brown had told him, "I'm running the ship." As Mr. Coas was relating this, Brown forced his way past him into my office. It was obvious that Brown had been drinking. I ordered him out of my room, but he refused to move. I said to Mr. Coas, "Go to your room and get me a set of irons." Once Mr. Coas was out of sight, I walked up to Brown, a big man, and picked him up, pinning his arms to his side. I carried him out to the passageway and dropped him to the deck. Then I ducked inside, slammed my door and locked it. I saw no more of Brown. Mr. Coas never returned with irons. He knew I had a set right there in my desk drawer and that I just wanted him out of the way so that he would not be a witness to my manhandling of Brown.

June 3 the chief steward and I went to the market for supplies. Even the best were of poor quality. On the way I bought three carved ivory necklaces and a brooch. June 4 we loaded jute and jute gunnies that had been shipped by rail overland from Calcutta. It was no longer safe to send ships there because of Japanese submarines in the Bay of Bengal.

As was the custom, before sailing, we mailed the owners copies of bills paid and advances made to the crew. This was to make sure that accounts could be squared and to minimize fraudulent claims should the ship be lost at sea. On all labor bills in India there was an allowance for officers doing the supervision and the usual cumshaw[2] on all bills for the captain. I accepted this money and subtracted it from the bills as I turned them in to the owners.

June 6 we finished loading 8,329 tons of ore and jute, secured the ship for sea, and sailed for Cape Town. We swung the boats outboard and posted extra lookouts.

June 8 saw fair weather, overcast with a westerly swell. I washed and ironed my soiled clothing and had the ship secured and washed down. AB Thompson had an epileptic fit and failed to stand his watch. I got bills, accounts, and the logs in order with the purser's help. It was very hot and I was suffering with heat rash.

The next day, Thompson reported for duty, but Lander claimed to have burned his leg on the after capstan. I had a metal guard put on it to prevent limbs from touching it when it was in use. The sea made up in the evening, so I had lifelines stretched to aid the crew in getting back and forth over the open deck.

June 10, with heavy weather, the ship was awash. Again I ordered the men to seal up all radios except for the one that I controlled and used to receive the news.

June 12 I held fire and boat drill but allowed no one on the forward deck because there was danger of being washed overboard. I worked on illness reports and my expense account. At 6:00 P.M. the ship's cat was washed overboard. We mourned her departure in silence.

On the thirteenth, with the weather moderate, I cleared up my desk, published the scuttlebutt for the bulletin board, and worked the stars.

War news: Germans were pressing the British Eighth Army at Tobruk in North Africa and were approaching Sevastopol and Kharkov in the Soviet Ukraine. Another contingent of American troops arrived in Northern Ireland, including a great many Negroes.

On the eighteenth, with fresh southeast winds, we had a good day's run, the best in ten days. The vessel rolled more and the wind became abeam and, to prevent damage to the lifeboats, we had to swing them in. We held Lyle gun drill. At noon Oiler McMasters failed to report for duty.

June 20 the weather moderated, but the vessel was rolling so heavily that the gunwale picked up water on each side. Corsetti told me he was treating himself for VD using sulfanilamide, the usual medicine in those pre-penicillin days.

War news: Germans in Libya drove the British back to the Egyptian border.

June 21 we were in Mozambique Channel with a good bright moon to light our way. We sighted several vessels. I studied piloting and looked for friendly birds.

War news: Axis forces were advancing in Libya and taking many prisoners and supplies. Tobruk fell to the Nazis under Rommel. The British retreated inside the Egyptian border. Sevastopol was still holding on after seventeen days of fighting on the Crimean Peninsula.

July 1 we approached Cape Town and arrived in the thirty-two-mile mine-swept channel just after dawn. For two full days we continued at anchor outside, awaiting our turn for stores, water, fuel, and routing. There was a cold westerly wind during the night. The "tablecloth" well covered the mountain behind the city. I had an urgent flag signal up all day for a boat. This was answered neither by a signal nor by the arrival of a launch. Although launches passed nearby, none heeded our hail. The crew chipped rust at the forward hatches. Seaman Corsetti failed to report for duty due to VD. I warned him that this was cause for stopping his pay.

On the third we still waited for our turn to enter. There was a northwest gale with rough seas and rain squalls. At 2:00 P.M. we found the vessel dragging, so we let go the second anchor. I wore myself out waiting anxiously for orders. I did not bother to signal for a boat because the weather was too severe to embark, but we did hold fire and boat drill. Next day the weather improved but left a heavy swell. At last we docked and took on fuel, water, and wonderfully fresh provisions. I had the doctor examine Corsetti and received a new supply of medicine. I met with the consul, the Naval attaché, the British Naval Control officer, and got our latest routing instructions.

I wrote home, but it was always a challenge to decide what to say. All mail went through the hands of censors, government agents whose job was to be sure no information that might be of value to the enemy was transmitted. We were required to mail letters unsealed and to write on just one side of the paper so that any words that the censor cut out would not affect writing on the opposite side.

On July 5 we sailed for Baltimore. Several vessels were outside Cape Town at anchor. I steamed over close to our *Columbian* and talked with Captain Johnson by megaphone. Then we slowly passed our *Montanan*, close enough for me to talk to my brother Albert, who gave me news of home, about which I had heard not a word in five months.

On sailing, we swung out all lifeboats and secured them. My directions were to follow four thousand miles up the African coast, then head for Trinidad, where I would join an American convoy to Baltimore. Otherwise we were to travel alone because of our slow speed.

At Cape Town we were fortunate to have taken on good, fresh provisions, including fruits and vegetables. These had not been available in Iraq, Iran, or India. We relished the nice mealy potatoes and sweet grapes. All were glad to be homeward bound.

War news: Germans were at El Alamein, sixty-five miles from Alexandria, Egypt.

On July 7 Corsetti resumed work. He had been absent from duty for five days, for which I stopped his pay. After checking on our blackout effectiveness, I wrote up the scuttlebutt and between news items added warnings and advice for emergencies. Our route was supposed to take us clear of known submarine positions, but we could never be certain as to their whereabouts.

On the eighth Seaman Thompson suffered a second epileptic fit and had to be relieved from duty. July 9 was overcast with an occasional break in the sky such that we caught a few sights for position. The purser and I were busy on paperwork. Thompson returned to duty. I held fire and boat drills.

War news: Germans forces were trying to cross the Don River one hundred miles east of Kursk and to the north of Kharkov in the Ukraine.

July 15 we met one steamer. No stars were visible. I varnished my bed frame and the bathroom brightwork and washed my clothes and curtains for the bedroom ports. We sighted several whales, surprising in this hot latitude, three degrees south. I held the usual drills. Once more Corsetti failed to report for duty. He had pains all over. I believed this to be from an overdose of sulfanilamide and had him stop the treatment.

War news: Germans were driving down the Don River towards Stalingrad on the Volga. In North Africa there was a stalemate near El Alamein.

Monday, July 20, we had a stiff southeast wind from astern that blew hot air from the fire room into my quarters. I sorted my personal belongings, getting ready to go home on arrival in Baltimore. I was hoping for my annual vacation. I checked with the purser and heads of departments, published the daily news, had the slop chest room cleaned, and painted the floor. This was the driest day of the trip, so we ventilated the cargo.

Wednesday, July 22 was fair with southwest monsoon and sea. At 1:00 P.M. we held fire and boat drill. At 5:00 P.M. the crew and junior officers were at supper. We senior officers were to eat, as usual, at 5:30. I was sitting in my office swivel chair with piles of the crew's overtime slips in front of me. I was checking each one against the log book for accuracy, and as I completed each sheet, I stacked it on the floor beside me.

5:14 P.M.: Explosion! The ship shook violently. I was on the deck, dumped backwards among a pile of overtime sheets. My desk tore loose from its moorings and overturned. The framed pictures shattered and ripped from the bulkhead. I had no doubt about what had happened. On the bridge there was glass everywhere from the broken wheelhouse windows, and the compass lay on the deck, popped right out from the binnacle.

Having practiced safety drills, we all knew what to do. The officers carried assigned equipment to the lifeboats. The engineers had orders to stop the engines and make for the lifeboats. With the engines stopped and using no steam, the boiler pressure built up and blew the safety valve on the top of the smoke stack, making a deafening sound. The radio officer, Mr. Sullivan, had the SOS message already prepared and only needed to insert our position, which the officer on watch gave him immediately. The message read: "AMERICAN STEAMER HONOLULAN. SUBMARINE ATTACK. POSITION 8–41 NORTH, 22–12 WEST. VESSEL SINKING. MASTER."

The crew rushed for the lifeboats. The torpedo had hit on the starboard side, just aft of the engine room bulkhead. Number three boat, nearest the blast, was demolished, turned nearly inside out. Those assigned to that boat took places in the remaining three. I went to the center of the boat deck, expecting to take charge of getting the lifeboats filled, lowered and away. Already boats two and four on the port side were on their way down. Number one boat on the starboard side, usually the captain's boat, was ready to lower but was not descending. I called, "Lower away," but the men at the falls hesitated. I was anxious to get the boats away from the ship since she was flooding with seawater, and there was danger she would capsize and take the lifeboats with her to the bottom if they were close by or still on the falls. Small was at the forward falls. He was the union delegate, and he and I had had several confrontations not long before. He wouldn't lower the boat. I got up close so that he could hear and I bellowed, "What are you waiting for?"

"You!" he replied. This was a compliment, coming from him, and I was impressed with his concern. I insisted, and he lowered the boat. Buoyed by the sea, all three boats automatically unhooked from the falls. The seamen doing the lowering slid down the falls to the floating boats. It was no more than three minutes since the explosion.

It was my plan to abandon ship but to rejoin her later if she remained stable. With the boats away, I went to the radio shack to be sure that Mr. Sullivan was broadcasting the emergency message. Sullivan said, "Look up and see if the antenna between the mastheads is intact." It was. From that high position in the radio shack I saw that the after deck was settling, awash. Much of the deck gear in the area was broken and adrift. However, I hoped that she might not settle any further. There was still a possibility of bringing the crew back aboard, a more comfortable place to await rescue than in lifeboats.

*At that point Dad did something he never mentioned for the public record. His frugality got the better of him. He went to his room, opened his closet doors, wrapped his arms around his hanging clothes, carried them to the rail and dumped them onto a raft. Subsequently, the evidence of this act went to the bottom.*

Most of the crew had not eaten supper. It was foolish to remain aboard and risk being caught inside the vessel should she roll over, but I went quickly to the officers' mess room and grabbed a white enamel bucket. From the icebox, I dropped in a dish of hard-boiled eggs, some cheese, and a dish of sliced cold meat. On top of these I put in a dish of sliced jellyroll from the supper table. Into a second bucket I put two loaves of bread. I rushed them to the forward end of the vessel where to my surprise I met Mr. Coas, my chief mate. I had thought that only Sullivan and I remained aboard. Coas was a quiet man but always on the job and I was greatly pleased to see him. He and I made up lines for passing the buckets to a near-by lifeboat.

5:28 P.M.: A second torpedo exploded beneath us. The whole vessel was awash. We swam for the boats, and the buckets of precious food sank to the bottom. (Afterwards the crew asked jokingly, "Captain, what did you do with the food?") We saw Sullivan step from the boat deck to a raft. As the ship sank, the sounding boom struck the raft, capsized it, and dumped Sullivan into the sea. The ship was out of sight beneath heavy foam as she slipped toward the bottom. Several hundred bales of jute floated low in the water. To our relief, Mr. Sullivan popped up among the debris. One of the seamen in my boat jumped overboard to part the bales of jute so that we could row the boat toward Sullivan. At last we came alongside him, a huge man made even larger by his lifejacket. It took several men to parbuckle him up the high-sided lifeboat. This operation was complete at 5:41 P.M.

Four minutes later a submarine, painted gray with no visible identifying marks, rose from beneath the surface near number four boat. The submarine commander and eight men emerged from the conning tower and ordered the boat alongside. They were all young and suntanned—they must have had a secret base somewhere in the South Atlantic. The men manned three guns on the after deck, one on the forward deck, and one in the conning tower. Another man held a machine gun and another a movie camera. All these devices were aimed directly at us. I let the weighted bag of secret codes slip to the bottom.

The U-boat commander asked Mr. Nelson, commander of number four boat, "What is the name of your vessel?" He spoke English well. Then he asked, "Of what nationality? From what port did you sail? Where were you bound?" After receiving Nelson's answers, he asked, "Where is your captain? Are he and the others all right? Do you have food and water? Do you have cigarettes?" With a negative response to the last question, the commander handed down two cartons of Overstoltz cigarettes and a bag of matches. Then he asked Nelson if we had the course and distance to the two nearest neutral ports, Bathurst, Gambia (now known as Banjul), and Freetown, Sierra Leone. He gave the headings to Nelson, advised the boat to shove off to avoid being hit by the sub's propeller, and called, "Good luck." In great relief, all those in Mr. Nelson's boat shouted, "Thank you, and good luck to you." The submarine disappeared over the horizon to the south.

It was dusk—being near the Equator, the days were twelve hours long. We took roll call, and it was then that we discovered Oiler McMasters was missing. We searched the jetsam for signs of him. We found none but recovered extra rockets and water from the rafts. The boats reassembled, and the men asked me to say a prayer for McMasters.

Afterwards, I explained to all that we were safe to stay where we were in deep water and that we had successfully broadcast the distress message and the ship's position. Now it was advisable to keep cool and await rescue. The officers and experienced seamen felt lucky to be in deep water. The others failed to be convinced that waiting was safer than risking a landing on a rocky shore in possibly hostile territory.

Homeward-bound sailors often try to figure the exact moment of arrival and reunion with loved ones. They count the weeks, days, and minutes, and conduct a pool, placing their bets. Our new situation made for a new game, with many worrying "if," not "when."

We moored the lifeboats together for the night, using a sea anchor similar to the one I had used on the *Sea Jack* in Boston's outer harbor. It kept the boats headed into the wind, riding at greater safety. Five hundred miles from the nearest land, we thirty-eight men spent a terrible night. The small boats rolled and tossed in the rough sea. The wind blew and heavy rain fell. There was no shelter and no place to rest. Although we were in the tropics, the brisk wind blowing over our wet bodies made us all cold. Most of us were seasick. In boat number one, only I and Mr. Lucas, the purser, were not, and he had never been to sea before. Once an hour, we shot a red rocket high into the sky.

At daybreak we saw a four-motored plane patrolling the area. At 9:30 it dropped a yellow package nearby, which proved to be a lifejacket and a container with chocolate, a smoking pipe, tobacco, and a message reading: CORVETTE[3] BE OUT AT 6 AM. MAN IN YELLOW LIFEJACKET 1 ½ MILES UPWIND. MUST LEAVE, SHORT OF FUEL. SERGEANT FELLARD, BATHURST.

All three boats immediately got underway. The men struggled to row those heavy, overcrowded, high-gunwaled lifeboats to windward against the heavy sea and rain. At 3:00 P.M. Mr. Coas's boat, which had the most regular seamen and best oarsmen aboard, discovered McMasters floating in the water. He was lifted on board.

McMasters had been in the water for nearly twenty-two hours. He had managed to put on the lifejacket dropped to him by the plane, but otherwise he was wearing nothing but short pants and a singlet. He had been walking on the after deck just as the torpedo hit and was blown overboard into the sea. Treading water, he had watched the ship travel away from him and had seen the dust fly from the ports when the second torpedo hit. Nearly spent, he had found a floating hatch plank to hold on to. The water was warmer than the air so he kept himself shoulder deep. He had been surrounded by sharks and had several times struck out at them. Once he had pulled a small fish from his leg. We found that the flesh had been stripped from his heels and toes and a hunk of meat had been gouged out of his thigh. His courage, stamina, and will to stay alive and afloat all night without the aid of any life-saving equipment was hard to believe possible. He had lost a lot of blood, but the wounds had been cauterized by the seawater, and he bled little after rescue. The men made a bed for him using the kapok from two of the boat's metal air tanks.[4]

Eventually everyone recovered from seasickness, but they did not lack for misery. At 9:30 P.M. we heard a plane circling overhead. No corvette arrived. There was, however, comfort in knowing that our distress signal had been heard.

Friday, July 24, we continued to have rough seas and pelting rain. The bilges had to be bailed frequently. I remembered having seen junks in the Orient carrying their lumber outside the gunwale, so I had our oars slung similarly, giving us a smooth, but not soft or motionless, place to sit. Our elbows and bottoms were already raw from the constant motion of the boats. With no real exercise, we had little desire for food. Warm water and crackers seemed to sustain us.

That night, beginning at midnight, I was on watch with a seaman. By then the sky was clear. Together we tended the lookout and the moorings and fired a rocket every two hours. At one point I had him watch for ships, and for a while I lay down on a thwart. I could see a heaven without limit. I watched the nearby stars and an endless number beyond them. Never before had I felt like such a small speck in the wondrous universe.

I was desperate for exercise and at daybreak I stripped off my clothes and dove overboard to swim, returning after a few minutes. I was quite proud of myself as I smoothly boarded over the high gunwale. Once aboard, my companion deflated my ego by pointing out seven sharks swimming under the boat. I thought about my responsibilities to my family and did not go swimming again.

Shortly, a four-motored plane arrived and circled the area for nearly three hours. Then it dropped a lifejacket, which we recovered. Tied in it were five cans of beef stew and a message reading, "CORVETTE 50 MILES AWAY. SHOULD ARRIVE IN 3 OR 4 HOURS. WE ARE LEAVING. SHORT OF FUEL. HEREWITH DISTRESS SIGNALS AND SOME CHOP. BEST OF LUCK FROM CREW H 204." We did not find the distress signals, but the cans of stew were intact. We fed some to McMasters. We had high hopes of rescue and all kept an intense lookout for the corvette. At noon we rowed my boat to within speaking distance of Mr. Nelson's to confer. Oscar Nelson, second mate and a veteran of the sea, was in charge of the number four boat. He was the navigating officer of the ship and had the navigating equipment in his possession. It was his duty to determine our official position, which he reported to be seventeen miles northeast from where we were the day before. Our drifting that far could have accounted for the corvette failing to locate us. After dark we heard a plane in the distance. It flashed to us in Morse code, "Corvette is coming," then disappeared. We saw no sign of the corvette. The men were restless. One man was really hostile and all wanted action.

Saturday, July 25. The monotonous waiting and the repeated promise of rescue enraged some in the crew. The crew in Mr. Nelson's boat angrily protested our failing to attempt a landing on the African coast. Mr. Nelson was about fifty years old, blond, freckled, friendly, and normally quiet. He had faith and tried to laugh off a threat of mutiny in his boat. He controlled the boat from his station in the stern where the steering was done with a heavy sixteen-foot sweep like the oars of ancient galleys. After reasoning with the mutinous crew, I told Mr. Nelson so that all could hear, "You are in charge and are responsible for the safety of your lifeboat and its crew. Although legally you are under my command, if you think another course is advisable, I hereby release you."

Up to this point Mr. Nelson had been very passive. But now at the limit of his patience, he took command with a firm voice, stated his case for staying with the other boats, and warned the hostile man, "Stay in the other end of the boat or be knocked overboard with a long sweep." He made it clearly understood that his boat was not to be wrecked on the treacherous African coast. He heard no more opposing views that day.

It had rained most of the day and night. My crew groaned and suffered as they tried to rest on the hard wooden thwarts. To freshen our mouths we fashioned makeshift toothbrushes by whipping small rope yarns into short bristles.

Once more on duty from midnight to 6:00 A.M., I mentally reviewed the situation. I felt certain that we would be picked up eventually, and I figured that it was my job to help the men be patient. I wondered how I could improve morale. Just before daybreak I woke the chief steward, Mr. Rocomonte, and asked him if he would make hot chocolate if I made a fire. Soon all thirteen men in my boat were intensely busy under the direction of Mr. Dancy, the third mate. One of the men chopped a hard ash oar into short lengths. Each piece was then cut into slivers by those who had knives. We transformed a metal breaker into a stove by chopping a hole in the bottom for a flue and another hole on the side through which an empty rocket can was inserted as a kettle. We set the whole thing up on the stern so that the wind would make a draft through it. Using waxed paper from chocolate bars, we started a fire, then added the slivers of wood. This made a lot of visible smoke. Cheers went up from the men in the other boats as they realized something was cooking. We soon dissolved shavings from the chocolate bars in water in the makeshift kettle. We had difficulty dissolving our milk tablets, but we finally solved the problem by shaking a few tablets at a time in a jar with water. We ended up with a thick, creamy syrup, which we boiled and diluted with more water. Using boathooks and buckets, we passed a share of the hot chocolate to the other boats. It was not safe to allow the boats to come too close to one another in the running sea. Then we made a second bucketful of this sweet, hot liquid for ourselves. The first hot drink in three days put new life into all of us. Frowns turned to smiles.

Before noon Mr. Coas and Mr. Nelson asked me how long I intended to wait for the corvette. Their men still wanted to get moving. I replied, "A reasonable length of time." Again I offered to release them to go their own way, but neither of them chose to do so. Later that day I finally decided that we had waited long enough. We set sails and got underway in "V" formation.

We sailed with the wind. The lug sails gave us little choice as to direction. I thought that perhaps we were headed toward more frequented steamer routes, where there would be a better chance of being sighted and rescued. Not once did the crews in the boats ask the destination. Everyone was relaxed because at last we were doing something, going somewhere. We were running free with my boat in the lead. During the night we placed a lighted lantern at the masthead. It waved as the boat floundered about in the sea and might be sighted by an oncoming vessel. We conserved the few rockets we had left.

Sunday, July 26. We had been under full sail all night. In spite of the rain, everyone was happy because we were moving. I was glad that there was lots of sea room ahead of us, and we did not need to worry about rocks, reefs, shipwreck, or the jungle for a long time.

At daybreak the weather cleared, and the sun came out for the first time since we had boarded the lifeboats four days before. Clothes, stores, and the boats themselves dried out. We made more hot chocolate. Some of the men towed fishhooks baited with white cloth torn from their clothing, but all the fish that bit were lost because the men had made the lines fast to the boat, and since there was no spring in the line, the hooks and lines were carried away. All we ate was crackers. More food was not a priority.

With the fresh southwest wind filling the lug sails full from astern and the waves heaving us ahead, it was easy to imagine that we were making great speed. In order to keep together in a regular formation, it was necessary for my boat, in the lead, to check its speed. This we accomplished by shortening sail just a little by squeezing the clew a bit. Even members of the engine department took part in the handling of sail and had fun doing it. The sailors in my boat sewed a six-foot "V" of small rope onto the sail with a bucket underneath the point to hold rainwater as it ran down the rope dam. Everyone was busy. Mr. Shukhart, the chief engineer, took it upon himself to build a shelter using metal from an air tank. Mr. Lucas, the purser, was busy working on the illness reports. Some men wrote letters, some read the few available magazines. McMasters showed an occasional smile.

The lifeboats were visible to each other when we rose on adjoining wave crests, invisible when in adjoining hollows. Flying fish skimmed the surface and the petrels, called Mother Carey's chickens, fluttered about. Occasionally we saw Swiss men-o-war (large jellyfish) shining in the sunlight. At night the skies were extremely clear, and once more as I lay looking up at the heavens, I was overcome by the wonder of the universe.

Monday, July 27. McMasters was now my major concern. A very sick man, he lay on the floor of number two boat on his bed of kapok, nursed and cared for under the direct supervision of the chief mate. He was now very much in need of medical attention.

At noon Mr. Nelson verified our estimated position with the use of his sextant and chronometer and by observation of the sun. He announced that since abandoning ship, we had traveled a good 242 miles to the east-north-east. We were now 250 miles from Bathurst, West Africa.

At dusk, during our routine securing the boat for the night, the second cook suddenly startled us by shouting, "Ship! Ship! Ship ahoy!" Amazed, we looked aft and stared. It was no mirage. There she was, over the horizon, hull part down, a beautiful ship heading at right angles to our course. Apparently her lookouts had not yet seen us. Immediately we fired our remaining rockets. Such excitement, so sudden. The ship turned toward us. This was the moment we had been waiting for, and it came when we least expected it. Most of us had given up on rescue, and we were resigned to saving ourselves.

The vessel was on us in no time, and we prepared for rescue. We dowsed the sails and masts, took our oars inboard, and threw the stove overboard, which brought loud protest from the other boats. We maneuvered the boats with the oars as best we could to go alongside the ship. The wind was from the southwest, and the ship was heading north for us. She passed to the leeward of my boat and to the weather side of numbers two and four. She didn't get her headway off until she passed us by. She was so high-sided that she drifted rapidly to the east before the wind. We had to row hard to bring my boat to her lee side. Luckily, the ship was ready for us. She headed just to windward of the boats and stopped by reversing engines at the full. The side ports were open on the lee side, and several Jacob's ladders were dropped to water's edge. The strong wind pressed the big vessel hard against the boats. There was danger they might capsize as they rose and fell in the swell against the hull of the ship. The men tried to ease the pressure with oars.

A wire stretcher basket was lowered from the ship, and McMasters was hoisted quite smoothly aboard, in spite of the bobbing. The ship's crew tried to take our boats aboard, but since their hooks didn't match ours and time was of the essence in these submarine-infested waters, they abandoned the salvage. We scrambled on board over the Jacob's ladders—thirty-eight men, tired, hungry, ragged, bearded, sore, weather-beaten, and, for the most part, barefooted. After six days in the boats, it was like entering a new world. The three lifeboats were set free, and the ship proceeded on her way.

Our rescue ship turned out to be the British *Winchester Castle*, a 22,000-ton transport vessel. She carried a crew of 470 but had not a single lifeboat. She was returning from northern Madagascar where she had landed 5,000 troops, using all her lifeboats.

I was ushered up to the bridge to meet Captain Newdigate. I gave him a brief account of our circumstances, stating our nationality and destination. The *Winchester Castle* was, to our extreme good fortune, headed for New York for repairs. On board was a British Army quartermaster who had soldiers' clothing for us. There were two medical men ready to help. We all needed to wash, shave, have our hair cut, and get into dry clothes. In addition to McMaster's medical problems, there were several cases of fractured ear drums sustained by crew members who had been below decks at the time of the first explosion, and a few men had broken their toes while climbing barefoot up the side of the rescue ship. All of us had skin problems from exposure. My nose was peeling and my cheeks had deep cracks in them, as was the case for most of my men.

We cleaned up and our rescuers served us a hot meal at one long table, gave us medical care, and found us a place to sleep. Captain Newdigate lent me a pair of his pajamas. He was short and round, and I, tall and long, which made for an amusing fit. I didn't care how they looked. They felt wonderful.

Wednesday, July 29, following a glorious night's sleep, I made an effort to dry my papers and my few clothes. I then made arrangements for each man in my crew to see the doctor and to receive supplies from the commissary and canteen. From the quartermaster I secured a British Army khaki shirt, shorts, a razor, handkerchiefs, stockings, and brown sneakers. Most of the officers and crew got about the same. McMasters was in the ship's hospital and was already responding nicely to treatment. The doctor confirmed that he had lost a lot of blood.

On the thirtieth, we had boat drill at 11:00 A.M. Assigned to life rafts, there being no boats, we were all given life preservers.

My crew and officers seemed to be having a fine time. The purser and I were trying to pick up lost accounts and records from memory. As best we could, we reconstructed the totals on overtime that each man had logged from Cape Town. We had to do some estimating and asked each crew member to help us. The officers in charge of each department and their men signed as to the agreed-upon number of hours. This accomplished, payrolls could be made up. That evening McMasters was well enough to enjoy a game of cribbage with Johnson.

Next day, July 31, homeward bound, the captain had me come to his office with one of my officers for a little chat and a drink. In the northeast trades, the air was getting nicely cooler. The *Winchester Castle* ran alone, zigzagging during the day. I spent most of the day with my officers making up reports. In the evening I called on McMasters in the hospital.

August 1 Captain Newdigate invited me to observe his crew drop depth charges. We went to the stern where what appeared to be sealed oil drums were arranged in a rack so they could roll off the stern one at a time. These barrels, filled with high explosives, were designed to wreck submarines below the surface. At the captain's command, the officers set one to explode two hundred feet below the surface, then let it go overboard. In a few seconds it reached its intended depth and exploded. The whole ship trembled, even though the explosion occurred well behind us. The object was to increase the sea pressure on a sub if one were in the vicinity and thereby crush it.

Sunday, August 2, I called on the crew and on Captain Newdigate once more, at his invitation, and then did some writing. The weather was fine. I took the rest of the day off. Next day I made out letters for each member of my crew, explaining the loss of normal papers. I also prepared a discharge for each, entitling them to free service at the Marine Hospital. At night it was muggy aboard with everything shut up for the blackout. Captain Newdigate once more invited me to his quarters for a visit.

Wednesday the fifth I had a haircut in the barber shop, paid for my Army clothing, and tipped the steward.

> *Weekly haircuts were the norm in the forties. A neat, clipped appearance was essential, especially for an officer in charge.*

I secured chits from the crew, paid the *Winchester Castle*'s purser for crew purchases, and advanced the crew what money I had. The purser gave me a picture of the ship.

Thursday, we met an outbound convoy headed for Europe. I busied myself with paperwork. In the afternoon we had boat drill, and at six the officers of the rescue ship entertained my officers. Later there was a party for my crew in the ship's lounge. I bought my crew three quarts of liquor for the occasion.

Friday, August 7, at nine in the morning, we arrived at New York. What a glorious sight to see the Statue of Liberty and the New York skyline beyond, welcoming us.

After we passed quarantine, McMasters was taken to the U.S. Marine Hospital on Staten Island, and the rest of us were questioned by Naval Intelligence officers. At 5:00 P.M. we were landed by small boat at Battery Park in lower Manhattan. From there we walked, double file, to the owners' office nearby. I was clothed in a British Army khaki short-sleeved shirt, short "K" pants of a different shade, no stockings, and odd-colored brown sneakers. My bare legs showed below the short, loose topcoat lent me by Captain Newdigate. All my men were similarly clothed. We truly looked like survivors. Union officials were among our escorts, and I overheard a crewman complain to one of these men about the regimentation he was being subjected to after six days of hardship in a lifeboat. The union delegate replied, "That's nothing. We have had several crews land here after having been thirty days, even longer, in open boats." After further interrogation at the office, each crew member was advanced $100 and dismissed for the weekend.

At the first chance to do for myself, I called Dorothy on the telephone. I was on schedule, and she suspected nothing unusual. I suggested she fly to New York. Because this required so much planning on her part, she said she would come in the morning. I said, "No, no, come this evening." She was so excited that when I asked her to bring me a full set of clothing, she agreed without wonder. I told her I would call her back in one hour.

Meanwhile I made reservations at the Commodore Hotel. It was Friday night and most of the stores were closed, but I managed to find a men's store nearby where I could get fitted out top to bottom. While doing my shopping there, I called my wife once more and told her that I had hotel reservations and to forget about bringing me clothing. Having had time to reflect, she asked, "Have you been torpedoed?"

We met at the airport that evening. Dorothy had carried the responsibility of the family alone for six months while I was on the other side of the world looking after my ship, crew, and cargoes. For the moment I was free from responsibility. Dot and I were together again. What else mattered?

Saturday was a busy day for me at the office of American-Hawaiian. That evening Dorothy and I took Captain Newdigate out to dinner at Schraffts, then to the Music Hall, where we saw the movie *Mrs. Miniver.*

Monday morning I surrendered the ship's register at the customs house and cashed the remainder of my letter of credit at the bank. With the assistance of the paymaster, my purser, and the ship's officers, we paid the crew off before the U.S. Shipping Commission. Each man was given a discharge as well as letters to help him renew any lost papers. I made arrangements for McMasters' care. On Tuesday I was tried before the U.S. Coast Guard for the loss of my vessel. Finding: "No neglect of duty." I spent most of the day being interviewed by the ship owners, the U.S. Maritime Administrator, the War Administrator, insurers, charterers, and Naval authorities.

That evening at the hotel we received a phone call from Dorothy's sister Jean, telling us that Dick had just survived an emergency operation for acute appendicitis. Anxious at first, we were tempted to fly home, but after reasoning that he was well cared for, we stayed on.

At noon on the twelfth, with representatives of the *Honolulan*'s owners, we gave a luncheon at the India House for the four officers of the *Winchester Castle* who had done the most for the survivors: Captain S. F. Newdigate, master; Doctor C. Crawford, surgeon; Captain L. M. Harrison, British Army quartermaster; and Mr. J. K. Kirtin, purser. Each was presented an award.

On August 13, 1942, five days after our landing, with my ship's business completed, I went home for a vacation.

# Notes to Chapter 16

1. Marlin spike: a pointed metal spike used to separate strands of rope in splicing.
2. Cumshaw: a tip or gratuity, pidgin English from Chinese "gamsia," an expression of thanks.
3. Corvette: a small, fast warship.
4. Since the war had started, all air tanks in lifeboats had been filled with kapok, a silky fiber used to stuff mattresses and life preservers, to retain buoyancy even if punctured by bullets.

# CHAPTER 17

# THE NAVY WAY

Having lost the *Honolulan*, I had lost my job. However, we had successfully delivered an important military cargo in time to help delay Hitler in his eastward advance.

Relaxing at home, the pleasure of being with family was wonderful. The boys and I swam, fished, and sailed together in the sloop. I told the story of my survival at sea to a group at the church and again at a clambake at the Ionic Club. My stay also proved to be a busy one, as I had to be ready for my next call to duty. The government had taken over the operation of most American merchant vessels. Many steamship company officials had volunteered for military service following the attack on Pearl Harbor. I did my utmost to prepare the family to carry on in case of my extended absence. Enemy submarines were sinking ships on our coast so rapidly that there was danger of the oil supply being cut off entirely. Since our home was heated with oil, I set up an emergency coal- and wood-burning stove in the kitchen, a coal grate in the fireplace, then laid in an extra supply of oil, coal, and wood. To prepare myself, I had my eyes and teeth cared for.

On September 7, 1942, I received orders to report for active duty with the Navy as commanding officer of the training ship *American Seaman*, subject to physical examination. The assignment, however, fell through.

*The assignment as commander of the training ship with the rank of captain never came about due to Father's political naiveté. His friend Fred Shaw had given him the news about the training ship assignment. Dad's response was, "I didn't volunteer. I'm still in the Merchant Service." This must have*

On October 9, 1942, I began four years of active duty in the Navy. I had been a lieutenant commander in the Naval Reserve for sixteen years. My career as an active Naval officer started in Portland, Maine, where I was appointed as port director at the Naval Yard. I had to learn the job from scratch and was kept busy with Navy correspondence courses. In spite of my ignorance, while I was there I advanced in grade to commander. I supervised the arming, manning, and supplying of all gun crews with ammunition and was responsible for the routing of vessels on the coast. Because the two Portland shipyards were turning out ships ahead of schedule, their guns were often not in Portland on time. In such cases we had machine guns sent up by truck from Boston so that no ship went to sea unable to defend itself.

I was given a beach wagon (station wagon) for transportation, one of the very last Oldsmobiles built before the production of cars was stopped due to the war. I secured my Maine driver's license and enjoyed having a car of my own, though the winter driving was treacherous. I kept busy learning the job and Navy methods. My evenings were taken up studying Navy course materials. I had a room at Mrs. Corey's place. She was always looking out for me and feeding me. Invited out to dinner quite often at friends' residences, I occasionally dined at the Propeller Club with other officers. Since Portland is only one hundred miles from Swampscott, I managed an occasional trip home and Dorothy and the boys came to see me.

On January 18, 1943, there was a very thin glaze of ice on the streets. In the late afternoon darkness I was driving to the shipyard, going down a grade with two lines of cars in bumper-to-bumper traffic. I had it all clear ahead when a car bolted across my path to go down a side road. It got across the road ahead of me but stalled on the ice, and I slid into its side. It was a beat-up old car carrying four shipyard workers. My left fender was damaged. There was no damage to the old car that anyone could tell. I took their names and other information and then asked, "What do you want to do about this? Shall we get an estimate of the damage?" They agreed to follow me to town for the estimate. I went ahead and their car stayed right behind me. I stopped in front of a garage in town. The driver and passengers from the other car joined me inside. The estimate for repair of my fender was $60.55.

"Now," I asked the driver, "What do you want to do about if?"

"I'll go home and get the money," he said.

"No, no," I said, "not on icy streets like these. Suppose I meet you at the shipyard first thing tomorrow morning?" In the morning I met the driver, and he handed me $60.55 in cash. I made out the Navy damage report and handed it to the officer responsible for such things, together with the cash and the written estimate for repairs. Dumbfounded, the officer hardly knew what to do. "I've never handled a case like this before," he said.

*Dad could be intimidating. He was a big man with a "lead, follow, or get out of the way" demeanor. A dreadful driver, he had many accidents with the car the Navy had entrusted to his care. He was inclined to operate an automobile as though it were a steamship. He once drove to Swampscott in a howling blizzard and I was amused to note that there was very little area on the car that had not been damaged and repaired at least once.*

The time went quickly. I continued to study, often until late at night. Dorothy visited me on several occasions, arriving by bus. Gasoline was rationed, so she could drive her car only on short errands at home. On March 15 a big snowstorm made it difficult to get around. That evening shipyard workers rioted when the local theater failed to produce the scheduled vaudeville show. On March 20, in spite of the icy roads, I drove home to Swampscott. Mother Allan was very ill. On April 3 I went home again, this time by bus. Now Jean was very sick.

*Mother Allan, eighty, had inoperable cancer. Nurses were tending her at home around the clock. Aunt Jean was suffering a recurrence of the cancer that had required a mastectomy five years earlier. She had seemed normal for about three years but then began having severe back pains. The cancer had spread to her bones.*

On April 24, 1943, I received orders to report to Camp Peary, a Construction Training Center, near Williamsburg, Virginia. My Portland port director's job ended just as I was getting things running smoothly. I took the train for home, having four days to comply with my new orders. Mother Allan was being given narcotics for her incessant pain. Jean was in similar condition at New England Baptist Hospital in Boston. My wife had two boys at home, a dying mother to care for, and her sister seriously ill in the hospital. I could not help her. I had to depend on my boys.

On passing through New York, I called Captain Schermerhorn and told him that I was not happy being transferred to Camp Peary for duty. He told me, "You got that duty because you objected to assignment as captain of the *American Seaman.*" Apparently, Captain Schermerhorn had recommended to the Navy that I get that job. This was all news to me. Master of a training ship was what I was best suited for. Stevedoring, my new job, was certainly not my choice. I regretted the misunderstanding.

*Indeed, a very deep regret. In 1975 Dad was writing his account of his life. Each weekend I would take a set of ten yellow notepads to read and often made notes in the margins. Once I noted, "It is not clear to me what the mis-understanding was or how it occurred." He never responded. Apparently it was too sensitive an issue.*

Now I was in the awkward position of being a line officer[1] about to serve with the Civil Engineer Corps (CEC) of the Navy Bureau of Yards and Docks. I was to be in command of a Naval Construction Battalion, or Seabee (for CB).

April 29 I left cold New England wearing winter blues and arrived in hot Virginia weather for which I was much too warmly dressed. I found a Navy beach wagon and driver to transport me from the railroad station to the camp. We sent up clouds of dust as we drove over newly graded, unpaved roads. Camp Peary extended over eleven thousand acres and newly bulldozed dirt extended for miles. There were many barracks but not a tree in sight.

I arrived at about nine in the morning, virtually caked with red dust. The metal administration building was hot. On entering the building, I found others sensibly dressed in khaki, which made me feel like a stranger from a foreign country. I presented my orders to the yeoman behind a desk. Noting my three stripes, he took my orders to the inner office. The executive officer, also a commander, came out to meet me. I introduced myself. He read my orders, handed them back to me, and said, "You are a senior officer. We have no duty for you here." Without another word, he returned to his office. My jaw dropped.

I found an open space on a long bench nearby and sat down to gather my thoughts. I was hot, dirty, and frustrated. I knew little about the Navy and wished I had not lost the assignment to command the training ship. In the Merchant Service from which I had come, a person knew how and when to do a job before ordering someone else to do it. Here I was all rank and no competence. I had looked forward to an opportunity to learn.

Sitting on the bench, I reread my orders, then stepped up to the desk once more. I asked the yeoman if I could talk with the executive officer again. The officers at this camp were all with the CEC, whereas I, wearing a star on my sleeve, was a line officer. I called the officer's attention to my orders, which called for my training of men. He insisted he could do nothing for me.

I said, "Suppose I ask you to train me?"

He replied, "Well, that's different. I think we can accommodate you on that basis."

I was accepted and assigned to a platoon and a barracks. At the barracks I met a new class of junior officers—ensigns, jg's,[2] and lieutenants, just in from civilian life. All were young and smart, none more than thirty years of age. I found myself in charge of about thirty of these men.

Camp Peary was a sizable operation, with forty thousand officers and enlisted men in training. As a senior officer, I was in charge of the platoon. Responsible for organization and order as well as taking the training classes, I had double duty. I had experienced some semi-military training at the Maritime Academy, which proved to be a good beginning. Basically we were all trainees, with rank forgotten. Many of our instructors were enlisted Navy men or Marines. A few were civilians. Wearing fatigues, who could tell?

Every morning we were called at 5:45 and marched to breakfast at 6:30. We had to be assembled for colors before 8:00. By then the barracks had to be thoroughly cleaned, beds made, and every shoe and hat placed just so for inspection. As the inspector looked down the long barracks, he had to see every shoe, hat, and coat at the same angle. We could not leave even a speck of dust for him to find.

When we went to meals, we marched to the mess hall, stood in line, and picked up a divided tray. The servers slapped food onto the tray as we passed by. Standing in line took quite a while and left no time for leisurely dining. In fact our whole day was spent hurrying from this to that. Captain Ware, the station commander, held mast daily and acted as judge. I attended as an observer at 11:00 each day so that I could learn the judging, Navy style. This would be a principal duty of mine when on my own.

We were assigned more reading than was possible to complete before the next class. The same was true on weekends. Friday's assignments were enormous. It was remarkable how these reserve officers studied every available minute. All lights had to be out at 10:00, but that didn't stop the studying. Between each barracks was a latrine building. The outer walls were just bug screening. Inside were the wash area and toilets, one big room with no partitions. The lights there were left on all night, and most nights these latrines were crowded with men studying.

Every weekday afternoon, we had physical exercise by going through an obstacle course. Managing the course took all of one's strength. Although forty-eight years old, I kept up with the rest of the younger men. Eventually I was stopped from doing so and was put in charge of men over forty-five and others who were younger but with physical limitations. Nevertheless, I continued to go through the regular obstacle course on my own. I was in good shape for my age and intended to stay that way.

At 1:00 on Saturdays we had inspection, after which all men had liberty until 8:00 Monday morning, but nearly everyone in my platoon stayed and studied. Some men had to go to Richmond on the weekends, their wives having insisted on coming there to visit them. The men met their wives, ate a meal, sent their wives home, and returned to the barracks to study for Monday's classes. There was a church service every Sunday, but most men used Sundays to catch up on reading and writing their lessons instead. These officers were in the service to do their duty toward winning the war. Never have I seen a more determined lot.

On May 5 I got 82 percent on my written examinations, far below that obtained by others who had fewer duties. The average score for my platoon was 76%. At least I ranked above the average.

By May 26, when we had finished four weeks of preliminary training as Seabees, I was transferred to a new barracks and assigned a new platoon with thirty-seven different young officers. This training was not required of me, but I had asked for it, hoping to excel in competence. Again I was the senior officer of the group and was responsible for its conduct and inspections. We studied telecommunications and learned about inter-office equipment, electricity, generators, and the operation of heavy equipment and engines, including the use and repair of earthmoving machinery.

On the thirtieth I went to Norfolk and visited my sister and brother. I was back on base by 10:00 P.M. Somehow on this trip I lost my reading glasses, so I telephoned home for Dorothy to send me a spare pair. On the thirty-first I was examined by a psychiatrist "to see if I was crazy," as it was said. This was done to all officers before they were put in command of anything. It seems some had lost their heads when under fire.

On June 1 I was made officer-in-charge of the Eleventh Special Construction Battalion and was given a list of the thirty-four officers assigned to be with me. I notified each and moved to a new section of the camp. There I studied the specifications for forming a battalion. It was a chore because my spare reading glasses had not yet arrived. The Eleventh Special was to consist of a headquarters company and four independently trained and equipped working companies designated A, B, C, and D, each commanded by a first lieutenant. I was given a list of the duties and ratings of the men to be in each company. Each company was to have a number of chiefs, chief petty officers, and warrant officers of each specialty, as well as so many carpenters, machinists, storekeepers, and various utility men. Since the men had been drafted according to age, not ability or training, we had far more men who had been storekeepers and far fewer carpenters than we required. To fill the slots, some storekeepers were arbitrarily designated carpenter's chief or carpenter's mate, and so on. This not only made for an inefficient team but created jealousies among the men as well.

The men were drawn from a pool of boot draftees on the premises. There were many Negroes in the pool. At the beginning of the war, the Navy Department did not approve of mixing blacks and whites. The first ten special battalions were all white. Thereafter the pools became so full of Negroes that Congress ordered the Navy to integrate subsequent units. In fact, the Thirteenth Special Battalion was half white and half black, and some that followed were all black. In my opinion, the Navy's fears in this regard were unfounded. As I saw it, the black men performed very well indeed. My battalion ended up with eight black men, all in the commissary department, and they gave us no trouble whatsoever.

Sunday, June 6, we moved all officers to battalion headquarters, and next day we received 892 men from the pool, each of whom had had just three months of boot training. In the afternoon I observed the Tenth Special Battalion in a formal military parade review, something my battalion would be required to perform later on.

On the eighth I attended Captain Ware's mast, and then I joined my men on the drill field, as I did almost daily. Our Marine training officers were very fast walkers. My men tried to keep up, but for many it was just too much, especially for those with short legs.

There were always a few men who wanted to get out of going overseas. They tried all sorts of excuses—sore backs, flat feet. They even wet the bed, but we broke up that racket. After being examined by the doctor and found to be healthy, the men were assigned to hospital bunks rigged one above the other. The mattresses were so thin that if the man in the top bunk wet, his urine would run down onto the man below. If this did not work a cure, we alternated the assigned top bunks. If that failed, we had the night guard lead them to the toilet every two hours. If this failed, we had them called more often. At one time my battalion had six men in treatment for bedwetting. Finally all six men were functioning normally, begged to be put back on regular duties, and gave up their pursuit of a discharge from service.

The doctor had sick call every day at 10:30 A.M. and every man had a right to line up to see him. Many of the men were continually put on light-duty status. As commander, I was supposed to have at least 65 percent of my men on productive work. I questioned Dr. Krakes, who explained that many of the men complained of sore backs or feet, and he felt he had to give them the benefit of the doubt. So I made it my business to be present on numerous occasions when the men lined up to see the doctor. I would ask a few in line, "What are you here for?" It took no more than that for many of them to drop out of line and resume their regular duties.

The medical officer had one man continually on light duty because of his flat feet. The doctor had recommended him for discharge, but the senior medical officer on the base sent him back for duty. Having often had trouble with my own feet, I was sympathetic. In my office I asked him about his trouble and took a look at his feet. They looked terrible. I personally sent him up for discharge, but the order was returned, "Fit for duty." Calling him to my office once more, I reviewed the situation with him, asked him to do his best, and told him we would see that he got a square deal. He was a member of Company D, and I had his commanding officer, Lieutenant Teague, with us at the time of this conference.

The next morning the battalion was on military drill and fell in together in formation. Lieutenant Teague stood near him to see that he was treated fairly and that he did his best. At the order "forward march," the man did not try a single step. Instead, he threw his gun to the ground. The company marched off, leaving him standing alone facing his commanding officer, who said, "Come on, now. I'll give you another chance. Let's you and I march double time together around the field, and I won't put you on report." The man refused. He was put on report and appeared before me at mast, where his lieutenant read the charge against him. He admitted his guilt. I locked him up: five days of bread and water. On release, he became one of the most willing men in the battalion. He never complained of his feet again in spite of how deformed they had looked to me. Some months later he was promoted. When I left the battalion, I shook his hand and said, "Thank you for being a good Seabee." Tears welled up in his eyes and he said, "Commander, you were not so bad yourself."

Military training led by the Marines continued. We were preparing for review. On June 25, a beautiful day, the Eleventh Special Construction Battalion passed in review, parading before Captain Ware. We received our colors and battalion standard. All in whites, 1,044 officers and men, we made an impressive spectacle.

Dorothy wrote me about things at home. I was impressed how well the boys were taking care of the place in my absence.

Saturday, June 26, I went to mast as usual in the forenoon. We had one man who was a Seventh Day Adventist and wanted to worship on Saturday instead of Sunday. At mast I tried to get him to go along with the battalion. I was not successful in persuading him, so I had the head of his church come down from Richmond to help me. I told the man that if I let him off on Saturday, I would soon discover that I had over a thousand Adventists in my battalion, that my battalion represented all religions, and that I wanted Seventh Day Adventists included. The man went along with me for a week or so. Then, as we got nearer to going overseas, he wanted to get nearer to God by resuming his Saturday worship. I listened to his story then asked him, "Would you assist a fallen brother even on a Saturday?" He allowed that he would do so. I told him to wait while I talked to my senior medical officer. It so happened that the medical officer needed more hospital attendants, so I transferred this man to the medical department. It worked. When I left the battalion nearly a year later he was working well as a hospital attendant every day, including Saturdays.

On July 5 the Eleventh Special and six other battalions took part in a regimental review and parade, during which I experienced the embarrassment of a lifetime. My battalion of five companies was at parade rest. On bringing them to attention, I gave the order, "right, dress," a carry-over from my earlier military training at the Maritime Academy. No one knew how to respond. The modern military order is "dress right, dress."[3] This was the first time I had made this mistake. I was humiliated before my entire battalion. Realizing I was making a mistake, I then ordered, "right dress, dress," even worse. I started anew with, "as you were," and began again, giving the correct command.

Since there was no ship available to take us overseas, my battalion remained in training. They granted us ten days' leave, and on the fifteenth I left for home. I got a ride as far as New York, where I boarded a train for Swampscott. Both Mother Allan and Jean were in a bad way, sicker than ever with cancer.

Back at Camp Peary on July 25, 1943, I received word from Dorothy that her mother at last had died. It was a sad day for me. Mother Allan had been a wonderful lady and a great asset to the family. We had always been fond of one another. Dorothy's letters had expressed concern that Jean might go before her mother. At least the parent did not have to live through the death of her child. Now Jean was hospitalized full-time.

We were ready to be sent overseas. The Eleventh Special had been trained to build pontoons, docks, and roads, and to do grading. We were also trained militarily to defend our battalion against attackers. At noon on July 29, 1943, we filled two trains of day coaches headed for Davisville, Rhode Island. The trains were hot and dirty, since soot from the coal-burning engine poured in through open windows along with needed fresh air.

After sitting up in coaches all night, we arrived at Davisville, twenty-five miles south of Providence, on the west side of Narragansett Bay. The camp was far more attractive than Camp Peary, with shade trees and forest, but the area had not been occupied for weeks and was overgrown with brush and weeds. We were there for advanced training, or so our orders read. In reality, we were simply waiting for a ship to transport us overseas. We were housed in tents or Quonset huts. Much of the so-called advanced training consisted of close order drill, which the men thought was not necessary. Many were disgusted. They had joined the Navy to fight the war, get it over with, and go home. Having to wait and wait was demoralizing. They no longer felt important or needed, but we set about to improve the camp and make it livable anyway. Such activity helped. A mock-up of a ship was set up to train men to load and discharge cargoes. We lived from day to day, not knowing how long we would be there. As morale broke down further, it became more difficult to maintain discipline. With no fences and no gates, it was nearly impossible to keep tabs on the troops, surely a test of my ability to keep order. My officers sympathized with the men and frequently failed to put them on report when they were AWOL.

When men were put on report for being absent from duty, I tried them at mast. I expected the officers to set the example, but, with their wives arriving from distant places, even they took liberties. Finally I had an opportunity to set an example to the whole battalion. A junior officer was absent without leave, and I restricted him to the station for ten days. This brought the officers together in rebellion. They sent the chaplain to me to plead for him. I reduced his restriction to five days. My officers were still not happy.

They had another gripe. There were a number of battalions on the station, and all had officers' clubs, where they could meet and buy liquor. None of the enlisted men were allowed to have even a can of beer. I thought this was unfair. My officers visited adjacent battalions' clubs. I had no objection to this, but after I restricted the officer to five days on station, my officers got together and elected a delegation to go before the base commander and complain about not being allowed to have a club. They claimed that I ran the battalion like a ship. (According to the written regulations, I was supposed to run things like a ship.) I was called before Captain Wilson and charged with stripping the officers of battalion club privileges. I took this from Captain Wilson for just so long. When I could take no more, I said, "Captain Wilson, if you don't want me in this battalion, just kick me out." He then did an about-face and tried to reason with me. This I accepted. In the end he ordered me to set up an officers' club in my battalion and in two weeks to invite him to it. Now that I had been given specific orders, the first thing I did was to direct Lieutenant Snyder, who was in charge of Headquarters Company, to set up an officers' club as quickly as possible. I was the first to buy shares in the liquor stock. Since I had orders to allow my battalion to deal in liquor, I was now convinced it was my duty to cooperate. When the battalion finally boarded a troop transport for overseas, the club carried liquor cased in several wooden boxes. On each side of these cases was a big red cross to designate it as "hospital supplies." All of this satisfied my officers, but my 1,010 enlisted men were not happy.

On Sunday, August 8, I was at home in Swampscott for the day. Dot and I drove to the Boy Scout camp near Amesbury to visit Dick. We watched a ball game where the boys played against the camp counselors. I cheered loudly for the boys' side.

On Sunday the twenty-second, we had orders that there would be no liberty whatsoever. I made every effort to see that the command was obeyed. Wives had come from all parts of the country to see their husbands and my men were not happy being restricted. The first night, sailor Anderson was caught outside the gate, so I confined him for five days. We had no news of our future and later the restrictions were eased. I stayed close by until Saturday night, September 4, when I went home for a quick visit. I was back on the base Sunday evening for another week of not knowing what was to happen next. On Saturday the twelfth we were again restricted to the base, and at noon we were notified we would embark at 6:00 A.M.

The *Santa Monica* was a C-2 troop transport, a freight ship operated by W. R. Grace Company. We were the first troops she was to carry. She had a crew of eighty-six men, all civilians and inexperienced in handling troops. I boarded first to make inspections and found a lot to be desired. On the thirteenth at 6:00 A.M., we were in battalion formation and lined up ready to board. At the gangway each man was checked with a full pack on his back. A Red Cross representative handed each man a green cloth bag containing sewing equipment, a roll or two of Lifesavers, and toilet articles.

We boarded together with five hundred Marines and two hundred Negro soldiers. I was dismayed to discover that the officers, who were to get cabins, would be given three meals a day. All troops, on the other hand, were to get just two meals a day, eat standing up, and sleep in the 'tween decks on fixed cots arranged three to five high. I sent off a telegram of protest to the authorities in Washington. I was inclined to do away with the special privileges for the officers altogether and let them all line up at the same barrels and eat the same powdered eggs and boiled potatoes as their men. However, remembering my encounter with Captain Wilson, I doubted I would get away with reform of such magnitude. My message to Washington was answered with a suggestion that I try to give the men a sandwich for lunch. As things worked out, we were unable to do this. September 14, by Morse code, I tried to get the port director to have the toilets surveyed. He answered, saying that a survey team would be sent. None came.

September 15, with 1,700 troops aboard, we anchored near New York, and at seven the next morning, we sailed for the war front. We had no idea where that might be.

Aboard, we were busy getting settled and making the best of what we had. As we were approaching the island of San Salvador, I gave a talk over the PA system about Columbus' trips to the West Indies.

September 23 the *Santa Monica* was anchored at the U.S. Naval Base at Guantánamo, Cuba. I tried to get refreshments from shore for the men, but without results. The toilets wouldn't flush. Drinking water coolers broke down. There was no one in the ship's crew to make repairs, but the Seabee motto was "can do." The men in my battalion came from various walks of life and were eager to exercise their talents. They did all sorts of repairs, and those who helped out the ship's force were accepted as crew members. They received no pay but were welcome to sit at the table and eat three meals a day, either with the officers, petty officers, or crew. It was a great privilege for them to be accepted as such.

September 27 we arrived at the Panama Canal. During our passage through "the Ditch," I described the canal to the men over the PA system. We were to be in port twenty hours. I tried without success to get liberty for the men, but I did convince the Army to allow my men to come off the ship by one gangway and back on board at a second. I also arranged with them to send truckloads of candy, ice cream, tonic, snacks, and toilet articles out to the dock. Any military unit was allowed to make a profit of 15 percent by law. The Army unit serving us that day really cleaned up, selling over $10,000 worth of goods to our Navy CB passengers.

The *Santa Monica* finished taking on fuel and water, then sailed at 7:00 P.M. with only one Marine missing. I still had no idea where the ship was bound. Perhaps the captain didn't either. He most likely had been directed to proceed to a rendezvous for further orders.

October 1 we passed the Galápagos Islands. The troops were kept busy standing watches, performing cleaning duties, and the like. We had a committee set up to handle entertainment. Every day different outfits organized contests in boxing, jujitsu, and wrestling. The chaplain led vesper services over the loudspeaker. There were also lectures and movies. October 8 the ship passed south of the Marquesas Islands and the next day, north of Tahiti and the Society Islands, I gave a short talk about them.

October 13 the ship entered the U.S. Naval Harbor of Pago Pago, American Samoa, and discharged the two hundred Negro soldiers. My battalion had three hours' shore liberty, a boost to their morale. The men who had never seen palm trees did their best to get hold of coconuts to carry on board. It came back to me that some went so far as to climb the trees in the commanding officer's yard. On the fourteenth we sailed once more for unannounced destinations.

It became a real challenge for me to get my men to clean the compartment where the black men had lived. The bunks the men had slept on were simply pipe frames with canvas stretched between. According to regulation, the canvases had to be unlaced, taken on deck, and scrubbed on both sides. The compartment deck, walls, and overhead required scrubbing. Many of the military men on board came from south of the Mason-Dixon line, and they detested cleaning up after black men. My officers and I had to go so far as to stand guard to see that the compartment's contents were not simply thrown overboard.

October 23, 1943, after being on board the *Santa Monica* one month and eleven days, we arrived in the port of Nouméa, the capital of the French island of New Caledonia, 750 miles east of Australia. The colony, loyal to the Free French, had been occupied by U.S. forces in 1942 to prevent Japanese invasion. My battalion had originally been sent to assist the Second Battalion stationed at Nouméa, but since the Japanese had been driven back, we were to have duty in a more advanced area. On the twenty-fifth I got orders that we were to be moved to Banika Island in the Russell group, forty miles north of Guadalcanal. Our mission was to set up and operate a supply base there. I went ashore each day, learning as much as I could about the Second Special Battalion's operations.

On the twenty-seventh the Marines disembarked. My battalion was still on board. Several thousand cases of beer belonging to my battalion were discharged from the ship, and I asked why. It was explained to me that our other equipment was coming forward with our supplies on another ship, which would pick up the beer for us. This sounded mighty fishy, so I insisted on leaving two of my men behind to see that it got to us.

I was to travel ahead to Banika with Mr. Trout, the lieutenant in command of A Company, to survey the area. Trout and I billeted at the Second Special's quarters while awaiting air transportation north. On the twenty-ninth, he and I and ten other passengers flew six hours to Guadalcanal on a mail and cargo plane. We could sit on the wooden bench or lie down on the mail sacks. There was one porthole but nothing to see.

On landing, we were driven to "Hotel de Gink," a twenty-by-sixty-foot Quonset hut on the edge of high land overlooking the plains below. The hut had a wooden floor and a curved steel roof that came down to within two feet of the floor. From there it was fitted with screening. There was a screen door at one end but no windows. Furnishings consisted of twenty portable canvas cots, each supplied with an Army blanket. Outside the door was a small, one-holer privy and a water pipe with an opening just above one's head. With a few boards to stand on, this was the shower. The man taking a shower was exposed to everyone, including the town below. There was no telephone, mirror, or other convenience. We could get meals at a small Quonset hut some four hundred feet from the edge of the cliff. A serviceman was there to wait on the "guests." The food was pretty good, considering the meager facilities.

On October 30 Mr. Trout and I rode the bus to town and learned as much as we could about Number One CB Battalion, already in operation on Guadalcanal. At noon we boarded another cargo plane for the Banika Island Naval Base, a twenty-minute flight. Banika was a pretty island, volcanic, about twenty miles long. The island was dominated by a single high mountain covered with mahogany timber. Later, most of the men, including me, climbed it. At the apex stood a lookout tower built by the Japanese before they were driven out. The summit was well above the treetops, and from there one had a view to sea in all directions.

We were introduced to Lieutenant Commander Harris, public works officer, who showed us where our camp was to be. It bordered on the water. The land was fairly level, about forty feet above sea level and covered with coconut palms. It was owned by the Australian Palm Olive Company and Lever Brothers, but the coconuts had not been harvested since the island had become a Naval base. They had fallen naturally and produced young trees three to six feet high. Snakes, rats, and land crabs were everywhere. Crabs covered the roads at night. Driving over them made a gruesome noise as our tires crushed them.

Mr. Trout and I each secured a jeep and drove back to our site, part of which was occupied by one company of the Ninth Special Battalion, soon to leave the island. We surveyed the area and made a rough layout on paper. At 4:00 P.M. the *Santa Monica* arrived and anchored in the harbor with my men and basic equipment—tents, food, and kitchen set-up. The lighters were towed to the beach, and there we loaded our stuff onto six-by-six Army trucks. The trucks were driven on soft roads through the woods to our area where the goods were unloaded to the ground under the coconut trees. Since it was dark under the trees, we borrowed the ship's portable lights, and made no effort to return them once most of the batteries had run down.

(The borrowed lights caused me considerable trouble later when the Southwest Pacific Command took me to task for the theft.)

The men worked through the night in the rain. Mr. Trout went to live with the Ninth Special, where conditions were much better. To set an example, however, I stayed with my battalion and made the best of what we had. I slept on the ground and ate from the same mess line as the men.

There were no paved streets, electric lights, theaters, or native inhabitants. This was not what the men had expected and they were disappointed, but after forty-one days on the crowded ship, they were glad to be ashore. At least we were warm, being in the tropics. The island was six hundred miles north of the Equator. At that latitude there are two seasons: wet and dry. Our arrival was at the end of the wet season and the beginning of the dry one.

We had no tents set up, no screening, and no lumber to build toilets. We made a galley of sorts from packing cases. Our eggs and potatoes were powdered. We had highly spiced beef stew from number ten (one-gallon) cans. We did have plenty of good canned salami, but the men soon got sick of eating it every day. We made our own bread but had no fat for it. Butter, so called, came in number ten cans and would not melt. It had a hard, waxy consistency. I drew five days' supply of canned goods from the Marines. (There were forty thousand Marines on the island, and they ran everything.) When we received our allotment, many of the cans were rusted and some had holes in them because they were stored in huge piles outdoors. We were given ten percent extra to compensate for the leaking and swollen cans. The only wood we had for fires was green or wet coconut logs. We tried to make an open fire to heat soapy water with which to clean our trays after meals. A second barrel with boiling water for rinsing was the specification, but since the wood was wet, we couldn't get the fire hot enough to boil the water in either barrel, creating a health hazard.

Our toilets were simply troughs dug in the ground. The mud and flies were awful and we all got dysentery. My officers and men were much disgruntled.

We spent from November 3 through the end of the year building a camp and getting needed equipment. We had to borrow barges and trucks from other battalions. No local help was available because all the natives had been moved to another island.

It was a major project to try to supply enough water for a thousand men. There was a well-drilling rig on the island under the control of Lieutenant Commander Harris of public works. He refused to lend it to us for obtaining water. Insisting it was to be used only for draining water to reduce the breeding of mosquitoes, he told us to dig. We tried it with shovels and a crane but, since we had no lumber with which to line the hole, the sandy sides kept falling in. There was lumber on Banika Island, but Harris would not allow its use in lining wells or building latrines. With no proper water supply, we towed water tanks behind our jeeps and got water, a tank at a time, from a Marine unit. With such a limited supply we had none for proper bathing. I secured empty gasoline barrels and, with borrowed tools, opened the ends so that we could collect and stow rainwater.

By the middle of November we were pretty well housed in tents, but our working gear had not yet arrived. With borrowed equipment, we began unloading ships and barges towed across the ocean from the States. Our main duty on the island was to operate a supply base for forward areas–Pacific islands that had no deep water docks to accommodate oceangoing ships. Liberty ships[4] sailed from the States with supplies, including food, fuel, ordnance, trucks, and tanks, all of which we unloaded. The supplies were first stored in a dump, then transferred to landing ship tanks (LSTs), which transported them to the front. LSTs could land supplies ashore directly onto a beach by dropping their forward ramps.

The men worked in gangs, six hours on and six off. They relieved each other at noon, at six in the evening, at midnight, and at six in the morning. There were no days off. Meals were served four times each day. Eating, sleeping, building camp, and digging foxholes were done on the men's own time. Foxholes were terribly hard to dig because the ground was of coral, so that instead of being round, the "pebbles" were jagged and interlocking. However, it was good for morale for the men to be working, doing their part to win the war.

At last, on November 17, our supply ship arrived with our working gear, and we set about discharging it. We received our first rations of butter and fat, a welcome event, since we had been baking without either for two weeks. We had no place to store our PX supplies–candy, beer, and the like. They just had to sit on the ground, unsecured. We secured the liquor inside our eight-by-eight-foot iceboxes, using a crane to place them door side down to prevent pilferage. On the twentieth we finished discharging our trucks, dump carts, bulldozers, cranes, jeeps and jitneys, iceboxes, and ice machines, all in a heap. It was a relief to have our own equipment at last and to start making improvements. Morale improved immediately.

On December 1 I sent in my initial monthly report. Most of my men were sick with dysentery and morale was low. My officers sympathized with their men and would not put them on report for failure to show up for duty. But this day, concerned about the general slowdown, Mr. Smith, a warrant officer who was in charge of camp labor, put thirteen men on report. At mast I disrated three petty officers and fined ten enlisted men two-thirds of a month's pay. I was forced by the book to give one man five days' bread and water.

I thought the chaplain and the postmaster were my best bets for boosting morale. The Ninth Special Battalion was moving off the island to a more forward area so I bought their galley, water tank, and piping. I assigned the galley, a thirty-by-sixty-foot wooden building, to the chaplain to be used for the men's recreation hall. The officers wanted a separate officers' mess room and club. I insisted they wait until after we obtained the enlisted men's mess room. They had some other complaints, too. At that time our hospital was simply a long tent with bare ground for a floor. I insisted on first things first, which I judged to include a floor for the hospital. Then, after the mess rooms were built, I designated the first Quonset hut we erected to be the armory, and the second I designated our post office. The postmaster had been operating from a tent with mail bags on the ground. Many of the other officers felt that I was favoring the postmaster. What I did favor was service to all the men, and I made sure that they got their mail from home. From my many years at sea, I knew what mail meant to men a long way from their loved ones. I wrote home with pride, "I have a wonderful recreation hall for the men, with books, lights, and music. The officers will have their comforts later. I insist the men come first."

> It was, no doubt, this insistence of his that caused him to be sent away. It also prevented him from advancing to captain, the Naval rank he could have had as master of the training ship, American Seaman.

My diary for December 6, 1943, had this brief entry: "Work by the men in all companies is running smoothly and morale is continuing to improve." On the twenty-fourth: "Officers' mess and club completed and moved in. A big lift for the officers."

> The officers' club came into being only after some officers wrote to Navy authorities in Washington complaining that their commanding officer was denying them their rights. Dad was ordered to provide the club. However, he continued to champion the underdog, no matter what.

Headquarters Company's Lieutenant Snyder, a very able engineering officer, managed to obtain the drilling rig to get us started on our own sources of water, but we were still unable to secure lumber to shore up our wells. Neither could we get lumber and screening to build toilets, although there was plenty available on the island under the control of Lieutenant Commander Harris, the public works officer. Screening for the toilets was essential to control flies, the cause of dysentery, which was making my men very sick. I had two supply officers, but neither had been able to procure lumber. CB Battalion Thirty-six, stationed not far from us, was about to be moved to a forward area. I thought that I might obtain some odd pieces from them. With a list of my essential lumber needs in my pocket, I drove my jeep close to the commander's office and trudged on foot the rest of the way in deep mud—it had been raining for about a week. I told the commander of my desperate circumstances and begged for any lumber at all. Surprising me, he asked, "Have you a list?" I gave it to him, and he said, "Where do you want it delivered?" Wishing I had made my list longer, I said that I would have my trucks come for it, but he insisted on using his own. "I'll have your lumber delivered to your camp tomorrow morning." And so it was. It seems that he had been in the same predicament when he had built his camp and, like me, had not been able to get the lumber from public works. Then a senior engineer corps officer visiting the island gave him a written order that immediately secured any and all lumber he wanted from Harris, the stingy public works officer. Although he and his unit were about to move on, he was tickled to exercise that order once more. At last we had our lumber and screening, built our toilets, and made a proper roof and screening for our galley.

We had wells ready for operation except for check valves for the lift pipe. The supply officers could get hold of no more than one of the five we required and no nails for our construction work. Again my supply officer gave me the list of needs. I went aboard a merchant vessel and finagled fifty pounds of nails from the chief mate. Then I boarded another and met a young chief engineer. His name sounded familiar, and it turned out that his father was a shipmaster whom I knew. I got the check valves from him and at last we were able to pump water. In time we had eight wells working and our own fairly reliable water supply. (There was no regular supply of fresh water on the island during the dry season. Although the sea level was the same under the island as around it, fresh water, being lighter than salt, rose in the ground above the seawater. Under this fragile body of fresh, the water was salty. If we sank a well and pumped too hard, the salt water at the bottom rose, and the fresh water became brackish. We had to stop pumping and wait for it to become fresh once more.) We laid pipes to the tanks, then piped water from there to our five company areas for cooking. For bathing we put empty gasoline barrels overhead in the coconut trees and pumped them full of water with a short hose. Since there were no women on the island, a naked man taking a shower under a barrel presented no problem.

Our work proceeded, unloading cargo from ships to barges, barges to the dock, and from the dock to trucks, where it was hauled to the storage dumps. The Navy barges were made of four-foot-square steel pontoons joined together. They made a poor floating dock, but they were all we had. The only tugs we had were made of a few pontoons joined together with one or two outboard motors for locomotion. The work of loading and discharging ships carried on day and night. Only when Japanese airplanes flew overhead was there a blackout for safety. Much of the time we loaded to wheeled landing craft for disposition to forward battle areas.[5] We used special techniques to insure quick unloading. To support this work there were all sorts of associated jobs.

We were now equipped with basic working gear, including crawler cranes and jitneys to haul loaded cargo trailers. The jitneys and trailers had ten-inch iron wheels with hard rubber tires. These were ideal for working on decks, docks, or paved roads, but not in our mud. Our roadbeds were

Seabee Commander Bamforth on Banika Island, 1943

made of coral that, when wet, became slimy. The jitney's smooth rubber tires spun, heated up, expanded, and came right off the steel rims. We were still lacking some of the essentials, such as rope, wire slings, and clamps. I was able to borrow some things from an outfit which had no power equipment with which to use them. Eventually we built docks on pontoons to facilitate the loading.

On Christmas Day we had not only turkey but our first fresh fruit, an orange apiece. Christmas, however, was a working day like all the rest. It was especially difficult for the officers because the men insisted on celebrating on the job and had liquor from somewhere, either ready-made or the product of secret stills. In my box of presents from home was some candy, much of which had melted, making a mess. The hard candy was in pretty good shape, and I took it to give the men in the hospital. Little things meant a lot to them.

By January 1944, the Eleventh Special Battalion had nearly completed building its camp. At long last our tents had wooden floors three feet off the ground. The beds were the old folding Army cots with blankets, no sheets. A foxhole alongside each tent was big enough for four men. Each of the five companies had its own area and was completely equipped so it could be moved as a unit to a more forward area if needed.

The terrain and climate made our job difficult. The coral roads had to be well crowned and scraped every day. In the wet season, the supply dumps (which were just a spot in the woods—we had no warehouses) became quagmires. Bulldozers and tractors had to haul out bogged-down trucks. About half of the six-by-six trucks were equipped with winches on the forward end. These were a great help, and many a time the driver had to attach the winch wire to a tree to pull his vehicle out of the mud. The roads were much easier to live with in the dry season, but the continual scraping eventually made even the high crowned center lower than the surrounding terrain. The ditches would fill with water a foot or more deep.

Most of the cargo we landed we sent to the supply dump loaded on trucks borrowed from the base, all driven by Marines. We didn't have any gear to secure the cargo within the trucks, so of course things got damaged. Imagine a load of big steel arch frames for a Quonset hut in an open truck being driven fast over bumps. The cargo often flew out over the sides. Then the road scraper would pile slime on top of the jettisoned material. I would send crawler cranes up the roads to reload the trucks. The Marine drivers were not assigned any responsibility for their cargo. If a driver arrived at his destination with no cargo in the truck, it having fallen out on the way, which often was the case, it was no concern of his. I was helpless to fix these problems, having no authority over the Marines. That lack of accountability was only corrected after my tour of duty in the islands was done.

During the rainy season a Liberty Ship with a full load of nearly ten thousand tons of cement in paper bags arrived with orders for its rapid discharge.

We had to move it several hundred yards through pouring rain to a Quonset hut near the dock, where we had no hatch tents or hold covers to protect the bags from the pouring rain. We should have had the bags on pallets, but instead we were forced to use net slings. We did the best we could to get the cement into the warehouse without breaking the damp bags, but inevitably some broke open in each sling load. Some just about dissolved from the constant downpour. I had left the island before that cement was removed from the warehouse, but by then it must have turned into a solid mass. I was disgusted with the operation, and so were the men and officers under me. Such conditions were bad for morale. I had to keep a stiff upper lip and lead them to do their best in spite of it all.

Most of the cargo was discharged from ships at anchor to barges. We had no boats to transport the men, not even for me or my control personnel to make inspections. Our men had to be transported on the barges. Once we completed a pontoon dock, handling of cargo became much more efficient. We could then have big trucks come alongside a ship and get sling loads of cargo dumped directly into them. Fully loaded Liberty Ships arrived frequently. These new ships had a king boom with a wire six-fold block topping aft. The heavy fall had also a four- to six-fold purchase[6] to handle up to fifty tons. However, we found the wire stiff, and the purchase would not overhaul because the cheeks of the lower blocks were not fitted with weights, and we had none on hand to use. To make the rig work, we searched the island for heavy weights, old railroad wheels or the like. Finding none, our men struggled to heave a single fall down from an adjoining hatch, a slow and discouraging process. In spite of all our difficulties, each month the work of handling cargo improved. We had sixty-five gangs working hatches on an average of six ships at a time.

The senior medical officer of my battalion was giving many of the men light duty because they had fungus growing in their armpits, ears, and crotches. The remedy was gentian violet, but he could get none. The supply officer had even gone to a hospital on Guadalcanal for some, but without success. He sought my assistance. There was a troopship in port, discharging cargo. Armed once more with my list of minimum requirements, I boarded and met the executive officer, Commander Khoury, who was a friend of mine. After greetings, he said, "Charlie, what can I do for you?" I handed over my list. He sent for his senior medical officer, introduced me and said, "See what you can do for my friend Charlie." The medical officer took me to his department, where his apothecary assistant started filling out the order. When he came to gentian violet on the list, he said, "Now I have five five-gallon cans. I can give you three of them" Nearly dumfounded, I blurted, "Oh, no!" We settled on my taking ten gallons and he kept fifteen.

When my list had been filled, I thanked Mr. Khoury and said, "I'll get a boat out to secure the materials."

He replied, "No, the medicine will go with you in the ship's boat."

It was so ordered. While that was being arranged, I told Commander Khoury that I had asked his doctor if he would like to go ashore on the island and was told he could get no liberty. I continued, "If you consent, I will drive him all over the island and see that he is returned." Khoury agreed. The cache of medical supplies, including the ten gallons of disinfectant, we delivered to my supply officer and eventually to my hospital and medical officer.

Dorothy wrote that her sister Jean had died of cancer on February 3, 1944. She and I had enjoyed mutual admiration and affection. Our boys, whom she adored, were devastated.

> *Aunt Jean's funeral took place at the Church of the Holy Name in Swampscott. The nave was packed with family and friends. Her instructions for her funeral service included the playing of "Finlandia." It was to be played twice should the U.S. cut off diplomatic relations with Finland. This had become a possibility as the war in Europe progressed and the Finns collaborated with the Germans. Jean had loved Finland, having visited that country on several summer excursions.*
>
> *My brother Dick was the student and I the mechanic. She loved and admired each of us, however different we were. It was ironic that before the funeral service, the organ blower failed, and I was pressed into service to fix it.*

I paid particular attention to the subject of safety. Men who were hurt could not work, so the fewer hurt the better from a production standpoint alone. I assigned a warrant officer to ride with the driver of the lead truck to see that he did not drive too fast. We also strictly insisted that the trucks come to a full stop before anyone got off. Since we handled hazardous materials, including bombs, ammunition, and gasoline, it was necessary to employ safe methods at all times. I advertised for safety engineers. To five of those who responded, some with rank, some without, I gave special assignments. These specialists worked with the men from place to place and ship to ship, enforcing safe practices in all activities. They reported directly to me. This system worked very well. However, there were several good boys in the battalion whose curiosity got the better of them when they were handling bombs and shells. More than once we caught one taking bombs apart to see how they worked. In spite of the hazards, we were fortunate in avoiding serious injuries. In over a year's time we lost only one man, and that was due to his own foolishness.

The Marines kept their beer in a Quonset hut on another part of the island. Our man, thirty-five and married, heard about the beer and decided to try to get himself a case. The Quonset hut was guarded at one end by an armed white Marine and by an armed Negro Marine at the other end. Our man chose the black man to persuade to give him the beer. The Negro guard dutifully warned my man to stay away, but he begged and begged and kept getting closer. The guard told him, "If you touch the cases, I will shoot you." Finally my man said, "You won't shoot me for one case of beer." He picked up a case of beer and was about to leave with it. The guard ordered him to drop the case. He ignored the order and the guard shot him. He lived but a few hours. Dying on the way to the hospital, my man was heard to say, "It wasn't worth it."

The Navy was always afraid of fights between blacks and whites. When such occurred, the Negro involved would be quickly transferred. In this case too, we immediately transferred to another island the man who had loyally done his duty.

We had continuing difficulty in keeping beer shipments intact. In fact, it was the main problem for officers in charge of the work. As a senior officer, I attended meetings of the Naval Base Conference. Each officer in command of a unit was urged to state his principal problem so that, as a group, we could come up with solutions. For the beer problem I agreed to accept the assistance of the base police force, but the problem just grew. I then had to protect the beer not only from pilferage by my own men but from the police as well. My officers objected to the snooping of the police and resented the fact that they weren't considered good enough to do the job alone. Their protests were justified: before long, they caught a police boat being loaded with cases of beer from one of our shipments. Once more it proved that if you have a dirty job to do, it is best to do it yourself.

In training, my men had been taught "can do," no matter what the circumstances: "If you haven't got what you need, get it." This philosophy encouraged stealing, often referred to as "moonlight requisitioning." They stole from other battalions, from their own battalion, and personally from each other. They did good work, but stealing was always a problem. For example, when a supply vessel came into port, my executive officer, Mr. Fitzgerald, assigned an officer-in-charge to supervise the discharging of that ship. The ship's chief officer commonly gave this man a room on the ship. Once, an officer-in-charge from D Company was assigned to supervise discharging from a ship with six staterooms comfortably fitted out with mattresses. When the ship arrived in her next port, none of the staterooms had mattresses. At that time headquarters officers, including me, slept on canvas cots.

I had been in the habit of inspecting all the men's quarters every working day but had not included inspections of the officers' quarters. After talking the affair over with Fitzgerald, I said, "Let's inspect the officers' tents in D Company." We found six officers with ship's mattresses on their cots. The officer responsible claimed he had been given the mattresses. I had them gathered up and returned.

The chaplain was in charge of the movie theater, a naturally formed, curving slope in the terrain, at the bottom of which was built a wooden platform with a movie screen erected at the back. The seats arranged around the curving bank were coconut palm logs, not what anyone would call comfortable. I was awakened one night about two in the morning by the sound of trucks. On investigation I found two of my trucks dumping loads of sawn lumber. My men had diverted it from another destination to their theater. They wanted to improve the seating. To my surprise, the chaplain was standing there watching. I asked no questions, simply ordered them to reload the lumber and sent it to its proper destination. The chaplain, whom I felt was more or less responsible, told me that he was shocked and glad that I had appeared. Maybe!

Our crawler cranes were left on the docks or at the shore unattended when not in use. Several times, when we came to use them again, we found the batteries missing. With no replacements, these machines were then useless to us. On March 1, 1944, the Thirteenth Special Battalion was due to arrive. It was under the command of an old friend and former colleague of mine, so I made it a point to see that the area designated for them was in proper shape. It had previously been occupied by the military police on the island. Removing a few tents left there, we found the dead batteries from our crawler cranes. Now we knew what had happened: the MPs had stolen our batteries to power their radios.

The Southwest Pacific Command ordered an investigation of the portable lights from the *Santa Monica* that my "can do" men had taken so that they could see to unload the ship. The investigators called all officers together for questioning. We all admitted using the lights, for good reasons. The case was dismissed. Nevertheless, I had the whole battalion muster, told the men about the investigation, and ordered them to bring all lights to a second formation. All came to the formation but brought no lights. After explaining that I wanted lights, not persons, and how I intended the routine to work, they returned with the lights, put them on the ground, and, on command, took four steps to the rear. With thirty lights on the ground (we had been charged with stealing only twenty-eight), the men were dismissed. I wrote the Command that we had the lights ready for shipment when ordered. That was the end of it. We never did receive orders telling how to dispose of them.

After we had been on Banika Island for several months, Commander McCarthy was sent to us to serve as regimental commander. He was a Civil Engineering Corps officer and had commanded the Second CB Battalion. He had done an excellent job in New Caledonia. When he arrived, he laid out his plans, and we cooperated. However, when he dealt with my battalion, he preferred to deal directly with my executive officer. This was apparently because my rank as commander-of-the-line was above his. I let this pass until my executive officer complained to me about his unreasonable and impossible demands. I protested personally to Commander McCarthy and told him that I would take his orders directly from then on and see that they were processed through chain of command, according to Navy regulations. "Just tell me what you want, and I will see that it is carried out," I said.

*Apparently those words were not well received. Dad might better have brought a bottle of liquor and had a friendly little chat. Alas, such was not my father's way.*

I never heard a word from Commander McCarthy following that meeting, but about a week later I received orders from Southwest Pacific Command that I was being relieved of my post with the Eleventh Special Battalion to be replaced by McCarthy's former executive officer, Lieutenant Young. Young himself said to me, "I do not appreciate the job."

It was a big shock to me to have to leave my men, but in the service, one does as ordered. On April 4 my officers came to wish me their best and to say that it had been a pleasure working with me. The last thing I did before leaving my battalion at Banika was to call on all the men with whom I had become best acquainted, including all those who had been disciplined. I said my goodbyes. I had done my duty to the best of my ability. Later I heard that Young lasted only a few weeks.

On April 5, 1944, I flew back to the States via Navy Air Transport Service (NATS) to Guadalcanal, stopping overnight at Hotel de Gink, then on to Espiritu Santo in the New Hebrides. Next day it was on to Canton in the Phoenix Islands, and, in the morning, on to Pearl Harbor via Palmyra Island. On the ninth I flew the Pan American Airways Clipper to San Francisco, arriving at noon. Of course I was thrilled to be homeward bound. I was entitled to a day and a half leave for each month overseas, a total of nine days.

# Notes to Chapter 17

1. Line Officer: one trained to command a vessel, as opposed to the CEC officer, trained in support services. Line officers are superior in rank to CEC officers with the corresponding title.
2. jgs: junior grade lieutenants.
3. "Dress right" tells the troops assembled in lines what the next maneuver is to be and shall be executed upon the repeating of the word "dress." To dress right means to turn the head to the right and extend the left arm. Each man shuffles into his position an arm's length from the adjacent man.
4. Liberty ships: merchant ships built in large numbers during WWII, carrying about ten thousand tons.
5. Some landing craft were amphibious boats with wheels. Smaller than LSTs, they were known as "Ducks" and could drive up onto a beach and beyond.
6. Purchase: a device, such as a tackle or lever, used to obtain mechanical advantage.

## CHAPTER 18

# DISTINGUISHED SERVICE

Arriving in San Francisco on April 9, 1944, I reported to Washington by phone. They told me to expect new duties within a few days, but as it turned out, I ended up waiting idly for a month. San Francisco was so crowded with servicemen that it was impossible to get rooms. I finally landed a cot, number 81, on the mezzanine floor of the Fairmount Hotel on Nob Hill. There were many Marine airmen with cots alongside mine. All of us complained about being kept in the dark about our next assignments. We had to report three times a day in person to the Federal Building, so we were restricted in our travels to a fifty-mile radius of San Francisco.

I spent most of my first day there getting my clothes ready so that I could appear in proper uniform. My blues were moldy from tropical humidity. I managed to get my suit cleaned and pressed in spite of the severe labor shortage in the area. There were "Help Wanted" signs in every window. Many of the streetcars and taxis were being operated by women.

I called on Captain Kane of American-Hawaiian. While others went to nightclubs and dances, I kept trying to call home. No answer. Finally I sent a night letter. I felt lucky to be within three thousand miles of home and in the States. Most men had been out of the country for at least eighteen months before getting a chance to go home.

April 15, still waiting for orders, I wrote Dot.

> I just returned from the Federal Building where many had received telegrams from Washington, but there were none for me.

310

The dry air here is wonderful, flowers, green grass, and clean, hard-surfaced streets. No more yellow sloppy mud.

There are all kinds of fruits available, and real eggs. Nice-looking women in colored clothes and many military men in dress uniforms. All that is missing is you, dear. I don't know what is next. It is exasperating. If only I could go home and get my orders from there. I'm sorry I told you I would be home this weekend, but perhaps after I mail this letter I will get orders. . . .

I eat breakfast at a restaurant near the Federal Building that serves the best hot cakes and delicious bacon. There are shortages, of course. No restaurants serve butter, for example. I was out to the Herberts' last night and had fried chicken. Mrs. Herbert told me that many eating places use their ration points for meat instead of butter.

I've tried to get into the St. Francis Hotel several times but find the lobby so full there is hardly standing room. As you have seen via the full page advertisements in Life magazine, "Don't come to Frisco until after the war."

I'm driven nuts waiting to get home. I might get duty here or get sent back to where I came from as have others. Orders usually come here within five days. I'm nearly frantic.

I spent many days reading in the park until I got cold. I was still unable to find more satisfactory living arrangements. Only allowed to hire the cot by the day, more than once I found it occupied by someone else. On April 18 I took a trip out to the fleet post office and tried to intercept my mail that was bound for the islands from whence I had come. I was told that could be done only if I had new orders. As I lay in bed on the night of the nineteenth, I decided that if I didn't find orders in the morning, I was going to consider myself still attached to the Bureau of Yards and Docks and report to the officer in charge of the Pacific Division. In the morning I found no orders, so I proceeded with my plan. I went directly to Captain Cotter, who offered the reason for my lack of orders. It seems that the Federal Building personnel were supposed to have told me to go to the Bureau of Yards and Docks. It was more of the same trouble I had encountered before, the confusion due to my being a line officer. Captain Cotter was pleased to see me and sent a special telegram to Washington. I had already spent nine frustrating days waiting in San Francisco.

At last, on May 11, I received my orders, which gave me ten days' leave before reporting to Camp Parks, California, for duty. I was to be in charge of training a Special CB Battalion there. I made the trip east as fast as I could arrange it. At home on leave, I was in heaven, but the stay was all too short. In New York, Dot and Dick and I were able to get together with Allan, who was on leave from Aberdeen Proving Grounds in Maryland,

Navy Commander Charles Nathaniel Bamforth
with Army Private Charles Allan Bamforth, 1944

where he was in training. He had finally been drafted into the Army after receiving a series of deferments because, as a G.E. machinist, he was in demand helping to supply the tools of war. At Aberdeen he was assigned to the Ordnance Department.

On May 23 I was back in San Francisco. I arranged transportation to Camp Parks, a so-called "Replacement Center" forty miles south of San Francisco on the east side of the bay, thirty-five miles from San Jose. The camp had about seventeen thousand men and nine nurses. The drill field in front of the administration building covered a full twenty-five acres. I arrived there on May 24 and did paperwork all afternoon. I was put in the training department and told to set a schedule for training special battalions and to supervise the construction of a dry-land ship. However, because of changes in Navy plans, I could not proceed.

A letter came from James Harris, my yeoman in the Eleventh Special. He was a wonderful man and had been a great help to me. He was pretty sore at the way things were going on Banika. He quoted one of Commander McCarthy's letters: "The former officer in charge of the Eleventh Special Battalion was relieved for failure to curb and control personnel in his organization." I wrote about it to Dorothy:

> I don't know whether this was a report or an answer to a request. The fact that [Commander McCarthy] didn't want me was not very complimentary. . . .
>
> There is a Navy rule that if I had failed in my duty, my superior must notify me in writing and include my reply in his fitness report. Since he did not bother to do this, his report must simply have been filed to clear himself.
>
> The whole affair has not made me happy and burns me up. If he were charging me with an offense, at least he could have notified me.

*I suspect Dad's faithful yeoman had quoted this passage because he thought it was so amusingly absurd. Dad didn't see the humor.*

By then Commander McCarthy had been transferred, and my field Commander Howard Gaidsick relieved him. Gaidsick had been an officer under me on the *Pennsylvanian*. I admired the man very much.

After a month at Camp Parks, I was reassigned. The command recommended they release me from the Bureau of Docks for general service. On June 25 I received orders: "Detached. Proceed. Report Amphibious Base, Oceanside, California." I was back into general service and happy to have something to do with boats, my line. Although I had five days to get there, I was eager to be useful again and I traveled immediately to Oceanside, thirty miles north of San Diego.

I arrived at Camp Pendleton Marine Corps Base on June 29, 1944, after a long, hard trip from Camp Parks. The camp covered a three thousand-acre tract, a dry, dusty place with nothing green growing since there was no rain. There were about eighteen thousand men, all Navy. All officers were of the line, like me, wearing stars. At the sea end of the Marine Base, the new camp was designed for beach battalions engaged in training for amphibious landings.

I was attached to Beach Battalion C, one of the first two battalions to be trained there. Battalion A had been trained elsewhere. Battalions B and C were to begin a six-week training course starting July 15. In the meantime, the place was just getting organized. So far, Battalion C had twenty officers and eighty-seven men. Most of the officers were just back from duty in Africa, Italy, or France. Although this battalion was only half the size of my Eleventh Special, it had as many officers of higher rank. The commanding officer was Captain Hoffman. I was made executive officer of Battalion C. Under me were three companies with three platoons each. The nine platoons were each under the direction of a lieutenant commander. Each platoon would have a doctor and thirty-five men when placed aboard a combat ship. I was advised right away not to send for my family since no housing was available. Then I was handed two big books with reading assignments for evening study. We studied all the time. On July 13 I received seventy-two men fresh out of boot training. I wrote home,

> Nice weather, very busy, studying and organizing. I have seventeen officers on board so far of the forty required: two lawyers, one schoolteacher, one professor, one paint salesman, two insurance men, one manager of a steel sash company. All are very smart. All eight are lieutenant commanders and have been in the Navy longer than I. Lieutenant Commander Emile du Pont, one of the lawyers, was a personnel manager. He is a member of the famous family that made a fortune in the chemical industry. He did a marvelous job with the landing on the Normandy beachhead and is here to train men for landing on Pacific beaches.
>
> I ate dinner with three officers. They insisted we play bridge afterward. They were to play for money. I told them I couldn't. They cut the stakes to one twenty-fifth, whatever that means, and insisted I join them. They were all expert players. We cut for partners. My side won the first round. I don't know their terms, but we won thirty cents apiece. I felt guilty as hell with the thirty cents and I still haven't put it in my pocket. I tried to buy colas but no one had nickels for the machine. One of the officers could hardly believe I'd never played for money. I didn't play after the first rubber. So you get this letter instead of my staying to play more.

To Dick I wrote,

I enjoyed your newsy letter. You are getting to be quite a man, earning hard cash. However, I feel the experience [as a salesclerk in a men's store] is worth more than the money.

We now have about thirty thousand men at this camp or school. About three times a week, my battalion spends all day with forty-five boats. We practice landing men on the beach in simulated assault attacks. Later on we will do it from ships. At present we board the boats from a mock-up wooden dock that looks like the side of a ship, and we climb down the rope nets. Then the boats form in rendezvous outside the harbor behind a line of departure. I supervise my control boat on which is the division beach master (myself or other commander), and, on schedule right to the second, we have the troops loaded. Boats dash for the beach through the heavy surf in waves of personnel spaced five minutes apart.

The boats get as close to the beach as possible. The ramps are let down and the soldiers, Marines, and sailors rush up to capture the beach. The beach party (our men) take charge of the beach and send "casualties" back by boat to the hospital ship.

Although this business is supposed to be secret, I notice pictures are being shown to the public on the movie screen and in newspapers.

Some boats are wrecked or broached-to on the beach. It is our job to refloat them, make repairs, and keep the traffic moving. It is very exciting work. Our men are soaking wet most of the time. We practice both day and night. After ten days' more schooling we will practice farther up the coast, making landings from ships onto APA (Ancillary Personnel Assault) vessels.

Although the battalion is made up of nine platoons, each consisting of three officers and forty-five men, each one will be placed aboard a ship and each platoon will be known as a "beach party" with a lieutenant commander as beach master. He will have one executive to assist, one doctor, one chief bos'n's mate, one first class bos'n, five signal men, five radio men, two first class carpenter's mates, two more mechanic's mates, three hospital corpsmen, and twenty-one seamen. While aboard ship they act as part of the ship's crew. Commanders like myself may have charge of several beaches at one time.

On July 23 I received two commanders, both junior to me. I seldom got to school or lectures. I was too busy organizing and keeping others in class. On the thirtieth I received seventy-four men. Though my battalion was still short by thirty-four, we were taking all the honors.

315

By August 5, Beach Battalion C was nearly complete, and my work was easing up. Captain Hoffman was pleased with the results and the outstanding reputation of my officers and men. The station training officers were telling new officers to watch how Battalion C did it. Battalion B, training adjacent to us, was envious.

On the thirteenth I wrote to Allan,

Nice weather here to train in. A letter from Mother said she was happy to get fifteen gallons of gasoline. Soon I expect to be separated and sent out as division beach master. I will supervise several beaches and beach masters and be on the staff of the commander of troop transports at sea. . . .

So far only three men have been up at captain's mast. One was disrated, the two others restricted. For minor offenses I treat them my own way as I did in the CBs. I form an "awkward squad" and give them an hour's duty, drilling hard under a good adjutant, or I drill them myself together with a little fatherly talk. This saves putting them on report and keeps their record clear. The method usually works. We are better friends afterwards. Some who were in that squad my first week are now my best petty officers. This also teaches officers how to handle their own men and not burden the commanding officer with their problems.

Today we had a lecture by an officer sent back from the forward area. He reported actual assaults on Guam and on an island near Saipan. We also had a lecturer who had been a beach master in the assault on Saipan. He gave us a firsthand picture. Meanwhile, we get better at this new kind of warfare. Unfortunately, so does the enemy. Two more weeks and my men will be authorized to wear the yellow Amphibious shoulder patch. . . .

Don't worry about my assignment being too dangerous. As has been proven in this war, we don't attack until we have superiority in numbers and equipment. Advantage is taken through the element of surprise. The U.S. has by far the best equipment, superiority in numbers, and control in the air. We have complete confidence that most of our men will come back alive. The job ahead is very exciting and interesting. If it's to be the Philippines, I've been all around them. If it's the China coast, I've been there too. Most of my men have never before been out of sight of land, and for many it's their first time away from home as well.

My beach battalion finished training in late August. The men earned the right to wear the gold and orange Amphibious insignia on the left shoulder. There were twelve who finished the course but because of their asinine behavior were not permitted to wear the patch.

Lieutenant Albert Seechts, U.S.N. retired, wrote to me. He was the one who had said he would make a real sailor of me when he ordered me up the main mast during my time on the schoolship so many years before.

C.N. Bamforth, Commander U.S.N.R.,

My best greetings to you, dear friend, and thank you for the very friendly and welcome letter. It is heartwarming to be remembered by those for whom one has a high regard. The war has brought you a title. I know you can carry on with credit and honor.

I am the old "has been" just giving Father Time a race, and rather sorry to be an inactive member in a war for human rights. However, I adopted the war in 1938; fought the Hitlerites by sending finances to England where I knew they needed it. I was in England when the war broke out and made my getaway on the S.S. *American Shipper.* She is now at the bottom of the sea.

My brother Francis, whom you met in the Philippines, has been murdered by the Japs. His last home was in Arion, Bataan, across the Bay from Manila.

I may be able to take the ferry across again. When I do, it will be the slowest I can find. The sea is my first love. You know, Charlie, with your Merchant and Navy service, you could and should write a book. I know you would do a truthful job. You will live to see reforms. I don't expect to.

I do expect to live to see Germany whipped and Japan also, within two years after the fall of Germany. Distances in the Pacific raise hell with any plans and the tropics knock out many men before they do much fighting.

That must have been a German sub that got your ship.

Again thank you for the kindly letter and "Hands Across the Sea" to you, my dear friend. Thumbs up!

Sincerely,
A. Seechts

On September 13, 1944, I wrote home,

I was told today I would be the next division beach master to go to San Diego for study. I'll welcome the change from responsibility. My captain told me today that another official has complimented me for the work I have done here. The executive officer of B Battalion has received six of my platoons and complimented me openly on what I have accomplished and added, "and you did it alone." It is nice to hear that from a competitor.

Allan wrote to me that he was being shipped to a camp in California. I was hoping to get a chance to see him. To Dot I wrote,

> I am one of six nominated for team's division beach master and I'm second on the list. As these new APA ships are completed, we should get going soon.
>
> If I had been allowed to stay in my own field of business, I would be a Navy captain by now, as several of those who have served under me are. But then I've had an interesting and varied experience and went where the Navy department wanted me most. I find many of the officers who have worked under me or trained under me are very complimentary, and that's a great satisfaction.

My orders came to report to Training Command Amphibious Forces, Coronado, California, just south of San Diego. As I was leaving Camp Pendleton, Captain Hoffman was making up the fitness reports. He laughed and said the only fault he had with me was that I worked too hard. I had been with him long enough that he, and everyone else, knew I meant business.

Since I had five days to comply with my orders, I went to Wilmington to try to find Allan. He was not at the port annex. Only Italian prisoners were there. Camp Anza was my next guess, sixty-five miles on the other side of Los Angeles. I first tried at the embarkation station. Allan was not there, nor could the station help me. I was treated with respect, but they were guarding against divulging secrets. Finally the senior officer said that I might look for Allan at Camp Anza. I found out that an Army truck driven by an Italian prisoner was sent there once a day with mail. I secured permission, and the following morning I rode out eighty-five miles in the back of a truck. At headquarters I was told that they had no record of a man by the name of Charles Allan Bamforth. I insisted he was there and that I must see him. I was given the round robin. Finally I got to his commander and was told that he was there, but I could not see him because he was out on a long march. I insisted that he couldn't be. I knew from Allan's letters that he had a sprained ankle. The officer finally laughed and sent me to Allan's quarters where I found my boy lying in his bunk. The company commander voluntarily gave him a twenty-four-hour pass. Together we went to the beautiful nearby town of Riverside and put up at a nice hotel. We had a good visit, and twenty-four hours later, Allan reported back to camp.

> *Indeed, the meeting was special. Neither of us knew for sure if we would ever meet again.*

After arranging for Dick, who was in high school, to stay with the Miller family next door, Dorothy came west to see me. On September 28 I met her at the train station in San Diego. I spent as much time with her as possible.

Commander Bamforth receives Merchant Marine
Distinguished Service Medal, 1944

I was in heaven. On September 30, 1944, she joined me for a small ceremony. A special band and troops assembled in formation. Then a captain of the Maritime Service, down from San Francisco, decorated me with a Distinguished Service Medal for my work done in saving the crew of the *Honolulan* when she was sunk by a German sub in 1942. The Maritime Commission had tried to make contact with me several times before but had been unable to catch up with me. The award read:

UNITED STATES MARITIME COMMISSION
WASHINGTON
OFFICE OF THE CHAIRMAN
May 22, 1944

The President of the United States takes pleasure in presenting the
MERCHANT MARINE DISTINGUISHED SERVICE MEDAL
to
CHARLES NATHANIEL BAMFORTH, MASTER
CITATION: for distinguished service in the line of duty.

His ship having been torpedoed, he calmly gave orders to abandon ship, but remained onboard with the First Mate and Radio Operator to obtain extra food and equipment for a lifeboat which was standing by close aboard. Just as this task was completed, a second torpedo struck and the ship began to settle rapidly. In company with the other two officers, he jumped over the side and swam to the nearby lifeboat. Mustering his crew on the three lifeboats and discovering that an oiler was missing, he conducted this search until the one missing man was rescued. Having received a signal from a plane that help was on its way, he kept the boats together in the vicinity for four days, and on the fifth day, with no assistance in sight, set his course for the nearest land and finally was picked up by an English steamer.

His calmness, which inspired his crew, his concern for the safety and comfort of his officers and men, his leadership in keeping the boats together were highly commendable and in keeping with the finest traditions of the United States Merchant Marine.

For the President,
Emory Scott Land,
Chairman

*Though my father makes the award sound very routine, the photograph of him receiving the medal tells a better story. He looks physically fit, giving testimony to his oft-described efforts to be so. Mother looks truly proud. The khakis he is wearing are typical of his lack of pretense. Though he does not make it sound so, the medal really was a big deal.*

I was happy to be with my wife for a few nights in San Diego. Then I was sent to sea in training as a beach master. Dorothy went to Long Beach to visit my brother Ralph, and I sailed on the Neville APA, whose master was Captain Anderson, formerly with American-Hawaiian.

Ships loaded with supplies, beach battalions and Marines sailed from San Diego toward an island on the coast. We simulated an attack. The destroyer in our company bombarded the island. Then men made landings on the beach and set up defenses. They dug foxholes and established communications. The boats then returned to the ships to bring supplies ashore. After the Marines "captured" the island, we returned the Marines and supplies to the ships. The whole operation took ten days.

Arriving back at San Diego October 10, I received surprising new orders: "Proceed. Report Pearl Harbor Command. Duty in charge of pilots. Proceed by air." I had five days to comply. I picked up Dorothy at Long Beach and we trained to San Francisco together.

# CHAPTER 19

# PEARL HARBOR

Dorothy and I put up temporarily in San Francisco at an old third-class hotel where we were lucky to get a room. I was booked on a Clipper seaplane, first class to Honolulu, scheduled to fly in the evening. I said goodbye to my wife, who went by train to Seattle the following day. For four consecutive lonely nights I crossed the bay to Oakland Airport from San Francisco and waited for the plane to fly, but it did not, due to fog. On the fifth day the Navy canceled my flight on the commercial carrier, and I was assigned to NATS (Naval Air Transport Service), whose planes were flying every night, fog or not. This was far from first class. Passengers sat in canvas chairs that tilted way back. The plane had six canvas bunks, three high. Being a senior officer, I had the privilege of using one, so I stretched out and slept for the night.

On October 18, 1944, I arrived at Pearl Harbor and reported for duty at the pilot station. Seventeen of the pilots on duty were Navy, but the senior pilot, Captain Atteson, was a civilian. He had tried for the Navy but had failed the physical examination. At the same time, he couldn't be let go because of Civil Service regulations. He was a good man and an experienced pilot. Although I was placed in charge, he was the senior pilot. He had been in charge for years and knew the ropes. Two other Navy commanders before me had been unable to get along with Merchant Captain Atteson and had resigned from the Navy. (My Merchant Service background may have been why I was assigned here.) We worked under the command of the captain of the yard, Captain Craven. Some staff, including our driver, came under me.

I was in charge of the pilots' establishment. Our office was in a former nurses' billet near number four dry dock and adjacent to an old hospital that had been turned into a BOQ (bachelor officer quarters). My quarters had been one of the hospital rooms. We had our own mess in the old nurses' quarters, our own cook and messmen, and our own station wagon and driver.

Pearl Harbor is located in the trade wind belt. The wind blows northeast in the dry season and southwest in the monsoon season. All the docks were oriented northeast and southwest. This way ships could come in easily under their own power. Most of the docks were wooden decked and supported by wooden pilings. The mooring crews placed pontoons alongside the docks, and tugs pushed the ships broadside against the pontoons. Ships had to land very easily or the pontoons would be pushed under the dock, breaking the pilings. It was the pilot's duty to avoid this.

On a Navy aircraft carrier, for instance, the pilot stood behind the repeater[1] to keep the ship on the proper heading. Because the pilot could not see the dock from the bridge of these huge vessels, officers aboard the ship were stationed within view of each pontoon to inform the bridge by telephone of the distance from the hull to the pontoon. The tugs were placed on the offshore side of the ship, one at each end. They were secured to the ship at right angles with their stems hard against the ship's side. An officer placed at each tug station relayed orders.

Navy tugs operated under regulations with a standard speed of fifteen knots. One-third speed was five knots and two-thirds, ten knots. The pilot might order, for example, "Forward tug, ahead one-third. After tug, back two-thirds." This system almost always worked satisfactorily. When it failed, pontoons inevitably broke the pilings.

In the forward wartime areas, beyond Pearl Harbor, the uniform of the day included khaki shirts open at the neck. Dress at Pearl was more formal, with the addition of a black necktie per order of the captain of the yard. He also issued a circular stating that there was to be no smoking on the pilot boats, all of which used gasoline for fuel.

I saw to it that all pilots complied with the rules, wore black ties, and did no smoking on the pilot boats. After I had been at Pearl a few months, however, it became evident that one of the pilots, whose rank was the same as mine, defied the rules when he was drinking. One evening at the dinner table, this pilot exclaimed for all to hear, "Well, I'm not going to wear a tie, and I'll smoke as I please on the boats." At the time I passed it off as just talk, but afterwards this officer did just as he had proclaimed. I put him on report to the captain of the yard.

We both appeared before Captain Craven, who told the smoker in very positive terms that any order coming from Commander Bamforth was to be considered as coming from the captain of the yard himself. Captain Craven followed this up by having a notice posted in the pilot station stating that I was the senior pilot officer. Things went much more smoothly thereafter.

*Here Dad recorded each of the vessels piloted, giving the name of the ship, her captain, and the date piloted. While this is of less interest than what he might have written in a diary, the rules said no diaries, and he followed the rules. His account of the years 1944 and 1945, consisting of excerpts from his letters home, was written in 1975 when he was eighty.*

*His daily routines at Pearl included administrative work as well as piloting one to three ships a day, each requiring about three hours. He was on the job at six each morning and often did not finish until eight or nine at night. There were many periods of waiting during which he read, played checkers, worked crossword puzzles, went to the movies, or wrote letters home daily.*

November 3, 1944
Dear Dick,

Here in the trade wind belt this time of year, the temperature ranges from seventy-one to seventy-eight, quite comfortable. One can always see rain clouds over the volcanic mountains and craters nearby. It seldom rains here, though only a few miles away it rains frequently. As I ride in the motor launches in the early mornings or just before sunset, it is fun to see the mullet jumping and playing above the surface of the sea. Today I had a big job outside the harbor. It was exciting to see many porpoise playing about, jumping and spinning in the air.

It is a good feeling to know that our family can have one man at home to take care of Mother and keep the home fires burning. We are looking ahead to the day when we will be home again together with peace on earth and good will toward all men.

Merry Christmas,
Dad

Dearest,

This job is the easiest I have ever had. The responsibility is very great but only for two or three hours at a time, a real vacation for me. Much of my time is spent waiting, reading, and playing checkers. I have a private room right near the office and mess room. The food is good, although bacon and a few other things are missing. I met many captains. We have very little night work here, the harbor being blacked out.

Before I came out here I was told, "All there is to do is drink." I haven't done so or even been outside the yard. Most anything I need can be found right here.

I heard the commissary officer say, "No butter this week." Lots of things are in short supply at times. One was soap powder. . . . The socks I got in Frisco are terrible, full of ink. My feet are blue even though I wash both feet and socks every day. . . .

I had letters from you, Allan, and Dick today. Both my boys sound cheerful, which convinces me that they are getting a lot out of life. They both make me very happy. Dick enclosed a photo of the dog and the house in his letter.

Dear Dick,

I'm glad you are doing so well at home and with schoolwork. We pilots have our own mess. We have a dog and a cat for pals. How they play together!

In my private room in BOQ, I have a bed, bureau, and clothes locker, and have finally secured two chairs, a table, mirror, and bed lamp. I have also put up five colored pinups on the wall...

Dear Dot,

One of the best coast pilots on the Pacific Coast is now my friend here. He is Lt. Commander Jacobsen. We go on hikes together for exercise. It's a joy to have him here with me. . . .

I found out that captains of American ships have 36 percent of their wages deducted for taxes at the source. We must get this war over with or we will all be broke. . . .

I was thrilled to meet my brother Albert, now master of his own ship, in Honolulu today. He is well and seems content. It was wonderful to be with family once more.

It might surprise you the number of friends and acquaintances I have met here. Yet I have never been to the officers' club except to use the telephone. I often meet captains from the American-Hawaiian Company, many of whom have served with me on merchant ships. Hardly a day goes by that I don't meet men in the Navy who have worked with me in the past. . . .

The saleswomen and workers here wear black pajamas and that takes away all the sex appeal.

Dear Dick,

Having wonderful time keeping the best Navy in the world going. Have you heard this one? It's about the moron who took a ruler to bed with him to see how long he slept.

Mother wrote of what a good job you were doing.

The natives here seem quite prosperous and wear good clothes. Quite a few women wear silk stockings. There is no begging on the streets as in most foreign countries. I will tell you more about it when I get home. I feel restrained. I am not allowed to tell things that would indicate my whereabouts. It might give the enemy the number of men in a certain location.

So ended 1944, another year away from home.

*Dad continued on at Pearl Harbor throughout 1945. He made over a thousand pilot runs by year's end.*

Dear Dot,

Dick wrote that he didn't believe that I have a beard. I have an advantage, being away from home where a man can act natural.

I had written to Betty, asking where Albert was. Then just a while later, he called me from the port by telephone. He came by cab and we had another visit, but he had to leave early as there is still a curfew at ten. Albert looks fine and is happy. He said he had expected to get fired because his cargo of sugar got wet. Instead the company gave him a new ship. He said he fired his mate and two days later had to rehire him because there was no one else available.

Dear Dick,

Our dog is now one year old and still playful. Pilots all go by number. When on a ship we hoist a code flag displaying our number. At first mine was number eighteen, now it is number four. None of the pilots wanted the unlucky number thirteen so we gave that number to Sandy, the dog. Last week number thirteen developed a boil on his head so we sent him to the hospital, the first time he had ever been away. Tonight the driver of our beach wagon brought him back. How glad Sandy was to see us. He rushed from one to the other, crying with glee and rolling on our feet. He must have been terribly lonesome at the hospital.

Mother writes that she is lengthening your trousers. Take it easy, son, don't try to beat the old man in everything.

You know those dark hairs I used to have on my chest? Now they are turning white and look like barnacles on the bottom of a boat. I'm feeling like an old boat that needs to go to home port for dry docking and be overhauled, scraped, and bottom painted, the rigging tarred, get a new suit of sails, have decks caulked and seams payed with pitch. You know an old man gets rusty just like a ship and needs caring for. My boilers are not down, however, and they don't yet need new tubes. Perhaps I could use new piston rings to build up my speed, although I truly haven't noticed much lag in efficiency.

Dear Dot,

I received yours with the clippings about returning veterans. Cheer up, dear, just think how much better off we are than those in London, Coventry, Rotterdam, Berlin, and elsewhere. It makes my head ache to think of the terrible destruction. I saw by the paper

326

where American-Hawaiian Company received $7 million by selling eleven ships, two of which I had commanded in the past.

It is a pleasure to hear Allan was promoted.

We are in pretty good shape financially. But if we have inflation it will ruin us.

All ships entering Pearl get pilots except LSTs, normally. The captain of one asked for a pilot before entering today. We answered that, because of a shortage of pilots (all working on larger ships), he should enter by himself. The policy is that pilots will be dispatched to such small craft only if disabled. He answered that one of his engines had quit, so we sent a pilot. Mind you, these 333-foot-long craft are commanded by young college men from inland homes, and most of them had never seen salt water before the war. What an excellent job they have done.

Do you want a picture of my beard? No, you couldn't stand it. But many good men have worn beards. Your father, for instance; Jesus and the disciples too. Now wouldn't they look odd without their beards?

Last evening during a blackout I visited with you in my imagination.

I just had a day off, the first since I've been here. I went all over the island with transportation provided by Mr. Eisenberg, a friend I had helped when we were in the Russell Islands. We returned at six and had dinner at the officers' club, where I met Mr. Du Pont, one of my officers at Oceanside. He had had some experiences for sure. On return I found one of my shipmates, Earle Hammond, who was leaving the next day. The captain of a merchant ship, he has a nice home in San Diego. He said he will quit when the war is over because the unions are driving him nuts.

The captain of a ship I was on yesterday had been third mate with me in '32. He is now a full commander in the Navy.

I have good reason to believe that my old CB Battalion is now at Okinawa with Mr. Trout in charge. Tonight I received another letter from one of my Eleventh Special officers. I piloted the *Santa Monica* today. She was the ship that took us to Banika in '43.

On a ship yesterday the captain asked where I came from. They all know I am from the Boston area because of my speech. He introduced me to his radio officer who had had Jean as a teacher. He sends regards to Miss Shaw.

Two days ago I received yours complaining of my short notes that were five days apart. We have been married for twenty-four years, stick by me. I had a letter from Allan. We call him "our boy," but he is really quite a man.

On May 8, Victory in Europe (V-E Day), I wrote home,

No celebration here that I know of. Work as usual. Just saw *Broadway Rhythm* for the second time.

We are the greatest bunch of old salts and as bad as young fellows in looking for our mail from home.

*Following victory in Europe, shipping at Pearl kept up a hectic pace because the battles in the Pacific Theater continued. After victory over the Japanese in August 1945, there was a short period of slackening, but then the servicemen who had accumulated forty-nine points or more were on their way home. At the same time younger men with less service were being shipped to Japan for the occupation. Several of Dad's pilots left and others, waiting for transportation, just drank. So the pressure continued.*

War is in full force here. Curfew as usual. Shipyards, pay office, and all are open seven days a week, nonstop. However, I find that since Germany capitulated, many officers who have been away from home for three or four years are sick of the war and want to get back. We have to curb that. The show must go on.

I had a letter from Mr. Fitzgerald, my former executive officer in the CBs. He says my old battalion is right up where the fighting is the hottest.

Last night I saw the best show, *Going My Way*, with Bing Crosby as the priest.

May 17, 1945

We are not so bad off here. We buy food for our mess both from the government and in private stores. No bacon or hams are available. Your long search for meat makes our food problems seem minor by comparison. A wife from Quincy writes she had difficulty getting food also.

I had a long letter from Captain Staley. Remember, he is the officer who married the German girl when we were on the *Mount Clay* together. He has been captain continually. He lost one of his ships by enemy action and after twenty-five days landed in a desolate part of Africa. Then it was six days before they were rescued.

Yesterday I met Captain Earle Vaux. He had put my old ship, the *Pennsylvanian*, on the Normandy beach. Sunk, it was used as break-water to facilitate the invasion.

## June 19, 1945

I met two Swampscott boys whom we should all be proud of, at least I am. Yesterday I was piloting a ship, U.S.S. (LSD) *Cabildo*, and when there was a break, Chief Quartermaster Forest Mason asked, "Aren't you from Swampscott? I recognized you so rushed to the log book to check your name." We were then old cronies. He told me of another Swampscott boy on a different ship in port. So tonight just before dark I went on board that ship, the U.S.S. *Chicago*, and asked the duty officer for Bos'n's Mate Second Class Walter Parrish. Being a large ship I imagined the officer would have to look him up on the crew list, but he said, "Oh, yes, he is in my division. I'll get him." I waited and I soon was happy and proud to see this fine-looking, upright man. He gave me a snappy salute and then a broad smile. His division officer had told me that he was one of his best men. As with Mason, they told of their experiences and I told them of Allan's. Both are proud of their ships and apparently get along well. Parrish informed me that he has been married for two years, has a baby, and was looking forward to the time when he can see them. He is proud that he learned seamanship from his fisherman father.

Mason had just met Parrish. Won't they have a good time when they meet again after the war. I must write to Allan. Seldom do I have much to interest him that would pass the censor.

## July 3

I had the afternoon off and went to the hospital to see a pilot who got hurt. I took along a checker board and he beat me five games out of eight. While in that building I met two who called me by name, Marine Lieutenant Rudziac and Navy Lt. Commander Ray. Rudziac had taught judo on our ship bound to the Pacific. He said he was upset about receiving no mail and then mentioned that he knew an Elizabeth Moore who teaches at the high school in Swampscott. I am writing you promptly so she or someone can write him a letter. I went into the next room to write down her name. I did not even hint I would convey this information. I know he would be very happy to hear from someone. I urged him to write her and told him he could get an answer in ten days. I think he was encouraged. I am including his address.

## July 14

At my regular job of piloting I have not been too busy. However, as senior officer and executive officer, I have been active lately. I have nineteen regular pilots with twelve more in training, ten boats and crews. I do most of the garden work myself in my spare time.

*He determined that it was more trouble than it was worth to get enlisted men to keep the grounds groomed, so he and his buddy Jacobsen did it themselves. The physical exercise was good for him, but had he put some of that energy into politicking at the officers' club, he might have had further opportunity to advance in rank. That, however, was not his style. On the other hand, he was admired by nearly all whose path he crossed. He continued to be somewhat of a loner, exercising his conviction never to drink, smoke, or gamble. At last he did go to the officers' club with Jacobsen to eat.*

*He also came to love the Navy. With twenty or more officers under him, together with two drivers and the staff of the pilots' mess, and his court duties, he was a big cheese. The fact that he was fully qualified to do piloting and was appreciated by his colleagues added to his growing like for the Navy.*

The curfew has been lifted. A lot to be said for and against it. It hardly affects the military men since their liberty hours remain the same.

My pal hopes to get thirty days' leave to Portland, Oregon. He hasn't had one day off since he entered the service four years ago. He just stepped in to say goodnight as usual.

Lt. Commander Fitzgerald of the Eleventh Special has been overseas for twenty-three months and is at last on his way home. He called on me. Since his rank was "spot,"[2] he is now back to lieutenant. I'm one of the lucky ones who did not have to go down a peg.

This week I went to the hospital to call on another sick pilot and he told me that Rudziac was thrilled about a letter he had received and wanted to see me. I hunted him up and was he ever like a big kid! Enthusiastically he said that he had heard from Miss Moore and that her mother knew Mrs. Bamforth. He couldn't understand how she got his address. He was very happy and has since had twenty-six letters one day and seventeen the next that had caught up with him. He is getting along fine. I'm glad I started the correspondence ball rolling for him.

One of the pilots just returned from thirty days' leave. He was twenty-nine pounds lighter. He said that there was lots of meat available at home, but he had no ration points to allow him to buy any. Here right now we have no eggs. But even then, we fare better than you do, I believe.

I received a copy of a confidential letter from the personnel selection board. They had met to select for promotion those commanders who had held rank for three years. They regretted that I was not on the recommended list. I was disappointed, but I have peace of mind that I've done my best.

The conflict over? We will be sure when MacArthur gets to Tokyo. The Japs are still everywhere to be cleaned out. At present I am in a very important post with no hope of being relieved, even with the required number of points. We have heard that jobs are not available at home, and as for American-Hawaiian, they will have no coast piloting until they reestablish their business. I have not yet contacted my old employer; neither have I asked to be kept in the Navy. Generally speaking, those over thirty-five years of age are not wanted. It's nice to know that you want me in spite of my age.

Victory over Japan, V-J Day, came on August 14, 1945, and ended World War II. The focus of our lives changed and a new set of challenges began.

August 26

Navy censorship regulations are still in effect. I've written to American-Hawaiian for a job. A lot of my group are going to Japan for the occupation, rather than home to the U.S. Civilian pilots are going on a forty-hour week, but those of us in uniform work seventy hours. Washington says all those with forty-nine points must be relieved. If replacements are necessary, Commands are allowed 120 days to get them. By that we should all be out in four months.

September 3

We are sending pilots to Japan and Korea.

Today, two weeks after V-J Day, and the day after the formal signing of surrender, there was a big notice in the post office allowing us to seal our envelopes, now that censorship has ceased. There was a big celebration in Honolulu, and I let as many pilots as possible attend. I saw about three hundred planes in the air overhead.

I had three young officers assigned to my office to train as pilots yesterday. Today they got word that they would be on their way to Korea in a week. They don't know much, but they are the best available. It shows you how much in need the armed forces are for essential services.

September 16

I piloted the *Neville APA A-12* to sea. This is the ship I sailed out of Coronado a year ago as beach master to bombard and land troops on an island off San Clemente, California. I am in charge of scheduling this week, and I assigned this job to myself for sentimental reasons. As I walked up the gangway, several officers gave me a broad smile and called me by name. The captain, a regular four-striper, was new to this vessel. He was unhappy because he had to sail on such a spit kit after twenty-eight years in the navy. He had hoped to make admiral before the war ended. Furthermore, he was obviously bothered because his officers were making such a fuss over me. I enjoyed it thoroughly! His officers and I had a fine time telling each other about our former shipmates and their new commands. The *Neville* had 1,400 officers and men aboard from the States. All were very young, being sent out to relieve the older men. You see we get them going both ways.

My pal Jacobsen just returned after thirty days' leave. He hadn't been home in four years. He says costs of everything at home are high and that he would be broke in no time if he stayed there. He says ship owners are disgusted with the government for spoiling their business.

Hundreds of officers around here are eating their hearts out. They have been ordered home for separation but are having to wait and wait for transportation. They report every day to see if their name is on the list. Some have been waiting for five weeks.

I received a reply to my letter to Captain Schermerhorn of American-Hawaiian. He suggests I stay in the Navy a while. "We have not received our ships back from the government," he said. When I do return I will be considered a senior master as before.

I told you what money I get in detail. Don't expect any more.

Yes, officers do accumulate leave up to 120 days, after deducting all leave except sick leave to be paid in cash when put on inactive duty. An officer gets thirty days' leave a year. An enlisted man is discharged without accumulated leave. However, during his active duty he usually gets more time off than an officer does. A man may request that his relief be extended beyond the 120 days at the government's pleasure. I had to make a quick decision: get out as quickly as they could release me, or make a request for an extension. I want to get home, but I need a job. Since I don't have a job lined up at home, I asked for an extension of six months. I had to state a definite time period. That does not ensure that they are going to keep me. It just means they have the right to do so.

The government has another way out: put pilots under Civil Service and pay them half as much. It is rumored they will do this soon. Some of the men are willing to take the Civil Service transfer. If a man puts in twenty years as a Civil Service employee, he is entitled to a pension. It doesn't seem advantageous for me. Few will be senior to me at American-Hawaiian.

At least in the Navy there are no labor troubles and no night work. As a civilian it is all night work. In civilian service at American-Hawaiian, I'd get only fourteen days a year leave and no chance for a pension. I'm glad you asked these questions.

October 6

I brought in the aircraft carrier *Villa Gulf*. As we tied up, the captain directed a lieutenant to escort me to the gangway. This lieutenant asked me "Do you come from New England?" I replied, "Yes." He said, "I could tell." I told him that many people ask me, "What part of Boston do you come from?" He said, "Well, I come from Swampscott." He was Lieutenant Nelson J. Darling, Jr. He went to the parochial primary school but took English with Jean in junior high school.

My pal, Lt. Commander Jacobsen, says that if they don't get him more work to do he is going to get out of here. Work is slacking off. He wants to go back again and fight the unions as he did before, except for the misery it caused his wife. The union men were always calling her on the phone and telling her terrible things, such as, "Your husband has been found with his head cut off," or, "His guts are out and he is floating down the river." But he thinks we can lick the hold the unions have now. We fought the war. Now we go back home and fight to earn a living. Cheer up, I have been very fortunate and I will make out some way or other.

I came back from my last job at 3:00 P.M. and worked for two hours in the garden. I could hardly hold the hoe by the time I quit. Right now it's difficult to get anyone to work in the garden, and yet we all have orders to have things looking their best for open house on Navy Day, the twenty-seventh, when the public will be invited.

We had a hurry-up call to send two pilots to Okinawa, and we sent two by air this morning. We had been holding two others who want to get out, waiting for reliefs. Now, one has been sent to Midway, and the other was sent home, sick.

I heard Commander McCarthy finally made Commodore. Well, I am far more fortunate than many, and I didn't buy my rank with liquor.

We are losing our cooks and messmen. Navy ships are very much handicapped, some dreadfully so. The point system is taking away so many of the experienced men there is no one left to teach the youngsters.

When I arrived at the office this morning, the eight Negroes were having a revolution. They had enough points but were not allowed to go home. They thought they were not getting a square deal. So I had to make sure that they were. I called them all together and straightened them out.

I visited an American-Hawaiian captain this morning and secured three charts of the Delaware. I'd been trying to get them for a year without success. I can now study up. The captain told me that seven of the company's former captains had to go back as chief mates.

This point system is raising Cain, causing a serious shortage of experienced men. There is a new directive from Washington requesting regular seagoing officers with experience to remain in the service another six months and any out of the service to volunteer to serve so as to help get the troops home. . . .

I find now I couldn't get out of the Navy if I tried. I bet Allan I'd be home first. It may be a tight race.

I'm having to calm my men. One pilot has taken to drinking heavily. I had him before the captain of the yard to correct him, but he has been drunk ever since. When a man's time is up he just goes to pieces. That is, some do. The Navy really is a wonderful service. Here we are, ferrying the troops back home, and I think we are doing a bang-up good job. My wife is doing a good job too in encouraging me to carry on. Oh, she is a peach.

December 24

I piloted the *Wakefield* with five thousand Marines bound for Japan.

An interesting letter arrived from Albert. He had been laid up in Eniwetok in the Marshall Islands for two weeks, at Ulithi, east of the Philippines, for fifty-seven days, and in Okinawa for forty-eight days. In two weeks they will start to unload his ship. I am surely better off here. He said there were 150 ships there waiting to discharge.

I piloted the *Manhattan* in yesterday and out today. She is the largest ship built in this country. She came into Boston during the early part of the war all burned out and was rebuilt there as a troop transport. She now has on board five thousand low-point Marines bound for China.

December 27

I piloted the *West Point* to sea. Bound for Manilla, she had no real seafaring men on board. I arrived at the gangway through a side port. The port door was at right angles, an inch or so from the dock with the tide going down. I got on the phone to the executive officer about this, but he showed not the slightest concern. When I reported the condition to the skipper, Commodore Hays, he immediately got it corrected and explained to me that the point system had taken all real seamen off the ships. He continued, "My executive officer has been manufacturing electric kitchen wares and has virtually no qualifications for the sea. It leaves me with a twenty-four hour job trying to keep the ship afloat."

And so ended 1945, a tumultuous year, what with the death of President Roosevelt in April, V-E Day in May, and V-J Day in August.

In an effort to get the ships and troops back home and to relieve the troops in the Far East, we were busy at Pearl and suffering losses of personnel. My future with the Navy was uncertain. Prospects for a job with American-Hawaiian were nil.

On January 1, 1946, I piloted the *Hermitage (AP 54)* to sea. She was bound for Japan with 5,700 troops aboard. On the third I had the day off, my second since coming to Pearl. In the evening I saw the best show of the year, *Knute Rockne.* It was good for my boys' morale. I got back in time to hear President Truman on the air.

The pilot office had word that three captured Japanese submarines were due to arrive. I assigned myself and two other pilots to do the honors on their arrival. There was no news as to their maneuverability, so we thought they must be being towed. When we met them, we found them operating under their own power. They flew the American flag under the United Nations pennant. The three commanders were sons of admirals. I boarded *Number 401* and happened to get the commander who was second in seniority. So *Number 401*, with me as pilot, was to enter second in line. The sub with the senior ranking commander led the parade.

It was getting late and would soon be dark. There were no lighted aids to navigation in the harbor. We were only halfway in when the lead submarine slowed down. I remarked to the skipper of *401* to keep our distance and added, "Too bad, it will be dark before we get in." He asked, "If you were conning, would you proceed?" My answer: "By all means!" Whereupon he pulled his executive officer back from the conning tower and said, "The pilot has the conn." I ordered increased speed and blew the passing signal. The lead commander signaled back, "Keep your distance," to which Commander Spruance of *401* replied, "The pilot has the conn." Then came the message from the lead vessel, "Request rank and number of the pilot." Of course I was senior to them all. They were all young and just recently promoted. So we on the second sub passed the first and all three got tied up before dark. These three young officers were classmates and competitors. The incident gave Commander Spruance a bit of a feather in his cap.

These three subs were surveyed by United Nations representatives, then taken out to deep sea and sunk intact. I piloted *Number 401* out to sea. Commander Spruance wanted to give me a souvenir, but this was forbidden.

February 1

Regarding the clipping [in the *Boston Herald*] about the 1941 attack on Pearl Harbor, the trouble was here, nowhere else.

*Dad is referring to the controversy over our vulnerability to the Japanese attack on Pearl Harbor. At a time when the public and isolationists in Congress were resisting U.S. involvement in the war, FDR thought we should be more active and that our involvement was inevitable. This led to speculation that the War Department, and even FDR, hoped for a precipitating event to spur American entry into the war, and that they were in some way involved in the lack of preparedness at Pearl Harbor. Dad believed none of this. He placed all the blame on the admiral in charge at Pearl.*

Admiral Kimmel was in charge of the Pacific Fleet. If he had been successful, he would have been a hero. He wasn't, so he should take the blame. It was Sunday morning after a big Saturday night. It was his duty to see that an adequate proportion of the men were on each ship. They were not. I ask these questions:
1. Was the net gate closed?
2. How did the Japanese subs get in the harbor?
3. Why was it the Japanese planes were so successful?
4. Were antiaircraft guns properly distributed and, if so, where was the ammunition?
5. Why were the bulkhead doors to watertight compartments left open on the weekend?
6. If the ammunition boxes were in the ready, near the guns, who had the keys? We all knew that war with Japan was threatening for months before December 7. After all, George Washington's troops surprised the Hessians in a surprise attack at Trenton, New Jersey, the day after Christmas in 1776. If you were a Jap, Sunday was a good day of the week to attack.
7. If you were Admiral Kimmel, wouldn't you guard against this very hour? He was paid and trusted to do these very things. It was his duty. I personally hope he will be held up as an example of failure, and I still have confidence that he will be.

On February 23, I piloted the *Saidor*, a tanker type. She was being fitted with photographic equipment for the atomic bomb tests. March 13 I took the *Carlisle APA 69* to sea. She was to load ammo to be used in the Crossroads experiment.

> *Operation Crossroads was the code name given to the experimental explosion of an atomic bomb over the Bikini Atoll in the South Pacific. The name referred to debate over the Navy's postwar defense plans and in particular whether large battleships that might not be able to survive the bomb should continue to dominate the Naval Fleet. The test was to take place June 30, 1946.*

One of our pilots heard from San Francisco that thousands of ships were being laid up and that there were no jobs stateside. I felt lucky not to be mixed up in the many labor strikes taking place at home.

March 17

I had a cold supper since, as is often the case on Sunday nights, the mess treasurer in charge (a pilot) had gone home. He had planned to have pigs' feet and the officers had looked forward to this treat. We were served nothing but the usual cold platter consisting of potato salad and sliced liverwurst. No pigs' feet. The officers started to rave. I went out into the kitchen to see the chef and asked, "Where are the pigs' feet?" He pointed to half of one and said, "This is all they left." Apparently, the cook and Negro boys who had eaten earlier liked pigs' feet. You can imagine how pleasant it's going to be for the mess treasurer tomorrow when he returns.

On March 19 I heard that Allan was advanced to sergeant.

My dearest,

I am enclosing a sheet which describes this place, one that we send to all ships for the benefit of men arriving here. It describes things pretty well from a sailor's point of view.

I'm glad Allan's recognition made you so happy. I share it with you. You're not the only one who appreciates the boys. I must go to the show. I don't know what is playing but it is a good diversion, otherwise one could go nuts.

Dear Dot,

This is between you and me. I cannot relax. I'm upset. Now that the war is over, ships are returning to be decommissioned with a surplus of stores. For the last two weeks I have suspected that our men have been given supplies unlawfully. While working in the garden today, I saw a mysterious box being slipped off a truck as it slowly passed nearby. Later I heard it contained one hundred pounds of coffee. I was exasperated and decided that I must do something about it or we could all get in trouble. So this afternoon on the quiet, I went to see the provost marshal, a colonel of the Marine police. I told him that I suspected government food was going out the gate in our beach wagon and that this reflected discredit on our mess and the command. I gave him the numbers on our cars and asked that they be searched when outbound to scare the hell out of any guilty ones and stop it. I understood that he would see that it was done. I had hardly reached my quarters when I got a telephone call summoning me to the office of the captain of the yard to report details concerning my request to the police. I will be up before the captain in the morning. It is a bad situation because I haven't any proof that anybody did anything wrong. Not only that, but the officer I suspect is regular Navy, and I hesitate to make trouble for him.

The next day, Friday, March 29, I went to the office to explain to Commander Waite why I had thought it necessary to have our cars searched at the gate. On Saturday Commander Waite called me to send the individual I suspected up to the captain of the yard. He was immediately relieved from duty. It had not been my wish to have him punished simply on the basis of my first observation.

Dearest,

My mistake in asking to have our cars searched was having gone to the provost marshal without going through the proper chain of command. The following day I had to give additional evidence concerning the movements of Navy stores by the truckload. The three regulars in my group who were suspected are very meek. I can imagine they got sat on hard by Captain Waite.

I went aboard a merchantman last night and had the captain send for the chief mate. I wanted to tell him how we made lines fast to buoys. On sight of him, I said, "How do you do, Mr. Mate?" He replied, "Say, you are one of the Haywire pilots, aren't you?" American Union Seamen always called American-Hawaiian the "Haywire Line." He had probably been a seaman on one of the ships that I had piloted before coming in the Navy. It hurt me, but I swallowed it.

On April 3, I made out a fitness report for my pilot, who was accused of accepting stolen property. Then I asked that the beach wagon no longer be searched. The man was kicked out of the Navy and made a civilian pilot.

Piloting and other activities at Pearl were gradually losing their importance. Several departments were consolidating, and more pilots were becoming civilians. Telephone numbers and exchanges were being eliminated every day. During the war, we had had thirty-two thousand civilians working in the Navy Yard, but now we had only twelve thousand. Ships for the Crossroads bombing experiment made some work for us.

*Seventy-three obsolete warships were transported to Bikini, where they waited at anchor for the explosion of the atomic bomb. The Navy intended to study the effects of an atomic explosion over water on various types of vessels. In addition, hundreds of ships carrying support personnel and equipment sailed to Bikini.*

On April 8 I took the *Rockingham PA 229* to sea. She was taking a full load of soldiers to Eniwetok to be used in the Bikini Drill. On the eleventh I piloted a C-4 to sea with three thousand troops aboard. Of the total, 2,500 were Negroes on their way from the States to Yokohama. In the evening I went to see the movie *Scarlet Street*. It was very good, but the film had five breaks in it. I got word that my niece Louise Ward Johnson's husband had died in Korea from a gunshot wound. I wrote home,

In my search request, I hurt some people. The irregularities have been stopped to save an awful scandal. I've never told anyone that I reported them. Neither have I denied it. All must know that I did, and I seem to have gained respect. I have wondered if I would lose some since I rather bungled the process.

April 18
Dearest,
Our drivers have been sent home. The point system determined that they go. I have a permit to drive government cars, but I'm not going to unless there is an emergency. This afternoon I walked up to the administration building for tomorrow's work sheet and picked up the mail. I found that the Fleet Post Office had been abolished. Things are winding down fast.

Every effort is being made to get men home. Our last cook has gone too. The pilots are being made civilian, have to live outside the yard and bring their lunches to work with them. They will no longer have servicemen's privileges. Those still in service can buy their food at the BOQ. Our boats and tugs are terribly inefficient because the point system has sent all experienced men home. . . .

339

I believe our officers' mess will be closed the first of the month. I'll have to stand in line and wait on myself in another place.

April 22, 1946

As to your coming out here, money is not a consideration. Housing is. To get a house one has to agree to stay a minimum of six months. At the end of March I had agreed to ask to stay until July 1, 1947, but delayed doing so, hoping that job prospects would become more certain.

First I must secure a letter saying they expect to keep me here for six months before I can get consideration for a house. Only with a house will they give me a transportation permit for you. There is no use trying to get here by beating the government. Others have tried it to their sorrow. There are hundreds ahead of me looking for housing. . . . As for hotels, one is only allowed to stay for five days at a time. I'll have you come out here if I can, and you won't have to pay one cent. I do know families here who wished they never came because of the housing situation. Please be calm and patient.

April 23

I went to see Captain Singer, the housing officer. He told me that I must get priority from higher up to get a place on the list.

Dot, I have slim hope of getting housing. If I do, then and only then can I apply for your transportation. You will have to agree to stay six months unless I get transferred.

I found out that the Matson Steam Ship Company will not take passengers since they are booked up for months to carry troops. Airplanes will not book passengers until after September. I did meet a chief engineer who got the union to get his wife a room at $10 a day, with toilet down the hall, limit twenty-eight days. I was advised by a Naval officer to do it the Navy way since the government controls everything.

If you don't stay six months, the Navy won't pay for your transportation. I have to get quarters first. Regular Navy officers have preference because they are likely to be here longer.

April 24

I appealed to Captain Kristian for priority in getting housing and, to my surprise, he granted it verbally. I'll get it in writing tomorrow.

April 26

The point system took our drivers, so more often than not I walk or thumb a ride. I feel better the more exercise I get. The captain of the yard tried to sell me on becoming a civilian pilot here when I couldn't get quarters. He wanted to keep me here as long as possible. That is the special concern I get for being a faithful servant.

I am asking that I be given urgent special priority. If I do get housing, you will then be obliged to come, now that you have started me on that track. If you come, it might be troop-type accommodations on shipboard.

This place has a wonderful climate. It is very Oriental. Because of the wind and dust, I wash my head every night. The wind makes the heat bearable.

I will try my utmost to get housing priority. Now that I've gone this far, I hope you will not let me down. Families must come to stay, not for just a visit. The Navy will pack and ship furniture free. If you get a chance to come, please don't linger longer than necessary. If you delay, your trip will be stopped.

On April 30 we had the last meal at our mess. I secured passes for our crew to eat at BOQ number six.

May 2

Captain Kristian wants me here longer, even if there is no piloting for me. If you fail to come out here when the date is set, it is doubtful you will get a second chance. Of course, if you are not coming, I will cancel my special request. I bring in many shiploads of dependents and watch their husbands waiting eagerly for them on the dock. This is a good time of year for you to move out here.

May 3

I have just been assigned number 232 B Ave. . . . Commander Neilen said, "Glad to meet you. So you are the one who really pulled the strings." He assigned me to a house with two bedrooms. . . . I am making application for your transportation, which I have to present in triplicate with my orders from my last regular duty station at San Diego. I went to the office to type these and I'll have to type more when I apply to have furniture, car, and whatnot shipped. I will borrow some things here. To get the house I had to agree to keep you out here until July 1947. On your transportation orders you will have to sign to remain for at least six months. On this request I put that you would be ready to travel about June 1.

The lower floors of all government buildings here are painted concrete. It's cooler and vermin-proof. Some people lay linoleum over the concrete. There is a big front room. The walls are brown, half-finished in plywood, which is odd at first but okay after you get used to it. There is a refrigerator, gas stove, and electric water heater provided. If you like it out here, perhaps you will enjoy staying the winter with me. *Change* is the Navy officer's life. After I get forms started, they go to the commandant for approval. He will forward them to the Twelfth Naval District in San Francisco. SF will contact dependents regarding rail transportation, together with other travel instructions. Water transportation will be provided from the port nearest to the dependents, when available. Please accept what the government offers. It will be the same as what admirals and generals get. Are you going to accept this trip? It is now or never.

Our house is a few blocks from the main gate, theater, bus, and commissary. I'll try to make it presentable by the time you get here. Automobiles cannot be bought here, so bring yours.

My Dearest,

I went to the housing office for a copy of regulations, then to see about repairs and reconditioning, to the telephone company, and to the transportation office to see if the commandant had approved my request. He had. Ten days from last Monday, you should be getting word from San Francisco, giving sailing schedules and asking you to make reservations two weeks in advance. I will send you certified copies of my orders. You must take them to the transportation office in Boston for detailed instructions.

The house has a bath and a storeroom upstairs. It has a big front room with adjoining breakfast or dining room. There is a big lawn with flowers; no trees, no garage, but lots of windows. I will get furniture. I can cover the lower floor with linoleum or paint. You better bring small rug, silver, dishes, toaster, radio, iron, linen, and clothespins. When you arrive, windows will require drapes. Roads are being improved and grass planted, and this is cutting down on the dust. Your sailing will be from San Francisco, Los Angeles, or San Diego. There will be room on the ship for your car. . . .

Please come. You will be at sea for only five days. I will send more details when I get them. There is no chance to fly. I've decided it won't pay to ship furniture here.

On May 11 I went to the administration building and found that my request for a telephone had gone through. I took rake, shovel, and hoe to our house and worked until six in my garden. I was back at eight, dead tired. The next day I found that some screens and lights had been repaired and the kitchen sink had been worked on. On the fourteenth I sent eleven complete copies of my orders to Dorothy.

My Dearest,

My orders read, "Your application for housing for yourself and your dependents has been approved and Navy housing has been reserved for you and your family."

You better come out and take care of your old man. It's getting more and more difficult to get meals as BOQs close up. You don't seem to be worried about how much I drink or gamble or carouse. Of course, you could delay until Allan gets home, but don't delay forever.

I saw today that the inside of the house had been cleaned. I've planted several vines and bushes and spread fertilizer, and I am getting ready to put in a small hedge at the border.

You had better rent the Swampscott home. I cannot keep two houses.

On the sixteenth I had a telegram from my wife. Allan was leaving his post in France on June 1 for Le Havre to get on a ship for home. I wrote,

As for Allan, I cannot arrange his transportation as he is not a dependent. I'm quite certain Allan could not come on a Navy ship as you are sure to. There are very few private ships running, and they are booked up months ahead. If he got here, I might take him in as a visitor. Article ten says, "Do not take in boarders or sublet."

The BOQ I've lived and eaten in is to be vacated and used as a Naval apprentice school. Perhaps Allan could get in that school. It is questionable whether he would be allowed to live in Naval housing with us. Civilians have had to move out and are making a big stink in Washington. You and Dick should come and be with me.

I'm exasperated to think you won't get out here, as your telegram says, until early August. I'm going to have trouble holding the house, let alone my job.

*Torn by conflicting loyalties, Mother was waiting for me to be discharged from the Army.*

May 17

I worked at our house receiving loam and planting a hedge. I've been out here two years, and I seem to be having an "H" of a time to get you out here with me. It's our twenty-fifth year together, or are we? I have asked . . . perhaps they will allow me to have Allan out here as a visitor. Sweetheart, I know you are torn between two fires. You and the boys or me. . . . Dick not wanting to come makes me half sick. All these years apart—seems that the least we could do would be to TRY and get together this year. Please come. I'm sure we can have Allan with us for a while, a vacation. I'll pay half his fare. Some privileges that you will be allowed as a dependent, he will not have. I've had a long day. I'm dead tired.

*Dick's memory of this period differs from Dad's letters: "I have no memory about being reluctant to go. I only remember the excitement and the farewell parties. Who knows what Mother was saying in her letters?"*

On Sunday, May 18, I was busy in the office all day, acting as dispatcher. I directed the moving of twenty-four ships at ten-minute intervals and brought in the last vessel myself so that all the boys could go home early.

Dearest,

Just twenty-five years ago tomorrow we joined in wedlock. I'm happy with you, and I think you will be pleased with your trip. Today I got to the house for a few minutes. I carried plants with me that I dug and watered for several days. I planted the hedge and spread the largest load of loam ever. I worked until six. . . . I am having carpenters come and correct some problems. Get your car out, and we will make out somehow. Fresh vegetables are hard to get, so I will set out some tomato plants. I'm so tired lately that I don't get a chance at the movies.

I told Mrs. Jacobsen on the phone today that you were tired of contemplating the move and apprehensive about the inoculations. She said it's not so bad. She said the Navy doctors and nurses were wonderful to her. I go to dinner at Jacobsen's at least once a week, and they help me whenever they can.

May 20

On the way to our house I stopped at the Navy ships' stores to borrow a wheelbarrow. Finding none, I walked in back of several houses to see if a wheelbarrow was available. At one place I introduced myself to a woman and told her about the loam I had to move and asked, "Do you know where I could borrow a barrow?" She did and I got a nice one. She told me that she and her husband had lived there eight years. I told her I would have the barrow back by six. I was wearing green trousers so she probably thought I was a Marine. Then I went to work. After a half-hour's time, a Marine jeep drove by. It went to the end of the street and came back. On his knee the driver was holding a one-year-old baby with just a diaper on. He stopped and asked, "Are you getting enough equipment?" I told him how generous one of the neighbors was. He said, "Yes, that is mine. If you need any more, just help yourself." I had supposed he was an enlisted man but half under his collar I thought I saw a silver or gold leaf like mine. Evidently he is a lieutenant colonel, USMC.

Most everyone here is younger than we are, and small children are numerous. People don't have much but share things. The Navy lends lawn mowers. You will need a vacuum cleaner, by the way.

May 21

I finally got the shipping and authorization form that was supposed to have been mailed to me. Then I went to the housing office to see about inspection but decided to delay since I would have to start paying rent right away. At least I can use the house to store things. I replanted four banana trees and two more three-foot hibiscus shrubs that I had grown down at the office from plants. I secured two Victoria vines to grow on strings to the telephone pole in front. All the heavy outside gardening is now done. A garden three feet wide by sixty feet long is full of flowers gone wild and needing to be thinned out . . . I'll clean windows inside and out, and by the end of another month, all should be looking good.

Everybody speaks of how unhelpful the clerks are in the stores here. They are mostly Civil Service workers. Don't expect too much and you won't be disappointed. Civilians in general don't like to give up housing to make room for military personnel. But Mrs. Hoffman, a neighbor and civilian, helps me all the time, even to watering my lawn each evening to get it green. She has three little brats. Her place looks very nice, but her man won't lift a finger. I find most of the civilians keep their places looking better than the military.

I've found out that visitors are allowed to stay for ten days only and must be registered. Boarders may be allowed with permission. I'll take care of that, but I cannot get permission until Allan gets here.

May 23

Most of the afternoon I dug in the garden. Then I finished cleaning and repairing the chairs, nice mahogany ones with white cushions and spring seats. Now I'll varnish them and they will be like new. I've planted six of the twenty-five hibiscus I had grown from small twigs five months ago. They are now in full bloom and quite beautiful.

I'm glad you are now happy, and I am happy planning for you. I have plenty of sheets and pillow cases. I'll have the drapes up on your arrival. The boys will have a wonderfully cool room with windows on three sides.

The kitchen is on the windward side of the house so it should be as comfortable as possible. Thanks for being helpful and for putting up with what I can provide.

On the twenty-sixth I took the dispatch job and also managed to pilot two ships. Then I spent three hours at the house. The next day I worked on arrangements for Allan to travel with Dorothy. On the twenty-eighth I took another Japanese sub to sea, dead and under the U.N. flag. I wrote to Dot,

On my return from taking a Japanese sub to her grave, I received approval for Allan's transportation. . . . If he makes it on the *Arthur Middleton* with you, my pay will be charged for the passage. I'll be glad to have him with us. Later I went to town and bought washers, bathmat, grass seed, tacks, varnish, and stain and worked three hours in the garden.

I'm afraid you will like it so well here you won't want to leave. Don't worry about curtain materials or anything until you get here. Getting here is the most important consideration.

I worked hard three hours at the house raking and watering. I planted an oleander bush five feet high in front of the dining room window.

When I was working outside, a reporter approached and asked my name. I begged that there be no publicity. I told her I was a sailor, but she knew better and thought it remarkable that I had done all the gardening myself. I made no comment. Apparently it was for a local housing paper.

I had May 30 off, the first day off in weeks. I worked hard at the house and was so tired at 7:30 that I lay down to rest and woke up at 4:00 the next morning. The next day I spent the forenoon arranging to get my enlisted men fed, since the BOQ had closed. I worked at our house all afternoon, with time out for dinner at Commander Jacobsen's. On June 1 I was the dispatcher all day. We moved only ten ships. I had a hard time finding a place to eat. I went to BOQ number eight for breakfast and to the receiving station for supper.

I heard from Dorothy that she had talked with Allan on the phone. He had just landed from Europe. I wrote home,

The work has slackened off after a very busy May. Most of the fleet and one hundred other vessels have left for Bikini and the bomb tests.

On my day off yesterday I varnished six chairs, a table top, and a small desk. After working outside, I was very tired and ached but feel all right today. This shows how soft I have let myself get.

Do you get a picture of what I am doing? My plantings include: seven hibiscus shrubs, and they are beautiful; tiger lilies; La Moana vines and wood rose vines; three kinds of fern; red hedge; cup of gold; wandering Jew; three Victoria vines; ginger; bakaki hedge; two bougainvilleas; several kinds of aloes and two mock orange bushes; one small poinsettia tree; one hollyhock transplanted; bulbs of canna; and one oleander tree, now six feet tall. I had fun getting them started, plus the four banana trees that I transplanted and one small papaya tree, seven feet tall. Today I will put in the four tomato plants that have been offered me, as well as some mint, chives, parsley, and maybe a pepper bush. All these should be attractive by the time you get here.

June 5

Today I piloted the *Arthur Middleton*. She is the ship you are scheduled to come out on. She came in with passengers and was met by the Army band and all the top brass.

It's been tough to get meals without going to expensive places, but I am learning my way around gradually. Better get out here. I need at least one good meal a day where I can sit and relax. I hope you were able to get Allan out of Fort Devens without delay. . . .

There was no walkway for twenty feet between the curb and the door. I secured some curb stones of concrete reinforced with steel wire. . . . Using a straight edge, a chisel, and a hammer, I notched the blocks where I wanted them to break. Then I dropped them on a board held on edge. They cracked nicely where I wanted them to, but then I had to cut the reinforcing wire. I now have them placed diamond-shaped, embedded in the lawn to the front door and from the back door forty feet to the rubbish and garbage barrels. It was heavy work, and I had to carry them by hand. The woman across the street said, "If you only didn't work so hard on your lawn, my husband wouldn't be so inspired, and I wouldn't have to get out and work like this." I think *she* is getting *him* out to work, if the truth were known.

The local housing weekly had a few lines in it about me being the hardest working man in the area. That was put in to inspire other Naval officers. Many other yards are nicer than mine.

Captain Byers told me he could always squeeze in an extra car or another male passenger on the *Arthur Middleton*. I do hope and pray that you will be on that steamer before I get change of duty orders. You should be here by Fourth of July.

On the eighth I had a letter from Allan and wrote him, asking him to come out. I was heartbroken to find both Dick and Allan were set on getting back early to go to school. But how could I want them to do differently?

*Again, Dick has different memories of this period? "It is news to me about wanting to return after a month. On the contrary, I distinctly remember planning to finish high school there and attend the University of Hawaii the following year."*

On Sunday, June 9, I had an encouraging letter from my wife. The next day was supposed to be my day off, but I brought in one ship. I then arranged to buy linoleum for the ground floor of our house and borrowed tools to work in the garden. I had just started work when I received a telephone call with the worst possible news: I was no longer needed in Pearl. The fear that this might happen had been in the back of my mind, but now it seemed like the least opportune time, when everything was finally falling into place after so much uncertainty as to Dorothy's wishes and all the work I had done. I had no recourse but to return to the office and start making arrangements to leave.

I sent a telegram to Dorothy: "Cancel Hawaiian trip. I will be discharged Boston about July 1. Stop furniture." I then went to "our house," mowed the lawn, trimmed the hedge, and moved all borrowed things out.

My Dearest,

I am a most disappointing husband. At least you have one to put up with. Either he stays away when he is wanted or comes home when you want him to stay away. It hurt me to stop your trip, and I know it messes things up at home. Today it happened. Orders started in Washington three days ago. I was notified that the Navy appreciated my offer to stay, but, with cuts in appropriations, they could not use me any longer.

After I get home in early July, we will go on a trip together. It will be September before I will want to leave home again. I was sorely distressed in having to stop your trip. Right now I am relieved for I am going home at last. I haven't seen you in almost two years. I'm going to hug you awfully tight. We will all be happy together.

On June 11, 1946, I turned my house over to Commander Petersen and I spent the evening going through my things. I noted that I had piloted ships 1,847 times in just ten days short of twenty months. I had to move out of my room at the office and found temporary lodgings just outside the Navy Yard gate. On June 13 I had a telegram from my wife saying that she would meet me in San Francisco. I sent her a telegram replying that my orders were direct to Boston, and I would meet her there about July 1.

June 14

I'm still at the pilot office, but with the door closed. Up until now it has always been open. I am not part of this establishment any more. I've gotten over my blue spell and am now happy to be going home. They had a ship going with troop-type quartering, but they are holding me for better accommodations as I am a senior officer.

While waiting for transportation, I was beginning to unwind. I had never been so sleepy before. I was on the beach all one afternoon and felt right at home. At dinner I had steak cooked on an open fire. After dark a group of us played bridge, then hearts. I won a long game.

On the seventeenth I learned I was to sail the next morning. I was up at six, ironed all my clothes, and at seven I was at Captain Jacobsen's to pay a farewell visit. I finished packing, then boarded the *Renville*. That evening she sailed for the U.S. I relaxed, having nothing more to worry about. I slept, ate, exercised, and played solitaire and checkers. On June 24 the weather was cool, and I was full of pep after coming from the tropic's muggy air. I was up early, looking for the Farallons, the islands off San Francisco. I packed up and went up to call on Captain McCracken to thank him for a pleasant trip. He told me that he had been taken prisoner by the Japanese and held for three years at Corregidor in the Philippines, where he had had to work barefooted in the fields most of the time. At 4:00 P.M. we landed at San Francisco.

The next day I boarded the ferry that connected to my train for Chicago, another leg of my journey home. Along the way I read, wrote letters, and enjoyed the scenery. I was utterly carefree, with no responsibility. Just before dark we crossed the Great Salt Lake where past centuries had made their mark at high water on the surrounding mountains.

On Friday, June 28, we were approaching Chicago. There were vast fields of corn about a foot high, as far as the eye could see, and not a tree in sight. Occasionally a farmhouse came into view. The scenery gradually changed, with shade trees appearing and signs of inhabitants and cultivated fields. In the busy city of Chicago the buildings seemed especially dark and dirty from smoke. As I sat in the waiting room, the people seemed to be in more varied dress than in the Islands or the West, where most people were in uniform. Here the military made up only a small minority. There were many women about, a welcome contrast to what I had been used to for three years.

At noon on the twenty-ninth, the train arrived in Boston. I called home, reported to Naval headquarters, then returned to the station where I met my loved ones, my wife and two boys, now men. We went to dinner, and while my family was off to a movie, I went back to the Naval office to register for separation. At 4:15 we all met at the North Station where I picked up my gear, and we drove home together.

The house and grounds seemed beautifully kept. After greeting the neighbors, we had supper on the back porch and I went to bed early, as I had not slept a wink all the previous night. It was good to be at home with the family for the first time in thirty months. I felt relaxed and very happy. The next day, June 30 I did nothing, just sat on the lawn in the shade listening to the radio description of the atom bomb test at Bikini. I wondered what had happened to the hundreds of ships I had helped to get out there.

*The atomic bomb sank two transports, capsized a destroyer, and severely damaged at least twenty other ships. All of the ships suffered some damage. The news reports of the day show a naïve view of the bomb with its awesome explosive power the sole focus of observers, while the effects of the radiation it produced were little understood.*

The following day I went to Boston and was officially separated from the Navy. I stopped at the American-Hawaiian office where I called on Mr. Farley, president of the company. Then I went to the market for meat. There was none in sight for sale. At home I planted the vegetable garden with Dick.

# Notes to Chapter 19

1. Repeater: a gyroscope compass.
2. "Spot" ranking: temporary ranking.

CHAPTER 20

# UNION HOSTILITY/SOVIET HOSPITALITY

On July 3, 1946, Dorothy, Allan, Dick, and I began a three-week trip to Canada, which took us to Ottawa, Montreal, Quebec City, and the Gaspé Peninsula. I spent the rest of the summer with my family, sailing, fishing, and gardening. We saw some baseball games and visited friends. In early August we put Margaret and the two boys on a steamer for a two-week visit to Nantucket. Then Dorothy and I drove on to Eastham on Cape Cod to visit old friends. At the end of the month we had a big dinner party in the backyard. The whole neighborhood joined us, plus Margaret, a total of fifty people.

## The S.S. *Mount Tamalpais*

I had told American-Hawaiian that I would be ready to go to work about September 1. A mid-summer letter from Captain Schermerhorn offered me a job as master on the S.S. *Rhoda Seam*, a new collier. I sent a night letter, accepting with pleasure. I packed my trunk and sea bag and sent them off to New York. On the first of September, the boys and I went to Chelsea to see the steamer *Clan Morgan Seam*, a sister ship to the one that would be mine in New York. We approved. That night I took the coach to New York.

352

On September 3, 1946, I reported to Captain Schermerhorn, who told me that my ship was to have a new name, the *Mount Tamalpais*, and that the owners would be the Mount Steamship Company, a subsidiary of American-Hawaiian. I reported on board and was busy all day getting acquainted. I checked on the ship's papers, slop chest, sextants, clocks, and binoculars. At the office I arranged Dorothy's allotment, made other business calls, and saw many friends. It was a grand welcome back to my old line of work. I was dead tired at night after climbing up and down the bulk cargo holds.

The more I learned about the ship, the better I liked her, not because she was especially comfortable, but because she should be able to make money, and that would mean a steady job.

On the fifth I made requisitions for the slop chest. I found out I would be paid at the senior master rate, which was higher than the ship rated. Alas, a seamen's strike commenced and all crews walked off the job.

> *The strike was precipitated by the refusal of the Wage Stabilization Board to approve a wage increase that the Seafarers International Union and the Sailors Union of the Pacific, both AFL affiliates, had negotiated with the shipping companies. The WSB denied the increase because it exceeded the raises won by CIO affiliates the previous June. The unions took the stand that they were not striking against the owners or the government, but rather against the WSB, a federal agency, in an effort to force it to reverse its ruling. Shipping companies also urged the WSB to reverse its ruling. Because virtually all unions, including CIO affiliates, honored the strikers' picket lines, all shipping on the Pacific, Gulf, and Atlantic Coasts was halted. The widespread economic consequences led to pressure on the government to intervene with the WSB, as well as to controversy among business interests over the wisdom of allowing labor to dictate to the government agencies.*

Except for passenger ferries, the harbor was dead, strikebound. Common stocks took another tumble due to unsettled conditions all over the world. I had a feeling that we would be lucky to keep what we had and that, if strikes persisted, public sentiment would surely turn against organized labor. I was glad that Allan and Dick were productively employed in work and study. With their mother's continual encouragement, they would surely go places.

By September 12, truckers were on strike too. Ships were strikebound on the West Coast by cooks and firemen in spite of the fact that they had a contract running to January. The companies were refusing to talk until those unions maintained security watches as they had agreed. On the thirteenth I was in the American-Hawaiian office all day studying. The *Rhoda Seam* was officially purchased from the U.S. government at one minute after noon. In the evening I relieved Captain Anderson and worked until midnight getting settled, putting my things in closets and setting up my desk. The next day a hurricane was threatening. I secured a certificate of inspection and letters of ownership. Chief Mate James Wachter reported for duty. I showed him around, then sounded the bilges. Pretty soon my crew included a purser and a watchman, along with the chief mate and engineering officers. There being no steam up, we ate ashore. On the sixteenth my purser tried to return to the ship but was stopped by pickets. I managed to cook a few things on the *Mingo Seam*, which was docked nearby. She had an electric line from shore.

September 18 I wrote home,

> Assisted by shore labor smuggled on board, we shifted this dead ship by tugs to the shipyard. Expect less trouble here. It is a pleasure to have lights and water on and the use of fans. I am serving as security officer since the unions allow no crew. I don't cross the picket lines more than absolutely necessary so as not to aggravate the unions, and I didn't want to ask for a pass from the firemen's union as others have. I'm glad to have lights on since I have so much office work to do. My purser was able to get on board, finally, this afternoon. As long as we can get a shore gang to prepare the ship, I'd just as soon not have a crew until we are ready to sail.
>
> This is how crew members work it. The company calls the union hall requesting personnel. The hall decides who they will send. The first day, on pay, they come on board at four in the afternoon, just in time to stop work. They don't bring their gear with them. If they decide they like the ship, they return the next day again at four, ready to quit, and get paid for the whole day. They begin work on the third day. Some racket!

*The strike issues became still more complicated when the National Maritime Union, CIO, and other unions amalgamated in the Committee for Maritime Unity, announced they would demand pay increases to equalize CIO wages with whatever the AFL unions eventually won. When the WSB held a second hearing and again denied the pay increase, the White House announced changes in the stabilization regulations, which effectively granted the strikers' demands. AFL affiliates immediately called off their strike, the National Maritime Union began its own strike, demanding pay parity. Federal arbitration led to their demands also being met, and the strike ended officially on September 21.*

Using shipyard men, we made progress getting the ship ready. On Saturday, September 21, my wife came to New York and joined me aboard the ship. Since there was as yet no crew, I made meals on the hot plate. On Monday after breakfast I sent Dorothy home again.

On the twenty-fourth we got steam up and had hot water, a big improvement in living. I did my laundry and enjoyed a hot bath. As the day ended we had nearly a full deck crew. At 5:00 P.M. the stewards and engine room crew reported, but none would start work until after midnight. The engineers had to do the firing besides all their other chores. They were working about twenty hours a day to get the ship ready. Of course, they collected overtime pay, but they had another reason to get the ship out to sea: they didn't want to be in port when their union went on strike the first of the month.

On the twenty-fifth I was solicited, and finally I relented and joined the American Masters, Mates, and Pilots Union so as to have a smooth-running ship. I would have had no crew if I had refused, so at long last I joined. It cost me $65 in dues just to the end of the year.

My second mate came aboard the next morning to work at 9:00 A.M. I told him politely that I expected him to act like an officer and start at eight to set a good example. The next day he came on an hour late again. He told me that life was too short to be on board at eight, and he quit. That morning we got orders to sail for Norfolk. The last of the crew signed on and we got away by 3:15. On the way out of the harbor, we calibrated the radio compass. I had a busy night on a new ship with a new crew and officers.

September 28 we picked up the Norfolk pilot at Cape Henry, then anchored off Sewells Point, Norfolk, ready to load coal for Europe as soon as we could get a berth. Next day we anchored off the coal pier and waited. I could make no contact so went ashore by launch to the owners' office with a letter to the charterers. After my mission had been executed, I went to visit my family in Norfolk.

The thirtieth was the first cool day of the season, with a northwest gale blowing. We increased the length of the mooring chain to sixty fathoms in order to prevent lifting and dragging. That day came a hurry-up order to go to sea. I drew money, then returned to the ship with an RCA technician to calibrate the radio direction finder. We landed him at the pilot boat, held safety drills, and anchored off Norfolk with forty other ships waiting to load coal, ten of them scheduled ahead of us. Time was of the essence. The officers' union was planning to go on strike for a closed shop.

October 1 the worst happened: the engineers' union went on strike. We upped anchor and moved to Norfolk Army Base to discharge our perishables since we would have no steam or refrigeration. I mailed a letter home,

All officers and crew are off my ship. The unions are giving the captains seventy-two hours to get off.

I just helped tie up Captain Pierce's ship. He also had joined the union, realizing that if he didn't, no crew would sail with him. Each of my officers and some of the men told me that they hated to leave this ship. They are all broke from the last strike. The ship was to go

355

on hire, but the charterers would not take her with the strike threatening. Can you imagine my walking a picket line with a sign front and back? I have to guard my job. When labor has control one has to go along, or else. I think that is the way the Nazis got everyone to go along.

*The Marine Engineers Beneficial Association and the Masters, Mates, and Pilots Association were each on strike for 35 and 30 percent wage increases, respectively, and for "union security," meaning a closed union shop. The strike had nearly been averted in last minute negotiations by concessions by East Coast operators, but Mr. Plant of American-Hawaiian, negotiator for the Pacific American Shipowners Association, refused to concede a closed shop to the unions.*

October 2, strikebound, I paid off the crew. My engineers began cooling the boilers and shut off the water and the lights. The union would permit no mates on board but did allow me a night mate. I appointed Mr. Wachter, my chief mate.

October 3, with Captain Pierce, I went to the Masters, Mates, and Pilots Union to report, get a picket line pass, and register with the strike committee. At the union hall we showed them our receipted cards. They then sent us to the strike committee, where we secured passes to allow us through the picket line. They registered us as doing union duty during the strike and sent us to the engineers' union to have our cards stamped. Captain Pierce and I went straight to the union desks, did our duty, and marched straight out. We didn't speak to any one of the hundreds on strike there. We wanted no confrontation. One captain had been stopped by pickets. They took his pass away and ordered him off his vessel. I made up my mind not to agitate or even get acquainted with any of them or give them a chance to order me off my ship.

On returning to the ship, we found that the union had called off all officers. Mr. Wachter left immediately for fear that, after the strike, no one would sail with him. That left the purser with me, but by Thursday he too wanted to leave for fear the crews would make his life miserable when he went to sea again. At his request, I paid him off.

Determined to avoid all confrontation with picketers or picket lines, I planned to stay right on board. I was at a safe berth, well inside the Army Base, so pickets at the gate were far from the ship.

On the seventh Chester came down to have lunch with Captain Pierce and me and brought us a radio. In the afternoon we heard that the union was not going to allow masters through the picket lines. This made me boil. I was more than ever determined to stay. I inventoried supplies. We had 1,800 pounds of new potatoes, 800 pounds of old potatoes, five bags of carrots, seven bags of onions, 125 pounds of lard, and fifty loaves of bread. I wrote home,

> Captain Pierce and I just had lunch together. Over the radio, we got the news. Two days ago the union took a captain's pass away, then after he paid his back dues of $350, they returned his pass for one day only. Another American-Hawaiian captain was ordered to the union hall to pay $1,000 back dues or stay off American ships forever. We also heard that the engineers' union voted not to allow anyone to pass the picket lines, meaning captains. If that makes you boil, then I am about to burst a blood vessel. I'll try to hold my tongue and be prudent. There is talk that if I stay, the union will assess me all my wages. We condemn just such things in Russia or Germany. What is the difference here? My family has to live. I'm doing my best. We will try to be discrete, come what may. I couldn't work unless I joined the union. Now they are trying to put me out of work. . . . It is a disgraceful situation. There is nothing in the world I hate more than to betray my trust to the owners. I'm still on board. I'm doing nothing to cause violence. The owners would be helpless to aid an individual. The strike may end when everyone is hungry. I'll try to be a good fellow and hold my tongue. I advise you to do the same.

October 8. Overcast and muggy, gales and rain. I kept busy looking after my ship. I wrote home,

> As I sit on the edge of my bed, outside the wind is blowing a gale with heavy rain. However, I will be up and around until the wind subsides to see that my ship does not get into trouble breaking away. This is the hurricane you will have heard about by the time you receive this.
>
> We now have an electric line to the dock and a hot plate on Captain Pierce's ship. We have a single bulb to light the gangway. I still have the kerosene lamps. Two are near my bed here as I write....
>
> There is an American-Hawaiian ship not far away and still in the Army Base. Her captain, I heard through the agent, has been on picket duty for the last six days. The owners have dropped him from their payrolls. Masters are no longer allowed to cross picket lines. We are fooling them, for the present at least, by staying on board as virtual prisoners....
>
> If the owners win this strike, we may get a cut in pay. If the unions win, we may get a raise. I think that the real stumbling block is union control over officers. It is rumored that the union will assess me 20 percent of my pay.

The next day the hurricane was passing offshore, and the air was hot and muggy with rain. Chester, Clara, and Captain Bill, Grace's husband, visited me with an apple pie. I gave Clara the last of the eggs and fifteen loaves of bread. I continued to work around the ship. A gale on the evening of the twelfth made the ships surge back and forth. We captains took up the slack in the mooring lines. I wrote home,

The captain who was on the picket line returned to his ship to find a notice from Mr. Plant: "All captains stay aboard your ships or resign." Apparently American-Hawaiian and Matson Lines are going to hold out for an open shop for captains and chief engineers.

The Virginia Railroad, for which Captain Bill works, depends on coal for 90 percent of its business. With colliers like this one laid up, the railroad too is idle.

I'm not growing a beard, but Captain Pierce and I are going to practice barbering on each other soon. It has been very warm here most of the time. Captain Pierce and I worked about our respective ships until 6:30, when I started supper of toast, peanut butter, cocoa, and canned figs. We have a hot plate, toaster, electric coffee pot, and electric lights in the mess room on his ship where we do our cooking and eating. We have cocoa and a full loaf of bread, toasted, between us every night. We are out of butter but hope to get some soon. We work hard, eat well, and he says we are getting fat. Yesterday I made split pea soup out of dried peas and part of a can of corned beef. Pierce says he wants pea soup again tomorrow. So, you see, he likes my cooking. I cook onions, potatoes, and carrots together in one pot. He says he wants mashed potatoes for a change.

The company has owned this ship for a month and she hasn't earned a cent yet.

Chester and Captain Bill came to visit me nearly every day, often bringing food. Clara sent food as well. I received an uncomplimentary letter from my wife because I wouldn't have her down to visit me. On October 17 I wrote home,

We are now laying up the ships for winter. I may not be kept by. I think this business never has had a darker outlook. How short-sighted the unions are. Yet by tonight's paper I see that the AFL is looking for a thirty-hour week. If these conditions continue, it may pay to move to South America.

I'm enclosing an interesting article on the strike. Captain Manning is here at Newport News, commanding the U.S.S. *America*, the largest passenger ship ever built in this country. I piloted her twice at Pearl Harbor. She was then known as the *West Point.*

Manning says, "I will not join the union." The union says the ship will not sail unless a union man is in command. Lots of us feel as he does. We would starve before we would join, but most of us have families to feed. I don't think Manning is married. I admire his resolve, but he might have been better off not talking.

As Masters, Mates, and Pilots Union members, Captain Pierce and I were ordered to a union meeting held just for captains. We went together. It was not a structured meeting, only a discussion. I guarded my temper and managed to lead the opposition. I started it and Captain Pierce and Captain Monroe carried on. It didn't all go our way, there being several agitators present. I stood at the rostrum and told the captains, "If the American flag is to remain on the seas, the captains must take the leadership." I was careful not to specify any person or group other than "the captains." Everyone was quiet when I spoke, and then I was cheered. They were not quiet nor did they cheer when the chairman of the strike committee spoke.

We found that the Masters, Mates, and Pilots Union had been forced to strike action by Harry Bridges, the powerful waterfront leader on the West Coast, together with the strong Seamen's Union of the Pacific. I was told that I was supposed to have been standing picket duty for the last three weeks, and that the union was charging me 20 percent of my pay for the support of the strike for each day that I failed to show up.

October 24

The settlement, as far as the owners are concerned, is a long way off. The unions have all they want except for their hiring of the masters from the union hall.

As far as I know, all captains are by their ships or playing both sides. The only fly in the ointment is a weak federal government, which may compel the owners to give in by forcing the ships into operation. If they do so, all real captains will be forced to quit the sea. I am much concerned for the support of my family. I haven't written you of the seriousness before in order not to bother you. I've been thinking of other ways of making a living. But let's wait and see what the outcome will be. . . .

Though I joined the union, I am not in good standing. Rather than pay fines of thousands of dollars to get in good standing, I'll dig ditches. Those on the picket lines are being promised the first and best jobs.

October 26

I'm hoping the ship goes back into service in the next few days, as the news seems to indicate. East and Gulf Coast operators have agreed with the union heads to end the strike. The unions now have to submit the proposal to the members for ratification. However, since American-Hawaiian ships are Pacific Coast operated, they have refused to negotiate so far. The tension on us masters has been relieved since East Coast operators have been successful in holding out for an open shop for masters (meaning that membership in the union is not mandatory). Now my chances for a job have improved. The small increase in pay is not important. We want to work in a businesslike manner.

Last Tuesday we were all ordered off the ships by the union. Clara drove down to get me to come home with her, but I declined.

Dorothy sent me an editorial from the *Boston Herald*, October 25, 1946:

Billion-Dollar Gyp

The maritime strike is a colossal steal from the American people for the express benefit of a few union officials. A total of 1,450 ships lie idle, the nation's ports are all but dead, the American merchant marine is tottering, seamen and officers are barred from their jobs, and the baleful consequences run through the whole economy of the country. To what end? More money and better living for the strikers? No, they are getting that. The remaining issue, preferential hiring for ship masters, is simply a device by which power-hungry union officials can extend their authority even to a ship at sea.

The operators have conceded to all other licensed personnel, mates, and engineers, the principle of preferential hiring. This means ship owners must fill vacancies from union members. It also means that an officer who is suspended or dismissed by the union must be discharged by the owners.

To apply such a rule to masters would be fatal to discipline at sea. A skipper's authority would always be subject to question by his subordinates, who could take their complaints to the union. The master, who is responsible both for the ship and the lives of those aboard, would be forever answerable to union executives, who have no responsibility for the ship or the lives of those on it. In making his decision, the captain would have the intolerable double obligation of safeguarding his charge and satisfying the often irrelevant demands of his men.

It is for this the Masters, Mates, and Pilots Union, AFL, is prolonging the strike, working hardship on its members as well as the nation as a whole.*

* "Billion Dollar Gyp," editorial from the *Boston Herald*, October 25, 1946. Reprinted with permission of the *Boston Herald*.

By October 29 most ships were back at work. Mine and twenty-six others operated by West Coast companies were still idle. Negotiations were to start shortly. All three of my Virginia families, Clara's, Chester's, and Grace's, came to the ship to urge me to come to their homes. They had read in the paper that all captains had to leave their ships. I refused.

On November 4 the mooring lines were drying out and becoming slack, so Captains Murphy, Pierce, and I used tackles and handy billies to haul them tight as there was no other person on the ship. I had my glasses in a carrying case in my vest pocket. In an attempt to get a big drift to haul on, I bent over the rail to put the Manila strap as far outboard as possible.[1] In so doing my glasses and case fell into the sea. I could see the case floating. Like a shot I leaped over two ships to the dock and ran up to the head of the slip where a float was tied up. I slipped off my shoes and outer clothing, dove in, and started swimming toward my glasses, hoping to reach them before they sank. I didn't get far. The cold water was a shock. I turned back toward the float, thinking that my life was worth more to my family than my glasses. In the afternoon I went to town on ship's business and ordered new glasses. I walked deliberately through the picket line looking neither right nor left. The pickets seemed bored and dejected.

The work of living and maintaining ships continued. Captain Pierce returned from a trip to Washington. He had paid his own way. He saw the head of the Shipping Commission and others. His object had been to impress on them the necessity of having ships properly run. He found that the commissioners were controlled by the politics of the Labor Department, so no changes could be made until after the union voting. The union still insisted on preferential hiring. The owners were holding out for hiring their own captains and officers.

November 11

The other day Helen talked to me about having you come down, and today Grace said, "I'd invite her if I had permission." Captain Pierce says that he has invited you already.

All three ships here are cattle ships except mine, a coal carrier. The captains call it the "coal hod." All the captains have served under me. They call me the Vice Commodore because I'm the second senior master in the company. It sounds ridiculous to me. I get less pay than any of them. My ship makes only eleven knots compared to theirs that make eighteen. However, any one of them would prefer my ship since theirs will be out of business on February 1.

My first mate and first engineer are standing by in Norfolk waiting for their jobs. I don't know when we will be in service, but we could be at sea in three days' time.

Orders finally came and on November 18 I got ready to receive a crew. The next day engineers came aboard and started steaming the vessel to prevent freezing. On the twenty-first my ship's name was officially changed to *Mount Tamalpais.* Dorothy arrived at noon. Chester drove to Norfolk to get her and brought her to the ship.

On November 25, 1946, we heard that the strike was officially over.

*The new contract, arrived at with the aid of federal conciliators, provided for a fifteen percent salary increase and a compromise measure on hiring.*

Mr. Wachter reported for duty, as did the stewards' department. Next day a bos'n and three ABs came aboard. On the twenty-seventh we sailed for anchorage. On the thirtieth Mr. Fuget, purser, reported on board from New York. I had him get accounts up to date. Sunday, December 1, I got ashore by launch and spent the day with family. I had planned to return to the ship, but the sea was too rough for any boat to operate, so I stayed at Chester's with my wife.

Monday I took the oath at the customs house for the change of the ship's name. I found no boat or tugboat would venture out in the harbor since there was so much wind and sea. I was worried—the only time I had left my ship, and then a gale came up. In the afternoon I took the ferry to Newport News and, in passing, I could see my ship was in trouble and needed assistance. There being no means of communication, I relied on my mate's good judgment. Later I learned that Mr. Wachter had stayed up on the bridge two nights and a day with the engines on standby should she drag. I counted five other ships high and dry, and other vessels had collided and tangled up. One American-Hawaiian vessel had been hit by two other vessels. Finally I got aboard Tuesday and found her sitting on the bottom. The northwest wind had blown the water off the coast, making the tide three and a half feet below normal. I had ballast pumped to the forward tanks to float her. The ship was aground all night, and I had no sleep, worrying. I had her trimmed by the head, and we steamed into deeper water and let the anchor go again. In my written report to New York and San Francisco, I didn't mention that I had been ashore when she got in trouble.

On December 6, at anchor off Norfolk, at last came my orders: "Receive crew, get up steam, and proceed Baltimore immediately." I signed on the crew and sailed at midnight. At Baltimore I requested a survey of the bottom because of the grounding and deposited the register at the customs house. I engaged a launch so the crew could get back and forth to shore.

December 13 the *Mount Tamalpais* was at anchor off Baltimore, waiting for a berth so we could load cargo. We had charter to take oil and oil well casings (pipes) to Odessa in the Soviet Ukraine, a nine-thousand-mile trip. I finally secured a second mate and arranged to get a box of books for the crew from the American Library Association.

I felt I had a good crew of officers and men. Only the purser was a problem. Though his union contract specified eight o'clock for starting work, he would not start until nine. He threatened to make my trip miserable if I made him go to work at eight. I quickly decided to get a new purser before we sailed, and on the seventeenth I ordered him to make out his own payroll. We were both very polite. The only comment he made was, "So, you couldn't take me to sea with you." Our new purser was a fine fellow, and we all liked him. On the twenty-second the chief steward fired the second cook and a messman. I wrote to Dot,

> I had a hectic time paying off two men today. They made unbelievable demands on the company. Many of their demands were not covered in the new union agreement.
>
> I received much Christmas mail including, believe it or not, a very funny letter from my first purser, who is now a shipping master in the New York office, just what he was angling for, no doubt. Several American-Hawaiian captains have been out of work since August and many are glad to go back as chief mates. The company gave me a job first, looking out for my interests as they had promised.
>
> We should be gone only two months. Many of our ships are going to India and China, much longer trips. I have a good crew but must handle them with kid gloves. So far, they seem to be exceptionally good. I'm lucky.
>
> So, you saw in the paper that Captain Monroe has his wife traveling with him. American-Hawaiian does not let families travel with the captains. They have found it doesn't pay. Texas Oil Company used to allow it until an incident took place at a port in Texas. While one of their gasoline tankers was at a dock loading, the captain's wife came on deck smoking a cigarette. She was asked to go inside if she wanted to smoke. It is reported that she responded, "You can't tell me what to do. I am the captain's wife." The captain was fired on the spot. Both he and his wife were ordered off the ship. In most cases, however, the practice was stopped because the captain was traveling with someone he only *claimed* was his wife. American-Hawaiian discontinued allowing wives aboard way back in 1900.

Mr. Wachter and I spent Christmas Day studying charts of the Dardanelles and the Black Sea. I tried to get in touch with a skipper from the Baltic, but the crew of the Russian ship would not let me on board. On the twenty-ninth we started loading. The owners and charterers expected to get only 2,000 tons of oil casings in the ship because of their awkward size. They were twenty inches in diameter, fifty and sixty feet long. Although made of steel, these pipes were more bulky than heavy, and there was bound to be lots of wasted space. I planned to take 3,400 tons through careful loading.

On the thirtieth we started filling the deep tanks with fuel. I had a letter from Captain Jacobsen, my pilot pal in Pearl. He said that he had been a fool to come to live with his in-laws, but that now he would be a heel to leave. He was painting houses to make money and keep busy and would start piloting January 15.

On January 2, 1947, I signed on a crew, or tried to. There was a dispute about overtime, creating a long delay. Finally, rather than delay the ship any further, the company gave in and said, "Pay it."

January 9 I was anxious to sail, but the second mate and the chief steward were down with bad colds. I sent them to the Public Health Service Hospital and waited anxiously for medical reports. The second mate returned, but the chief steward was admitted to the hospital with pneumonia, and I had to secure a replacement. To compound the delay, although I had expected the loading to be completed already, the longshoremen chose to stop work at five without finishing.

The next day we finished loading and secured the ship. The deck load was ten feet high. We had 3,354 tons of pipe aboard, close to my goal of 3,400, and significantly more than the 2,000 tons expected by the charterers. We also had 13,400 barrels of oil and 430 tons of fresh water. I bought a Russian-English dictionary and all the latest magazines. At 4:50 we sailed and I was up most of the night going down the Chesapeake. With a new crew there was no relaxation. At daybreak on the eleventh we discharged the pilot and took departure for Gibraltar. I sent a letter to Dot with the pilot.

Our route, the Dardanelles, the Black Sea, and the Ukrainian port of Odessa in the Soviet Union, is new to our owners. Our government seems to know very little about the area. There is no British or American consul in any Soviet port. We have no agents there either. The United Nations Relief and Rehabilitation Administration (UNRRA) does have an agent in Kiev. In spite of all that, I look forward to a successful voyage. I have a good ship well-stored, and a good crew. I will stop at the British Naval Routing Office in Istanbul for a route through the mine fields in the Black Sea.

I tried to buy linen through the company for home as well as for the ship, but stocks are very low everywhere. I got most of what I wanted for the ship via the company from surplus government stock. Prices are very high. I'm learning navigation again. I made up a Russian alphabet to be posted for the crew's information.

We crossed the Atlantic in strong winds and rough seas. I was getting into the swing of working the stars again, although I was terribly rusty. On January 23, in strong headwinds and rain squalls, we saw the lights of Gibraltar reflected on the clouds sixty miles away. In sight of the coast of Spain, we headed up the Mediterranean into a whole east to northeast gale at reduced speed. With decks awash, the *Tamalpais* proceeded off the north coast of Africa in a full winter gale. On the twenty-seventh we passed Cape Bon where the German Army had finally surrendered in the North African campaign. We passed through the Greek and Turkish archipelagos and by late evening we were off Canakkale quarantine station in snow and an easterly gale. We waited for a pilot, hoping to get a response to our flag signals to the station, but none came. So we returned to Cape Helles, twelve miles back. We signaled using the international code for thirty-five minutes, then anchored off Canakkale, Turkey, in the Dardanelles, waiting for a pilot and pratique.[2]

On Friday, January 31, at 8:20 A.M., the pilot came aboard. We were issued pratique and proceeded. It was a fine day and the waters in the narrow passage smooth. At ten we anchored off Istanbul.

The next morning a launch arrived to take the purser and me ashore. We first stopped at the British Naval Routing Office, where we received directions and local information for the Black Sea. I received a welcome letter from home. It had taken fifteen days in transit. Then we went to the agent's office and talked over conditions. Since there would be no laundry facilities at our destination, I left the ship's linens at Istanbul to be picked up on our return. One of our ships, the *Mount Sunapee*, was two weeks ahead of us. A telegram arrived from her master, Captain Griffin, informing me that he was icebound and short of water. I had the agent send out a barge with two hundred tons of additional fresh water for us so as to avoid a similar fate. We ordered fresh stores, left the mail, and bought postcards. Then the purser and I engaged a guide to show us the old part of the city. We went through the famous Sophia mosque, once the major cathedral of Eastern Christendom, now a museum, and at the Blue Mosque we viewed a beautiful windowed room. The floors were covered with rugs, but there was not a single piece of furniture. We were obliged to remove our shoes.

February 3, 1947, my fifty-second birthday, we were proceeding towards Odessa. It was overcast so we got no sights. At 8:30 A.M. the radio direction finder broke down. With much difficulty and uncertainty, we followed the route laid out by the British Routing Office. We managed to make the approach point and pilot station by 4:00 P.M. We had to run at reduced speed for the final four hours because of ice two to seven inches thick. It had been an unusually cold winter. We anchored in thirty-three feet of water at the lee side of Lundra Peninsula, thirty miles outside Odessa. Around us at anchor were five Russian ships and two American, one a Liberty design, the other a Victory. At 3:00 A.M. the *Terre Haute Victory* and all five Russian ships started in. The wind had turned northerly, blowing much of the ice southward, out of the entrance.

We got news by radio that the ice was thicker on approach to Odessa and that the *American Victory* had tried and failed to get out. We waited at anchor until February 9, when a pilot finally arrived and took us in. At 2:00 P.M. the ice at the entrance to Odessa Harbor was too thick for us to proceed. We were stuck, and anchored once more just outside the harbor breakwater. The next day a big double-ended ferry, acting as an icebreaker, made a channel to us. A second icebreaker helped by backing and filling around the ship. We were able to move ahead some, but, for fear of damaging the propeller, I stopped the pilot from backing the ship. One icebreaker took a head towline. With this arrangement and our engines going ahead, we were able to reach a berth alongside an American Liberty ship. We were securely tied up to her by 8:30 that evening. The ice was a full three feet thick in the harbor, although kept well broken up by icebreakers. The harbor, bounded by a breakwater, was at the mouths of three rivers, the Dniester, Bug, and Dnieper. The combination of all the fresh water draining from these rivers and the severe cold temperatures accounted for the heavy ice.

At 11:00 P.M., as soon as the gangway was in place, the boarding party arrived. All units came together. In the States they come aboard separately. There were thirteen people in all, most of them women: two from INFLOT (a branch of the Soviet secret service), plus horticulturist, quarantine doctor, radio engineer, customs officers, immigration personnel, and interpreter. Most of them spoke at least some English. They were very thorough. The customs officers searched the quarters with a representative of the crew present. Then they searched the ship and found several bundles of ship's linen hidden in the deck load where members of my crew had secreted them, ready to smuggle ashore for sale on the black market. The bundles were turned over to me. The immigration officials picked up our passports and took them ashore to be examined and copied. We were required to wait twenty-four hours for their return. The copies were our passes for us to get ashore. By midnight the boarding party had finished their work. Two armed Russian soldiers were placed at the shore end of the gangway to see that nothing was smuggled in and that the local regulations were enforced.

On Tuesday, February 11, the port authorities returned our passports along with the copies they had made. The authorities advised me to see that my crew were back on board each night by midnight since there was not enough electric power in the city for lighting to assure safety after that hour. We were required to declare the amount of money we had, and we were each told the maximum that we would be allowed to spend. All of my officers accepted the many regulations imposed, except for one young officer. He and the rest of the crew detested such limits on their freedom. I issued cigarettes to the crew, just two cartons per person to minimize what they could sell on the black market.

The next morning, Mr. Day, the agent, and Mr. White, representing UNRRA cargo, arrived. They filled me in on rules of the port and customs requirements. I offered them newspapers and magazines from Baltimore, but they couldn't take them through the gate. No printed matter was allowed off the ships at any time.

When we passed in and out through the gate, each of us, officers as well as crew and longshoremen, were searched. There were bars erected to keep people in a single line. Each Russian was consistently and thoroughly searched for contraband, whereas we foreigners were only touched on the outside of pockets to see that we carried no magazines or newspapers. We were treated with the utmost respect, both officers and crew. Returning to the ship we had to show our passes to soldiers who were stationed at the foot of our gangway. These guards could not be bought and never shirked their duty. It was clear that they had been tested.

In the afternoon, two young women representing the International Club boarded. They had lists of programs and activities for the week: sightseeing tours, concerts, plays, and dances, all of which were free under the Soviet Society for Cultural Relations. The International Club (something like a USO) was in a large, beautiful building, formerly the "Bourse" or stock exchange. Postal facilities and refreshments were available there. I was told that air mail normally took a month to reach the States.

On the thirteenth I found it necessary to warn two crew members who were late returning from leave. I fined two others for longer absences. My crew members were supposed to be on board at midnight. The guards allowed one hour more, after which they would pick up the passes from returning crew members. Next morning I was notified which passes had been picked up. If I decided that I still wanted the individual involved to have liberty, the guards would surrender the pass to me. If not, they would hold it for me as long as I wanted them to.

We spent most of the day trying to get the ship alongside the pier using the engine, winches on the mooring lines, and men on the dock with long boathooks pushing big cakes of ice away. The engine was on "ahead" only, and I had the chief engineer stationed aft so that if any big cakes of ice came close to the propeller, he could have the engine stopped. Finally at 4:30 we tied up to the pier.

The docks were well equipped with new electric cranes. The Germans had blown up the hydraulic cranes when they retreated. Discharging proceeded normally, though there was much delay. The docks were piled high with incoming cargo because the railroad capacity was inadequate. By the fourteenth we had discharged only 235 tons, barely seven percent of our total cargo. Clearly, at that rate we would be delayed.

In Baltimore a gang of twenty-two men had loaded the ship one pipe at a time. Contrary to the inefficiencies we expected of the Soviet system, in Odessa the Russians discharged the cargo two pipes at a time, six men to a gang, with ease. They had one or two men stationed in the ship's hold to hook lines to the pipes and another man on deck as signal man. There was a woman operating the crane and two men on the dock to unhook the pipes. The work went on deliberately, efficiently, and continuously. There was no shelter or place for workers to hide. The Russians were working proudly *for* something. The unionized Americans were *against* everything but more money.

The port was secured by a high brick wall. Employees came and went through a central gate. Women with babies left their offspring at the first floor of the gate building where they were cared for while the mothers worked. Each dock employee brought his or her own lunch to work. It consisted of a loaf, or part of a loaf, of black bread carried in a black cloth bag. When they ate the bread, they broke off a piece and ate it plain, without butter, cheese, or anything else. With it they drank nothing but water as far as I could determine. No Russian worker would accept an invitation to eat with the crew or be found in or about the crew's quarters.

Dear Allan,

I met a General Electric engineer who had just arrived. He is to work at a huge dam being constructed.

There is a wonderful big opera house here running seven performances a week. On the thirteenth I saw Glazunov's ballet *Raymonda* as a guest of the International Club. We were escorted in groups of six. My group was led by Shirley, a university student. She speaks grammatical English and can understand if you speak slowly. All seem to be well clothed.

It is odd to see so many women working cargo. They also serve as captains of ships, ship's officers, crane operators, stevedores, and agents. There are as many women as men in these positions.

Everyone works in Russia. They all seem to be happy and work with a will, having faith in the revolution. The devastation of the war is evident everywhere. More than ten million men were killed.

The women are allowed to raise their children until they are five to eight years old, after which the state takes them over to be reared. So none of the really young women are to be seen doing heavy work. One sees how the world can get along without men.

The ship's agent, Tania Rodina, comes on board each day. She is about twenty-five years of age and speaks good English. With great vigor she climbs easily over the deck load of pipes.

I found the pilots to be quite competent and everyone is very polite.

February 15 I had to fine another man for being absent from duty without leave. The International Club sent invitations for all of us to attend a Red Army Concert at nine. It was a good show, with about fifty soldiers in uniform singing and dancing. On Sunday the sixteenth I went to the International Club once more. There was dancing until nine then a concert until ten when dancing resumed. I was back aboard at 11:50 to find my messboy, Hirstron, in irons. In a drunken frenzy he had slashed a Russian longshoreman across the forehead with a butcher knife and had chopped three of the ship's doors with an axe. Together with three other officers, I went off to obtain depositions from crew members who may have witnessed the deed. This procedure took until 3:30 in the morning. We had the depositions typed and then signed by the witnesses.

Dear Dot,

We were delayed a week in the Black Sea getting through the ice. The icebreakers are all coal-burners. The pilot told us that all the firemen on such vessels are women. . . . The stevedores work two shifts, seven days a week. There are more women longshoremen than men.

A woman is in command of a very nice-looking Russian ship nearby. The senior pilot who brought us in told us that five of the ships in this port have women as captains. Twenty chief mates and thirty third mates are also women, as are all radio operators on Russian ships. I asked where the men were. I was told that they are serving in the Army or had been killed during the war.

All of our officers except the one on watch went to the opera. There was a cloak check room where an attendant received one's coat and gave a check, but tipping was not allowed. The building was really cold. We sat in a box and could see uniformed officials seated below in red velvet-covered seats. In several of the seats the covering was partly gone, worn away or eaten by moths. Many of the buildings and the steps to them are much in need of repair.

Our guide told us that it cost a couple of rubles to sit below our box seats, and that seats higher up cost three to five rubles. She emphasized, "The price is low enough so that even poor people are not deprived of a good show as they are in the USA." As guests we were charged nothing for our seats.

On the seventeenth of February we were shifting ballast forward and taking water in the forepeak tank to tip the ship by the head so that we could see if the propeller had been damaged by ice. We were again delayed in discharging due to a shortage of railroad cars. That evening I saw Tchaikovsky's ballet *Swan Lake* with Shirley.

On the eighteenth Lieutenant Dresher, the U.S. Naval Attaché, boarded, and we reviewed Hirstron's attack on the Russian workman. We decided to offer 1,000 rubles in damages to settle the affair.

The temperatures remained low on the nineteenth and drainpipes froze up. I personally worked with the engineers to clear them. The bypass hose supplying water amidships froze and another had to be used. Later that one froze also. In the evening we went to the movies and to a dance at the club.

By Thursday the twentieth, with the temperatures moderating, the engineers got the water pipes thawed and I was able to take a bath. The dock was completely blocked with cargo so that no more could be discharged.

Miss Rodina, the agent, ordered me to move the ship to another berth under our own power, a difficult order to carry out with the ship down by the head, the propeller out of the water, and the harbor crammed full of heavy ice cakes. I couldn't move her without damaging the propeller. Nevertheless, it was most important to get the cargo out since we were on time charter[3] to the Soviet government. I asked for tugs to move the ship but none could be supplied. We remained where we were for the time being and examined the propeller by jacking over the engine to view each blade in turn as it came to the top. No significant damage was revealed.

On the twenty-first the weather warmed to thirty-five degrees, and the agent ordered me to move to number ten berth. I refused to use the propeller in the ice. The agent then directed us to move the ship ahead just 180 feet. Using mooring lines and the engines ahead on slow, we made fast to a new berth. Next evening my chief engineer and I went to see the operetta *Stony Mountain* with Shirley. It was a first night performance and we found it very entertaining. As always, we were guests of the government.

When we went ashore, we had to walk up a long hill to the town. Invariably Russian tradesmen walked abreast of us and muttered, "I will give you fifty rubles for a carton of cigarettes or a sheet." If you indicated agreement, he specified which back alley to meet you in to do the business. One night, about the stroke of twelve and curfew, a fireman from my ship arrived in a designated alley to sell smuggled goods from the ship. The Russians stripped him completely, including his socks. He ran naked over snow and ice back to the ship.

One of my men complained of having contracted VD. Through the government agent, I ordered a doctor to examine him. The doctor was a middle-aged woman with a black bag in which she had medicine and washed, secondhand bandages. She treated my man but would accept no money. Nor did the agent. Such services were free to all in Russia.

On Sunday, February 23, Red Army Day, the weather was fair and warm with the snow and ice melting rapidly. I went for a walk about the town. On the corner of every building was a loudspeaker broadcasting the news and describing how much better the government was doing in the latest Five-Year Plan. Such indoctrination went on continuously.

I walked through the bazaar. At one open lot there were various secondhand wares displayed on tables. Other odd products lay in piles on the ground. Included for sale were a few rusty, bent nails, secondhand screws, old doorknobs, and such. It was a sorry-looking flea market by American standards. I was back aboard for supper. Then at 7:30 I went to the club once more for dancing until 10:30, when an hour-long performance by the Red Army Band took place. It was a wonderful show.

I spent most of the twenty-fourth at the INFLOT office before the officer in charge of the port police, regarding the attack by my man Hirstron on the Russian longshoreman. I had restricted Hirstron to the ship ever since. The injured Russian was now out of the hospital and back at work.

Lieutenant Dresher offered the injured man the 1,000 rubles compensation we had decided upon before the trial, but the authorities found no fault on the part of my ship or her personnel, and the victim refused the money. The reason: the Russian had violated the rules by his presence in the crew's quarters. That was the end of our official concern in the case.

Arrangements had begun for us to obtain a return cargo of six thousand tons of ore, but I received a cable from the owners in New York canceling the deal. We would have to return in ballast only.

One evening Chief Engineer Flood, First Engineer Smitka, and I went to the opera for a performance of *Madam Butterfly*. The scenery and acting were great; the singing, not so hot. As usual, Shirley was my official escort; Sonja was Flood's; Vera, Smitka's.

There had been some damage done to the ship by the stevedores in getting those bulky pipes out of the hold and to the dock. I tried to get repairs made, but there were no repair men or women available. The only men working in the shipyard were German prisoners of war.

Many of the ships had ice-damaged propellers. Ours was intact since I had insisted we do no backing in the ice. Damaged propellers on the other ships could not be straightened or have blades replaced. No replacement parts, straightening gear, or workers with the required skills were available. To make the damaged propellers usable, they torched off the bent ends as much as eighteen inches, considerably reducing their effectiveness.

A carton of cigarettes from my slop chest cost my crew the equivalent of just six rubles but could bring ten times that on the black market. I was required to collect all Russian money from the crew and get a dollar back for every three rubles, as allowed by the Soviet government. My crew must have been active in the black market because they tried to return more rubles than I had issued them. I refused to accept more than I had issued in the first place. However, turning back the same amount as received provoked the Russian officials to question me extensively, wanting to know how it was reasonable for us to have stayed three weeks, had a good time, and spent no money.

On March 3 we sailed with a Russian pilot and passed out through the breakwater. I followed the track laid down by the British Routing Office at Istanbul to avoid mines from Odessa to the Bosporus. On the fifth we had fine weather in the Black Sea and slowed to make the Bosporus by daybreak. I wired for more fresh water and for a doctor to meet the ship.

Dear Dot,

March 6, 5:30 A.M., approaching the Bosporus. I've been on the bridge since midnight. Expect to take a Turkish pilot aboard in an hour. Homeward bound, no cargo, no passengers, in water ballast only, six thousand miles to go. Today I stop at Istanbul for routing, water, and the laundry we left on our way inbound. I have ordered a doctor to examine the boys. As usual, they are suffering from misconduct. Many have VD. I have one man with a broken arm, another with a broken finger.

Later: With a Turkish pilot on board, we passed through the Bosporus, the net gate, and along by the picturesque forts and buildings and steep banks. Eastbound, all had been covered with snow. Now most all is green.

We anchored off Istanbul as ordered by radio. A barge with fresh water came alongside. The doctor arrived in a launch and examined my nine ailing men, and the laundry was returned. My purser went after penicillin to treat my patients. (We had had plenty of penicillin, but it had been stolen on our second day in Odessa and likely sold on the black market.) The purser carried a pharmacist's mate license and assisted me in caring for the ailing men.

We had strong headwinds and rough seas. It was difficult to steer a good course to Doro Channel between the rocky, poorly lighted Greek islands. We passed ten miles off Cape Passero on the southeast end of Sicily near midnight. The chief cook, Sam Hills, came down with a fever, temperature 104. We isolated him in his room. I had the purser and chief steward caring for him while I pondered at which port to seek medical help.

March 10 the cook was not better and was weaker from lack of nourishment. I made plans to go into Algiers for assistance, but then he seemed better, so I decided to stop at Gibraltar for medical help. I wired the consul to have a doctor meet the ship in a launch outside the harbor.

At 4:30 the doctor arrived and diagnosed Hill with pneumonia. He had to be hospitalized. I turned the ship over to Chief Mate Wachter and told him to heave-to outside the port. I went ashore with Hills via launch, leaving him at the Colonial Hospital. There were no port charges imposed since the ship did not enter the harbor. I wrote to the owners at San Francisco and New York and sent a note off to my wife.

March 14 we were relieved and relaxed after seeing the cook safely into the hospital. We had fair weather and cleared the straits by midnight. After setting the course well out into the blue, I had a good night's rest.

On Sunday, March 30, we docked at Pier 2, Army Base, Norfolk, Next day at 11:00 A.M. I paid off the crew. The officers and engineers took their money, but the crew refused to take theirs unless I canceled all fines. They tried to force the first assistant engineer off the ship for reporting to me their absences from duty in Odessa. The crew's union officials threatened me with loss of job if I didn't cancel the fines. They told me that they would see that I never got a crew to sail with me again. I stood firm, and finally the union officials agreed that the men would take their money and that they would give me a new crew. The fines stuck. So ended my voyage to Russia. The kindness of our Soviet hostesses had added pleasure to a harsh winter trip and provided a welcome balance to union harassment.

## Notes to Chapter 20

1. Drift: the part of the rope not in use.
2. Pratique: the temporary quarantine of a vessel arriving from foreign ports. A temporary certificate of pratique is issued to the master by the local health officer if he is satisfied as to the state of health aboard and accepts the bill of health issued the ship at the last port. If the certificate is granted, the ship is unrestricted; if not, it is quarantined.
3. Time charter: a contract that included a time limit beyond which fines would be imposed, thus providing an incentive to get the job done on time.

# CHAPTER 21

# THREE TRIPS TO BELGIUM

After a brief visit with Dorothy, on April 4, 1947, I was again on board the *Mount Tamalpais* alongside the C & O Coal Pier, Norfolk. We loaded 9,600 tons of coal for Antwerp. Between April and August, I was to make three trips to Belgium.

April 5 we entered the Gulf Stream, which would help to carry us across the Atlantic. The ship was deep with a full load. The decks were awash. I opened the slop chest and issued cigarettes out of bond (meaning they were free of federal tax). To discourage black-marketeering when we reached port, I sold no more than two cartons per customer.

April 19 we entered the West Schelde River with a Dutch pilot. At the border we changed to a Belgian pilot and waited for the tide to rise. While waiting for our turn to go through the locks at the Port of Antwerp, the ship touched bottom at the turn of each tide.

To avoid problems on arrival, I collected all cigarettes over the one carton that the crew had declared to the authorities. On the twentieth, with tugs assisting, we tied up at a berth and discharged coal using two cranes on the dock side and a third crane on the offshore side discharging to a lighter. I entered the ship and had the bottom surveyed.

At noon, while I was ashore, Belgian authorities searched the ship for contraband. They found three extra cartons of cigarettes in one seaman's room and fined him 600 francs. Then they searched the stewards' storeroom with the chief steward present. When they came to the fish box, the chief steward claimed he didn't have the key. The customs inspector insisted he open the door, so the steward cut the lock. Inside they found forty-three cartons of cigarettes. The chief steward was fined 43,000 francs or $1,000. He did not have enough money coming to him to pay the fine since he had left a big allotment to his wife. I wired the owners in New York to stop paying her. I paid the fines, expecting to collect from the man later. I wrote home,

Apparently the Dutch are in a very bad way, ruined by the war. Holland was flooded with salt water and lost her overseas colonies. The Belgians fared better, except for the Ardennes where the Battle of the Bulge took place. . . .

I wrote you two long letters the other day. Then I tore them up. They were all about ships, job, travels, and lack of money, things you are not interested in. . . .

We expect to sail at five in the morning if this gale lets up. The ship is so light, she would be unmanageable in such gusty winds. All have had a good time here. The purser told me that he had the best time of his life. There is everything available in the stores, although prices are higher than in the States. All the people seem to be clean and respectable and so is the city. The buildings are spic and span. The people dress well. All appear to work hard at their jobs.

I talked with the young American ex-serviceman who drives the bus for the agent. He returned here after the war and married a Belgian girl. He says that he likes Belgium very much, especially compared with France. He claims all the Belgians are energetic and ambitious.

The agent's boy escorted me about the business places and said to me, "We always try to make it pleasant for foreigners." Then he interrupted himself, "Acht, I don't consider Americans foreigners any more, there were so many here in the Army." Ninety percent of the movies here are American. We feel well acquainted.

We sailed on April 25. After leaving the English Channel, we were battered by headwinds for three days. On the thirtieth the wind abated and we were able to increase speed. I washed clothes then searched the ship for contraband, being careful to note the search in the log book. If the customs officers later found illegal goods, I could then defend the owners. We arrived at Cape Henry, then docked at Norfolk after passing quarantine. Chester came for me. Dorothy had arrived by rail, and we stayed at Chester's for the night. Letters from my sons were waiting for me also. Dick's read,

Dear Dad,

You must be making very interesting trips. I would like to talk to you about Russia. In school our graduation project is making a study of foreign relations, trade, and world peace. Please send me more information about Russia, what you did or didn't see. I was interested when you told of the university students speaking English. I think the Russian language should be taught on a wide scale in the U.S. That language is going to play a large part in the future of all countries.

I am anxiously waiting to hear of my acceptance at Williams or Bowdoin. Several from my class have been accepted by Dartmouth, Brown, and New York University.

I have had a busy and hectic year. I am getting a thrill playing in our new band. We start marching soon. We will go to the Eastern Massachusetts Band Festival in Medford. I guess Mother told you of my grand experience at the New England Music Festival in Vermont last month. That is one of the greatest thrills of my life. I also went in a group of fifty to Washington during our April school vacation. Thank you for the financial assistance. We really had a marvelous time. I appreciated everything so much more seeing it for the second time.

I just returned from a Young People's Fellowship meeting at church. Next Sunday a Salem group is visiting us. On Saturday I am to attend an all-youth convention at St. Paul's, Boston.

Yesterday and today Allan and I were cleaning up the grounds for summer. Daffodils are in bloom and tulips are up several inches. I think I will only grow beans and tomatoes in the vegetable garden this year. I am having a good time and being busy. Life is more interesting when one is not loafing.

I am anxious to hear more about your recent trips.

Love, Dick

It was soon afterward that I learned Dick, age 17, had been accepted by Bowdoin College for the fall. Allan wrote,

Your letter about Belgium and Antwerp was very interesting, confirming what I found there myself. I hope you had a smooth trip home, "home port" that is. I doubt that we will see you until after a couple more trips.

My latest hobby is radio. . . . I want a high fidelity receiver and record player and eventually a recording unit to go with it all. My friend and I built a small amplifier. I have a microphone and I bought an old tuned frequency radio (TFR) that works out just fine for a bargain price of $4.00 I am now remodeling the cabinet to suit. . . .

I took a look at the brake linings on the car and decided they should be replaced and had that done. Had the clutch replaced also. The clutch suffered from Mother's driving (shucks) and the adjustment not having been maintained while I was away in the Army.

Some drivers aren't as fussy as I am. We can be confident that the old bus is in tiptop shape now.

I can hardly believe it. I'm on my last week now as a G.E. apprentice. I'm going to talk to the assistant superintendent tomorrow to discuss my fate. I'm still studying at Franklin Institute and expect to continue all summer and start at Lowell Institute in September. It is a tough grind.

You must be due for a vacation soon, aren't you? I get two weeks this year. I am going to take a cabin with two buddies at a camp in New Hampshire, my second week. We ought to have fun. One of the fellows had been before and says we'll be outnumbered by the fairer sex, which sounds okay to me. We three are thinking of forming a bachelors' club. All the other veteran apprentices are married or becoming so, four last week alone. I'm still enjoying myself when I get time, with two or three on the line.

Dick is very busy with school, a real student. He has lots of extra activities too. A swell guy.

I hope to see you sometime. I could use your help with my woodworking.

Very affectionately,
your son,
Allan

The *Mount Tamalpais* went on hire again, but we were delayed at anchor for a week waiting for a berth. To my great surprise, a Mrs. Barrett and her three small children arrived as passengers. Immediately I went ashore and called our New York office to protest sending this group on my deep coal ship. It was no place for them. Apparently they were sent by higher authority. I went back aboard by launch. A tug from the coal company came to shift us but found they had the wrong ship. I went back to Chester's for the night.

On May 14 the new chief steward was not on the job, a miserable situation with passengers on board. Sunday the eighteenth we were still waiting for a berth, making it a week that Mrs. Barrett and the children had been with us. It was hot and muggy and promised to be even more uncomfortable when we started loading, since we would have to close everything up to keep coal dust out of the living quarters. We finally docked and started loading on the twentieth. I wrote home,

It is hotter than Hades. The barrels of garbage on deck stink. We wash down every two hours. The chief steward has been missing for three days. The extra messman, hired on the fourteenth, came on board at 6:00 P.M. on the fifteenth, fell overboard, and didn't work the next two days. He tried to get the officers to allow him to operate the medicine chest, claiming he was a druggist. On the eighteenth he worked three hours and then asked me for something that would put him to sleep for eighteen hours. I refused and told him, "If you don't feel well, lie down and rest." He replied, "I will if you give me a hypo." I refused. So he told me that he wouldn't sail with me and left the ship. He had been hired as an extra to wait on the passengers and had been on pay for six days. He had done no more than three hours' work. Good riddance. Everything else is running smoothly.

Mrs. Barrett wondered what the company had in mind rushing her down here a week ago. I am glad that none of the children have been hurt, not yet at least.

I enjoyed our visit together. Too bad I had to be out at anchor so long. You think I stick to the ship too much. . . .

I love my family and sometimes wish I didn't have to put up with ships.

We completed loading by 4:00 P.M., took on fresh water, and went to anchor to secure the ship. I left the anchorage for shore by launch and managed to get a replacement steward. We sailed at 8:00 P.M. for Antwerp, one wiper short. Wednesday, May 21, we hit the Gulf Stream. It was hot and muggy, and the passengers were seasick. The stewards' department lived aft, so I had to give the passengers my personal attention. I spent much of my time caring for them. May 24 we had a favorable current. Mrs. Barrett felt normal for the first time. She came on the upper deck in white shorts, exposing herself to the men below. I was tempted to tell her, "Get yourself covered before these hungry men attack you."

On the twenty-fifth the wind hauled northwest as we approached the Grand Banks. The weather was grim with an icy chill. One of the children caught cold. The next day was overcast with rough seas. The passengers were seasick again.

May 27

A week at sea. I'm all rested with work caught up and clothes clean. The new officers and men have learned to do their work as wanted. The children have recovered from seasickness and have learned their way around, and so far have not been seriously hurt, so that I have had time to relax and read. Mrs. Barrett is a very charming person though seasick most of the time. I just carried her a cup of coffee. . . .

Last week, May 18, was our wedding anniversary. Or was it your birthday? Just like a man, your man, to forget. The date has worn off the inside of my ring. Believe it or not. Of course it was May, we had such fine weather and so many apple blossoms.

Helen said to me when I was in Norfolk, "Dorothy is so happy this time." It was a honeymoon all over again, I think. . . .

Today while getting ready for supper, I washed the hands and face of the five-year-old boy. The girl and he went aft to supper with me. As usual, he rode on my back. I cut up their meat like their mother does when she is at table. Freight ships are not a place where the stewards make things appealing to children, serving great big man-sized portions. I had to order half-size helpings for the children. . . . Mrs. Barrett did come to meals one day but had to rush out and leave the children with me. It seems the vibration of the engines back there bothers them. One day I had the three children there with me, and after eating, the little girl threw up all over the table. What a life!

The little boy is now in my office with me. He is sitting on the floor shooting marbles, and how well he shoots, talking to them all the while. It is fun to watch him.

As we get up into the English Channel, I hope Mrs. Barrett will be out of bed since I will be too busy to care for the children.

One morning I had to go through Mrs. Barrett's bedroom to correct something in her bathroom. Her children were in the other room. She was still in bed but feeling better. I heard her say, somewhat under her breath, "Oh, if you only knew what I would like to do to you." I acted as though I hadn't heard her.

June 1, 1947, we found that the heavy seas had damaged piping on the after deck. As the waters calmed, the passengers got out of bed and were jolly, a wholly different mood. On the third we were passing up the English Channel. After daylight the fog cleared, and the passengers saw land, to their great delight. Mrs. Barrett gave me a new book, *Anything for a Laugh*, by Bennett Cerf, illustrated and autographed by her artist husband. On the fourth we had a good clear night in the channel. We took a pilot aboard and anchored to wait for favorable flood tide.

Mrs. Barrett was on the bridge as we passed through the locks at midnight. I went into the chart room to sign for money and had word passed to the crew below that I would advance money to them as soon as we tied up at Antwerp. Mrs. Barrett asked, "Why do you do that at this time of night?" I told her, "So that the men can go ashore." She said, "My God, I'm glad my husband is not a seaman." June 5 at 1:38 A.M., we tied up at a berth. At 2:00 A.M. I went to the mess room and advanced the crew the money they had asked for. I helped Mrs. Barrett and the three children off and accompanied them to a hotel near the railroad station and said goodbye. They were very glad to be on land.

On the previous voyage to Antwerp, we had taken all the cargo out before taking on water ballast. We were delayed several hours until enough ballast was aboard. On this trip I thought we might save time by taking on ballast as the cargo went out. I discussed the possibility with Mr. Flood, the chief engineer, and he agreed to the scheme.

Having been on the bridge most of the previous two nights, I went to bed shortly after supper. Next morning I got up at the usual time and went to breakfast, where I learned that during the night the ship had been in difficulties. The second engineer and the second mate were on duty. The cargo was being discharged by an offshore crane and by two inshore cranes on tracks close to the edge of the dock. As the crane took the coal off, the ballast water was flowing on board to the bottom tanks. The ballast water flowed in faster on the dock side, causing the ship to list toward the dock, held in tension by the mooring lines. The mate and engineer on duty were playing cards and didn't notice. Mr. Flood came on board at 2:00 A.M. and discovered the ship lying against the two shore cranes. The shore workmen were frantically trying to move the cranes away so that they would not be damaged. Most of my crew had escaped to the dock, fearing the ship might capsize. Mr. Flood scrambled aboard and into the engine room where he adjusted valves to direct the incoming water to the high side only. The ship soon began to straighten, and he located the engineer on duty, who was mighty embarrassed to learn what had been going on during his watch. In a short while the ship was back on a level and discharging resumed. By the time I reached the breakfast table all was normal. It seems that I was about the only one ignorant of the problem, although I was ultimately responsible. I was very grateful to have a capable chief engineer.

The ship was charged for some minor damage to the two cranes on the dock. The Belgian workers were conscientious and highly ethical in claiming only actual damage.

June 11, we were bound for Hampton Roads, Virginia. After a good night's rest, I did paperwork. On the thirteenth I sent a radio message to Dick, who was graduating that night from high school. The whole eastern seaboard was tied up by another seamen's strike. Later we heard it was over. Ships had been tied up only three days.

On the twenty-third I was at Chester's with Dorothy for the night. Next day I paid off the crew, signed on a new group, and shifted the ship to the coal pier. Mr. Wachter was a good mate, and I was able to leave him in full charge of loading. I gave him a quart of whiskey in appreciation.

The next trip with coal to Antwerp began with Mr. Smitka, our first assistant engineer, falling off the ladder when getting aboard. He had to be hospitalized. We loaded 10,372 tons. I thought to myself that the ship must be touching bottom, but the loading had been approved by the surveyor. I said goodbye to family members and fetched Mr. Smitka from the hospital to sail with us even though he would not be able to work for a few days. The chief engineer was pleased that he had Mr. Smitka with him, working or not. Then we were off, still short part of the crew.

July 10 we arrived at Antwerp once again. We had to use four tugs because it was the custom there for tugs never to come in contact with the ship. Instead, each pulled on a towline, and therefore they had to pull against each other. It was safe but not efficient. I wrote home,

We have a better chief steward this trip, which improves life for us all. In fact we have a fine group of officers and most of the men are good fellows and are doing a decent job. I have the work lined up and can now relax and wonder what my family is doing. I have no interests here in Belgium and look for none, but my men like it very much. I asked my room steward, a Negro, why the crew liked it so well and what they did. His reply, "Because it is so clean." However, the places they visit are the barrooms and the houses of entertainment. I have heard all over Europe that the darkies are very popular with the white women. The officers say they are popular with a certain class. I guess it is because they are so jolly, free, and easy. My officers go to the nicest homes here. You see, your husband is a stick-in-the-mud. As my mate says to me, "Your tastes are different." My officers meet American Army officers in the hotels here who are on duty in occupied Germany. They come here for a few days' holiday, away from the people they know. Some come with a nurse or friend, having made extra money on the black market in Germany to spend on their holiday.

We sailed for home once more on July 13 with lots of fog. In the English Channel it was soup thick. With no radar, we had to pass close enough to the headlands to hear the fog signals and keep a fix on our position. We had to keep a careful check on the depth of the water and the revolutions of the propeller to judge the speed. It was always a complicated and anxious procedure.

On the eighteenth I played Mr. Flood three games of Chinese checkers. In my spare time I studied Atlantic coastal piloting, including the waters of Chesapeake Bay. On the twenty-seventh I joined my wife and family once more at Chester's.

The next day I reported to the ship. She was ready to load. Since there was but a single seaman on board, my boy Dick, who had come to Norfolk with his mother, helped the seaman, the mate, and me open up the steel hatches so that the ship could load. I obtained a new crew and the ship went to anchor on the twenty-ninth. I stayed on board in case she should be needed at the loading berth. Next day I was notified by the company that I would be relieved by Captain Adams. Being captain of a collier wasn't all that grand, and I looked forward to something different.

August 3 Dick, Dorothy, and I left Norfolk in our own car, arriving in New York at 5:00 P.M. We stayed at the Paramount Hotel, had a nice dinner and spent the evening at Radio City Music Hall. The next morning I reported to the American-Hawaiian office and sent Dick and Dot on their way home. There being no specific decision as to my assignment by three in the afternoon, I was ordered to go home. I took the four o'clock train and reached Swampscott at nine, just before Dot and Dick arrived by car.

## CHAPTER 22

# RISKS AND CHALLENGES

In August 1947, American-Hawaiian decided to make me a company pilot again, and I served in that capacity for the next five years. I studied piloting at every opportunity and traveled on all kinds of ships to get in the required number of observer trips to obtain further licenses. As I earned additional piloting endorsements on my license, the number of waters in which I could do piloting increased, as did my worth to the company. I also made recommendations to the company on modifications to our ships that could make loading more efficient. I continued taking correspondence courses, and to keep up with the changing technology I studied electronics and navigation.

I was often away from home for days, traveling from one port to another along the coast to do my jobs. I had to travel by boat, train, plane, bus, taxi, and shank's mare to get to the ships I was called upon to pilot. I served much of the time at night, a necessary condition of my profession. Meeting many old friends and colleagues in the course of my work was one of the pleasures of the job. I also enjoyed the challenges and always tried to serve the company by keeping costs of tugs down to a minimum. Frequently I turned the ships by backing on a spring line to the pier. On occasion I decided that a single tug was sufficient to aid a ship's maneuvers, but the tugboat captains often refused to do the job unless I engaged a second tug. Sometimes after reassessing the risk, I dismissed the first tug and did the job myself with no tugs. I piloted twenty to thirty ships a month and saved the company thousands of dollars in tug expenses alone.

Arriving at the docks in New York, I could take a long taxi ride to the railroad station. However, I usually walked across the Central Vermont

Railroad tracks, followed a path through rough weeds at the water's edge, then crossed a trestle directly to the station. In crossing the freight yard, I had to climb up and over between cars. In daylight it was easy, but after dark it could be treacherous. Since there was no lighting, I preferred crossing in daylight.

*His taxi fare would have been among expense account items paid by the company, but Dad was willing to risk his life to save a few dollars for his employer.*

Although I did not often pilot ships through the Cape Cod Canal, the Army Engineers required pilots there to have made a trip within the previous three months. This assured that we were familiar with the changes continually being made by currents and shifting sands. I made sure I got in trips as an observer so that when the opportunity arose, I would be qualified to do the job. I earned no extra money for the time and effort spent, but I wanted to make myself as useful to my employer as possible. In turn, the company was always ready to do as much as possible for me.

To make me eligible for a government retirement pension at age sixty, I maintained my status in the Naval Reserve by serving thirty-five days' active duty each year and taking correspondence courses, which I enjoyed. American-Hawaiian did not provide a pension but had a policy of giving a year's salary as severance pay.

There was both a lot of hurrying and a lot of waiting in my job. When there were delays aboard ship, I worked in the ship's carpenter shop. I made new swing seats for my playground at home, a couple of baseball bats, and a canvas hammock for the yard. I read all the current books, another pleasure.

At home, my room in the basement was my haven. The rest of the house was Dorothy's domain. I had the telephone on the long cord kept handy and a radio on a long cord for the baseball games when I was in the garden. I built a ledge for the telephone outside one living room window so that I could hear it ring should I get a call to pilot. I maintained the house and grounds and did a lot of repair work for the church, especially anything high up where no one else would venture. I also continued to maintain the swings and teeter board in my play yard for the little children in the neighborhood. It was a delight to me and I made them happy. They all called me "Skipper." When they got to quarreling or there were too many gathered at one time, I sent the older ones away.

I was able to attend church and my lodge more often than when I had been at sea for long periods, and I joined the men's club at church. Dorothy and I were avid Red Sox fans. We went to Fenway Park to see games in the flesh and took friends and relatives with us on occasion.

*Those happy times degenerated as time went on. They argued heatedly over players and the umpires' decisions.*

When Dorothy was in Norfolk or on one of her trips, and Dick away at school or on one of his summer jaunts, Allan did the cooking for the two of us, that is until he married and got his own place.

My job frequently took me to Norfolk. I stayed at Chester and Helen's, and Helen treated me royally. Dorothy loved to visit there too and was good friends with all my family in the area. I spent lots of time with them, with Clara and her family, and with Grace and hers. Chester's family made several visits to Swampscott.

During these years, Dick attended Bowdoin College. He worked in the gold mines of Alaska one summer, made a tour of Europe on bicycle with a youth hostel group the next summer, and improved his language skills at Middlebury College the following summer. He graduated cum laude and took a job teaching high school Latin and French in Augusta, Maine. During the Korean War, he joined the Army, and after learning Russian at the Army Language School in Monterey, California, he served in Germany on the edge of the Soviet occupation zone. Returning home, he went to Berkeley Divinity School at Yale to become an Episcopal priest.

Allan completed his apprenticeship at General Electric and became a shop foreman at the company's Everett plant, where they made jet engine components for aircraft. He married Janice Laumann, moved to his own home, and gave us our first grandchild, Judith Ann, on January 18, 1952.

Most of my piloting trips were routine, but occasionally there were mishaps. One June day I joined the *Carolinian* at Castle Island, South Boston. It was usual on this ship for the chief engineer to check the steering gear but, because his wife was aboard, he had delegated the chore to his first assistant. The second mate was checking things on the bridge before sailing. He had made a trip with me when I was master of the *Pennsylvanian* and we had not gotten on well. I watched him test the whistle, telegraph, and emergency gong. Then he contacted the engineer in the engine room and asked him to test the steering gear. His reply was, "I tested my end. The rest is up to you." The second mate had turned the wheel but did not check to see if the rudder went over. Then he made his entries in the log book, testifying that he had found all in working order.

I was the pilot outbound, leaving the dock without tugs. Cautiously I put the wheel over and slowly came ahead on the engines. Immediately it was obvious that the steering gear was not working. I backed the ship and tried the wheel the other way. The ship did not steer. I called Captain Hansen, who hailed his chief engineer and asked him to look at the steering gear. (The engineer was on the lower deck saying goodbye to his wife on the dock.) Then Captain Hansen asked me if I could hold the ship in the confined space even though all lines to shore had been let go. There was no wind, and I assured him that all was safe enough. After the chief engineer saw the condition of the steering gear, he called the captain to come aft to witness his findings. The steering steam engine had been disconnected from the gear. It was customary in port to do this while working on the engine. The engineers were able to get both ends of the system to work together by simply dropping a bolt in a connection. I don't know what Captain Hansen said to his second mate, but you can see why the mate and I had not gotten on well in the past. His carelessness made piloting dangerous.

One winter Sunday, the ship that I was to pilot sailed for Providence, Rhode Island. At seven in the evening I docked her. Although it was dark, I did not call for tugboat assistance. There was a strong wind blowing offshore, and there was a dredge in the way. I managed to bring her alongside the dock successfully. Captain Sungals was the master and an able pilot himself in waters for which he was licensed. It was his practice to be on the bridge while maneuvers were being performed in close quarters. He was warmly dressed and stood outside where he could see what was going on, sucking on his pipe all the while, ready to take charge if, in his judgment, the safety of his vessel demanded it. After docking was completed, he said to me, "Under the circumstances, you did a wonderful job to get the ship up against the wind. But I want to ask you one thing. Why did you drag the inshore anchor?"

I replied, "To help me hold the ship up against the wind." I had lots of practice using anchors and spring lines in lieu of tugs.

One winter as I was piloting the *Mount Greylock*, approaching Boston, there was thick snow blowing from the east. The ship had no radar. As we approached the light vessel, the wind was strong on the beam. The snow was thick, and we were running at reduced speed. She was only lightly loaded and making a lot of leeway.[1] I didn't feel that it was safe to go beyond the light vessel, since any ships which might be anchored beyond that point would be trailing broadside across our path. I said to Captain Strong, "I plan to anchor out of the channel to the west of Boston Light Vessel." After passing the light vessel, a quarter of a mile east, I started to haul west. Captain Strong asked, "What are you doing?"

"Captain," I replied, "I thought you approved of anchoring in a safe position."

He said, "I think she will make it by proceeding."

Knowing he had the final authority, I replied, "All right, sir." I steadied her on her course again toward Graves buoy, but on slow speed I could not determine the leeway and said to the captain, "You are asking me to do the unreasonable. If a ship is at anchor ahead of us, she will be headed into the wind and lying across our path. We won't be able to hear her anchor bell and are liable to cut her in half."

Strong responded, "All right, let's anchor."

Once more I gave orders for hard left rudder and got the ship swinging west to a safe position behind the light vessel. However, on slow bell, I could not get her to swing into the wind. I planned to let out just a little anchor to drag to help the turning procedure and then later let out as much chain as needed for anchorage. I gave the order to let go the anchor to drag. As she started to take up, Captain Strong commanded, "Slack away, give her more chain." The mate responded as ordered. The ship drifted faster to leeward with the chain running out at an accelerating rate. The mate attempted to brake the chain, but by then it was running out so fast that it jumped the wildcat and ran out faster and faster. The brake would not hold. Sparks flew and the brake burned up. At last the chain ran to the bitter end and carried away. "What do we do now?" asked Strong.

"Let go the other anchor," I replied. I was allowed to handle the ship on my own from that point on.

Usually my judgment prevailed. While waiting for the traffic light to turn green to proceed through the Cape Cod Canal, an Army Engineer's boat came up to the ship. Its agent notified the ship's master, Captain Greenlaw, that all the lights were out in the canal, but that if he wanted to go through under those conditions, the canal would "show the green light." Greenlaw said he would proceed. When he told me, I objected. I told him that it was unsafe to go through the canal even in the light of the full moon. Shadows from the banks would mislead us. I offered to take the ship out across Nantucket Shoal and around Cape Cod. The master bowed to my judgment.

During a maritime strike in the fall of 1949, Dorothy and I drove to Greenfield to visit my sister Bea and her husband, Bill. There I talked on the phone to Mr. Twomey, Boston operating manager for American-Hawaiian. The strike looked bad. The company had laid off the officers and crews and put all of us captains on half pay. So Bill and I went to Roger Peck's orchard to pick apples at 20 cents a box. At noon we took twenty minutes to eat the lunch that Dorothy and Bea had brought us. We stopped picking at 5:00. I picked fifty-four boxes of apples. This was the first apple-picking job I'd had since I was seven. Bill was experienced at this game and picked two more boxes than I. It was now a contest. I was determined to pick more than Bill. I was able to pick fifty-nine boxes the second day. Bill beat me again. The next two days were alternately hot and rainy. Bill and I continued picking apples. I finally beat Bill, filling seventy-eight boxes in one day.

The company called and told me to report to the strikebound *Mount Greylock* at Erie Basin, Brooklyn, where I was to relieve her master. I was at the New York office at noon next day. I brought a few apples with me and distributed one to each desk. On board the *Mount Greylock*, I tried to study piloting and get rested after a hard month's work at home and apple picking. I boiled two eggs in an electric coffee pot and ate them with plain bread for lunch. At supper I had bread, cereal, and coffee. The menu and the routines were familiar from my past experiences aboard strikebound ships. Masters and chief engineers, plus a watchman, were the only ones aboard any of the tied-up ships. During my inspections I found that a ship's clock had been stolen from the chief steward's room.

*I had always wanted a ship's clock, preferably a genuine Chelsea, and thought Dad would have liked one for his basement den, too. There must have been many opportunities to get such treasures legally. For instance, all such items must have been salvaged from the old* Pennsylvanian *before she was sunk to make a breakwater at Normandy Beach for D-day. Dad, however, never looked for such opportunities.*

The ship was at the Robbins Lines pier. The shippers had special machinery in the ship that they wanted to get to destination at any cost. It was not possible to discharge it at this open pier, so the company planned to tow the ship to Newark where pickets could not get anywhere near her.

At eight in the morning laborers were sent on board to handle the lines, but they would not pass through the row of pickets. The strikers warned them that if they moved the ship they would be met by more pickets in Newark and would not be able to get ashore there. I convinced the laborers that I would get them ashore safely, and finally all eight passed through the line. At 9:00 A.M., four tugs succeeded in moving the dead ship to Newark. We tied up at 1:00 P.M. and I got the men safely ashore as promised. We began to discharge the machinery using office personnel. Later I was assigned to various other strikebound vessels, caring for them and their cargoes. My pay was reduced further as the strike continued.

Saturday, November 27, 1949, the longshoremen on both coasts voted on whether to accept an increase of 13 cents an hour for days and 19 cents an hour for night work. All except a few locals accepted the proposal. On December 6 newspapers reported that the longshoremen's strike on the West Coast was over, but the Seamen's Union of the Pacific was holding things up.

On the seventh of December, with the strike over, my pay was raised back to that of ship's master and I was able to return to the job of piloting. I sat for my Chesapeake pilot's license and received an endorsement on my certificate in Boston. However, on the last day of the year, the longshoremen decided to take an early holiday. Making money in the shipping business was a tough job. Longshoremen acted on their own and often stopped work if the weather displeased them, even though we were willing to provide the shelter of tarps when it rained. Then when the weather became perfectly clear and they were called back, they often refused. An idle ship loses money. This bothered the shortsighted longshoremen not in the least.

Once in 1951, when I was aboard a ship about to sail from Boston, a storm came up, then calmed abruptly. I knew we were in the eye of the storm. I called Captain Murphy and urged him to get underway and sail outside the harbor, where there was more room, before the wind came in the opposite direction. He consented and we took the ship to sea. It was terribly rough. She dove and rose and dove, the engines racing as the stern came out of the water. We could make very little headway, so we hove-to as the wind roared. It raised the tide so high in Boston that all the docks flooded. My decision to move out of the harbor had been correct.

Once when I was the pilot of a ship out of New York, the master interfered with my orders. He was the only captain I ever had serious problems with, and I was to have more later on. He was a sick man. I seldom wrote in my diary anything that might cause unpleasantness for anybody else, so I will try to tell the story from memory.

We were going up the Delaware in fog. As we approached the Newcastle Range, the vessel ran out of the channel and grounded. At high water we hove her back into the channel. She had no damage, and we proceeded to Philadelphia. On the way the weather cleared, and I sat down on my stool. As I did so, the captain said to me, "When on duty, *I always* stand up."

I replied, "Well, in good weather, I have learned to take it easy and be ready to get back on my feet when extra caution is required." His remark had seemed a bit queer, but I learned that the officers on this ship were fully aware of the hounding he gave pilots.

On leaving Philadelphia, after we were clear of the dock, the master went aft to take supper for himself. This was contrary to the usual custom of captains seeing to it that the officers ate first. Leaving the chief officer in charge, I got something to eat for myself and returned to the bridge where I looked for the pilot's stool. It had disappeared, and I could get no officer to tell me what had happened to it. I said to the chief officer, "When the captain comes back, watch me get the stool." Shortly thereafter the captain stepped into the wheelhouse, and I asked, "Captain, what happened to the pilot's stool?"

"I have no idea," he lied. I insisted on having the stool, but the captain continued to make out that he knew nothing about it. I was determined, insisting that I have the stool. Finally the captain said to the chief mate, "Get the pilot's stool." While I had been getting something to eat, he had directed the officers to take the stool out of the wheelhouse and to stow it inside a large box. This had required removing two heavy falls from the top of the box. Now the three of them reversed the procedure and at last got the stool back in the wheelhouse. The captain did not abandon his harassment, however. He later told me that he would have the carpenter make me a nice mahogany chair, sarcastically implying that I felt I needed a throne to sit on. As though his insult had gone over my head, I replied, "I don't want a chair, just a stool so I can rest my legs on the long trips."

Later, after this ship had made a round trip to the West Coast, I once more came aboard as pilot. Reporting to the bridge, I found my stool missing again. When I asked the mate for it, he pointed it out to me. It had been mounted on top of a cargo king post and painted with company colors like the smoke stack, buff with a blue band. I tried to go along with the joke. They got it down for me, and I made the trip with the same captain and officers. I had the stool and all went smoothly.

On sailing from Philadelphia, however, the captain remained in his room. The officers went there to consult with him on procedure. When it became essential for him to be on the bridge and sign the tug captain's chit, he remained in his room until we docked seventeen miles farther down river to load lubricating oil. Then the captain made an appearance as we approached the dock. He was in shirt sleeves and showed himself just long enough to order his chief officer, "Get me a five-gallon can of that lube oil for my car"—odd behavior indeed.

We loaded one thousand tons of oil in bulk and sailed. The captain appeared for a few moments as the lines were let go. He sang out to the linesmen something entirely out of place, turned, and went below. It was obvious to each of us on the bridge that there was something very wrong with him. As the ship left the inland waters of the river where it was usual for the master to relieve the pilot, there was no sign of him or his instructions. His officer on duty called him several times. He acknowledged with a "Yes," but stayed in his room and gave no directions. I stayed on the bridge, conning[2] the vessel toward New York. By then I was very tired. Finally, in desperation, I turned the ship over to the officer on watch and went below. On the way to my room I woke the chief mate, told him the situation, and advised him to go on the bridge and take over for the captain.

I went to bed but couldn't sleep. For hours I debated whether or not to report the captain to the company. I finally came to the conclusion that I would be doing wrong if I failed to report the situation to the owners. Next morning I took the ship into Newark. The captain appeared not at all, not even when docking. I signed the tug captain's chit myself.

I called the marine superintendent at eight sharp to catch him when he first came into the office. I said, "Captain Bain, something is wrong on this ship that you had better investigate."

He said, "What's wrong, the captain?"

I said, "Yes, sir." He instructed me to get off the ship immediately so as not to become involved. I found out later that the assistant port captain found the master intoxicated in his room, not from liquor, but from Phenobarbital. The drug had long been used to treat epilepsy and at the time was a popular tranquilizer. Apparently the captain recovered because later he worked for other companies successfully.

In addition to my piloting jobs, I was occasionally given some special assignments. I represented the company at a conference about the proposal for a sea-level canal in Panama. I listened to the pros and cons. On my return I recommended against the proposal, and although Captain Schermerhorn was in favor, I stuck to my decision and made my report in writing.

Once I was asked to give a short talk on celestial navigation and piloting to the Institute of Navigation in Washington, D.C. I took quite some time preparing it and getting it down to size. I was happy to hear from the president of American-Hawaiian, Mr. Farley, that he was pleased with my performance.

In Boston, Philadelphia, and New Haven, I spent several days surveying docks as directed by the company. While surveying Commonwealth Pier 5, Boston, on the east side of which a Dollar Line vessel was loading, I was accused by the Dollar Line superintendent of spying on the cargo. We exchanged some words, and neither one of us was complimentary. A few days later the incident was reported to the American-Hawaiian district manager in Boston. He was shocked by what I had told the Dollar Line man and admonished me.

In October 1951 I received a special assignment to make a survey of iron ore shipping from Canada as the company was considering entering the business. I flew to Sydney in Nova Scotia and, armed with a letter of introduction, called on the assistant to the superintendent of shipping of the Dominion Iron and Steel Company, Ltd. Then I phoned Dorothy to come up to be with me, since I was to be there several days. The port warden lent me the St. Lawrence pilot book, from which I made copies of the data. The following day I visited the piers and noted loading procedures. I studied the wooden cribbing used to retain ore being shipped from a mine in Newfoundland. Dorothy and I took a bus to Glace Bay, where coal was mined, and we toured the mines. We went down the shaft and met the men at work. Dorothy had claustrophobia and was happy to get back on the surface. We were given a piece of coal as a souvenir. On its surface was the perfect image of an ancient fern.

On October 28 I saw Dorothy onto the plane for home, then took a bus to the S.S. *Easton* with Captain Fawlow in command. He had received word about me, and I was welcomed. The ship finished loading steel rails and sailed for the port of Sept Iles, Quebec. The *Easton* was a little laker or stem winder, with her bridge on the bow and engine room aft. The bridge had been raised one deck on top of the old wheelhouse, where I slept. Below the old wheelhouse were the captain's quarters. The windows around the front of my room were covered over with solid shutters on the outside to keep the seas from breaking through.

Crossing the mouth of the St. Lawrence River, we encountered a gale from the southeast. It was too rough for me to go to or from the wheelhouse, so I wedged myself in my bunk against the bulkhead where I felt reasonably secure, although sea water was leaking in around the protected windows. Seas began breaking over the stem, one after another. Then a big one came over, dismantling my room. The shutters and windows were shattered. I yelled to the bridge above but got no response. Apparently the windows in the upper wheelhouse were also broken because seawater began pouring through the overhead into my room, ending up in the captain's quarters below. I got hold of a floating board and knocked on the overhead to notify those above that we were taking on much water. Finally a sailor came down and told me that they had plenty of troubles above and had no time to fix anything else. I peeled off my wet pajamas and pulled on my wet clothes.

All the following day the *Easton* remained hove-to in a gale. By radio telephone we learned that many other ships in the vicinity were also in trouble. Several made it into the shelter of nearby harbors, but we were too far out. Our radio telephone broke down. I spent the night in the captain's room below, bailing with a bucket. The wind, still gale force, veered to northwest.

On the thirty-first, as the wind changed direction, we were able to resume our course, and by three in the afternoon we anchored in the sheltered harbor of Sept Iles. We could make no contact with the shore. Our little ship was out of fresh water and desperately in need of it for the boiler. At least no more seas came through the broken windows. I got the captain's room bailed out pretty well, made a bed for myself on a couch, and studied my Navy course.

November 1 we still had no contact with the shore, but at three in the afternoon we hailed an iron ore boat. It took me to shore, where I registered at the Sept Iles Hotel, a new wooden structure. I took a taxi to the iron ore company, where I met the chief engineer of railroad construction and the superintendent of the terminal construction operation. The ore venture, called the Canadian Iron Ore Company, was financed by Hanna and Cleveland Iron and Steel, with interests by other American steel companies.

There were no highways, telephone, or telegraph connections. The sole means of transport was by ship and communication by radio only. The mines were well to the north in virgin wilderness. All mining equipment had to be flown in from Sept Iles. The building of roads, railroads, living quarters, bridges, and tunnels was then in progress.

The ore had to be mined in subzero weather. One big problem at this terminal was getting the ore out of the freight cars. It had frozen to the cars, making the ore and car one solid piece. Even when they turned the car upside down, the ore would not come out. They succeeded only after heating the cars.

A short while before my visit, the area had been inhabited by Indians, who were moved out for the operation to proceed. The Canadian government built a community of homes for the Indians a few miles in from the harbor. These were, by Canadian standards, very decent homes, with flush toilets and all that we would consider necessities. The Indians stuck to their traditional ways and would not use the flush toilets.

November 2 I met the captain of the *Navaport*, a 328-foot-long vessel with a new 125-ton diesel railroad locomotive on deck riding thwartships,[3] waiting to be discharged. The *Navaport* was well above the pier. The locomotive was sitting on a section of railroad track that extended from gunwale to gunwale, the locomotive's length about the same as the breadth of the vessel. There was no big crane in the port, so the stevedores were building a railroad track at right angles to the ship from the shore abreast the locomotive. The foundation for the track was made of crisscrossed ties. The rise up to the deck at the gunwale was about eight feet. They built the track up in a gradual incline to meet the locomotive, then bolted it to the track section on which the locomotive rested. The connecting tracks at the gunwales were only about three feet long, with loose joints to allow for the ship's roll as the locomotive moved. When all was ready, the motorman drove that engine right off the ship onto the shore. The ship was starboard side to the solid quay. As the engine moved, the ship listed first to starboard, then to port, then to starboard again. Everyone except the motorman in the cab stood clear. I could hardly keep my eyes on the operation. A disaster seemed inevitable, but it all worked perfectly. This method of discharge was the way it was regularly done, since there was no other means of getting rolling stock from ship to shore.

While at the port I met the chief engineer who had been in charge of building the terminal. I told him that one of the reasons I was there was to see if ships could be docked and undocked safely without tugboat assistance. He assured me emphatically that there was no danger docking under any conditions because the dock was built on solid ground and faced with steel pilings. He insisted that the dock could not be damaged. I tended to agree but wondered how a ship, which is nothing but a shell, would fare when running into such an immovable object. Ships coming there to load would be flying light with their broad sides exposed to the mercy of the wind. He hadn't thought of that. I was sure tugs would be necessary.

On Saturday, November 3, there was a northeast gale blowing with deep snow on the ground. The women waiters had to walk to work. They wore high shoes and long fur coats. There were few vehicles of any kind in the area. The storm raged, delaying my departure, and I had plenty of time to observe such things. I was fairly comfortable in the hotel, though it was drafty. A lot of money was changing hands. Men from the forward mining area had arrived to stay for a few days for rest and relaxation. The scene was much like the gold rush days, with plenty of wine, women, and song.

I was trying to get to Montreal and Cleveland, but planes had been grounded and ships could not sail in the storm. The S.S. *Easton* began discharging her cargo of steel rails successfully but had to stop at three in the afternoon. The wind blew the ship so far off the dock that there was danger of losing her, as well as the crane that was working her. Next day, Sunday, with continued gale winds, the *Easton* hung on to the dock as long as it was safe, then let go, and the wind blew her out into the harbor where she anchored. Eventually the wind moderated and changed direction. The *Easton* was then able to leave anchorage and tie up to a small, broken-down dock. There were no passenger ships in port. Planes did not fly on Sunday. I walked for exercise and then worked on my Navy course.

On Monday morning the weather was fine. I went to the pier only to find that a ship on which I might have taken passage had sailed at midnight. I booked passage to Montreal on the S.S. *North Shore*, which would be sailing the following midnight. At five in the afternoon I checked out of my room and hung around in the lobby to await sailing. The ship was delayed, which left me in the lobby waiting until the next day at four in the morning, when at last I boarded. The *North Shore* was an old Navy corvette, 250 feet long with a draft of only fifteen feet. She carried a crew of forty-nine and had space for ninety-five passengers.

As soon as passengers were on board, we sailed up the St. Lawrence River. I struck up a conversation with a fine fellow who had an interesting story to tell. He was a carpenter who worked at the ore project and was on leave for a few weeks. Bright and congenial, he had been brought up speaking French and had attended a Roman Catholic school that had a high fence at the back separating it from an English-speaking school. His school forbade all students to fraternize with the English. When he left school and went to work, he could not speak English and looked upon all who did so as inferior. In Quebec he continued his education at a Catholic school where only French was spoken. There he was encouraged to look upon all who spoke English as evil. Afterwards, at his job, he worked with all nationalities, learned to speak English, and was surprised to learn that English-speaking people were ordinary folk much like himself. This turned him against the Church and the French, realizing that he had been deceived. He was a most likable fellow and being with him helped to pass the time most pleasantly.

On November 7 we arrived at the city of Quebec, which was very different from the small villages we had stopped at along the way. The ship was to be in port for fifty minutes, so I took a taxi to town and bought charts of the big river. At noon the next day, we docked at Montreal. I took a taxi in the rain to the Laurentian Hotel, where I had a busy day making contacts with officials of Alcoa, Kennecott Copper, Clarks Steamship Company, the port warden in the department of transport, and the board of trade. I booked passage on a plane for Ohio in the morning, and at eight I was on my way to Cleveland. On arrival I went to the M. J. Hanna office where I met the manager. Later I observed their lakers working ore, noting how they were maneuvered, manned, equipped, and operated. Just before the end of the day I phoned our New York office and reported that I had completed my survey. I took the morning plane for Boston ending a seventeen-day adventure. For a seasoned mariner, I had learned a lot.

For the first four months of 1953, I continued as coast pilot for American-Hawaiian. Then on April 23, hamstrung with labor problems, the company I had admired and stood up for all those years went out of the shipping business for good. It was a sad time for a proud, fine company. Those of us at sea were all let go. No pension or separation pay was offered us. The company policy had been to give captains a year's pay in lieu of a pension, but once the company sold out, we were to get nothing. This ended my thirty-seven years of continual employment with the company and I was disillusioned. I felt my company had let me down.

*After all his efforts to save the company money, sometimes even at risk to himself, it is no wonder he was disillusioned. The management in charge of closing down the business had categorized him as office help, for which no severance pay was provided.*

I wrote to Mr. Gray, operating manager for American-Hawaiian, detailing where and how I had saved them money. I protested that I was let go without severance pay or other consideration. I observed that when it had been favorable to them, they had categorized me in the sea division, and when it had been to their advantage, I had been designated part of the shore staff. I said I would settle for $3,500 for all the money I had saved the company. I continued to follow up with letters, but none of them was answered. After some weeks I called on Mr. Gray personally. I told him I was very sorry that I was leaving the company under less than amicable terms. He said, "Didn't you get your check? Mr. Farley signed it." I was pleasantly surprised. With the help of my lawyer I also received six months' pay. That plus the $3,500 came to $7,970. It was worth having put up a fight.

After American-Hawaiian went out of business, I was engaged immediately by Captain Anthony, operations manager for Waterman Steamship Company. They hired me to pilot their ships to and from Boston at favorable terms, although I was paid by the job and had to pay my own expenses. Getting work immediately with Waterman helped ease my disappointment after so many good years with what had been such a fine company.

Waterman's ships in the coastwise trade were manned by regular crew members. Many of them were married and lived in Florida ports, which the ship visited once each trip, so that they got home often. It was a pleasure to sail on these ships. It was a different story, however, with their ships in the foreign trade. They were typically manned by unmarried men who signed on for a single trip and signed off when they got back to the U.S. It was evident when I piloted those ships that the crew lacked any enthusiasm for their jobs.

In those days there were many ships, passenger and freight, running both the coastwise and foreign routes. Monday mornings they were crowded together entering the harbor and running slowly so as to make their berths at eight, the time the cargo handlers started working at straight time pay rates. Longshoremen worked directly for stevedoring companies, who in turn contracted with the ship owners to work cargo at so much a ton. Longshoremen working on ships in the foreign trade got 65 cents an hour straight time. On coastwise vessels they got a dime less.

While most other companies delayed docking until after seven or eight in the morning, when linesmen and tugs became available at regular rates, Waterman never delayed unless for better reasons. For instance, when a Waterman ship arrived in Boston, she docked and linesmen were there regardless of the hour. Mr. Kiernan, the district manager, was always present and made everything happen like clockwork. He kept me well informed by phone, and I was never at a loss to know what to do. Everyone did his part. This teamwork was a pleasure for me.

When Waterman's coastal steamship business diminished, I began to work on my own, freelancing for many companies. Later, the difficulties of engaging work myself were lessened when I joined Captain Begleman's agency, Maritime Coast Pilots, Inc. His New York office received requests for pilots and assigned the jobs. It was a big improvement for me as I didn't have to solicit work, job by job, on my own. I was lucky to have any work at all. Many younger captains were idle. I was on commission for specific duties, which often did not include docking and undocking. When I did dock or undock ships, I had to use tugs far more frequently than I had in the past because the ships were unfamiliar to me. When I had worked for American-Hawaiian, I had piloted the same vessels over and over and knew them intimately. As a freelance pilot, I found myself piloting many different ships that were often much larger and deeper when fully loaded than those with which I had become closely acquainted. Of course, I also no longer had a personal incentive to avoid the use of tugs.

As an American-Hawaiian Company pilot, I had stayed on board for lodging whenever possible. My schedule had been arranged to have me travel from port to port and ship to ship so that I would not have to use public transportation from one job to another or to pay for lodging. Now, as an independent, I traveled by public means and found it necessary to use hotels at my own expense. I also got aboard or off ships via tugboats or pilot boats, whereas in the past I had usually stayed aboard a ship until it got to port. The hazards of boarding and leaving via the ladder were considerable. I piloted over one hundred ships a year under these conditions, and I loved it.

I still loved baseball and the Boston Red Sox. Now and then I took others with me to the games at Fenway Park in Boston. Visiting relatives and neighborhood boys were my usual guests. Dorothy was a fan too and joined us occasionally, but she and I often disagreed about the plays, the players, and the umpires' decisions. After having expressed my opinions, I would clam up and let her rave on until she was satisfied that she had had the last word.

In 1954 I did a lot of work for the Ionic Club, the home of Wayfarers Masonic Lodge, for which I was an officer and on the board of directors. The clubhouse was in dire need of attention. It was a large, brick building on the waterfront overlooking Swampscott Bay. In its heyday there had been over a thousand members, but by the mid-1950s, membership had dwindled to just 356 dues-paying members, so there was no money for upkeep. The roof leaked, there were heating and plumbing problems, and a lot of general maintenance had not been attended to.

I went about fixing things in earnest. I worked in the boiler room, put glass in a door, fixed pipes, repaired a side door, surveyed the leaky roof and repaired it. I cleaned out the shop and the room that adjoined the bowling alley. I removed ashes from the boiler room. The furnace had long since been converted to oil, but nobody had ever thought to get rid of the huge accumulation of ashes from the days of the coal-fired furnace. Many days I spent carrying ashes to the shore in a bushel basket that rested on my hipbone. (I think this was the cause of my undoing.) I repaired the floor and broken windows, nailed loose clapboards, and repaired several inside doors and a dormer. I sanded and varnished and painted inside and out. I built and installed storm windows, cleaned and painted toilet rooms, and built a storeroom for the old lodge room. Meanwhile, I piloted my usual number of ships, took care of the house, and attended many meetings at the lodge.

I began to get sick to my stomach but carried on and seemed to get better. Then I got a sore on my penis. I talked to the doctor on the telephone but kept my usual routine of work, including repairing the roof at the club. I was sick again and took aspirin, but I could hardly stand up for a piloting job. Next day I was very sick and went home by train. I got into bed with a temperature of 104, and on April 23, 1954, was admitted at Hahnemann Hospital in Brighton, near Boston. My sister-in-law Margaret's medical connections brought the whole staff to my bedside. My entire groin was swollen from my infected hipbone. I was treated with penicillin and gradually improved. There were no ball games to listen to on the radio but plenty on the Army-McCarthy quarrel.

> Senator Joseph McCarthy had begun a wave of anti-communist hysteria in 1950 with his unsubstantiated claim that the State Department had been infiltrated by communists. In 1954 he and the House Un-American Activities Committee held hearings in which the military was accused of harboring communists. It was an intensely exciting time when people were glued to their black-and-white TV sets or their radios. Soon afterwards McCarthy was discredited and censured by the Senate for misconduct.

May 4 I was released and went home but developed a bad case of hives from the penicillin. On the fourteenth I worked two hours in the garden and was exhausted. Slowly I got my strength back, and after twenty-five days of being laid up, I went back to piloting. In spite of all that, I managed to pilot fifty-seven ships from January through June.

Allan and Jan had a baby boy at the end of May 1954, Charles Henry. Another Charles, his middle name came from his maternal grandfather and his paternal great-grandfather, so both families were happy. Little Judy stayed with us for a few days at that time. By the end of the year I had piloted another fifty-four ships, for a total of 111 in 1954.

I resumed work at the Ionic Club, repairing and making the building more secure from the winter cold in order to conserve fuel. My legs were giving me trouble and I had to rest frequently. I got some professionals to work on the bowling alley, repaired a dozen chair seats, painted the roof, repaired the front door pillars, and moved a lot of furniture. Dorothy complained that she was a Masonic widow.

In July 1954, Dorothy and I drove downeast to Maine and visited Captain Pettegrew, a colleague from American-Hawaiian days. He showed us around his two houses and blueberry fields near Machiasport. Then we drove on to Jonesboro where I looked for another associate, Herb Whitney, but we learned that he had died two years before. We had been shipmates on several vessels. In my sixtieth year, my old friends were starting to leave the scene.

Mrs. Foley, our neighbor, had lost her husband and needed help with her place. I repaired gutters there and contracted to paint her house for $200. It took me 182 hours. I made little more than a dollar an hour, but Mrs. Foley was very appreciative.

On April 9, 1955, Waterman Steamship Company gave up the intercoastal business as unprofitable. From then to June 30 I managed to get a few other ships to pilot on the coast. Some of these jobs I solicited directly from the owners and some from Maritime Coast Pilots, Inc. In addition to maintenance work at the club, I did considerable upkeep work at the church on the stucco exterior and the cellar steps at the rectory.

I piloted the *Marine Currier* from Norfolk to Baltimore with a load of sulfur. We tied up at Fairfield to discharge and I went to sleep, as I had been up all night. At two in the afternoon I awoke and found that all the discharging was taking place on one end of the ship only. I was concerned the ship could not be brought to the proper draft to get through the shallow C & D Canal. I went to the captain to explain the circumstances and regulations at the canal. He assured me that he would have all requirements complied with. At 7:00 P.M. we sailed for Chester, Pennsylvania. At eleven we were off the western entrance to the C & D Canal. The draft was twenty-two and a half feet forward and twenty-five feet aft. The Coast Guard boat registered a reading of over twenty-five feet, but in a heated discussion with the second mate, the guard conceded that a few inches more or less would make no difference. The twenty-five-foot figure was agreed upon and reported to the dispatcher, who allowed the vessel to proceed. The ship was, however, too deep at one end to go through the canal.

At number two buoy she squeaked on the bottom as she rounded the curve. At the Chesapeake City turn, we met a barge that swung and hit us a glancing blow. At one the next morning, the vessel failed to make the turn at number eighteen light, and the bow grounded on the south bank in mud. The tide was falling. The Guard boat came to assist but could do little to help. I had her take the port anchor and lead it out toward the port quarter. I then ordered the mate to heave on the anchor with the winch. At the same time the Guard boat pushed on the stern to keep it in the deep water of the canal. Sparks shot into the air from her stack. I wondered if her engine would quit. Her captain dared not stop the engine for fear it would seize. At 7:00 A.M. as the tide rose, the mate heaved the bow off the bank with the anchor, and we proceeded to the Tidewater terminal and discharged sulfur. I had to go to Philadelphia to report the grounding to the Coast Guard. The moral: Always follow regulations.

August 23, 1955, Dorothy helped Dick move to New Haven. He had completed his three years in the Army and was about to begin divinity school.

By 1956 I was in business entirely for myself. Most of the jobs I arranged were for Luckenback, Isthmian, Rhode Island Pilots, Federal Pilots, and Maritime Pilots Associations. I piloted over one hundred ships that year. Most of them were American flag vessels under enrollment where I piloted dock to dock. All those with foreign cargo on board were under register, and state law required that a state pilot also be aboard.

One mid-December I piloted an oil tanker with a deep draft from Breton Reef to Boston. I had to anchor at the west end of the Cape Cod Canal. When getting under way on slow bell, though the charts showed plenty of water, she dragged to a stop on soft mud where the area had shoaled. I said to the captain, "She is not moving on a slow bell."

"Oh, hell, hook her up." he said.[4] I put her on full ahead, and we went along just fine. On the way I said to the captain, "I suppose now we have to report this."

"No," he said, "if I reported every time I touched bottom, I'd be doing nothing else." However, with my training and background I felt differently. When I got to Boston, I saw the port engineer and reported it to him. Later on, Captain Church, from whom I had gotten the job, heard of the grounding and was put out with me for not reporting it to him. Moral: Do it right or don't do it at all.

On February 4, 1957, I piloted the *Waltham Victory*. At 1:00 A.M., while docking in Philadelphia, she collided with an unlighted derelict barge. When the lookout spotted the barge, reported its presence to the bridge, and the order was given to steer clear, the bow did not fall away, because the captain had failed to make sure the ship was properly trimmed. Her bow was lower than the stern, making her pivot near the bow instead of amidships. As a result several railroad cars on the barge were knocked into the drink. For this I was tried by the United States Coast Guard. Later in court the owners won the case against Reading Railroad because it had failed to have a light burning on the derelict barge.

I piloted 99 ships in 1957 and 103 in 1958. Several of my jobs were canceled due to strikes after I had incurred the expenses of travel.

Dick graduated from seminary in June 1958 and was ordained at St. Paul's Cathedral in Boston. We had a reception for him at the house after the service. I upset him by inviting the wrong girlfriend to our party. Allan saved the day by escorting her away. A week later Dick left to begin his ministry in Missouri. In 1959 he married Patricia Pennington of Kirkwood, Missouri. That year I piloted one hundred ships. I was never paid for one, the *Wang Pioneer*, from New York to Baltimore. This rarely happened, but it was another of the disadvantages of being on my own.

During 1960 I made 104 trips as pilot. I was sixty-five years old but had no thoughts of quitting. From September 26 through 29 I was in Admiralty Court in Philadelphia for the case of the *Waltham Victory* versus the Reading Railroad. I was cleared of all responsibility. My attorney, Wilbur E. Dow, represented me at these proceedings. A fully licensed master mariner as well as a lawyer, he was retained by Maritime Pilots Association on a regular basis. Mr. Dow liked his whiskey. At his hotel in the evening, he would order a fifth from room service and consume the whole of it while planning for court next morning. This seemed not to diminish his performance.

On November 4, 1960, Dick and Pat produced our third grandchild, Margaret Anne, in Poplar Bluff, Missouri, where Dick was rector of the Episcopal church.

During 1961, I piloted eighty ships. That year I had my prostate removed and spent fifteen days in Lynn hospital after the operation.

> *My father continued to be, to me, an authority figure and "the captain." However, I had never realized the depth of my bond to him until I visited him in the hospital following the operation. He lay in bed, pale and vulnerable. I had always taken pride in never letting myself be seasick on watercraft or wince at gruesome spectacles. This time, however, I nearly fainted dead away when I saw my ailing father. It was then I knew how much I loved him.*

I had scheduled the operation for winter when the rivers would be frozen and work opportunities few, but I had arranged to take a course in radar in New York during my second week of recovery. In the hotel I studied with an ice bag in my lap to relieve the pain of a swollen testicle. I was in agony. On my return home, my surgeon removed the offending gland.

I made ninety-five trips as pilot in 1963. On May 10 Dick and Pat gave us our fourth grandchild, Jeanne Louise. On November 22, the day Kennedy was shot, I was piloting, ironically, the *American Leader*. It was a routine piloting job for me but a sad day for the nation. Dorothy was visiting Dick's family in Missouri. Although no fan of John Kennedy, she wept bitterly for his mother. On November 30 I attended the annual meeting of Massachusetts Nautical Schoolship Alumni at the Boston Yacht Club. There were eighty members present.

I was pilot eighty-four times during 1964. There was a towboat strike in New York, which held things up for a time. I received yet another pilot's endorsement, this time for the port of New Haven, Connecticut.

In 1965 I made 140 trips as pilot. During a longshoremen's strike that tied up all ships except tankers for thirty-three days, I did harbor work in the port of New York. I piloted fifty-one trips during that period alone, docking and undocking without using tugs. February 22 I piloted the *Good Hope* from New York to Port Jefferson, Long Island, where we collided with American Oil Company pipes. I was sued for $100,000. The captain claimed he did not know that there would be no tugs. Later it was proved that he did know, and I was exonerated of any responsibility for the accident.

There were more strikes in 1966. In spite of them I piloted 102 ships. On January 5 I piloted the *Alcoa Voyager* from Baltimore to sea. The pilot boat was to meet the ship inside Cape Henry at 4:30 P.M., but the boat did not arrive. The master of the boat had not been able to get out of the creek because of an extra-low tide. My concern was that the ship lose no time, so I was carried on to Savannah, Georgia, where I had the pleasure of meeting past shipmates but had the extra expense of having to travel back north.

In September Dick and his family moved from Missouri to Rockport, Massachusetts, where he became rector of St. Mary's Episcopal Church. It was good to have them back within easy visiting distance from Swampscott.

# Notes to Chapter 22

1. Leeway: the amount a vessel is carried to leeward by force of the wind.
2. Conn: to direct the steering or course of a vessel.
3. Thwartships: crosswise of the decks; from side to side.
4. Hook her up: put the ship on full power.

# CHAPTER 23

# NAUTICAL NIGHTMARE

When I was seventy-two, I was given one more opportunity to command a vessel. On Friday, September 8, 1967, I received a special assignment to serve as pilot on an excursion vessel taking passengers to view the America's Cup races off Newport, Rhode Island. The job was to last about ten days. I was to pilot the *Potomac* from Baltimore to Newport, and from there I was to pilot the ship with passengers to the races each day.

The *Potomac* was designed to take passengers on day or evening runs only. She was 618 gross tons, 420 net tons, and just 200 feet long, with an overall beam of forty-four feet. The draft was a meager twelve feet. Like a big balloon on the water, she looked something like a double-ended ferry boat except that she had only one pilot house forward and one propeller aft. The main covered deck was lined with glass windows on either side. Each of these windows had a sheet of unpainted plywood nailed over it, apparently a temporary means to protect her from the seas when she went up the coast. She was fifty-eight years old, rather ancient for a steel vessel. It was generally understood that her speed was between ten and fourteen knots, although she was advertised to have a sprightly nineteen knots of go.

I found the *Potomac* at the recreation pier at the foot of Broadway in Baltimore. A big party was underway with the band playing and people dancing. Mr. Brown, the operating manager's assistant, met me at the gangway. He told me the party would end at 1:00 A.M. and that she was to sail an hour later. He introduced me to a Captain Bryant, who, it was implied, had been in command on a previous trip. I asked to see the current master, and Mr. Brown told me that he would be on board later. Then I asked for a place to lie down and rest so that I could be ready for night duty. Brown showed me the captain's room with its brass bed, a small wall desk, and little else.

I lay down on the bed for an hour or so, and when I woke I lifted the top of the desk. There was nothing inside. I saw only rumpled-up papers as one might expect to find in a wastebasket. I was beginning to have serious doubts about this operation. I rolled up again in the blankets for a little more shut-eye, convinced that this job was to be no cinch. However, the money was good, and it was a job. I had committed myself and I would go through with it. At seventy-two years of age, I still enjoyed a good challenge.

At 2:00 A.M. I was called to duty and met Mr. Casey, the operating company's manager, who noted that the master was still not yet on board. An hour later Casey told me that the captain had been contacted by phone, and that he had resigned! Mr. Casey urged me to take the job of master as well as pilot for the trip to Newport. I was not pleased. I had been hired by the day with just piloting duties. This was something else again, but I could see I was needed and agreed to accept the summons.

"All right," I said, "so long as the law will be complied with to the letter."

"Of course," Mr. Casey said. I asked to see the ship's papers. Mr. Brown and I searched the ship and eventually, under the scraps of paper in the captain's desk, we found an envelope which contained the enrollment.[1] On a bulletin board under broken glass was a certificate of inspection issued in Washington three years earlier on May 7, 1964, allowing her to carry 1,700 passengers in the Baltimore area. An amended certificate in the envelope limited the number of passengers to 800, reflecting her recharter to carry passengers from Newport to the races each day. I was very happy to find this document, but the amended certificate read, "daylight sailing in other than inland waters." This complicated matters. I was told the *Potomac* had made this trip up the coast several times before, even as far as Boston. However, I had found darned little of an official nature to reassure me.

Also on the bulletin board was Mr. Bryant's license. I installed my license alongside his as required by law. Mr. Bryant was the only deck officer on board. I had been told by Mr. Brown that although Mr. Bryant had captained this ship on previous occasions, his pilot license did not extend his authority beyond the Chesapeake Bay. Later I found out that Mr. Bryant had never served as captain of this ship, but only as pilot. His regular job was skipper of tugboats in Baltimore harbor, in which capacity he piloted larger ships within the harbor. He had previously served as mate of the *Potomac.* I glanced at his license but did not read it in detail, relying on what I had been told. Bryant seemed a valuable man to this venture. He knew the vessel, was enthusiastic, and seemed to be a hard worker. I was happy to have him aboard, at least until I found his license was limited, whereupon I was forced to sign him on for a lesser rating.

The ship had no regular crew. The only ones I knew of were Mr. Bryant, who was to be mate; the purser; and Mr. Reeves, the chief engineer. I made every effort to get a crew signed on as men became available.

It was three in the morning. The ship had been scheduled to sail an hour earlier. I had to see that she was seaworthy—stored, equipped, and manned for the intended voyage. When I had been a commander of a Seabee battalion during the war, our motto was "can do." I took that approach now, practicing it with determination.

I set up a card table near the gangway and directed the purser to sign on crew members as they boarded. I could find no printed articles. On a piece of brown wrapping paper, I printed the items required: name, address, nationality, rate of pay, certificate, starting date. I could not fill in rates of pay since Mr. Casey was making a separate deal with each man as he boarded to be interviewed.

I pondered over the wording in the amended certificate: "daylight sailing outside," bearing in mind that nothing stood the test unless it was reasonable. I concluded that the main reason for the restriction must be the limited crew and people to stand watch. I made it my main objective to sign on the required complement of willing crewmen. Since it was a Saturday, I asked Mr. Casey to make arrangements with the customs house and the Shipping Commission to have a man on duty with whom we could communicate. Casey implied that he would take care of that "when the time came." I warned him that this was serious business and that noncompliance could delay the vessel's departure. Meanwhile, I studied the ship's papers, the enrollment, the charts, navigational equipment, fire equipment, the lifesaving equipment, and boats. I tried to make myself as familiar with the vessel as possible.

The crew was then complete, but there were still some irregularities. Mr. Casey supplied extra men to work with the crew as workaways. I signed them on as such since they had no certificates. For this the Coast Guard later gave me some difficulty, but I pointed out that the wording of the charter included the term "others in the crew." Mr. Aiken, who was hired to share piloting duties with me, did not have his license with him. One seaman did not have his certificate with him; however, from his discharges as an AB on larger vessels, he had letters to cover him in lieu of a certificate. Finally, the eighteen-year-old Negro cook who had been assigned care of women passengers as well as mess duties, claimed to have passed the Coast Guard requirements but had failed to pick up her Z card. Mr. Casey told me that he had been to the Coast Guard office with her and verified that she was legal. These items were not on the articles or the crew lists that I submitted to the authorities. The discrepancies could give the authorities grounds for charging me with negligence should they ever uncover them.

At 1:00 P.M., Saturday the ninth, we finally got a full crew signed. the ship had been stored, and I was ready to clear her at the customs house and get my name on the enrollment. Mr. Casey's father, who conveniently showed upon the scene, drove me uptown to the customs house, where I found the doors locked. I tried calling by telephone. No answer. I spied a customs house officer coming out of a nearby appraisers' building, ran to his side, and pleaded with him. He ordered me out of his way, got in a car, and drove off. I tried to enter the appraisers' building. It was locked. Next I tried a nearby dock where a Coast Guard cutter was usually tied up. There was none there. Having run out of options, I returned to the *Potomac* at 3:00 P.M., planning to fulfill customs formalities at the next port of call. I mailed the crew list to the Coast Guard before sailing.

On board again, I checked each department to see that all was ready. The ship had been fueled to capacity, 6,100 gallons. I checked distances on the various legs of our intended journey. There were no records, so we had to estimate the speed and rate of expected consumption. Later she proved able to make eleven knots on 140 gallons an hour and to have enough fuel capacity to steam for a run of twenty-four hours, at least in good weather. We were bound for Newport, Rhode Island, via Bayonne, New Jersey, where we would refuel.

There was no telephone to the engine room, so I walked down to check with the chief in person, then returned to the pilothouse to get her underway. As I was walking up the deck, the vessel began to move. I hurried to the pilothouse and found Mr. Bryant operating the vessel without my authority, moving the ship from the dock. He was trying to maneuver her clear of the many small craft crowded about her, and he was having trouble. He had failed to consider the wind blowing against the high-sided vessel. She was crosswise between a dredge and the surrounding craft. I took charge. We did make contact here and there with other craft before we got clear of the mess, but there was no damage, thanks in part to the rubbing beam or bumper that surrounded her. I made it very clear to Mr. Bryant that, as master, I was responsible and from then on would handle the vessel personally in close quarters and to and from all landings.

The weather promised to be favorable, and we sailed down the Patapsco River and up the upper Chesapeake Bay through the Chesapeake and Delaware Canal. We then steamed fifty-six miles down the Delaware to Cape May where inland waters ended. On the way I held emergency drills and tested lifeboats and fire hoses. The ship was cleaned and made ready for passengers.

We arrived at the mouth of the Delaware at 3:00 A.M., two hours before daylight, on Sunday the tenth. The weather was good. It would be dangerous to kill time by stopping to wait for daylight since we had barely enough fuel to take us to our destination. There was no place to refuel on the way. Before going into outside waters before daylight, I was assured by the crew and officers that they were willing to proceed. The visibility was good, and I judged that our inland lights could be seen by other vessels.

After considering the situation, I decided it was safe to proceed and dangerous to delay in spite of our being in violation of the requirement to proceed in daylight only.

We had some anxious moments. About to enter the channel to New York, we were delayed by a dredge pulling a cable across the entrance. At the same time, Mr. Reeves, the chief engineer, reported to me that we were short of fuel. The dredge people told us that the entrance would be closed for forty-five minutes. With our low fuel, we could not afford to idle at all, so we cut in around the dredge, far out of the channel. We managed not to run aground and proceeded on our way, aiming to get fuel at Berth 17, Bayonne, it we could make it.

We steamed into New York Harbor and through the Kill Van Kull to a point off Berth 16. Using our primitive megaphone, I called to men onshore, "Which way to Berth 17?"

Two men bellowed in unison, "There ain't no number seventeen!"

"Where can we get fuel oil?" I shouted. We maneuvered a little closer to where the men were standing.

"Number seven," they shouted and gave us directions. That required retracing our path, a half-hour run to Berth 7. If the chief engineer's report of low fuel were correct, by now we should have been out of fuel altogether. With this in mind, I decided that if we ran out, I would simply ask a passing vessel to shove us close to a wharf. Desperate, perhaps, but it seemed my best alternative.

At 2:30 we tied up at Pier 7 and took on oil to capacity. We were also in dire need of fresh water for the boilers. As it was Sunday and not a normal port of call, I did not try to contact authorities at a customs house. There was no fresh water available at Pier 7, and we were forbidden to tie up at an adjacent pier. I was advised to get water at Pier 6, Staten Island, a distance of three miles. So at five in the afternoon we sailed from Bayonne to Staten Island in search of water. There was a fresh northeaster blowing. We backed clear of the pier at Constable Hook, steamed out of the Kill Van Kull waterway, and started into the long slip between the vacant piers at Pier 6. The water connection was at the bulkhead at the inside end of the slip. The wide-bodied *Potomac* with her shallow draft was like a balloon before the wind. It was impossible to keep her from settling down on Pier 6 to leeward when we slowed down.

Pier 6 was an old dilapidated relic that had originally had an apron and landing built on wooden piles, but the piles and apron had been worn away. It was posted with a big sign reading "UNSAFE." The *Potomac* came to rest against the pier halfway in the slip. I stopped her there. There was danger of getting her stuck under the pier itself. The wooden guard around the ship rested against the wooden piles, the tops of which were fastened to nothing and waved to and fro in the breeze. The wind kept the vessel hard against this wreckage. This was the worst mess I could remember ever having been in. Cautiously I maneuvered her out of the slip and back out into New York Bay. Still in need of shelter and water, I finally worked her over to the Brooklyn shore. After talking it over with the officers, we tied up at the foot of Columbia Street near a fire hydrant. There were no bits or cleats to tie onto—apparently this pier was never intended to be used as a ship's berth—so we passed lines around the pilings.

We tried to take on water, but our hose connection would not fit the hydrant. I watched from the bridge as several of our men were vainly attempting to make the connection. I walked out on the pier and said, "Why not call the fire department? After all, this is an emergency."

The chief advised, "Take it easy, Captain. We have no authority to touch this hydrant." I supposed that the engineers were more familiar with the city ordinances than I, so I did not press the point. They assured me that they would have water soon, and they did. I contemplated sailing as soon as the water was on board, but the strong wind would be right ahead of us, so we took water to capacity and lay at our unofficial pier in the lee until five the next morning, Monday the eleventh, when the wind moderated some, and we sailed.

Hugging the shore of Long Island Sound, we were able to keep in the lee enough to have smooth water and to make good progress. Then the radio telephone broke down. There was no radar or gyro, so we steered by the magnetic compass, which was in good shape though of small diameter and difficult to read.

I figured that if we needed more fuel or water we could get it by going into New Haven or New London on the way. When we were off New Haven, Mr. Reeves reported that the fuel was getting low again. I hoped that he was playing it overly safe. Based on our recent experience, I was quite sure we could make it as far as New London. We continued, passing New Haven and New London, chugging along nicely. Our destination was Pier 4 in Newport Harbor on the east side of Goat Island. Big ships on which I had sailed before couldn't get in such narrow, shallow waters, so I was not familiar with this miniature harbor normally used only by small pleasure craft. However, I knew Goat Island had been joined recently to the mainland by a causeway at the northern end of Pier 4. We were to tie up at an abandoned Navy torpedo boat dock.

By evening we were in Newport Harbor approaching our destination at slow speed among many small boats anchored on each side of the narrow channel. The chief engineer once again warned me that we were dangerously short of fuel.

When we reached the end of the pier, adjacent to the causeway, we could see Mr. Casey waiting anxiously on the dock for us. The wind carried his voice to us so we could hear him shout, "Where have you been?" I did not attempt to answer against the wind. I just muttered, "It's a long story." When we were within talking distance, Mr. Casey said, "We don't want you here. Go back around Goat Island and dock at the north side of the causeway where an oil truck is waiting to supply you with fuel."

I turned the vessel around and steamed back down the harbor and out into Narragansett Bay to the north end of Goat Island. It was getting dark and I was in doubt about the harbor. My chart didn't show the causeway, nor did it specify the depth of water. I approached with great anxiety, but when we spotted the lights of the oil truck, I was reassured we were heading in the right direction. Now, however, the wind was blowing this big balloon of a ship onto the causeway. The only oil filling line was on our port side, aft. I had to turn the vessel in order to land port side to. This meant backing in the slip where the depth of water was in doubt. It was also more dangerous to back in, as this put the rudder and propeller in danger of getting in the mud and fouling the intake. In spite of these difficulties, we tied up safely. Then the truck driver refused to deliver the oil until he was assured of payment. I passed the word back to the purser, who convinced the driver that he would indeed get his money. We took fuel to capacity.

Again we rounded Goat Island to our berth just to the south side of the causeway and tied up for the night. The pier turned out to be long, narrow, wooden affair with a deck only four feet wide, with no railing. I backed her in, port side to the dock, to be ready to sail with passengers in the morning. Mr. Casey had cars ready to take the officers and crew to town for a meal and sleeping quarters. The next morning the same cars drove us all downtown to a restaurant for breakfast and then to the ship. The entire crew was on board at eight. The same procedure for food and housing took place each night.

The boilers had been shut down so we had no lights until the engineers got steam up at about 8:30. The passengers had begun arriving twenty minutes earlier. We held them back as best we could, and then they crowded on board. The band had set up and was playing on the navigating bridge just back of the pilothouse. The music helped to create a jolly spirit amongst the passengers. The noisy din was in competition with other nearby excursion boats, which had their own bands playing.

I tried to get to the customs house to put my name on the enrollment, but instead, to my surprise, Coast Guard officers came aboard and were setting up to make stability tests, demanding all my time and attention. In the rush and confusion of this first day of sailing, without an organized crew, it didn't help matters to have the Coast Guard officers interfering.

At 10:30 there were 797 party-mood passengers on board, and we set sail for the races, five miles away at sea. The race was to start at eleven and the day was bright and sunny. There was a stiff breeze blowing, promising a lively race. The contest was between the defender, *Intrepid*, for the New York Yacht Club, and the challenger, *Dame Pattie*, from Australia.

As commanding officer, I handled the *Potomac* to and from her berth and through the traffic in the harbor. When clear of Newport Harbor, I turned the control of the vessel over to the pilot, Mr. Aiken. We had to be very cautious because there were many other excursion boats and small craft also on the move. There were literally thousands of floating craft of all descriptions at these races. It amazed me that there were not many accidents. The *Potomac* was surrounded by a crowd of small boats only a few feet away, riding a rough and boisterous sea. On the viewing line running parallel to the racing sloops, the smaller boats were nearest to the racers. Then just outboard of them were the excursion boats, and farthest away were the larger vessels, such as revenue cutters and men-of-war.

Our wide ship rolled in the rough sea. We stretched lifelines for safety. Many of the passengers were seasick, which occupied them completely. Others were making an effort to take pictures of the contestants. Some young men scrambled for the highest vantage point, even to the top of the small pilothouse, which was not fitted with a railing. This was unsafe and we had to forbid it, but they continually defied my orders. I wore my uniform hat and tried to be courteous in my attempts to persuade them. This had no effect, so I took off the uniform cap and put on my old straw hat. With a loud and determined voice I ordered, "ALL MEN OFF THE PILOT-HOUSE ROOF, NOW!" I was ready to fight to see the order was carried out. Still defied, I started to climb up on the pilothouse myself and only stopped my progress when the last man got off. That done, I told the people who were crowded about that my initials were S.O.B. I never had to chase them off again. Later several women passengers confided to me that I was the nicest S.O.B. they had ever met.

My main concern was the safety of passengers. After I asked one lady to get back of the rope marking the navigating area, she told me that she was an officer's wife. I said to her, "Please step back. It is necessary for the safety of the ship and passengers. Other passengers paid full fare and have equal privileges." I took her arm and helped her to the other side of the rope.

The Coast Guard officers were checking the main deck when a big sea demolished the steel doors. Salt water boarded and threatened to run down into the engine room and dynamo room. One of the officers sent word to the wheelhouse to slow down and head into the sea. At last Mr. Bryant and his crew temporarily shored up what was left of the steel doors by sawing up a gangway and a Coca-Cola case, there being no lumber or other shoring materials to be found.

Once the steel doors were secured, we were able to maintain a favorable position so that passengers could enjoy the race. Once an hour I relieved Mr. Aiken, the pilot, and I did the steering. This gave me a hands-on feel for the ship. The band was playing right behind the wheelhouse. The officer on duty couldn't hear the radio telephone. I had Mr. Casey get the band to move. But each time I relieved the pilot, I found the telephone turned off. I turned it back on as required by law. Later I discovered that the Federal Communications Commission had called us. Their message had not been received or answered as required. The FCC complained that the deck officers had improper radio licenses. In response, Mr. Casey hired a regular radio officer that night.

The *Intrepid*, the defender, led all the way, ending the race with a lead of six minutes for the fifty miles in four hours.

On returning after the first race, the Coast Guard gave me written demands for specific repairs to be made before the ship could sail for the second race. Mr. Casey had men working all night in port making these repairs. Early the following morning the repairs were completed, and the ship's papers were returned to me so that we could sail.

I still did not have my name on the enrollment. At 9:00 A.M. I left the ship for the customs house but could find no customs officer. The officer on duty was on a ship in the harbor. Just before sailing, I phoned the U.S. Coast Guard in Providence in desperation. All the passengers were on board. I pleaded for permission to sail. This was granted, "this one and last time only."

Two FCC officers from Boston boarded the *Potomac*. They brought charges against the ship and its master for negligence in the non-use of the radio telephone. With so many official complaints against me, I phoned Maritime Coast Pilots, Inc., my agent in New York, and ordered a lawyer. That evening, as the *Potomac* was approaching the pier after the second race, my old friend Wilbur Dow was sitting on a piling waiting for us. He was a sight for sore eyes.

After the passengers disembarked, Mr. Dow and I went to the hotel in town, where I explained the situation. One of the Coast Guard's charges against me was that the chief mate, Mr. Bryant, was not licensed to perform his duties on a ship of the *Potomac*'s tonnage. The next day, the day of the third race, Mr. Dow, who himself possessed an unlimited master's license, was hired to replace Mr. Bryant. This also made Mr. Dow better able to defend me at a trial.

Another charge, this one from the FCC, stated that my radio permit was obsolete. Actually it was good indefinitely. The FCC also complained that I had failed to answer their radio calls and that watch officers lacked third-class radio telephone licenses. This last complaint had been addressed with the hiring of the regular radio officer.

On the day of the third race, the sea was calmer and fewer passengers were seasick, so they were better able to enjoy what they had come to see. By afternoon the passengers became better acquainted with one another and the ship, and were happy. Perhaps the liquor at the bar helped.

The Coast Guard raised several additional charges against me, and I was ordered to appear for a hearing on Friday the fifteenth. Fortunately, there was no race that day, since the *Dame Pattie* had asked for a lay day and was hauled onto dry dock for bottom polishing. All of the *Potomac*'s officers and most of the crew, plus the charterers, had to spend the day at the hearing in Providence. There were seven charges against me. It was four in the afternoon before we were dismissed. The civilian judge planned to study the case and proclaim his decision in ten days.

The hearing dealt mainly with the qualifications of the crew and whether or not they had proper papers. The cook with no Z card, whom I had signed on based upon Mr. Casey's insistence that she had earned one, became the reason for a legitimate charge against me. It turned out that she had failed the physical examination and had never been issued a Z card. Mr. Casey was very embarrassed by this revelation. Apparently the girl had lied to him. She was immediately discharged and sent back to Baltimore. From then on we sailed without a cook and had no one to care for the female passengers. Men had to clean the ladies' room by roping it off, barring the men from the men's head, directing the ladies to the men's head, then washing down the ladies' room with the fire hose. There was still a lot of seasickness, so the use of the fire hose speeded the cleaning process.

The Coast Guard also charged us with violating the lighting requirement. The argument had to do with the time of sunset on a particular night. A phone call to the Goat Island Lighthouse for the official time of sunset there proved that the *Potomac* was not in violation.

On the sixteenth we were to be at the oil berth at 5:00 A.M. for refueling. The weather was clear when we left the pier, but soon after getting underway, dense fog shut in. We crept around Goat Island without the benefit of radar. On reaching the causeway, we had to back her in. A revenue cutter had tied up at the mouth of the slip, giving me six feet less room in which to make the turn. Pressed for time, I put the stem of the *Potomac* against the stone jetty and, with teamwork, we accomplished the turn without damage. We took on fuel. The weather cleared, making for a decent, though humid, day. Four hundred and seventy passengers boarded. Interest in the one-sided race was dwindling.

The weather was clear inside the harbor, but outside dense fog set in, and halfway to our destination off Castle Hill Lighthouse, the fog was so dense that it was unsafe to proceed. We stopped, as did many other vessels. Word came that one excursion craft had run aground and that a second had broken down and had to be towed into port. We stopped the engine, drifted, and tooted the whistle. The weather gradually cleared, but the race was delayed and then finally postponed to the following day. Our passengers could at least enjoy watching the hundreds of boats returning to shore and take pictures of them.

When my passengers had had enough, we returned to our loading berth and called it a day. The passengers were given a rain check to ride another vessel, the *Martha's Vineyard,* whose passenger numbers were also drastically reduced. The one-sided race had left the public bored so that many abandoned their excursions altogether. Thus ended our primary mission.

The charterers next planned to use the *Potomac* on another assignment in Philadelphia. The original officers and crew all left. They had taken jobs mainly to see the races themselves, with their wives as passengers. Meanwhile, we lay all night at the fueling berth. Mr. Casey fed us ashore and put us up for the night. On Sunday it took all day to assemble a new crew.

Monday morning, September 18, we again had a full crew but still needed fresh water. There was none available at the fueling berth so we steamed around Goat Island again to the torpedo dock. At 11:00 A.M. we had our water aboard and sailed for Camden via New York. Just before sailing, many members of the crew had doubts. They were afraid they would not get paid at the final destination, Philadelphia. I assured them that I would take care of that at Bayonne where we were to stop again for fuel. We had no cook on this voyage, so I assigned an ordinary seaman to keep the galley clean and the coal fire burning. This young fellow was lazy and had to be forced out of bed in the morning. Each one made his own meals.

When we were just off New Haven, Mr. Santos, the new chief engineer, reported to me that he only had three hours steaming fuel left. I pondered this. Should I go into New Haven or Bridgeport for more fuel? Mr. Santos was new to the ship. He had been left with no data or measurements. I assumed that he was playing it safe with a pessimistic estimate of fuel reserves. I reviewed the fuel consumption during the previous two voyages that we had already made to Bayonne and to Newport. I also checked with the elderly oiler, Hicks, who knew the ship well, though he could not read or write. He reported to me that both wing tanks were full and that there were eighteen inches of fuel in the center tank. Good enough. I took the bull by the horns and proceeded, bearing in mind that if we really got short of fuel in the East River, I could get to a dock along the way by asking some other craft to shove us into one. Most of the city was lined with docks so there was bound to be fuel available.

At 1:30 P.M. we tied up at Bayonne and refueled. We could not take on water there but were allowed to get some at an adjacent pier. At this point the officers and crew again hesitated about continuing on the voyage. They were still afraid of not being paid off. I settled that by making a written demand of Mr. Casey: "Pay off in advance or else!" He paid us. I then had the crew with me.

We were allowed to lay over for the night at an adjacent slip. Getting there was a tough job against the tide. We parted the best of our rotting mooring lines while doing so. I set sailing time for five in the morning because of our restriction, "outside waters in daylight only." I wasn't about to steam in darkness and run the risk of being cited by the Coast Guard for violations again.

Next day I was up at 4:00 A.M. preparing for the ocean voyage down the New Jersey coast. Mr. Casey arrived on the pier a few minutes after four while we were topping off the water tanks. When he noted that we had finished and were taking in the hose, he asked me, "If you are ready, why don't you sail?" I explained that I had to comply with the Coast Guard's order to the letter and not cross the inland water line before 6:41, the official time of sunrise that day.

The sky was burning red as we left the harbor. We crossed the line just at 6:41 and entered the fact in the official log book. The weather was fine as we ran down the coast, proceeding at moderate speed to conserve fuel. My instructions for destination were Seventh Street Pier near City Park, Camden, four blocks beyond the Benjamin Franklin Bridge on Cooper's Creek. I had told Mr. Casey that I had never been there and that I would not enter the creek before full daylight at the earliest. My chart showed no details of Cooper's Creek.

At 11:00 P.M. Mr. Santos reported to me officially that he was short of fuel and that he would be out of fuel at four the next morning. My tide tables showed high water at Cooper's Creek at 4:00 A.M. That would be the most favorable stage of the tide to enter. However, if I did get stuck in the mud at that hour, the tide would be dropping, leaving us stuck there until the next high tide.

At 1:15 A.M. I tied her up at the end of Pier 34, Philadelphia, near the tugboat office. I tried to find a local pilot to take her into Cooper's Creek. None would attempt it. They told me that only barges went in there assisted by tugs. I phoned dispatchers of three towboat companies. None of them were interested or would help. So I steamed across the river to Camden and tied up at the Becket Street Terminal on the Delaware, as near to our destination as possible. Unwelcome there, we were ordered away by the watchman. He said he had a merchant ship coming to take the berth shortly, but we tied up in spite of his protests. I told him that the *Potomac* was in distress and could not move.

I lay down on the brass bed for two hours. At 6:00 A.M. I got up and checked the remaining fuel as accurately as possible. Then I took a taxi to the berth on the creek to which we had been directed. There, on an open field dock, I found Mr. Casey with a Miss Eagan, representing the owners in Washington. They were there to meet the ship and to turn her over to the new charterer. Before I could explain, Mr. Casey asked, "Where is the ship?" I was introduced to Miss Eagan and Mrs. Rasmussen, the new charterer. I explained my situation and examined the creek, which had not been visible from the Delaware. It was crooked and had old barges and dredges tied up at the entrance. At my insistence, Mrs. Rasmussen hired a barge captain to accompany me as my guide.

At 8:00 I was back on board, anxious to get into the creek before low water. We proceeded immediately, steaming up the Delaware for about a mile to the entrance, then started into the creek slowly with my guide advising. We got in about a thousand feet and grounded in the mud. Fortunately we were able to back off and out into the Delaware, at which point the chief engineer protested that we were out of fuel. I ignored his report and started

413

the *Potomac* into the creek once more. My own experience told me that the deepest water was usually on the outside of each turn. Even though the tide was falling and the current was against us, we made it and tied up at the new berth to the surprise, satisfaction, and blessed relief of all.

The crew had already been paid off, so I turned over all ship's papers to Mr. Casey's assistant, who had appeared on the scene. I was at last relieved of a nightmarish burden. We were all happy to get ashore, go home, and sleep for a couple of days, our mission completed.

At home a few days later, I phoned the FCC and learned that charges had been filed against me. I was told that actions would come from Washington, but as it turned out, I never heard anything further from them. Mr. Casey had all charges quashed through contacts with his friends there. I felt some kinship with Casey. He had had a job to do, and he had done it to the best of his ability.

On September 25, as required, I notified the Coast Guard that in four days I had carried 2,001 passengers safely. I sent in my reports to Mr. Casey, the Coast Guard, and Mr. Dow. The important facts in my favor regarding the voyages of the *Potomac* under my command were that there had been no loss of life, no property damage, and no injuries reported. Besides, we had had a lot of fun and excitement on this weird excursion.

*It is unclear if Dad was penalized, and he does not mention having to pay for Mr. Dow's services out of his own pocket. Either way, the penalties were nothing compared to the fun "The Skipper" had telling the story.*

**Note to Chapter 23**

1. Enrollment: a document giving all the facts relating to the legal use of the vessel, issued by the customs authorities to vessels in domestic trade.

## CHAPTER 24

# SIXTY YEARS AT SEA

After my nightmarish job on the *Potomac*, I gladly went back to piloting. In 1968 I piloted 110 ships, many of them foreign vessels. I especially liked Portuguese ships for their excellent food and service.

On July 9 I took the *Calmar* from New York to Baltimore. Her master, Charles Doane, was being relieved because his sixteen-year-old fox terrier had died. He was in deep mourning.

On October 15 I was busy at home making a fallout shelter under the front porch, following government specifications. To build it I had to remove big stones using block and tackle. I built a stone wall inside and under the porch to complete the project.

On June 6, 1969, I piloted the *Yorkmar*. Outbound from New York, we collided with a fishing boat as she crossed ahead of us and got under our starboard bow. The fisherman returned to port, and we followed her, fearing she might be damaged. She would not communicate. I reported the facts to the owners and to the Coast Guard and conferred with Mr. Dow, my lawyer. After he read my report, he said, "There is nothing to do but wait and see what happens." The fisherman never reported any problems. Perhaps the boat was not damaged after all. But why did she return to port? Some suggest the boat may have been engaged in smuggling.

I was almost always treated as a guest aboard ships. I usually stayed on board, had a nice room and bath, and ate with the officers and captain. On occasion I had a chance to go ashore for a look around. On one ship I reminisced with the chief engineer, who had been with me on the *West Hampton* as a deck engineer when she had been in Army transport service to France in 1918.

I was trying to secure a radio telephone, since I had had some embarrassing experiences without one. (I was once caught in dense fog in the East River while piloting a seven-hundred-foot, deeply laden tanker being pushed ahead by the tide, and I had not been able to warn ships ahead about our lack of control.) I couldn't buy a new or used telephone at any price. I finally rented one for $47 a month. I owned the crystal, which had cost me $104. Eventually I got a new one for $1,200, after waiting six months for delivery. Then, before I could get it written off, the government required all ships to carry their own and changed the channels.

On February 1, 1970, New York tugboats went on strike. In the two months of the strike, I handled fifty-four ships in New York Harbor without use of tugs. The winter weather was tough on crews and linesmen who had to handle more lines than usual. Busy almost every day during this period docking and undocking ships, I did manage a quick trip home occasionally.

On the fifth I piloted the *Desert Princess* from Stapleton on Staten Island to the Greater New York Terminal. We turned off College Point at 5:30 A.M. At 8:32 we were making a turn when the stem grounded at the edge of the channel. We shifted cargo aft but were unable to free her. At noon I called Captain Campbell, the marine superintendent, and told him the ship was in danger of leaking oil. I recommended he send salvage barges to us and asked him to notify the Coast Guard. The agents were doing everything possible to secure barges to take off cargo and lighten the ship. The ship owners sent a salvage tug, which took a towline aft to pull her off at high water. With the vessel lightened by removing cargo, she finally freed. But by towing her backwards, we had no directional control, and she grounded against the opposite bank near North Brothers Island. At the next high tide, the tug pulled us clear once more, and we steamed to College Point anchorage. When the tide was right, I made a second attempt, this time making the turn at North Brothers Island successfully. We tied up at midday the seventh, at Greater New York Terminal, and discharged the balance of her cargo of oil.

On the eighth I joined the *Desert Princess* once more. After dark the ship was ready and the tide was favorable. To make sure there was no misunderstanding between me and the Greek crew, I went to each end of the ship and personally gave instructions for getting the ship hauled back to the end of the pier. I saw to it that the officers fore and aft had the lines right for backing on stern spring lines around the corner of the pier. I was extra careful to make sure that everyone understood the maneuver, since leaving a berth without tugs was something they had never experienced before. When all was ready, I returned to the bridge to take charge and was surprised to find Captain Peterson, the state pilot, present. I asked him how he had gotten on board, since the gangway had been up for over an hour. He said he had boarded offshore from the pilot boat. The captain of the ship

417

told us that the owners had sent him out to pilot the vessel after we were clear. I said, "Yes, after I get her all clear and ready for sailing." That meant extricating her from the hole she was in and turned toward College Point for sailing when the tide was right. I said to the captain, "Let me do all the damage. When fully clear, I will turn it over to the state pilot."

Successfully getting the *Princess* clear, we headed east to College Point, anchored, and turned. I said to the captain, "Now I have your ship ready to go out," and turned command over to Captain Peterson. The tide was at full flood but, when Captain Peterson directed the turn at Hell Gate, he miscued. The ship's bow ran up into the Harlem River before he could get her stopped. She lay against the rocks. Fireboats and city boats crowded about but they could not help. I got ashore by a city fireboat and called the Maritime Coast Pilots office. At first Captain Begleman thought that I was responsible for grounding the ship a third time. He was relieved to learn that somebody else had done it. When the tide started ebbing, the *Princess* freed herself and Captain Peterson backed her into the East River and on her way. I went to my room at the Seamen's Institute for a night's sleep and to make out my written reports to the owners, the Coast Guard, and to my lawyer, Mr. Dow.

Next I piloted the *DeGauya*, bound for Newark. Another ship tied up in our intended berth and refused to move. Her pilot was waiting for the wind to subside—a mistake, since he could have used the wind to his advantage, but he didn't see it that way. Finally, to get a move on, Maritime Coast Pilots sent a different pilot to Newark to sail her. The new pilot did the job, clearing the berth for us to enter.

On February 23 I piloted the *Dauntless* to Stapleton. To get out of the slip I had to run stern lines to the end of the narrow pointed dock. The men handling lines were not convinced it could be done and didn't seem to understand what I wanted. I went on the dock myself to show them. In doing so I found the end of the dock cut off from the rest. Linesmen told me that a ship had done the damage several nights before. A day or so later I was accused of having broken the dock. The owners were charging me and my employers with the responsibility. The charges were dropped against us when lawyers handling the case were satisfied with my testimony concerning the truth of the matter. I was even excused from the hearing.

February 25 I piloted the S.S. *Penmar* from Newark to Stapleton. I brought the vessel in and wanted to turn her so as to be ready to sail, but her master didn't want me to. When it came time to sail, the wind was hard on the dock. How were we to manage? Only one way: put the stem against the dock and force her into the wind. The captain did not want to be involved in such a maneuver but agreed that it was the best way. It took two hours to turn her, a job that could have been avoided entirely had I been allowed to turn her on entering. Afterwards I met Captains Crossin and Thompson at the landing. They were doing docking and undocking during the strike just as I was. We commiserated. Al Thompson was an expert pilot. He and I did jobs for one another from time to time when there were scheduling conflicts.

I was asked to pilot a Polish ship, but a twenty- to thirty-knot wind was blowing her against the dock, and I refused to take her out. The state pilot was more courageous than I this time, and he did the job successfully.

While waiting on Staten Island for the *Oriental Explorer*, I went to Snug Harbor, the home for retired seamen, and called on Captain Strasser. He was eighty-four years old and suffering from an injury sustained when he had fallen into a ship's hold years before. He had sailed as mate with me on the *Nevadan* in 1922.

Occasionally I took a turn as dispatcher of pilots at the New York office of Maritime Coast Pilots, Inc.

March 19 I piloted the *Mandarin Core* from Newark to Stapleton. The Core ships were nicely fitted out to carry fruit and were fast at twenty-four knots. I finished at 9:00 P.M., having boarded just two hours before. I took the ferry for New York and by 9:30 was in my officer's room with private bath at the new Seamen's Church Institute at the Battery overlooking the harbor. These lodgings were ideal for my work, being close to shipowners' offices. They were also near the ferry, and most subways converged there. In the building there was a restaurant and a cafeteria. Rooms were $7 a day and meals were reasonable. Although there were no telephones in the rooms, there was one close by in the hall. Captain Begleman, other pilots, and I met for dinner now and then at this fine facility.

*Dick stayed at the new Seamen's Church Institute in 1983 while at a conference at Trinity Church on Wall Street. The Bamforth name was still well known there.*

On the evening of March 29 I was standing by at the landing in Stapleton waiting for the Norwegian vessel *Lisianne* to arrive from sea. She was delayed by northeast gales and snow. Because of the bad weather, the boatman refused to leave the landing to take me out to the ship. So by telephone I changed the docking time to 6:00 A.M. I stood by on the rickety wooden dock until the boat could take me out. I had nothing but a backless wooden bench to sit on. At 3:30 A.M., March 30, I finally boarded. I truly had to love my work to put up with such hassles.

Soon afterwards I piloted the German ship *Senator Russell*. She was loaded with sugar, with a draft of thirty feet. I boarded off Stapleton and took her to Erie Basin, turned around in a narrow area just touching soft mud, and then took her into Sucrest Sugar Refinery at the foot of Richards Street, Brooklyn. As with many of the places I went during the tug strike, it was a challenge for me, but rewarding when every thing went satisfactorily.

April 1, 1970, the tug strike was finally over and I went home to Swampscott for a rest. Two days later on April 3, I piloted the German vessel *Ida Isle* from Boston to New York. A new small ship, she carried containers only, 154 boxes. There were just nineteen in the crew. The first all-container ship in Boston, she had an eight-year charter to run from New York to Bermuda. These container ships were operating under foreign flags, where all the business was going.

After the strike Captain Begleman tried to get me to handle tankers at the docks without tugs. I was sure it would be unsafe and I refused. It had been risky enough maneuvering these huge fuel tankers without tugs when there was an emergency, but to continue the practice when the safety of tugs was available seemed foolish indeed.

April 18 I wrote to Captain Rea, U.S. Coast Guard, recommending navigational changes. At home I made two wooden window boxes for Dick. He was by then well established as rector of St. Mary's Episcopal Church in Rockport and wanted to improve the appearance of the rectory.

On July 1 I piloted the *Nepco Energy* from Block Island to Port Jefferson anchorage. At 4:00 A.M. we anchored one mile outside the sea buoy to discharge some of the oil to barges because, at forty-four feet, she was very deep. No normal port could accommodate that much draft. When we arrived a huge tug was standing by with a fifty-thousand-barrel capacity barge. At 5:00 A.M. the tug placed the barge alongside, and then it went to the harbor to get the boarding party of government officials. No pumping of cargo could start until they had passed the ship. A special dining room had been set up for the boarding party. Several bottles of liquor were included, along with sandwiches, coffee, and smokes. It was profitable for the ship to be passed promptly. These officials examined the ship's papers, which the captain and his assistants had already prepared: manifests, crew lists, passports, and health certificates. By random selection, they called in members of the crew to appear before them, carefully examined the store list, identified and measured the cargo, and searched for contraband. A prescribed amount of tobacco was allowed for use by the ship's company while in port. The rest was sealed. The whole inspection process took about an hour. The ship's agent helped to move things along.

Immediately after the ship was cleared by the officials, the crew expended great energy in discharging the cargo. Pumping of oil began at 8:30 A.M., and by 2:00 P.M. the barge was taken away by the big tug and towed into Port Jefferson.

With part of the cargo now out, the ship's draft was reduced to thirty-nine feet. I piloted her to Northport, the next port on the north side of Long Island, twelve miles to the east. Here two tugs from New Haven met the ship and assisted her alongside a concrete pier a mile and a half offshore in deep water. The pier was much shorter than the ship. A derrick on the pier had eight-, ten-, and twelve-inch diameter flexible hoses hoisted and ready to connect to the ship's pipes amidships. A flexible pipe lying on the ocean floor carried the remaining cargo of fifty-two thousand tons of oil to shore. Great care was required to avoid puncturing the hull of this heavy ship. As with all modern ships, she was made only of frames with steel skin about an inch thick separating her cargo from the sea.

As pilot, I directed the operation of the tugs and the ship's engines and communicated with the tugs by a radio telephone. One tug was made fast at each end of the ship so that she would land gently against the pier. They pushed or pulled as I directed. When she was in precise position against the pier, spring mooring lines were secured to the dock so that the ship could not move. While the mooring lines were being secured, the tugs kept pushing the ship against the pier. After the spring lines were secure, one of the tugs moved amidships to keep her pressed against the pier, while the second tug ran three mooring lines from each end of the ship to mooring buoys. The operation was complicated by working after dark in a heavy wind. With foreign crews, there was frequently a language barrier to overcome as well. The tying-up process often took considerable time. In this case we began tying up at 5:30, and pumping did not start until three hours later. Once fully secured at all four points, I reported to the captain, who was seeing to the boarding party's departure. Satisfied that the ship was properly secured, the captain dismissed the tugs. My job was complete.

On the Fourth of July I again boarded the huge *Nepco Energy* to pilot her from Northport back to Port Jefferson. Assisted by one tug, we sailed and anchored two and a half hours later, again one mile outside the Port Jefferson entrance buoy. The big tug maneuvered the emptied barge alongside. Official oil surveyors measured the barge and oil on board, and the rest of the cargo of oil was discharged to the barge. The barge then left the ship, which now was drawing only twenty-four feet of water.

With the cargo out and the hull down to a moderate depth for safe maneuvering, the captain was ready to sail immediately. The water was smooth. He told me, "We will sail with good weather and ballast her on the way out." He needed to add water ballast to lower the propeller and rudder deeper into the water for navigating in rougher conditions, which he would surely encounter farther out to sea. Usually it took five to seven hours to get the required ballast on board. In this case it would all be on board before the ship got to sea outside Block Island.

At 6:30 P.M. we sailed east in Long Island Sound. At midnight the ship was met by the pilot boat *Lispaso* off Block Island. I climbed down the long rope ladder to the bobbing pilot boat. One hour later, at one in the morning of July 5, the pilot boat tied up at Galilee, Rhode Island. I rested on the boat until nine and then got the first bus to Providence. I was at home by 1:00 P.M. I had been away five days on this single operation.

On July 19, 1970, I piloted the *Nepco Energy*, this time from Sandwich to Block Island. The next day we collided in fog with a barge being towed across the channel. We stopped the engines. We had heard a towboat on the port bow blowing one long and two short blasts. We supposed it was coming up the channel parallel to us. Instead she was crossing before us, and we had steamed between the tug and the barge. We did not see either tug or barge but felt the impact of the collision. Apparently, we had parted the line between the tug and the barge, resulting in some damage to each, as well as to the ship, but there were no personal injuries involved. We proceeded slowly outside the channel and anchored. At daylight a boat was lowered to inspect the hull. A cut in the plates well above the waterline was found on the starboard side. We waited for an official survey by the Coast Guard. The ship received a seaworthy certificate from them at 4:00 P.M. and she was then able to sail for the West Indies, where she would be repaired. Meanwhile, the Coast Guard brought charges against me for negligence. I was given notice in writing to stand trial.

My lawyer, Mr. Dow, once more came to the rescue. As a result of his efforts, I received a written apology from the commandant at the Coast Guard station in Providence stating that I would never hear of the charge against me again. It was determined that the blame lay entirely with the tug and barge.

For the year 1970, I served as pilot 149 times, including the fifty-four ships I had worked during the tugboat strike.

In 1971 I was seventy-six years old but still loved my seafaring life, even though I worked at all hours of day and night and had to travel to and from assignments with lots of time in buses, planes, trains, taxis, and on foot. Sometimes when boarding in a rough and confused sea where it was difficult for the ship to make a lee, and seas were rolling over her deck, I had to make more than a single stab at getting aboard from the pilot boat. Several times I was knocked about and got soaking wet but never was hurt in the least.

Dorothy had often complained that I never took her anywhere. For our fiftieth wedding anniversary, I wanted to plan a trip as a surprise, but I quickly realized I would need her cooperation. Margaret, who had just returned from the Hawaiian Islands, persuaded Dorothy that she should go there. When she told me, I put my foot down and said, "No! I'm taking you to Europe." Then she had no choice. Together we worked out the details for a guided tour of Portugal and Spain in mid-May at a cost of $1,400.

On May 6, 1971, I experienced great difficulty getting up the pilot ladder.

*While climbing the pilot ladder on the* Lionados, *which was riding light, necessitating a long climb, Dad couldn't make his legs work. He struggled, but halfway up he could only cling to the ladder in agony. The crew could see that he was in trouble and offered him a breeches buoy, such as used to rescue personnel from a ship in distress. He refused. It was his pride. He would rather have fallen off and drowned right then and there. With supreme effort, he managed, haltingly, to get aboard under his own power.*

422

The next day I went to see our family physician. He advised me to give up my work or face the possibility of being an invalid or of jeopardizing the safety of ships. I decided I would call it the end of my career.

On May 9 I wrote to the senior warden of the church, terminating my part in the cleaning project that I had joined. In the evening Allan and his family, including his mother-in-law, Kathleen, brought anniversary gifts and had dinner with us. The next day I went with Allan to Filene's and bought clothes for the trip to Europe.

*I helped him get outfitted in a light blue sport jacket, slacks, and a red tie. He had never before in his life worn such colorful clothes. He was like a kid, full of enthusiasm for the upcoming trip, forgetting for the moment his decision to quit the sea.*

Later, as I was puttering around the yard, Captain Begleman called to give me an emergency job piloting. I had to tell him that I was finished. I had sadly accepted my doctor's recommendation. I sent for refunds on the bus tickets that I would no longer use. I seriously thought my life at sea had ended.

Our trip to Europe lasted from May 13 to June 2. I decided to keep a daily log of our sightseeing adventure.

*He described every minute of every day through Portugal and Spain and a side trip to Gibraltar, filling six yellow pads listing every last detail. His motivations for writing were mixed. From the practical point of view, the trip was expensive, and he wanted to get his money's worth. The log also kept him occupied and freed him from conversing with other passengers. Fully confident in things nautical, he was shy and withdrawn with those he considered his superiors in education, accomplishment, or wealth—at least until he felt comfortable with them. Most of all, his jottings demonstrated his lifelong passion for life and learning. He drove Mother crazy as he wrote furiously, quoting the guide's every word and describing everything he saw. But his log also allowed him to give Mother an account of what she was missing. Handicapped with arthritis, she was unable to do the walking tours and stayed in the bus.*

*His log reads like the flicking frames of old-time movies as he recorded what passed by:*

flowers in bloom
vineyards
olive groves
cork trees
elderly people riding donkeys and carrying umbrellas
wild red poppies
Moorish castles

a bullfight arena
a field of sheep
rice paddies
people waiting for buses
concrete telephone poles
girls walking, with red scarves on their heads
a mule drawing a two-wheeled cart
children waving to us
scotch broom in yellow blossom
white calla lilies
fig trees
well-filled clotheslines
pine grove
grapes
a car, motorcycle
wisteria
fruit trees
town of Muta Gouch
corn
warehouse with corrugated steel roof
waste rocky land
pedestrians
grazing
mountain village
boulders
Guorda on top of hill—highest in Portugal
wool factory
Renault assembly plant
school
olives
We climb to Guorda—35,000 population
this beautiful town on NE slope of mts—the oldest in Portugal
ruins dating back to Paleolithic era
grapes, rocks, pines, wool
church, machinery center with 5-story buildings
can see the country for miles below
bus climbs and climbs
women walking, with cans on head
12:15 lunch, 1:30 Cathedral of 12th century, 2,500 ft elevation
down we go
two women walking, with bags on heads
gardens
pedestrians
almond trees

walkers, with stores on top of heads
houses here and there
a little walled-in cemetery
barren mts
deep valley ahead spotted with villages and gardens
natives selling cherries.

*He was fascinated by everything on their trip, including the dinner menu on the airplane and the fun of resetting watches five hours at a time as they crossed the Atlantic in less time than it took steamships to travel three hundred miles. He was impressed by the cleanliness of the cities and annoyed at having to drink bottled mineral water. He enjoyed the luxury of first-class hotels but felt guilty to be seen in a gambling casino. Once, out of curiosity, he pulled a dangling chain next to his ample hotel bathtub and was embarrassed to have the floor nurse walk in to scrub his back. He delighted in the village marketplaces and once bought "a pink and red carnation to take back to my love in the bus." He soaked up the historical background poured out by the tour escort and was amused by the inane questions of his fellow travelers. However, when a discussion on controversial politics took place among the passengers, he noted that they were mostly southerners and conservatives and did his best to squelch the conversation.*

*He waxed almost poetic when in Estoril he managed to hire a two-horse hansom, delighting in taking Mother for a ride through an area of beautiful gardens and homes. "The driver couldn't speak a word of English but whistled and talked to the horses all the way. The route was hilly, and when he rested the horses, they kissed and communicated."*

*He had never before been so relaxed about leaving the navigation to others and obviously enjoyed the trip. Away for nearly a month, one of the longest times they had ever been together, he and Mother returned home refreshed but not any younger. The family celebrated their anniversary with a dinner party at Pat and Dick's home in Rockport.*

I had considered myself semi-retired after the difficulty I had had climbing onto ships from the pilot boat, but after ten days at home following the trip to Europe, I went back to piloting. A tug strike in New York meant there was very little work on the coast but, in spite of the strike and my ailing legs, I piloted a total of fifty-six ships during 1971.

*Jack Greenley, the husband of Dad's niece Louise, was very fond of her Uncle Charlie. Jack was a specialist in public health, serving as a Naval public health officer in Boston. Jack listened to Dad's symptoms and suggested he consider a change of doctors, noting that Dad was eligible for free services at U.S. Public Health facilities. Jack's suggestion turned out to be a godsend, since the family doctor hadn't done any recent blood tests. He had simply attributed Dad's problems to old age, telling him that he needed to slow down. Mother seemed to have little interest in her husband's physical problems and strongly disapproved of his decision to enter a public hospital. He got himself there on his own, using train, bus, and shank's mare.*

On December 31 I went to our family doctor for a checkup. I told him it was getting so I could hardly walk and that I was considering going to check in at the U.S. Public Health Hospital. He threw up his hands and gave up on me in disgust. He was connected with the Lynn Hospital and considered the public hospital inferior.

January 3, 1972, I piloted the *Portmar* from Baltimore to Philadelphia. I had come down on the bus and was given the pilot's room in which to rest. Piloting at night, I began to see all kinds of imaginary lights, and I failed to check the radar. At ten minutes before midnight, I grounded the ship on the edge of the shoal at Smith Point. A ship with a state pilot was following at the time and had asked to pass on two blasts of his whistle. Then by radio he asked me to get over and let him pass. I did so and went too far. I wondered if my judgment was slipping. We pumped out all ballast and got off the shoal on our own power. At 1:30 P.M. on the fifth, the *Portmar* tied up in Philadelphia and I took the bus home. Something was wrong with me.

On the sixth I went to Rhode Island to get my state license for Block Island. Afterwards I made an appointment to enter the Public Health Hospital in Boston on January 24, a time that would not interfere with my work. Meanwhile I carried on. On January 8 I secured a license for Rhode Island over state waters to Long Island Sound so that New York would allow me to pilot in those waters.

On the nineteenth I saw Dr. Weiner at the U.S. Public Health Hospital. Blood tests showed a low red cell count. He confirmed my need to enter the hospital on the twenty-fourth.

January 21 I was at Breton Reef in the pilot boat to meet the *Tien Hong*. I was to pilot her from Block Island to Bridgeport. She was under the Liberian flag, with a Chinese crew. We could not make radio contact with her. But Captain Govostes, a coast pilot who was passing Point Judith westbound, reported seeing a ship southwest of Block Island. As I could not keep the pilot boat at sea indefinitely, I ordered her down to west of Block Island. To our surprise and relief, there was the *Tien Hong* at anchor. We had a lengthy delay while the engine and radar were being repaired, so I didn't get home until the twenty-third. The next day I checked in at the hospital and was put to bed and given many tests. Jack Greenley called on me.

On the twenty-sixth I was given further tests. Bone marrow was taken from my sternum. My granddaughter, Judy, a student at Garland Junior

426

College in Boston, called on me. Next day fifteen public health doctors plus Dr. Sullivan, a specialist from St. Mary's Hospital, summed up my case.

On Friday the twenty-eighth I went home for the weekend with orders to report Sunday night at St. Elizabeth's Hospital. Jack Greenley drove me in. I made more trips between the Public Health Hospital and St. Elizabeth's and went on a twenty-four-hour urine test. Tuesday morning the urine drill ended. It turned out my trouble was pernicious anemia due to failure of the marrow to produce red blood cells. To stimulate the marrow I was to take B-12 shots once a month for life. February 1 I was discharged and declared fit for full duty.

On the fifth of February, 1972, I went back to work, piloting the *Phoenix* from Sandwich to Block Island and had other piloting jobs on the sixth, seventh, and fourteenth.

For three days I attended a hearing with my attorney, Mr. Dow, at the customs house in Baltimore regarding the grounding of the *Portmar*. I received a penalty of one year's probation.

February 28 I was back for a checkup at the Public Health Hospital.

*Mother made no attempt to offer him a ride, so again he used his feet and public transportation.*

I painted the cellar and also refinished woodwork on Jack Greenley's sailboat. March 8 I was back on the job ready to pilot, but there was hardly any work, what with longshoremen's strikes or threats of them. I painted out the pantry at home and rebuilt one set of garage doors and the teeter board.

I piloted the *Oriental Trader* from New London to New York. Her master was Captain Chang H. Yang. She had a full cargo of plywood from the Philippines. Her crew were all Hong Kong Chinese.

Another checkup at the Public Health Hospital declared me fit for duty. I registered for a course in radar.

On October 6 I piloted the *Yamataka Maru* from Boston to Philadelphia and docked her during a tugboat strike. The captain had me escorted to the bus station on landing. I went by the name of Murphy.

*Presumably he didn't want the strikers to know he was the one doing the strikers' work. The name Bamforth was well known among them.*

On October 11 I piloted the *Yamakimi Maru*. I docked her with no tugs and was off at 10:00 A.M. with an escort through the picket line. Tugs were still on strike and I was paid as both pilot and docking master.

In November, at Wayfarers Lodge, I received my fifty-year membership pin.

I began 1973 by taking the radar course at the Seamen's Institute in New York. I had a room in the same building.

From February 9 to the end of the year I piloted forty-two ships. Most of the ships were under foreign flags and were new: one, two, and three years old. American merchant ships were becoming more and more scarce.

On September 30, 1973, I piloted the Panamanian ship *Lachine Trader* from New Haven to Boston. She was due to sail at 6:00 A.M., October 1, so I intended to get on board by midnight. I took the evening bus to New Haven, then a taxi to the terminal where she was supposed to be tied up. I arrived at the pier at 11:30, dismissed the cab, and walked to the pier, where I was surprised to find no ship. Inquiring of the dock watchman, I found she had sailed at six that evening. I called my pilot agency in Newport and was told she had had to go out to anchor to make room for an incoming vessel. The agent had called my home, but I had already left. He suggested I go out with the captain at nine in the morning. So I had a whole night to kill. It would be expensive to call a taxi, go to a hotel, and be back in just a few hours.

I looked about. There was a workmen's shack nearby with a gas heater, a few hard chairs, and a wooden bench. I lay down on the bench with my bag for a pillow. The bench was very hard. The watchman making his rounds every hour came in to punch the time clock or get a drink of water. The light was on continuously, and the noisy gas heater went on and off automatically, over and over again, but I managed to get some rest. At daylight I was up so as not to miss the captain going out in a boat. Soon he and I boarded a launch for the ship. He gave orders to get underway. At noon the anchor was up, and I was the pilot to Boston, a 180-mile trip via the Cape Cod Canal.

I quickly discovered she could make only five or six knots since she had but one boiler working. She was bound for Boston to have the second repaired. She had no deck officers and only one engineer on board. I figured I had a lemon, but I had to make the best of it.

At 2:00 P.M. the second boiler broke down, so there was no steam to run anything. There was a radio operator aboard, and a radio that should have been able to run on auxiliary batteries, but the batteries were dead. The captain wanted to communicate with the owner. I had my trusty walkie-talkie, which was of limited range as specified by FCC regulations, but I was able to use it to contact a Coast Guard station and have them relay a message to the owner to ask for a tug.

In the meantime we were adrift. Normally a ship anchors in deep water under these emergency conditions, but we dared not anchor because we had no steam to get the anchor back up. Our draft, fortunately, was only twenty-five feet. I kept an account of the drift and assured the captain that, with the wind and tide as they were, we would be safe and afloat if a tug arrived within a reasonable time.

Without steam there was no heat or even a galley fire. The captain and crew rigged an oil barrel on deck to burn old dunnage, and meals were cooked over the fire. The coffee was hot, and the captain remarked that the rice was better than it had been when cooked on the regular stove.

At 9:00 P.M. the tug arrived. Her master asked, "Will she steer?" I had previously arranged with the captain to prepare the hand steering gear aft, and I so advised the tugboat. The tug put a towline on board and started pulling. We got underway but soon found we could not steer at all. The rudder was small and needed screw current against it to make it work properly. With no screw current and only a five-knot tow speed, we could not steer and had to abandon the hand steering setup. The tug continued to tow, but since the ship's head kept veering thirty degrees on one side and then thirty degrees on the other, half the time the tug was towing the ship broadside.

We now were able to communicate ashore via my telephone to the tug, which relayed messages through the tug's more powerful set. On the way to the Cape Cod Canal, I persuaded the captain to radio for two more tugs that could tie up alongside to steer the vessel through the canal. The owner sent back word that he would only pay for one tug. I told the captain, "I will not pilot the ship without two tugs to steer." The owner then tried to get someone else to pilot the ship through the canal. No one else would, so the owner finally sent two tugs from New Bedford. With the three tugs we got through the canal safely, and then the two additional tugs returned to New Bedford. The first tug continued to tow the zigzagging *Lachine Trader* toward Boston.

Since the ship had no steam, and the batteries were dead, she had no lights. I insisted that the captain put kerosene lanterns in the side lights, but the tug master said he could not see them—they were too dim. Via our radio relay system, I warned meeting vessels to keep clear.

We had started October 1, passed through the canal on the second, and arrived off Boston at 7:00 A.M. on the third in dense fog. I had piloted all the way to Boston Lightship. Over a year later, I still had not received a cent of pay for my work. I turned this problem over to lawyers to try to collect something.

October 30 I had a physical examination by Dr. Gerrish in Lynn. I passed and continued piloting.

On December 7 I sent Form 15-11 to the Bureau of Alcohol in Boston. Although a teetotaler, I had become fascinated with the process of making wine from local fruit and needed the proper credentials. My homemade fallout shelter turned out to be a dandy wine cellar.

I decided to retire for good come December 31, 1973, having served at sea for sixty years. I was close to eighty and it was getting hard to maneuver in cold weather. Once again I thought I had said goodbye to the sea. There were only a few ships left operating. The rest simply went out of business. High oil prices proved to be the last straw.

In Swampscott I joined the Friends of the Library and had a marine exhibition displayed there for a month. It was well received, and I was asked to set up a second one. I also joined an IRS class on federal income tax and assisted other people in filling out their income tax forms.

In the spring, at the request of a neighbor, I gave a knot-making demonstration to a Brownie Scout troop.

April 22, 1974
Dear Skipper Bamforth,
This note is to thank you so much for taking the time to come to our Brownie meeting.

All the time you took to prepare for our meeting was very much appreciated and it certainly proved worthwhile. We all enjoyed your visit and will remember your stories and you for a long time.

Thank you again,

Sincerely,
(Here each of the fourteen Brownies signed her name.)

Once more I came out of retirement and returned to piloting. It seems I could not give up the sea. June 5, 1974, I piloted the *Stream Hawser* from Boston to Breton Reef. A new ship with a Korean crew, she had brought in a full load of cars from Japan and was bound for Japan with grain.

I had a novel experience piloting the *Bay State*, the successor to the Massachusetts Maritime Academy training ship *Ranger*, from Buzzards Bay to Sandwich through the Cape Cod Canal. She was headed for the Azores on a summer cruise, to be gone for seven weeks. A C-3 type vessel, she had gross tonnage of nearly thirteen thousand tons, quite a bit larger than the long-since-retired training ship on which I had learned my trade.

During the summer, I raised flowers and vegetables in the garden. I picked blackberries, raspberries, grapes, and elderberries and put up twelve lots of wine. In addition, I took on odd jobs in the neighborhood—painting, trimming shrubs, roofing, repairing furniture, and putting new sash cords in windows— and earned $1,000. In August I put up blackberry jelly from wild blackberries, using a hot plate in the basement. In September I put up elderberry jelly from wild berries that I had picked in the rain from the bog down the street. My arms were well scratched, and I was soaked, but I got a big load of nice berries. Then I put up twenty quarts of tomatoes from my garden.

*At a family dinner he actually drank a little of his own wine, made from raspberries he had grown. It was clear and red with a marvelous aroma. It was the only time he ever tasted alcohol except for the sips of communion wine he received in church—and some he had consumed unknowingly at my wedding!*

Grace and Bill spent a few days with us. Beatrice and her Bill did the same, as did Jack and Louise Greenley and their daughter Katherine. In August our granddaughter, Judy, was married.

*The ceremony took place in Swampscott at the Church of the Holy Name, with the reception at the Ionic Club, the home of Dad's Masonic Lodge. It was the first and last time I saw Dad dance, and dance he did, although not with Mother.*

November 7 I piloted the *Omnium Ranger* from Boston to Philadelphia. She carried 7,600 tons of sugar from Brazil. Since there was a sugar shortage, it surprised me that the ship had taken twenty days coming from Brazil at a cost of $5,000 a day, twice that of a usual round trip. It was profitable nonetheless because sugar prices were so high. When fuel oil reached $12 a barrel, however, even foreign ships stopped running on the coast.

Some jobs left me truly exhausted. I had been having so much trouble getting aboard vessels, and with my breathing in cold weather, that I reconfirmed my vow to retire for good. I sold my radio telephone and that sealed the deal. Although my hearing was very good, and my eyes were corrected to 90 percent, it made good sense to call it quits.

In all of 1974 I piloted only nineteen ships. I did not have a single ship in Long Island Sound, so I did not renew my license or incur any further similar expenses. My federal pilot's license was to run out in May 1975.

---

Lying in bed at night, I can tell when the wind is southerly and there is poor visibility in Boston Harbor. Even in winter with storm windows in place, I can hear the Graves Light fog signal blowing its two blasts over and over and the bell buoy's ring five miles away.

Today is the third of March, 1975. I fully retired from the sea the first of this year. I am eighty years old and a little forgetful. Before it is too late, I am glad to have this chance to get down on paper some of my memories. I have been more than sixty years at sea.

Captain Bamforth, coastal pilot at home, 1970

# EDITOR'S EPILOGUE

Although Dad wrote only that he had trouble breathing and maneuvering, in fact he was being treated for heart disease.

Mother was forever dropping spoons and forks into the disposal in the kitchen sink. The device would jam, and Dad would lie down on his back under the sink and work his hands overhead. One of these incidents brought on an attack of angina. The Swampscott police transported him to Lynn Hospital. When he was asked who his doctor was, he named his former local physician. When I visited him in the hospital, he was feeling fine and raring to go. When I got home, I thought it important to make sure the doctor was aware that Dad was a regular patient at the Public Health Hospital. I telephoned his office and left my message. The next thing I knew, Dad was on the sidewalk waiting for Mother to pick him up, abruptly discharged by his unsympathetic family doctor.

After that angina attack, Dad was under the care of a cardiologist in Lynn. He had another attack early in the fall of 1975, this time with damage to the heart muscle. Tests indicated that this was not his first heart attack, maybe the second or third. On questioning, he admitted to the doctor that he'd had other attacks he'd told no one about. One, he related, came on after pursuing a raccoon that had been nesting in the chimney. He had covered the chimney with a grate but the raccoons removed it. He tried fastening screening over the chimney. No good. Speculating that their access route came via an oak branch that hung low over the roof, he sawed the branch off. Later he spied a raccoon limping along the ridge pole. He grabbed his heavy wooden extension ladder, scrambled up the roof, and chased the varmint away. Before he got the ladder put away, he was hurting.

On hearing the story, the doctor said, "You must have been in severe pain. What did you do?"

"Well, I crawled to my cot in my basement room and sweated it out. When Dorothy called me to meals, I told her I wasn't hungry."

He now kept Nitrostat tablets in his pocket and at various points around the house, including the garage loft. Refusing to pamper himself, he continued to climb trees to trim them and allow more sunlight to reach his garden. Though he was fully retired from piloting, he kept as busy as ever doing odd jobs around the neighborhood, keeping out of Mother's way. Evenings at the high school, he taught a course in small boat handling. He was also writing his memoirs.

I visited him almost every weekend. He was no longer the captain and father figure to me. Instead, for the first time in my life, he treated me as an equal. He listened to what I said, and together we worked on his memoirs. We often became engrossed during these sessions. I found myself closer to my father than ever before. At one point I said, "I love you, Dad," the words falling from my lips quite naturally. Just as easily, he responded, "I love you too, son."

One Saturday I arrived to find him standing in the garden instructing a teenage helper how to plant tulip bulbs. He had lost weight and for the first time needed help with this fall ritual. His doctor had arranged for him to have heart bypass surgery, but he said not a word about it to me. I learned of the arrangements only after he died, when notices came in the mail directing him to report to the hospital. As he stood in the garden, he said to me, "Time is getting short. We have to think about things after I'm gone."

"No, you have a long time yet," I said. I had convinced myself that he would never die. I refused to think about the inevitable.

On the evening of November 19, 1975, I was alone at home in Lynnfield. Jan was at dinner with some of her colleagues from her work. I was about to view the nightly news. I called Dad to say that I would come for a visit afterward.

When Mother answered the phone, she said, "He's under the sink again freeing the machine."

"Oh," I said. "He had an attack the last time he did that." I turned back to the television but within ten minutes Mother called back.

"He's having one now. He is putting pills under his tongue. I never heard of such a thing. I've called the police."

"Good," I said, "I'll be right along." When I arrived, two policemen were trying to figure out how to get Dad off the breakfast room settee where he lay helpless.

One grabbed the built-in table. I said, "Oh, no, it'll wreck the table."

Dad took in all the air he could and ordered, "Take my feet and drag me out." On the stretcher he looked very gray. His arm hung limp. I picked it up and put it across his chest. He rasped, "Call the doctor and tell him I'm sufferin'."

The police asked me if I wanted to go in the vehicle with him, but I said, "No, I'll drive myself," believing that this was just another angina attack. I said goodbye to Mother and left for the hospital. There I waited anxiously for word. I kept looking down the hall from the waiting room toward the room in which he lay. At one point the doctor came out and went to another room. He had a smile on his face. I relaxed, but within another ten minutes, the doctor came to me with a nurse.

He said, "I'm sorry. I did all I could. He's gone."

I fell apart. My tears began and I screamed, "What do I do now?" The nurse and doctor ushered me quickly into the quiet of an examining room. The nurse said, "When asphyxia took over, I told him his family was here, and he nodded."

"Bless you for telling me that," I croaked, blinded by tears.

The doctor said, "Go be with your mother."

From the hospital I called St. Mary's Rectory in Rockport to tell Dick. His wife, Pat, answered. Dick was at church. It took a long time for me to get the words out. Pat, as always, took care of everything. When I got to the house, the Reverend John Barrett from the Church of the Holy Name was outside waiting for me. He and I went in, and I told Mother that Dad was gone. Without emotion, she said, "I'm not surprised."

A few days after his death, we had a memorial service at the church where he and Mother had been married in 1921. The nave was filled with family and neighbors, with colleagues from the Merchant Marine and the Masons, with associates of mine from General Electric, and with parishioners from Dick's church in Rockport. We sang,

> The strife is o'er, the battle done,
> the victory of life is won . . .
> God is our hope and strength,
> a very present help in trouble.
> Therefore will we not fear . . .
> though the hills be carried into the midst of the sea;
> though the waters thereof rage and swell . . .

When it came to the final hymn, it was a struggle for many to sing,

> Eternal Father strong to save,
> whose arm hath bound the restless wave,
> who bid'st the mighty ocean deep
> its own appointed limits keep:
> O hear us when we cry to thee
> For those in peril on the sea.

The captain's presence was represented by a folded flag provided by the Veterans Administration. True to form, Dad had arranged everything ahead of time. To minimize expense, he had donated his body to Harvard Medical School.

More than a year later, when the body was of no further use to the school, they informed us that the remains were ready for burial. Between a fine black marble stone engraved BAMFORTH and the simple Veteran's ground plaque with his full name and dates, a plain, small wooden box was lowered into the ground.

I remained dry-eyed until the undertaker handed me my father's wedding ring. After all those years, it was misshapen, and the inscription was just barely discernible. It symbolized all the joys and all the sorrows of his fifty-four years of marriage and a life at sea. My hero, whom I admired and loved, was finally at rest.

Dick, as grief-stricken as I, but more accustomed to burial rites, read the words of committal and these verses from Psalm 107.

> Give thanks to the Lord, for he is good.
> Let all those whom the Lord has redeemed proclaim that he
>    redeemed them from the hand of the foe.
> He gathered them out of the lands; from the east and from the
>    west, from the north and from the south.
> Some wandered in desert wastes . . .
> Some sat in darkness and deep gloom . . .
> Some were fools and took to rebellious ways . . .
> Some went down to the sea in ships
>   and plied their trade in deep waters;
> They beheld the works of the Lord
>   and his wonders in the deep.
> Then he spoke, and a stormy wind arose,
>   which tossed high the waves of the sea . . .
> Then they cried to the Lord in their trouble,
>   and he delivered them from their distress.
> He stilled the storm to a whisper
>   and quieted the waves of the sea.
> Then were they glad because of the calm,
>   and he brought them to the harbor they were bound for.

Note: Excerpts from *The Hymnal* 1982, © Church Pension Fund, used by permission.